Bread, freedom, social justice

T0321569

About the Authors

ANNE ALEXANDER is a research fellow at the Centre for Research in the Arts, Social Sciences and Humanities (CRASSH) at the University of Cambridge. She has published widely on Middle Eastern politics, social movements and digital media, and is the author of a biography of Gamal Abdel-Nasser (Haus, 2005).

MOSTAFA BASSIOUNY has more than a decade's experience as a reporter and editor in the Egyptian and regional press. He was industrial correspondent for *Al-Dustour* newspaper between 2005 and 2010, reporting on the mass strikes by textile workers in Al-Mahalla al-Kubra in 2006 and 2007, and the uprising which rocked the town in 2008. He reported on the overthrow of Ben Ali in Tunisia in January 2011 before returning to Egypt to participate in the uprising against Mubarak. Between 2011 and 2014 he was Head of News for liberal daily *Al-Tahrir* and is currently Egypt correspondent for the Lebanese daily *Al-Safir*.

Bread, freedom, social justice

Workers and the Egyptian Revolution

ANNE ALEXANDER AND MOSTAFA BASSIOUNY

Zed Books | LONDON

Bread, Freedom, Social Justice: Workers and the Egyptian Revolution
was first published in 2014 by Zed Books Ltd,
7 Cynthia Street, London N1 9JF, UK

www.zedbooks.co.uk

Designed and typeset in Monotype Bulmer
by illuminati, Grosmont
Index by John Barker
Cover designed by Kika Sroka-Miller

A catalogue record for this book is available from the British Library
Library of Congress Cataloging in Publication Data available

ISBN   978 1 78032 431 9 hb
ISBN   978 1 78032 430 2 pb
eISBN 978 1 78032 433 3
ePDF 978 1 78032 432 6

Contents

Tables and figures

Acknowledgements

As well as taking three years to complete, the process of writing this book spanned two languages and two continents. While it is a joint work, for which both authors take full responsibility, the book is also the product of a division of labour between us. Anne Alexander wrote the introduction and most of chapters 2, 7, 8, 9 and the conclusion. Mostafa Bassiouny wrote most of chapters 3, 4 and 6. Chapters 1 and 5 were jointly written. Mostafa Bassiouny's sections of the book were written originally in Arabic and translated by Anne Alexander. Some of these contain updated and revised versions of material which has previously appeared in Arabic articles and research papers published by the Centre for Socialist Studies and Al-Ahram Centre for Strategic Studies. Sections of Chapters 6 and 7 likewise contain material which was previously published in English in articles for *International Socialism Journal*.

Very many people beyond its authors contributed to the making of this book, and we are profoundly grateful to them all, not only those we have mentioned here by name. First, and most importantly, we want to thank the activists whose tireless struggle to build the Egyptian workers' movement through dictatorship, revolution and counter-revolution is not merely the subject of this book, but its inspiration. Our discussions with colleagues from Mahalla, the Property Tax Agency, the Cairo Public Transport Authority and Egyptian National Railways have been particularly important in shaping the arguments we present here.

The project of writing began to take form following a workshop held at the School of Oriental and African Studies in 2009. Gilbert Achcar played a critical role in convening that workshop, and we would like to thank him for his continued support over the following years, in the course of many rich and stimulating discussions.

Kim Walker, Jonathan Maunder and their colleagues at Zed Books showed remarkable tenacity in sticking with us through what turned out to be a far more lengthy process of writing than either of us imagined: we are very grateful for their patience and professionalism.

Special thanks go to Sameh Naguib for reading several drafts of the whole manuscript, providing not only invaluable advice and critical comments but encouragement and support throughout the project. We are likewise grateful to Philip Marfleet and John Rose for their enthusiastic engagement with the book from the beginning, and for their rigorous appraisal of our arguments at every stage of the project. We benefited greatly from comments by Charlie Kimber, Colin Barker, Joseph Choonara, Neil Davidson, Jack Shenker, David Renton and John Molyneux. Discussions with Hisham Fouad, Haitham Mohamedain, Mohamed Shafiq, Alex Callinicos, Simon Assaf and Bassem Chit also played a vital role in shaping our analysis.

We are particularly grateful to the many comrades and friends who in the midst of the revolutionary struggles gripping Egypt and the wider region, took time from the pressing needs of the day-to-day battles to engage with our project.

Without the love and support of our partners, David and Beesan, the book would never have been completed. Our gratitude and respect for them far exceed whatever we can express in a few lines here.

Finally, we cannot introduce this book without emphasizing that writing it has been as much a political project as an intellectual one. For us, the book's real value cannot be measured solely by assessing its impact on debates about the causes and nature of the Arab Revolutions among academics or journalists, but rather whether it plays a small role in the process of winning some of those who have experienced and been inspired by the Arab Revolutions to revolutionary socialist ideas. We are not neutral observers and commentators, but first and foremost political activists, whose main goal is to make whatever modest contribution we can to the victory of the struggle for bread, freedom and social justice. Despite all the difficulties and darkness of the road ahead, we remain convinced that the most important lesson of the 25 January Revolution is the glimpse it gave us of the potential of ordinary people, when the power of the organised working class drives their struggles forward, to create a world free of exploitation and oppression.

Anne Alexander
Mostafa Bassiouny
July 2014

Acronyms and abbreviations

When rendering Arabic proper names, we have adopted the spelling most commonly used in English, where possible respecting the spelling favoured by the individuals themselves (thus Mohamed ElBaradei, rather than Muhammad al-Barada'i). Other Arabic words have been transliterated using a simplified version of the system adopted by the Library of Congress which is widely used in academic literature. We have retained the inverted apostrophe to represent both the Arabic letters *ayn* and *hamza* in the middle of words, but not at the beginning or end of words, and we have avoided the use of other diacritical marks or special characters. We have rendered the Arabic letter *jim* with the English letter *g*, following common Egyptian pronunciation.

In order not to burden the non-Arabic speaking reader, we have translated, rather than transliterated, names of organisations in the main text, however a list of these is presented here, along with their English acronyms, and other abbreviations and acronyms used frequently in the text. In the case of the property tax collectors' union, RETAU, we have chosen to use the acronym based on the American English translation of the union's name, as this is the form adopted by the union itself in its English-language correspondence.

AFL–CIO	American Federation of Labor – Congress of Industrial Organizations
BIWU	Banking and Insurance Workers Union (*al-niqaba al-amma lil-ammilin bil-bunuk wal-ta'miniyyat*)
CAPMAS	Central Agency for Public Mobilisation and Statistics (*al-gihaz al-markazy lil-ta'bia al-ama wal-ihsa*)
CTUWS	Centre for Trade Union and Workers' Services (*dar al-khidamat al-niqabiyya wal-ummaliyya*)
CSS	Centre for Socialist Studies (*markaz al-dirasat al-ishtarakiyya*)
DWR	Doctors Without Rights (*al-ataba bila huquq*)
EDLC	Egyptian Democratic Labour Congress (*mu'atamr ummal masr al-dimuqrati*)
EFITU	Egyptian Federation of Independent Trade Unions (*al-ittihad al-masry lil-niqabat al-mustaqilla*)
ECESR	Egyptian Centre for Economic and Social Rights (*al-markaz al-masry lil-huquq al-iqtisadiyya wal-igtima'iyya*)
ETUWW	Egyptian Trade Union and Workers' Watch (*al-marsad al-niqaby wal-ummaly al-masry*)
EISC	Egyptian Iron and Steel Company (*al-hadid wal-sulb al-masriyya*)
ERSAP	Economic Reform and Structural Adjustment Programme
ESCO	Egyptian Industries for Silk and Cotton (*sharika al-mahallat al-sana'iyya lil-harir wal-qutun*)
ETUF	Egyptian Trade Union Federation (*al-ittihad al-am liniqabat ummal masr*)
FUC	Factory Union Committee (*al-lagna al-niqabiyya*)
FJP	Freedom and Justice Party (*hizb al-hurriya wal-adala*)
GUTW	General Union of Textile Workers (*al-niqaba al-amma lil-ammilin bil-ghazl wal-nasig*)
HTU	Health Technicians Union (*al-niqaba al-mustaqilla lil-fanniyyin al-sahiyyin*)
ILO	International Labour Organization
ITUC	International Trade Union Confederation
LE	Egyptian pounds
NCW	National Council for Wages (*al-maglis al-qawmi*

	lil-ugur)
NDP	National Democratic Party (*al-hizb al-watany al-dimuqraty*)
NGO	non-governmental organisation
PPP	public–private partnership
PR	proportional representation
PSI	Public Services International
PTA	Property Tax Agency (*maslahat al-al-dara'ib al-aqariyya*)
PT	Public Transport Authority (*ha'it al-naql al-am*)
RETAU	Real Estate Tax Authority Union (*al-niqaba al-amma lil-ammilin bil-al-dara'ib al-aqariyya*)
RS	Revolutionary Socialists (*al-ishtarakiyun al-thawriyun*)
SCAF	Supreme Council of the Armed Forces (*al-maglis al-ala lil-quwwat al-musalaha*)
Al-Tagammu	National Progressive Unionist Assembly (*hizb al-tagammu al-watany al-taqadamy al-wahdawy*)
TE	Telecom Egypt (*al-misriyya lil-itisalat*)
UGTT	Union Générale Tunisienne du Travail (*al-ittihad al-am al-tunsi lil-shughal*)
USAID	United States Agency for International Development
WCNL	Workers' Committee for National Liberation (*lagna al-ummal lil tahrir al-qawmi*)

From the Republic of Tahrir to the Republic of Fear? Theorising revolution and counter-revolution in Egypt 2011–14

> Welcome to Tahrir Square ... the republic of possible dreams.
> In this liberated corner of Egypt, protesters are experimenting
> with self-rule, and inventing forms of resilience. Veteran com-
> munists, critics and writers, members of Al-Azhar and priests ...
> all the sections of this revolution which the youth are leading. As
> for the presenters on the regime's TV stations, they have no idea
> how to deal with the truth which is becoming increasingly hard
> to deny.[1]

Exactly three years after the greatest popular uprising in the
Middle East for a generation, the hopes inspired by Tahrir's
'republic of possible dreams' seemed a distant memory. The
square filled again with crowds on 25 January 2014, but this
time they were carrying pictures of Abdel-Fattah al-Sisi, Egypt's
new military leader and cheering on his ruthless war against
opponents of the regime. Around a hundred were killed on the
streets that day, shot down for daring to mark the anniversary of
the revolution in defiant protest. With tens of thousands filling the
prisons and uncounted numbers disappearing into the dark places
of what veteran Islamist leader Abdul-Moneim al-Fotouh called
the 'Republic of Fear',[2] many within Egypt and far beyond are

questioning whether January 2011's demands of bread, freedom and social justice can ever be realised.

Yet, despite the confidence of Mubarak's generals and secret policemen that they can crush all resistance or co-opt dissenters, the social and political contradictions which detonated the revolution in the first place have not been resolved. As we outline in this book, the specific character of the Egyptian Revolution poses enormous problems for those hoping to re-stabilise the authoritarian regime. This book uncovers in particular how the workers' movement has shaped the Egyptian Revolution, and presents evidence for our contention that the organised working class has a special role to play in the struggle to realise the political and social goals of the January 2011 uprising.

In this chapter we set out the theoretical framework for the rest of the book. We focus first on the interdependence between states and capitals at national, regional and international levels and then address the relationship between political and social revolutions. We also present our approach to understanding the Islamist movement and outline our analysis of the role of the trade union bureaucracy. Finally we explore how the concept of 'permanent revolution', developed by Marx and Trotsky in response to the defeats of the 1848 and 1905 Revolutions in Europe and Russia, can be applied in an Egyptian context.

States and capitals in the Middle East: some observations

The global capitalist economy developed in a highly uneven fashion, as states which adopted capitalism early were able to win and defend opportunities for 'their' capitalists at the expense of their competitors. Yet, as Marx and Engels argued in the 1840s, capitalism cannot be contained with the borders of any national economy, as the capitalist class ranges the globe tirelessly in search of new sources of raw materials, new labour markets and new customers for its products.[3] Our analysis of development of the capitalist state and capitalist class in Egypt therefore lies within a broader historical perspective on the uneven development of the relationship between states and capitals on regional and international levels. The history of capitalism in Egypt likewise cannot be separated from the history of imperialism in the Middle East, which we understand as a specific stage in the development of global capitalism characterised by the fusion of processes of military and economic competition between the most powerful capitalist states, and not simply as another term for military conquest.[4] Rivalry between the various imperialist powers that have sought to dominate the Middle East in order to secure privileged access to its natural resources and strategic locations has shaped the way in which these powers have exercised domination over the people living there.

In contrast to a perspective that sees the state as separate from and counterposed to 'civil society', we see the state as a brutal instrument of class power – a weapon in the hands of the ruling class. However, the state is at the same time a set of institutions which *appears* to mediate in *all* the conflicts of capitalist society. State institutions apply laws to employers and employees, arbitrate in disputes between neighbours, enforce taxation on rich and poor, and often regulate working conditions and wages. The state's 'mediating' role in conflicts between workers and their bosses is, however, a carefully crafted illusion: where the state appears to take the workers' side, this is based on a calculation that the *general* interest of the capitalist class is best served by concessions even if this is detrimental to the interest of the particular capitalist party to the dispute. The real mediator in this situation is the trade-union bureaucracy, if one exists – a point to which we will return later. The state's role as mediator between the competing interests of different *capitals* is, however, perfectly genuine. It is the paternal authority conjured up from the imaginations and needs of a 'band of warring brothers', as Marx termed the bourgeoisie. As Colin Barker argues, the state is a 'field of intracapitalist conflict' which takes on its specific form as 'an impersonal mechanism of public authority isolated from society' precisely in order to be able to arbitrate effectively between different capitals.[5]

The idea of the state as an 'impersonal mechanism' is, however, also a critical component of the ideological apparatus that helps to sustain those already in power. As we explore in more detail in Chapter 9, one of the most potent weapons in the ideological armoury of counter-revolution has been to invoke a vision of the state as an autonomous, neutral machine, which must be preserved at any cost, unless society is to risk complete breakdown and disintegration. Defending the inviolacy of the state (*al-dawla*) was in this context a key mechanism for the rehabilitation of key elements of the pre-revolutionary regime (*al-nidham*). Grasping the impossibility of separating 'the state' from the social antagonisms that make necessary its existence is important if we are to go beyond understanding the state as a set of institutions, or even simply a charmed circle of personalities. Such a narrow conception of the state is a major weakness in Kandil's exploration of the Egyptian Revolution through the lens of rivalry between the Egyptian state's military, security and civilian leaderships.[6]

As Barker remarks, one of the problems with Marxist debates about the state is that they often seem to assume that 'capitalism has but one state', whereas unfortunately 'the beast is numerous'.[7] It is important to emphasize that the beast is also *varied*. Capitalism in Russia, for example, emerged in a highly uneven, concentrated form, thanks largely to the efforts of the pre-capitalist state, which 'hothoused' the development of both a bourgeoisie and a working class in sectors directly connected to its military and economic competition with the European powers, such as shipbuilding and communications infrastructure.[8] In the case of the capitalist states that developed in countries that were colonised by the same European powers in the nineteenth and early twentieth centuries, analogous processes can be observed. Here the colonial authorities steered the processes of state formation in directions that suited the perpetuation of their own rule. Often at the same time they actively or passively impeded the development of indigenous capitalism, which might disrupt an imperial division of labour relegating the populations of the colonies to the subordinate position of producers of raw materials and consumers of finished goods. Anti-colonial rebellion after 1945 in large parts of the 'colonial world' involved a would-be local ruling class seizing the state and using it to begin a process of 'hothoused' economic development (in some cases in political alliance with and in direct emulation of the rulers of the Soviet state).

In Egypt, the seizure of power by junior army officers in 1952 under the leadership of Gamal Abdel-Nasser represented just such an attempt to overcome the blockage imposed by the political alliance between the colonial power (Britain) and large landowners, led by the royal family. One of the Free Officers' first acts in power was to reform land ownership with the aim of mobilising agricultural surpluses in order to fund industrial take-off. This was followed by the transformation of large parts of private capital into state capital and the massive expansion of the state's activities in production through a programme of import-substitution industrialisation under the guidance of Soviet economic planners.[9] We discuss in Chapters 1 and 2 what happened when this strategy of accumulation reached an impasse locally with the entwined military and economic crises of the late 1960s, and internationally with the global shift in strategies of accumulation with the end of the post-war boom.

The roots of the Egyptian Revolution of 2011 lie in the transformation of the relationships between the state, capital and labour that took place over the previous thirty-five years on both a local and a global scale. In Egypt, this transformation was initiated at the highest level of the state by Anwar al-Sadat with his adoption of the project of *infitah* (economic and political opening) following the death of Gamal Abdel-Nasser in 1970. *Infitah* represented a strategic realignment for the Egyptian ruling class on two levels simultaneously. On a geopolitical level Sadat shifted from dependence on the Soviet Union towards a new relationship of dependency on the United States. From the beginning, however, it was understood that implementation of liberal economic reforms following the model that was appearing on a global scale during the 1970s would be a critical component of this realignment. The emergence of what would later be called 'neoliberalism' signalled the beginning of a global shift away from economic policies centred on developing the state as a provider of public services and direct producer through the expansion of welfare systems and nationalised industries. The turn towards neoliberal policies on a global scale has often been equated simplistically with the notion that the state is shrinking, a view fostered by the supporters of neoliberalism themselves. Yet, as Naguib notes,

> The policies of neoliberalism were never about dismantling or even reducing the role of the state in the economy but rather about increasing the role of the state as facilitator of capitalist profit-making at the expense of the working class. This created an even more intimate relation between state and capital.[10]

The 'retreat of the state' was a much more specific and limited process, confined to the abandonment of an ideology which projected the state's key role as a guarantor of a minimum standard of social equity through its direct intervention in the process of production, distribution and redistribution of wealth. By contrast, neoliberalism protected the state's role in facilitating the process of capital accumulation. Nor did the state completely withdraw from the provision of welfare or public infrastructure, but rather neoliberal policies meant the partial cannibalisation of these economic sectors in order to transfer some of their costs directly to the poor, *and* to facilitate their transformation into machines for making profit. Some of the mechanisms which had been used during the previous generation for a limited redistribution of surplus wealth *downwards* were reconfigured as means to redistribute wealth *upwards*. State-run industries would undergo a similar process. Some elements would be directly sold to private capital; in other cases the state partially divested to share profits with private investors, while others faced neglect, decay and eventual closure.

This history gives a partial glimpse of how the multifaceted relationships between states and capitals have developed. States provide a host of 'services' for the capitalist class as a whole, including enforcing discipline on their workforces, organising the reproduction of labour power through a variation on the welfare state, and making workers contribution to the cost of their own maintenance through taxation. The state may also secure and distribute external sources of income, such as various forms of rent and aid, in addition to the function discussed above of mediating between different capitals in their collective, 'national' interest. Chris Harman argues powerfully that states and capitals should be seen as 'structurally interdependent':

> The groups of capitals and the state with which they are associated form a system in which each affects the others. The specific character of each capital is influenced by its interaction with the other capitals and the state. It reflects not only the general drive to expand value, to accumulate, but also the specific environment in which it has grown up. The state and the individual capitals are intertwined, with each feeding off the other. ... Neither the state nor the particular capitals can easily escape this structural interdependence.[11]

Capitals and states bound together within such systems are the product of specific histories and geographies, which constrain

capitals' ability to uproot themselves at will should the conditions for accumulation become less favourable. Likewise, Harman
argues, the structural interdependence of states and capitals sets
limits on the autonomy of the state bureaucracy. These insights
provide an important starting point for addressing the question
of state autonomy in the context of the Middle East, an issue
which has traditionally been focused on the debates over the
theory of the 'rentier state'.[12] Such accounts have emphasised
the distorting effect of access to 'rent' for the exploitation of
major deposits of oil on the development of state bureaucracies.
Such state bureaucracies have been able to free themselves from
the need to raise revenue through taxation, proponents of this
theory have argued, and thus can act with a degree of autonomy
and capriciousness, which is an important factor in sustaining
authoritarianism in the region. Analysis of the Gulf has frequently
assumed that in such 'rentier states' the dynamic, productive role
is entirely taken up by foreign capital. By contrast, as Hanieh's
work clearly demonstrates, massive conglomerates spanning all
three circuits of capital accumulation in the Gulf (productive,
commodity and financial), have emerged in recent decades, which
knit together Gulf private and state capitals across the region.[13]
Foreign capitals and states still play a critical role in this system,
which is predicated on the Gulf's particular place within the
global economy as a key source of the most important commodity in twentieth-century capitalist development: oil. However,
they now relate primarily to a rising capitalist class, which has
emerged as a central player in the political economy of the wider
Middle East, not to a collection of pre-capitalist tribal elites. As
the capitalist class in the Gulf has matured, so too has its thirst
for investment in production. Again, as Hanieh demonstrates,
Gulf capital investment in Egypt is found across a wide range
of sectors, with major investments in food production for both
domestic and regional markets, textiles and transport as well as

finance and banking and real estate.[14] These investments create a very direct material interest in restoring suitable conditions for capital accumulation on a regional scale for Gulf capital by financing counter-revolution in Egypt.

The tendency to refer to states and capitals in the singular is, as noted above, a convenient simplification but often misleading. Similar problems also arise when we scratch the surface of the labels 'state capital' and 'private capital'. Rivalry and competition between different capitals is, as discussed above, a central reason for the existence of the state in the first place. However, it is also important to recognise that where the state acts as a capitalist, this will give rise to a *system* of interdependent state capitals, in the plural, not a monolithic bloc of 'state capital' in the singular. In the case of Egypt, one particular form of state capital – military capital – has benefited from the shift towards neoliberal policies, while the fortunes of other state capitals, in particular civilian public-sector manufacturing, have declined. In fact, it may be justifiable to claim that the rise of military capital as a distinct form of state capital in Egypt is a product of the period of neoliberal reforms. For, although military appointments permeated every level of the state bureaucracy under Nasser, and army officers played a key role in *managing* the drive to build up public-sector manufacturing in particular, the military's creation of its own manufacturing empire dates from the 1980s, at the very moment when state policies were moving towards disengagement from the public sector in preparation for eventual privatisation.

Political and social revolutions: preliminary notes

There is no space here to do justice to the debates over the nature of political and social revolutions, nor to reference properly the voluminous literature generated by these discussions.[15] We will focus therefore on the application of a particular understanding of revolution to events in Egypt. This understanding of revolution is not the 'common sense' interpretation of the word, which, as Hal Draper observed, appears frequently as 'either a bogey or banality, depending on whether it is seen as a sinister plot or reduced to a mere synonym for change'.[16] In fact, the sheer scale of popular mobilisation in Egypt after 25 January 2011, followed by a sudden crisis at the top of the state apparatus and the army's dramatic removal of Mubarak from power, temporarily made it more difficult to reduce 'revolution' to either of these meanings.

Nevertheless, there remained a sharp difference in perspective between characterising 'the Egyptian Revolution' as a spectacular *event*, generally associated with the eighteen-day long uprising against Mubarak, and as a longer-term *process*. As this book makes clear, we do see revolution as a process, although one in which specific events play a critical role in the transition from one phase to another. In addition, the outcome of particular struggles can alter the overall balance between the social and political forces engaged in the process. The outcome of the massive street protests in November 2011, for example, differed sharply from the outcome of the 18 day uprising earlier that year, and as a result both counter-revolutionary and reformist forces hoping to halt the revolutionary process gained greater room to manoeuvre.

So what kind of revolutionary process unfolded in Egypt between 2011 and 2014? At one level, it can be understood as primarily an attempted political revolution, in the sense that a 'transfer of governmental power'[17] was partially accomplished, even if the process of transfer was halting and protracted, and then swiftly reversed. Moreover, the people to whom governmental power was partially transferred, the leadership of the Muslim Brotherhood, had little prospect of achieving this outcome by any other means in the pre-revolutionary period. The partial and qualified nature of this 'transfer of power' is, however, very important. As we emphasise throughout, the pace of change in the institutions of the state throughout the period 2011–13 remained glacially slow, reflecting both the resilience of core institutions of the Mubarak regime and the unwillingness of their reformist opponents to challenge those institutions directly. This 'transfer of power' did not, therefore, in itself, put the nature of the state in question. Nor did it necessarily presage a shift away from authoritarianism, even to the extent that some Western politicians assumed was happening as they attempted to fit the Egyptian Revolution into the well-worn paradigm of a 'transition to democracy'.[18]

However, a primary goal of this book is to demonstrate that at another level it was the social aspects of the revolutionary process which shaped its trajectory. It was not the commitment of Egypt's reformists to a different vision of the state that gave the political revolution its motive force. Rather, it was the fact that after 25 January the revolution's political and social demands were raised through mass mobilisations in the streets and workplaces. As we discuss in detail later, the 'social soul' of the revolutionary process was a critical element from the start, with the interwoven pattern of strikes and political protests weakening the grip of the regime in the years before 2011, and strikes playing a critical role in the consummation of the 18 day uprising. However, the political aspects of the revolutionary process were initially entirely driven by mobilisation from below, coalescing around massive street protests animated by the slogan 'the people want the downfall of the regime' after 25 January 2011. Later, as we explore below, mainstream reformist politicians and even counter-revolutionary generals became more adept at turning the waves of street protests to their advantage. This was not the case in January 2011: neither the political nor the social mobilisations from below in the early stages of the revolution were conjured into being by sections of the elite to aid them in a fratricidal conflict. (This kind of popular mobilisation, where it is different figures within a warring ruling class who call protesters into the street, was famously described by Marx in *The 18th Brumaire of Louis Bonaparte*.) Rather, they were an authentic embodiment of the refusal of millions of Egyptians to continue to live under the neoliberal authoritarian regime which had ruled them for more than thirty years.

The popular character of the revolution is also the reason why the Egyptian Revolution was closer to becoming a revolution that bursts social boundaries in the process of a transfer of political power (a 'political revolution with a social soul', as Marx put it) than many other revolutions in recent history. Lenin, writing about the 1905 Revolution in Russia, pointed out that although it lacked the 'brilliant successes' of the contemporary Portuguese and Turkish Revolutions, it should be considered a 'people's revolution':

> since the mass of the people, its majority, the very lowest social strata, crushed by oppression and exploitation, rose independently and placed on the entire course of the revolution the impress of their own demands, of their attempts to build in their own way a new society in place of the old society that was being destroyed.[19]

In Russia, the independent political mobilisation of 'the mass of the people' crucially took on an institutional character in the form of the St Petersburg Soviet, or council of workers' deputies, which led the October 1905 general strike, and found expression in mass revolutionary organisations rooted in the organised working class. Both of these elements were missing in the Egyptian case. Nevertheless, the kinship between the Egyptian Revolution and Russia in 1905 can be seen in other aspects. In both cases it was the social struggles of the poor, and particularly those by organised workers, which opened the space for the democratic demands raised by narrow layers of opposition activists to become the rallying cry for millions. Yet a democratic revolution was clearly necessary for workers to win their key social demands: mass waves of strikes for better wages and conditions might bring some piecemeal changes from individual employers, but not the kind of social reform which would make a difference to the lives of wider sections of the poor. Rosa Luxemburg, in her writings on the 1905 Revolution, introduces a concept of 'reciprocal action' between the social and political aspects of the revolutionary process; this has been important in shaping the analysis advanced in this book. She argues:

> the economic struggle is the transmitter from one political centre to another; the political struggle is the periodic fertilisation of the soil for the economic struggle. Cause and effect here continually change places; and thus the economic and the political factor in the period of the mass strike, now widely removed, completely separated or even mutually exclusive, as the theoretical plan would have them, merely form the *two interlacing sides of the proletarian class struggle in Russia.*[20]

Reciprocal action is the process by which these 'interlaced' aspects of class struggle during a revolution interact. In one sense it is a sideways movement, with the relative weight of the economic and political aspects of the class struggle constantly shifting in pendulum-like motion. But it has to have overall a movement forwards, penetrating simultaneously further into the heart of the capitalist labour process, and upwards towards the apex of state power.

It is no accident that the January 2011 call for 'bread, freedom and social justice' expresses both the social and the democratic aspects of the revolution. The slogan could be read as expressing an unformed but powerful desire for a kind of 'Social Republic': a social-democratic compromise which unites democratic reforms with state intervention to redistribute wealth, provide jobs and offer basic services. The workers of Paris died on the barricades in June 1848 for the 'Social Republic': the Egyptian workers' movement has yet to articulate a democratic agenda of its own.

This is the other side to the Egyptian experience since 2011: the social and democratic souls of the revolution did not simply embrace; their relationship was marked by constant tension and occasional conflict. The catastrophic consequences of that conflict could be seen in the wake of the 30 June protests and the military coup against Mohamed Morsi in 2013. Instead of the waves of strikes and apparent signs of workers' self-organisation which preceded the 30 June protests paving the way for a new phase of the revolution, it was counter-revolutionary forces, led by the military, which reaped the benefits. By substituting 'Order' for Freedom and putting a trade-union leader in the cabinet to make false promises of 'Bread and Social Justice', the generals were able to turn the contradictions between the social and democratic aspects of the revolution to their advantage. Morsi's end illustrates therefore that 'reciprocal action' between economic and political struggles is not a process that points inevitably in a single direction. Despite the depth and breadth of the wave of social struggles during his year in power, the politics of the counter-revolution came to dominate the political protest movement, setting the process of 'reciprocal action' temporarily into reverse. Following the army coup against Morsi in July 2013, the political and social aspects of workers' struggles took on an even more contradictory relationship, with workers in some cases defying the military regime's repeated injunction against strikes, but holding aloft pictures of Minister of Defence Abdel-Fattah al-Sisi as they urged his intervention to resolve the dispute in their favour.

None of this was an inevitable outcome to the phase of the revolutionary process which began in January 2011. And one important reason for hope is that the experiments in self-rule and new forms of resilience that characterised the 'Republic of Tahrir' were not restricted to the hundreds of thousands who passed through the Square during the 18 Days, but were carried into workplaces and neighbourhoods across Egypt on a historic scale between 2011 and 2014. Grasping the implications of this process requires a deeper understanding of 'democracy' than parliamentarianism. On its own, the democracy of the mainstream reformists proved incapable of imagining more than cosmetic changes to the authoritarian state. The uneven way in which the revolutionary process reached into different sections of society, particularly the gap between urban and rural areas, made it absolutely necessary for revolutionaries to defend and participate in the institutions of liberal democracy against counter-revolution. However, the weakness and cowardliness of the reformists in the face of the 'Officers' Republic'[21] confirms the urgency of nurturing the institutions and practices of a different democracy. We return at the end of the book to discuss the potential for developing forms of popular democracy rooted in the everyday struggles of the Egyptian people which have the democracy of the organised working class at their heart. Until this democracy-from-below is able to offer a genuine alternative to the bureaucratic-military machine of the bourgeois state, its defenders will have to make careful judgements about when to stand *with* and when to stand *against* their vacillating reformist allies.

Analysing Islamism

Analysis of the political and social movements which have been variously labelled 'Islamist', 'Islamic fundamentalist' or belonging to 'Political Islam' has been a matter of considerable debate for decades. On the left, these movements have often been characterised as entirely reactionary, expressing the needs of either a section of the bourgeoisie or the petite bourgeoisie and generally working in the interests of the region's imperialist powers. Gilbert Achcar, for example, argues that the Islamist movements are 'reactionary responses' to the problem of underdevelopment and unevenness between core and periphery.[22] Their social base is to be found among the traditional middle classes and intellectuals, but neoliberalism has reinforced the appeal of Islamist movements by creating spaces for them to act as substitutes for state welfare services.[23] Fred Halliday has argued that Islamist movements pose an existential threat to the values and organisations of the left and that there can be no ground for common action between left-wing and Islamist organisations.[24] Versions of this negative analysis have been reflected in the practice of most left-wing organisations in contexts where Islamist movements have gained mass support, from Egypt in the 1940s to Iran in the 1970s, Algeria in the 1990s and beyond.[25] Mainstream analysis of Islamist movements has often been polarised, with some writers celebrating their potential to advance an agenda of democratic reforms against authoritarian regimes and others arguing that Islamist movements are fundamentally opposed to 'Western democratic values'.[26]

This polarisation of views has intensified since 2011, reflecting the role played by Islamist movements in the revolutionary crisis across the region. In Egypt, Tunisia, Bahrain, Yemen and Syria, Islamist movements constituted the largest opposition movements in the pre-revolutionary period, and as such naturally became the repository of both hopes and fears of change as the revolutions unfolded. Egypt's Islamists, of course, have experienced extremes of triumph and despair since 2011: with the Muslim Brotherhood's ascent to power in 2012 followed by catastrophe in 2013 when massive popular protests combined with a counter-revolutionary offensive by the military, removing Mohamed Morsi as president on 3 July.

Achcar, writing before the Brotherhood's experiment with power in Egypt was abruptly terminated, claims that the Islamist movement's influence was ebbing even before the 2011 revolutions. Repression in Algeria, Tunisia and Egypt; collaboration between Hezbollah and the Syrian regime; damage to Hamas as a result of its own ascension to power in Gaza after 2006; and the crisis of the Iranian regime left the major Islamist forces ill-equipped to deal with the rise of new mass movements.[27] 'The fundamentalist movements that have gained prominence thanks to the uprisings in the region have all joined a movement started by others', Achcar argues, noting that the metaphor of an 'Islamic tsunami' is particular apt to describe the rapid advance and retreat of the movements since 2011.[28]

Echoing earlier debates on the social base of Islamist movements, Achcar argues that it was the Brotherhood's mobilisation of big business, and not its Islamist version of state welfare, that defined the social character of Morsi's regime.[29] Hanieh comes to similar conclusions, arguing that conflicts between the Brotherhood leadership, the military and Mubarak's allies during 2011–12 are 'best seen as competitive struggles within and between fractions of the same Egyptian capitalist class and state apparatus'.[30] Hanieh likewise sees the Muslim Brotherhood as representing an 'attractive partner' for Western powers in their quest to stem the tide of revolution, because of the Brotherhood's willingness to work with the military, combined with its enthusiasm for neoliberalism and strong connections to the regional powers of the Gulf, the latter being a 'key element to a further deepening of the Gulf's political penetration of the state apparatus'.[31]

Analysis of the role of the Islamist movements since 2011 in the media has been often contradictory, by contrast. As Philip Marfleet notes, the electoral success of the Muslim Brotherhood in Egypt and Ennahda in Tunisia was greeted by a wave of pessimistic articles which claimed that the Arab Spring was turning into an 'Islamist Winter', without addressing the social and political challenges faced by the new Islamist governments.[32] The overthrow of Morsi, however, prompted more sympathetic coverage, with the Muslim Brotherhood depicted as the victim of anti-democratic, counter-revolutionary forces. Notably, however, key Western officials did not seem to share this analysis, with US

Secretary of State John Kerry giving the new military regime in Egypt his backing in the wake of Morsi's fall,[33] and British Prime Minister David Cameron going so far as to announce an inquiry into the Muslim Brotherhood's activities in April 2014.[34]

Our understanding of Islamist movements in general, and their main representatives in Egypt in particular, is based on the approach outlined by Harman in an influential essay written in 1994 in the wake of the bloody repression of the Algerian Islamist movement.[35] In contrast to a perspective which sees Islamist movements as ultimately one homogenous, reactionary bloc, we argue that analysis of such movements must always be rooted in an assessment of the context in which they arise and the specific configuration of social forces which they mobilise. As Naguib argues in a powerful critique of the Egyptian left's attitude to the Muslim Brotherhood written before the revolution, failure to make such an assessment has often led to tacit or active support for the state's attempts to crush Islamist movements.[36] The counter-revolutionary outcome of the popular protests against Morsi in 2013 underscores the point that a nuanced understanding of Islamist movements is both necessary and difficult.

In this book we cannot go beyond a preliminary sketch of the role of Egypt's principal Islamist organisations in the revolutionary process. However, our analysis here is based on the premiss that when assessing the role of Islamist movements in the revolutionary process, it is important to do so from two perspectives. First, any analysis must start with an understanding of the organisations' specific history and development. Second, it must take into account their position in relation to the state – do they propose to reform it, overthrow it, or maintain it unchanged? This question is, of course, an issue that causes sharps divisions within and between Islamist movements.

Taking the case of the Egyptian Muslim Brotherhood, it is important to set the organisation's role in 2011–14 in the context of its social composition and historical development. We see the Brotherhood's appeal resting largely on the frustrations of the organisation's core cadres in the modern middle class with the failed promise of modernity. As Naguib argues, in the decades before the revolution of 2011 the core of the Brotherhood's organisation was firmly rooted in a layer of university-educated would-be professionals who were frustrated by the contradiction between the promise of fulfilling, well-rewarded work in an expanding economy and the reality of dead-end jobs or unemployment.[37] The other central element in the Brotherhood's ideology spoke powerfully to the same social layer: in response to the humiliations imposed by Western powers on the military, economic and cultural levels, the Brotherhood offered both explanation and remedy for the failure of national liberation under Nasser.[38]

Islamist movements have often proposed 'solutions' for both of these problems which presuppose that fighting the 'enemy within' – whether in the form of other Muslims, non-Muslim communities, unveiled or 'immodest' women or the left – is a route to achieving social and political renewal. However, this may be combined with attempts to win support for programmes of social and political reforms or mobilise popular anti-imperialist movements. Moreover, the balance between these different elements is constantly shifting, reflecting the contradictions of such movements as they are torn between conflicting pressures reflecting the tensions between the expectations of their membership and the constant compromises of their leaders. As Harman notes, the most useful comparison is not with fascist movements but with other Third World nationalist movements which have attracted the support of similar social layers.[39]

However, we also assess the Muslim Brotherhood's role by asking where the organisation sits within a range of responses to the state. Egypt has witnessed over the past century the rise and fall of Islamist movements which have proposed answers across

the political spectrum – from electoralism with the aim of securing reforms, to the exemplary violence of revolutionary guerrilla
warfare, to attempts to create a pious society through internal exile
and withdrawal. The balance between reformist and revolutionary
currents has also continually shifted, although there have been
several repetitions of a pattern where the repression of reformist
currents has led to a minority drawing the conclusion that the existing state must be overthrown and as a consequence turning towards
armed struggle. Thus it was the repression of the Brotherhood in
1954 by Nasser which propelled Sayyid Qutb towards formulating
ideas that were taken up by jihadi groups in the 1970s, while when
Sadat turned on the Gama'a Islamiyya at the beginning of the 1980s
this prompted a new wave of radicalism which fed into the armed
struggles of the 1980s and 1990s. The wave of repression against the
Muslim Brotherhood which began in the wake of Morsi's downfall
is clearly already producing very similar results.

Thus, while we recognise the specific character of the Brotherhood as an Islamist organisation, with a particular ideology,
history and social composition, we argue that it is also important
to understand it as a *reformist* organisation. By this we mean
that the Brotherhood advocated reforms to the political system,
while rejecting fundamental changes to the form or content of
the state, not that it is a 'reformist' organisation in the sense
sometimes understood in a European context, where the term can
appear as a synonym for 'social democratic'. The Brotherhood is
not, and never has been, a party of the organised working class,
despite having large numbers of workers as members. Nor has
the Brotherhood's programme ever had much social-democratic
content – the organisation's stance on issues such as privatisation,
labour law reform, land ownership, defence of public services and
the welfare system has generally been weak and hesitant.

It could justifiably be argued that the Brotherhood's reformism
in relation to Egypt's political system was also in general weak

and hesitant. As we discuss in more detail in Chapters 8 and 9, the Brotherhood did not even strongly advocate any serious programme of political reforms aimed at expanding democratic governance or checking the power of the military or security forces. And the reforms that the organisation championed most strongly once in power, such as the judicial reform programme, alienated even the Brotherhood's former allies among the judiciary. Yet we believe that seeing the Brotherhood as merely another faction of the ruling-class-in-waiting (despite the fact that its leaders clearly hoped it would be) risks underestimating the organisation's powerful appeal as an apparently viable reformist alternative to the old regime.

The reasons why so many Egyptians projected their hopes of reform onto the Brotherhood were both positive and negative; in other words they expressed both what the organisation *was* and what it *was not*. The Brotherhood, it is critically important to emphasise, was by far the largest political organisation in Egypt outside the old ruling party, and in 2011 had never been tested in power, not even in local government. It had only once, in the 2005 elections, won more than a handful of parliamentary seats. This brief period of respite from repression had ended with the 2010 parliamentary elections where the ruling party had reasserted complete control of the electoral arena. Although some of its leaders, such as Khairat al-Shatir, had in other ways impeccable establishment credentials as millionaire businessmen, they were alternately persecuted and marginalised in the pre-revolutionary period. The fact that it took a revolution to force open a space in which the Brotherhood could even begin to play a meaningful reformist role (in the sense of advocating reforms that the organisation might be in a position to test in practice) underscores this point still further.

The negative reasons why millions invested their hopes in the Brotherhood relate to the weakness or absence of the political alternatives. As we discuss in Chapter 8, the Brotherhood's electoral success in 2011 reflected not only the legacy of the organisation's long history in opposition to the regime, but also the advantages conferred by access to organisational resources and funding which their opponents lacked. Secular reformists such as the liberals Ayman Nur or Mohamed ElBaradei, who, like the Brotherhood, had been marginalised or persecuted by the old regime, had no organisation which could even begin to compete with the Brotherhood on a national level. Hamdeen Sabahi, the Nasserist figure with the biggest national profile, began the revolutionary period in a similar position, and rejected the option of building an independent organisation, instead focusing on creating a relatively loose coalition of supporters, the Popular Current, which was quickly infiltrated by elements from the old ruling party in many areas. The revolutionary youth groups and the very small forces of the revolutionary left likewise lacked the organisation and numbers to compete with the Brotherhood on the electoral terrain.

Nor, it turned out, were the Brotherhood's reformist or revolutionary opponents capable of using their influence outside the electoral arena in order to maintain the momentum of the revolutionary process. The secular reformists, principally the Liberals and the Nasserists, as exemplified by ElBaradei and Sabahi themselves, formed an alliance with figures from the old ruling party such as Amr Moussa, who had fallen out of favour with the regime in the immediate pre-revolutionary period. The National Salvation Front gave political direction to the massive waves of street protests which engulfed Morsi in November–December 2012 and June 2013. Although its members lacked the organisational forces to mobilise for them directly, it was the politics embodied by the Front's leadership which prevailed. This included, as we discuss in Chapter 9, an even more insipid version of the Brotherhood's milk-and-water reformism. Rather

than advancing a political programme of their own and mobilising
their supporters for expanded democratic and social rights, the
Liberals and Nasserists instead opened the door to the political rehabilitation of the military and the security forces, under
the cloak of defending the 'independence of the judiciary'. The
final catastrophic consequences of this approach played out in
the crisis of 30 June 2013 and its aftermath, when the military
intervened against the Brotherhood in order to turn frustration
with Mohamed Morsi in a counter-revolutionary direction.

Reformism and the workers' movement

The mainstream Islamist and secular reformist currents in Egypt
were thus both strong and weak across different dimensions. They
were strong enough to undermine the impetus of the revolutionary
process, and divert the energies of the popular movement away
from the assault on the core institutions of the old regime which
had begun with the 18 day uprising against Mubarak. However,
they were also weak and pliable in the face of counter-revolution,
in large part because they feared the half-formed spectres of a
potentially much deeper revolutionary process which the rising
tide of social struggles was beginning to unleash. One of the
key themes that this book will explore is the absence of workers'
voices on the national political stage, despite their evident social
power. The mainstream Islamist and secular liberal reformist
currents gave no expression to workers' social demands. The
Nasserist Hamdeen Sabahi appeared to offer a potential break
from this pattern during his presidential election campaign, which
promised a strong programme of social reforms. However, as
noted above, Sabahi prioritised the making of political alliances
against Morsi with the *feloul* above mobilising independently of
these political forces in support of the social demands of workers
and the poor.

We also discuss 'reformism' within the workers' movement in later chapters, from a perspective that goes beyond examining how workers engaged with the various political organisations claiming to offer a programme for the reform of the state. In Chapters 3 and 4 we explore how the struggle for day-to-day reforms at a workplace level, in the shape of battles over pay and conditions, transcended the expectations of those who argued that this kind of everyday 'reformism' was inevitably self-limiting and could not connect with the growing agitation for political change. An influential current within academic writing about the Egyptian workers' movement has argued that workers' resistance to the early stages of neoliberal reforms was best understood as the operation of a 'moral economy', where protests were triggered by workers' attempts to restore the patron–client relationship with the state which they had experienced during Nasser's rule.[40] We disagree with the contention that workers' everyday struggles for reforms were therefore only capable of expressing a nostalgic desire to restore the social relations of the past. In Chapters 3 and 4 we examine how changes in the form and content of workers' collective action after 2006 demonstrated that workers had begun to reject the reformism of previous generations, which focused on winning concessions through the existing trade unions and professional associations rather than by means of their independently organised struggles.

This rupture with the past did not, however, mean that the pressures for a reformist solution to the social and political crisis lessened. Rather, they reappeared in different guises. In Chapter 5 we examine how the birth of the independent unions created a space for new reformist practices to take hold, with the emergence of a trade-union bureaucracy. Despite the counter-pressures on strike leaders such as Kamal Abu Aita from a democratic culture of rank-and-file organising, the pull of various kinds of bureaucratic reformism within the independent unions proved surprisingly strong. We identify in Chapters 4 and 6 several different sources of the pressures towards the development of a new trade-union bureaucracy. These include the nature of trade unionism itself, which as a form of workers' self-organisation is inevitably focused on mitigating the effects of exploitation rather than removing the source of it altogether. The role of the state was critical in this respect: at crucial moments in the independent unions' development sections of the state bureaucracy were prepared to accord the new unions' leaders de facto recognition as legitimate bargaining partners (even if other state institutions continued to harass them legally and physically). In the case of two of the first independent unions, the Property Tax Collectors' union RETAU (Real Estate Tax Authority Union) and the Independent School Teachers Union, relationships with the international trade-union bureaucracy and in particular the active interest of the ITUC in forging links with the emerging independent unions was an important factor in hastening the development of bureaucratic practices. We also identify a model of 'NGO trade unionism' which was partially connected to these links with the international trade-union bureaucracy, but which could also operate independently. In this model, the most important function of the emerging trade-union bureaucracy was not bargaining with employers, but campaigning and lobbying on behalf of different groups of workers. We argue that this model was strongly evident in the development of the two main federations of independent unions in Egypt, EFITU and EDLC.

The pressures towards the dominance of the bureaucracy were, however, always subject to counter-pressures from below. We outline in Chapter 4 how the tensions between highly democratic forms of strike organisation and the tendencies towards bureaucratisation played out in RETAU. In Chapter 6 we explore how this process was repeated on a bigger scale with the explosive growth of independent unions in the wake of Mubarak's fall.

The experience of Egypt validates, we argue, key elements of the approach to understanding the role of the trade-union bureaucracy which has been developed by Marxist and Marxist-influenced theorists.[41] Cliff and Gluckstein's classic statement of this position emphasizes two central points. The first is that full-time trade-union officials occupy a unique position in capitalist societies: they are neither employers nor workers, but are positioned as mediators between the two and subject to pressures from both sides. However, as their sociological function is determined by the maintenance of the reformist machinery that they control, they will inevitably tend towards conciliation with employers and the state where possible.[42] Second, a conflict of interests between the trade-union bureaucracy and rank-and-file union activists and members is a permanent feature of trade unionism. A recent restatement and defence of this approach by Darlington and Upchurch argues that, contrary to the critique developed by Hyman in the late 1970s, the division between bureaucracy and rank and file in trade unions is 'a meaningful generalisation of a real contradiction within trade unionism'.[43]

Darlington and Upchurch argue that a combination of four different aspects of the trade-union bureaucracy (by which they mean full-time officials in the leadership of national unions) help us to understand their unique position: 'their social role, their bargaining function, their relationship with social democracy, and their power relationship with union members'.[44] Although this approach was formulated specifically to analyse the nature of the trade-union bureaucracy in the British context, we argue here that an analogous combination of factors helps to explain the role of the trade-union bureaucracy in the independent unions in Egypt. In the Egyptian case, the most important features of the bureaucracy's social role were not the comfortable salaries and secure jobs that trade-union officials in Britain enjoy, but rather their relative isolation from the day-to-day pressures of the workplace and the prestige and influence they obtained from their position. And while the leadership of EFITU, for example, did not wield the organisational power of their British counterparts, they were able to mobilise resources which most workplace activists could not: access to the national media, access to national politicians and employers' representatives, and access to the international trade-union movement. And while social-democratic politics of the British or European model was absent (a point we discuss more fully below), the Nasserism of trade-union leaders such as Kamal Abu Aita proved in practice to be its functional equivalent. In Chapters 8 and 9 we analyse how this was expressed in the role played by a key layer of trade-union activists in Hamdeen Sabahi's presidential campaign, and later by Abu Aita's acceptance of a ministerial role in the post-Morsi cabinet appointed by the Armed Forces in July 2013. Finally, the pressures inherent in trade-union officials' bargaining role are common to both contexts, although – as we discuss in Chapter 6 – in Egypt these tended to operate most strongly on the actual strike leaderships rather than necessarily on the very small layer of officials around the national federations, who largely performed campaigning and lobbying functions in relation to strikes.

These factors go some way towards explaining the strength of reformism within the workers' movement. However, as we indicated above, reformism in this context as well as the domain of national politics was also in many ways surprisingly weak. One obvious expression of this weakness can be found in the failure of the workers' movement to articulate its own *political* agenda – of either a reformist or a revolutionary kind. This was despite the strength of workers' collective voices in not only raising demands for social justice in an abstract and general sense, but in putting forward a series of concrete demands, which if implemented would have constituted a considerable challenge to the neo-liberal authoritarian regime that both pre- and post-revolutionary governments upheld. Their principal demands were the return of privatised companies to the state; a rise in the minimum wage and the redistribution of wealth through the enforcement of a maximum wage; job security for precarious workers; more state spending on health and education; and legal protection for the right to strike and organise. The inclusion of Abu Aita in the post-Morsi government and the unfulfilled promises he made at the time of meeting these demands can be read as a deflected recognition by the military of the power of the social agenda of the workers' movement.

Yet the circumstances in which these promises were made, in the midst of a counter-revolutionary offensive by the Armed Forces and the Ministry of the Interior, also points to the political weakness of the reformists within the workers' movement. They were unable to win any of the mainstream reformist parties to their cause, or even to force meaningful concessions on any of the movement's key demands from the state. Nor were they capable of creating a reformist party of their own, either in a social-democratic or a populist mould. Instead they vacillated between a defence of trade-union neutrality in narrow syndicalist terms, arguing that 'politics' had no place within the trade-union move-ment, and capitulation to the nationalist agenda of the military leadership, which dressed up its counter-revolutionary intentions in jingoistic 'anti-imperialist' language.

There are a range of potential reasons why the Egyptian Revo-lution did not give birth to a mass reformist workers' party. There is not space in this volume to give this question the attention it deserves. However, we can observe that the most important reasons are likely to involve the following combination of objec-tive and subjective factors. On the objective side, it is easy to forget the effectiveness of the Nasserist model of state capitalist authoritarianism in reducing to almost nothing the space for workers to gain independent organisational experience in the pre-revolutionary period. In contrast to, for example, Bolivia, where the explosion of a revolutionary crisis in 2000–2005 was preceded by decades of workplace, community and electoral organising by trade unionists and indigenous activists, the organisational experience of the Egyptian workers' movement was relatively impoverished until a mere five years or so before the revolution itself.[45] On the subjective side, the presence of Islamist currents as the main reformist organisations limited the space for other kinds of reformist political organisations to grow. The political choices made by the Islamists' opponents, in particular the strong influence of Nasserism on key figures such as Abu Aita, was also a critical factor in pushing reformist trade-union leaders in the direction of political accommodation with the state, as we discuss further in Chapter 9.

Towards 'permanent revolution'?

In 1850, as the storm of counter-revolution raged across Europe, Karl Marx and Friedrich Engels wrote an address for the Central Committee of the Communist League, the revolutionary organisation which had helped to lead the revolutionary upheavals of the previous two years. In the similarly difficult circumstances of Egypt today, we have looked to their theoretical insights to point to the potential for a different future. Although Marx and Engels were still hopeful that the revolutions which had convulsed half a continent were not yet defeated, they recognised that the revolution in Germany revealed challenges that they had not even imagined back in 1848. Like most of their comrades in the embryonic revolutionary socialist movement, they thought then that alliance between the radical and bourgeois opponents of the absolutist regimes of Europe was still possible. During the course of events it became clear that the bourgeoisie feared the spectre of the 'Social Republic' – the form of radical republican regime which united radical democrats from middle-class and artisan backgrounds with their working-class allies – even more than the monarchy. Yet Marx's hopes that the radicals and organised workers alone could triumph over absolutism were also dashed, as the radical democrats followed the same path as their bourgeois counterparts and turned on workers and the poor. The only real alternative to counter-revolution, Marx concluded, was proletarian revolution, even if this required a period of 'protracted revolutionary development' of workers' independent political organisation, and the internationalisation of the revolution through the victory of the workers' movement in France.[46]

Leon Trotsky, in the jail where the defeat of the 1905 Russian Revolution had left him, expanded and reworked Marx's 1850 call for 'permanent revolution' into a theory which would allow Russian revolutionary socialists to overcome a similar set of challenges. Like their German counterparts in the mid-nineteenth century, they found that their weak and vacillating bourgeois liberal allies collapsed into the arms of autocracy at the first opportunity, terrified by the spectre of working-class self-organisation in the mass strikes which shook urban Russia during the course of the revolutionary year. In response he proposed three connected ideas: first, that the organised working class could turn the uneven and combined nature of economic development in Russia that we discussed above to its advantage. The concentration of workers in large, modern enterprises, in sectors of the economy critical to the state, would give organised workers the necessary social weight to take up the political leadership of the 'democratic revolution' over autocracy. Second, rather than voluntarily hand back political power to the bourgeoisie, which had been incapable of leading the struggle against the tsar, the working class should turn the democratic revolution into a socialist revolution, bypassing the need for a phase of capitalist democracy. This would leave the working class in 'backward' Russia far in advance of the working class in the more developed countries of Europe, having assumed state power in a country without the material resources to make socialism a reality. Trotsky solved this problem with a final component of the theory: the internationalisation of the revolutionary process, which would spread from East to West and end the isolation of the Russian vanguard.

While there is not space here to explore the development of either Marx's or Trotsky's conceptions of 'permanent revolution' and debates over the relationship between them,[47] we argue that the central concerns of both versions of the concept remain critically important to understanding the dynamics of revolution in the context of Egypt and the wider region. Both versions of the concept attempt a theoretical resolution of the tension between the social and the democratic 'souls' of the revolution. The political organisation of the working class appears in both as the force which implements the democratic revolution in the course of achieving social revolution. In Trotsky's version of the concept, this can be seen as the working class turning the 'explosive amalgam' of contradictory social and political relations created by uneven and combined development in its favour at a national level.

Likewise both versions of the concept propose a theoretical resolution of the tension between the national and international elements of the revolutionary process, through the internationalisation of the revolution. Marx and Engels in 1850 only referred to the internationalisation of revolution in a positive sense, as they outlined hopes that the victory of proletarian revolution in France would compensate for the relative political and social backwardness of the German working class and accelerate its development. History demonstrated, of course, that it was the internationalisation of absolutist *counter-revolution* which eventually snuffed out the revolutionary hopes of 1848 – a fact that loomed large in the minds of subsequent generations of revolutionaries. Again, this can be seen as switching the operation of uneven and combined development at an international level from a process favouring capital accumulation in the most powerful states and capitals into one which transmits the explosive instabilities from the periphery of the global system back into the core by uniting workers across national boundaries in a common revolutionary struggle.

The 1905 Revolution, however, provided Trotsky with an element that was necessarily missing in 1850: the institutional form which moved the resolution of the contradiction between the democratic and social revolutions from the realm of theory to that of practice. The council of workers' delegates in St Petersburg, which Trotsky himself chaired, was the first example of the practical means by which the Bolsheviks would later put Trotsky's theory into practice in 1917. The Soviet was both the organiser of the social struggle, through its leadership of the mass strike, and the embryonic form of the future workers' state. It reached for political authority as a consequence of its command of workers' social power, making actual what was only latent in the mass strike itself. Without soviets or institutions of the same sort, Trotsky's insights remain at the level of an abstract theory within international political economy. And it was Lenin, rather than Trotsky, who developed a fuller understanding of how the elemental attributes of the future workers' state could be found in the actual institutions created in the course of revolutionary struggles, using the Paris Commune and the Russian soviets as examples.[48]

What is the relevance of the concept of permanent revolution in the Egyptian context, however? Here we can only hope to sketch the bare outlines of a response, by sharing what elements of the concept we have found most useful in guiding our analysis. A first, and critically important, point here is that by referring to permanent revolution, we are not implying that Egypt needs a bourgeois revolution. The capitalist class is already in power and has been for several decades – even if this has been somewhat obscured by the fact that for much of that period state capitalist elements have dominated. Moreover, the 'combined' features of development which shape Egyptian society are combinations of different phases of *capitalism*.[49] Nor are we saying that institutions of a soviet type appeared in Egypt during 2011–13, even though some of the conditions making possible the creation of such institutions were present, including extremely high levels of strike action and a strong culture of democratic organisation at a workplace level in the context of a profound crisis of the state.

Nevertheless, the experience of Egypt between 2011 and 2014 confirms that the central questions which the concept of permanent revolution sought to address are still the axis on which the fate of the revolution turns. We have focused on one of these more fully in this book, namely the contradictory relationship between the revolution's social and democratic souls. However, the partnership between the Saudi capitalist class and the Egyptian military in the counter-revolutionary coup of July 2013 confirms once again that nationalism is no defence against the internationalisation of counter-revolution. The relationship between the national and international dimensions of the revolutionary process can also be seen as characterised by oscillation between unity and contradiction. The January Revolution mobilised national symbols against the Mubarak regime: from the cross and crescent of the 1919 Revolution scrawled on the burnt-out walls of the ruling party's headquarters to the sea of red, white and black national flags. It triggered an international tsunami of protest and inspired movements across the globe. Yet July 2013 showed it could be eaten up by nationalism, expressed even before Morsi's fall in racist posturing by politicians over the dispute with Ethiopia over the Nile waters, xenophobic attacks on Syrian refugees, and eventual collapse into uncritical support for the army by many who identified with the January revolution.

In Chapters 1 and 2, we examine how the shift from a largely state capitalist to a more neoliberal economy created an explosive amalgam of political and social relations which was detonated in 2011 as the result of the *interaction* between social and political struggles against the regime over the previous half-decade. Chapter 3 discusses how strikes and protests were enmeshed in a mutually reinforcing process of reciprocal action where the social and democratic souls of the struggle against the regime became every more tightly interlaced. Chapters 4 and 5 look at this process in detail from the perspective of the workplaces, analysing first the crisis of the Nasserist model for managing workers' discontent and then the historic leap from temporary strike committee to independent union.

Chapter 6 examines the dynamics of reciprocal action between social and political struggles, during the revolutionary process launched by the 18 Days uprising against Mubarak in January 2011. However, as we discuss in Chapters 7, 8 and 9, the social and democratic souls of the revolution did not only 'interlace' and occasionally embrace – they were also in constant tension. Chapter 7 explores the successes and failures of the workers' movement after Mubarak's fall: an explosive growth of independent workplace organisation, but also the rapid bureaucratisation of a layer within the new unions' leadership and the failure to force the state to meet workers' political demands. The tensions between the social and democratic struggles in the electoral arena are the subject of Chapter 8, while Chapter 9 analyses the challenge of *tathir*, cleansing the state.

In the conclusion we return to the question of the institutional forms and practices which offer the greatest potential for the resolution of the contradictions between the social and democratic, national and international, aspects of the revolutionary process through the realisation of the demands of bread, freedom and social justice.

CHAPTER 1

From Nasserism to neoliberalism: a new amalgam of state and private capital

On a sunny winter's day, just as 2010 was drawing to a close, a ship called *Al-Hurriya 3* (*Freedom 3*) careered down the slipway into the blue waters of the Mediterranean. Behind the crowds of cheering shipyard workers, anxious engineers and managers, Egypt's most senior army officer, and Minister of Defence, Field Marshal Hussein Tantawi watched the 10,000-tonne container vessel settle gently into the waters of the dock. For Tantawi and his colleagues, the launch of *Al-Hurriya 3* represented more than a routine official engagement. Rather, it was a chance to see first-hand the fruits of an investment made three years previously in August 2007 when the Ministry of Defence took over the Alexandria Shipyards from the state-owned Holding Company for Shipping.

Just like other investors, Tantawi and his colleagues had benefited from more than a decade of preparatory work before the sale of this prized state asset to new owners.[1] Failed attempts to privatise the shipyard in the 1990s had demonstrated the need for more government investment in the infrastructure surrounding the yard.[2] Naturally the workforce had been 'streamlined' and 'restructured', with 3,600 workers forced into early retirement on terms which benefited the government rather than the workers themselves, who continued to protest that they had been cheated out of their full pensions as the sell-off date approached.[3]

A gushing news report on the private satellite channel Dream congratulated the Armed Forces on *Al-Hurriya 3*'s launch. Accompanied by stirring martial music and panoramic shots of the shipyard, Rear Admiral Ibrahim Gabr al-Dasuqi emphasised the new owners' successes since acquiring the yard:

> Since the Alexandria Shipyard was transferred to the Ministry of Defence, we have begun a programme of complete development in every sector. We have rebuilt our client base after a period of falling orders, trained the workforce to the latest technological and technical standards and won ISO accreditation.[4]

The 'privatisation' of the Alexandria Shipyard fits uncomfortably with standard narratives of how neoliberal reforms have restructured the Egyptian economy over the past forty years. Rather than private capital rescuing an ailing state industry, it was another part of the state that stepped in. The 'sell-off prize' touted to international investors in the early 1990s turned out not to be so attractive to private capital after all.[5] Or did Tantawi's acquisition of the shipyard indicate that the military was acting to subtly frustrate neoliberal reforms, protecting not only its own interests but also those of a wider 'national' faction of capital, which saw 'the state, not global capitalism as their meal ticket', as Paul Mason puts it?[6] By intervening to 'support the development of national industries' (in the words of Dream TV's reporter), was the military defending the legacy of Gamal Abdel-Nasser, who ordered the building of the current shipyard in 1960 as part of his state capitalist programme to develop a local manufacturing base?[7]

As we explore in this chapter, the fate of the Alexandria Shipyard tells an important story about how the transition from a form of state capitalism under Nasser in the late 1950s and 1960s to the current neoliberal regime has never been simply about the retreat of the state from the economy. Rather, neoliberal reforms have created a new amalgam of state and private capital. A glance at the order books of the Alexandria Shipyard illustrates neatly that this amalgam is increasingly composed of transnational and regional as well as local state and private capitals: one of the yard's biggest clients in recent years has been Nile Cargo (formerly the National River Transportation Company), part of Nile Logistics, a platform company owned by private equity firm Citadel Capital.[8] Citadel brings together some of Egypt's biggest private capitalists with representatives of leading Saudi business groups, a UAE sovereign wealth fund, and the Qatari royal family.[9]

The rise of Nasserism

To understand what neoliberalism means in an Egyptian context, however, we have to go back to the heyday of Gamal Abdel-Nasser's regime in the 1950s and 1960s, in order to explore the nature of the state capitalist policies the neoliberal reformers apparently rejected. The political economy of Nasser's regime was shaped by the interaction of three major sets of factors. As a form of state capitalism, it was made necessary by the crisis of accumulation which the Egyptian ruling class had failed to solve during the final years of the monarchy, despite the development of increasingly interventionist policies designed to facilitate the build-up of sufficient capital to achieve industrial take-off.[10] The particular form that this state capitalist regime took was made possible by a specific conjuncture of geopolitical and domestic circumstances, however. The seizure of power by junior officers in the Egyptian army in July 1952 was on the one hand an expression of a general trend across much of the colonised world, and their success was enabled both by the retreat of the old empires and the rise of a mass, popular anti-colonial movement.[11] The workers'

movement played a crucial role in the development of this mass
movement from below as independent workers' organisations
emerged for the first time from the shadow of the liberal nationalist movement of the previous generation, the Wafd, and shook off
the tutelage of ruling-class patrons such as Prince Abbas Halim.[12]
The Free Officers took power on the cusp of the 'Long Boom', a
period of sustained expansion in the global economy driven by a
combination of the adoption of policies which privileged the role
of the state as the principal organiser of capital accumulation and
the diversion of excess value into military spending by the USA
and the USSR.[13] This created an opportunity for the Nasserist
regime to balance its *political* suppression of the independent
workers' movement with its *social* incorporation, by a limited
shift in the distributive and redistributive policies of the state in
favour of the poor in general and urban workers in particular.
The workers' movement which had emerged during the social
and political struggles of the 1940s and early 1950s was too independent and well organised to be ignored or easily crushed. On
the other hand, neither was it strong enough to impose its own
leadership on the wider popular movement, which challenged
both continued British occupation and the monarchy itself.

The modern history of workers' organisation in Egypt is generally accepted to have begun with strikes by workers in cigarette
factories in 1899, which led to the establishment of embryonic
trade unions.[14] The economic restructuring that took place during
the First World War, as a result of the interruption of trade and the
greater reliance on Egyptian production either by the Egyptians
or the British occupation forces, saw the working class grow in
number and importance. Even before the end of the war strikes
erupted among the cigarette workers and tramway workers of
Alexandria. Strikes by workers likewise played an important role
in the 1919 Revolution led by the liberal nationalists of the Wafd
Party against continued British occupation. The first national

federation of unions was established in February 1921 with twenty-one local affiliates representing around 3,000 workers.[15] By the beginning of 1924, the new unions had mushroomed: in Alexandria alone local unions counted between 15,000 and 20,000 members.[16] Compromise between the nationalist leaders of the Wafd and the British authorities paved the way for the repression of the trade-union movement by the Wafdist government which took office in 1924, however. The 1930s saw the slow revival of the workers' movement, although largely under the patronage of leaders from outside the working class, including Prince Abbas Halim, a maverick member of the Egyptian royal family who presided over the establishment of a number of workers' organisations. The Wafd, particularly during its increasingly lengthy spells out of government, also nurtured its own trade unions.[17]

The 1940s saw a qualitative change in the nature of the trade-union movement. As during the First World War, the economic needs of the British military provided the impetus for a further expansion of Egyptian industry. The workers' movement began to take shape across a wide range of economic sectors, from the textile mills of Al-Mahalla al-Kubra, Alexandria and Shubra al-Khaima, to the sugar refineries and cement works in Hawamidiyya near Helwan, and across the expanding modern transport infrastructure. However, this period not only saw the expansion and deepening of trade-union organisation, but also witnessed a dramatic shift in trade unionists' political consciousness. Democratic practice in trade-union organising strengthened the movement in the face of the authorities' attempts to repress it.[18] The trade unions' living interaction with political issues and organisations did not compromise the movement's independence, as is clear from the debates in the trade-union press and literature of the period, which displays a refined awareness of the question. A generation of working-class leaders such as Yusif al-Mudarrik and Taha Sa'ad Uthman emerged to lead the trade unions, which were established in the course of industrial and political struggles. The broad experience of political activities across the workers' movement indicates the expansion of workers' political consciousness. The nascent Egyptian trade-union movement made its first international appearance with the arrival of Egyptian delegations to the 1945 Paris conference of the World Federation of Trade Unions.[19]

The Workers' Committee for National Liberation (WCNL), which was founded in 1945 by leading activists among the textile workers' union in Shubra al-Khaima and other trade unionists, is one example of how worker activists sought to articulate a distinctive contribution by the workers' movement to the struggle against the British. Within a few months of the WCNL's foundation, the rising tide of strikes and protests provided the opportunity for the development of new and broader forms of practical coordination and leadership within the growing movement calling for British evacuation. The National Committee of Workers and Students brought together student and worker delegates to organise massive joint protests and strikes on 21 February and 4 March 1946 in response to attacks on student protesters.[20] Worker activists' consciousness of being part of a wider battle for 'national liberation' from colonialism extended beyond the borders of Egypt. Suez Canal workers organised to resist the passage through the canal in 1947 of the Dutch vessel *Volendam*, which was en route to suppress the national movement in Indonesia.[21]

The nature of the relationship between the 'economic' goals of the workers' movement and the 'political' aims of the popular anti-colonial struggle was the subject of intense debate. Communist activists, who played an important and very influential role in the leadership of many of the new trade unions, argued that there was an organic connection between the battle to improve workers' pay and conditions, on the one hand, and the struggle for British evacuation and domestic political change, on the other. Moreover, they believed that workers' organisations should play a role in leading the political movement against the British. This perspective was challenged from outside the workers' movement by the liberal nationalists of the Wafd, on the one hand, and the Muslim Brotherhood, on the other, which both sought to subordinate workers' independent political action to their own direction. Within the trade unions there were also non-Communist working-class leaders, such as Anwar Salama of the Eastern Tobacco Workers' Union, who were supportive of the idea that trade unions should concern themselves with supporting workers' demands for improved conditions at work and shun political activism. The British authorities also purposely cultivated a small reformist, anti-Communist trend among leading worker activists, and recruited the leader of the Cairo Chaffeurs' Union, Ibrahim Zayn-al-Din, as a paid agent to promote this view.[22]

Despite the efforts of the British to promote a brand of reformist trade unionism modelled on the practice of the British Trades Union Congress, the perspectives of the Egyptian Communists were in many ways much closer to the experience of the tens of thousands of workers who took part in protests and strikes during this period. The space in which reformist trade unionism could operate was extremely narrow. Not merely state repression of workers' strikes and the periodic suppression of the trade unions, but the very intimate relationship between the repressive apparatus of the Egyptian monarchy and the British occupation reinforced the Communists' messages. Moreover, the trade unions were growing in a context where waves of political and economic struggles were inextricably interlaced, culminating in the great wave of protests and strikes in the winter of 1951–52, which saw demonstrations of around 500,000 in Cairo and 250,000 in Alexandria and the explosion of guerrilla warfare against the British in the Canal Zone.[23]

The Free Officers' coup was initially welcomed by large sections of the workers' movement because of the officers' declarations of support for the anti-colonial movement and their hostility to the monarchy. The first direct encounter between the officers and striking workers was an exercise in brutal repression, however. The army suppressed a strike by textile workers in Kafr al-Dawwar in August 1952 and transferred workers to a military tribunal, which hastily issued sentences of hard labour and executed two of the strike leaders, Mustafa Khamis and Mohamed al-Baqari. The response to the strike split the trade-union movement, with most of the unions supporting the position of the Free Officers and denounced the strikers as 'terrorists'. The Founding Committee for a General Federation of Egyptian Trade Unions issued a statement denouncing the Kafr al-Dawwar strike as motivated by pro-imperialist interests, while Communist activists toured workplaces in the company of army officers, appealing for calm.[24] Despite these expressions of support, the Free Officers launched a campaign of repression against the trade unions and banned the planned founding conference of the Federation.[25]

The events of March 1954 were another turning point in the relationship between the workers' movement and the military regime. Conflict within the ruling Revolutionary Command Council spilled out into the streets and workplaces. A minority faction, led by President Muhammed Naguib and supported by left-wing cavalry officer Khaled Mohi-el-Din, argued for the return of the army to its barracks and the restoration of some form of parliamentary democracy, while Gamal Abdel-Nasser led the majority of his colleagues in support of the continuation of military rule in order to ensure the evacuation of British troops. Both factions attempted to win the backing of the trade unions, and the workers' movement was split between support for Abdel-Nasser and Naguib. Despite the opposition of trade unionists in Alexandria and Kafr al-Dawwar, Nasser's control of the Interior Ministry, however, gave a decisive advantage to the minority of trade unionists who were working with the Revolutionary

Command Council. He mobilised the police and the state's newly created mass organisations such as the Liberation Rally and the paramilitary National Guard to create an impression of widespread popular support for a strike by Cairo transport workers demanding the continuation of military rule.[26]

Although Nasser owed an important part of his victory over Naguib to this alliance with sections of the trade-union leadership, it was not until 1957 that the regime felt secure enough to permit the formation of a national federation of trade unions. The founding congress of the Egyptian Trade Union Federation (ETUF) took place on 30 January 1957, attended by 101 members representing seventeen unions and professional associations with 242,485 members, under the presidency of Anwar Salama, whose candidacy for the post of Federation president had been approved by Nasser.[27] The congress represented a decisive break with the past and the consummation of a new relationship between the trade unions and the state. Although the unions represented at the founding congress had their roots in the independent unions of the 1940s, the Federation created a new, centralised structure for the trade-union movement which was shaped fundamentally by the needs of the state, rather than responding to pressure from below for greater coordination across the workers' movement (see Chapter 4 for more details on the ETUF structure).

The incorporation of workers' organisations into the state played a pivotal role in the political economy of Nasserism. The single officially sanctioned trade-union federation assisted in the repression of workers' protests and strikes, mobilised workers to meet production goals and monopolised their remaining legal channels for political expression through control of nominations to the various representative bodies set up by the regime.[28] It was, however, also a key partner in a limited redistribution of wealth, which the Nasserist regime achieved chiefly through investment in workers' social welfare, education and housing, combined with subsidies on basic consumer goods and fuel, as much of this was organised directly through public-sector workplaces.

The role of the working class in the Nasserist system was shaped by a number of different factors. First, because – unlike in the USSR itself – industrialisation took place in the context of an expansion of global capitalism, it was not accompanied by the systematic driving down of urban workers' living standards.[29] Workers' wages rose significantly during the first phase of state-led industrialisation between 1960 and 1965.[30] Both ideologically and practically, this system of social welfare was made conditional on workers' economic and political quiescence. As Joel Beinin notes, the word 'strike' literally disappeared from the political discourse during the early years of Nasserism.[31] The incorporation of the trade unions into the state lay at the heart of regime's relationship with the working class. It was a policy designed to maintain peace on the shop floor and make the trade unions watchdogs of productivity. There was also a corresponding political impact, as the officially sanctioned unions came to control a large proportion of the nominations to the representative bodies of the regime. From the mid-1960s 50 per cent of seats in the National Assembly were reserved for workers and peasants. The bureaucratic apparatus that managed the trade unions on behalf of the state developed in parallel with the wider state bureaucracy which managed the public-sector enterprises. Although some of the trade-union leaders had played roles in the independent unions that had emerged in the 1940s, their role in the Nasserist system was much closer to that of other members of a class of state administrators and managers, than to a trade-union bureaucracy. With union dues collected by compulsory deductions from wages, the trade-union leaders' positions did not depend on their ability to maintain independent organisation and wrest concessions from the bosses or the state, but rather on their effectiveness in policing workers' discontent. The integration of the trade-union leadership into the wider Nasserist bureaucracy did not preclude some or even the majority of trade-union leaders occasionally acting as a relatively coherent bloc to protect their own interests against attempts to redistribute material resources and political power *within* the ruling class. It is in this light that the opposition of some of the trade-union leaders to the economic liberalisation policies of Nasser's successor, Anwar al-Sadat, is best understood.

Infitah and the long crisis of the Nasserist state

The first Five Year Plan of 1960/61 set ambitious goals for the rapid transformation of the Egyptian economy through industrialisation and increased agricultural productivity. Having failed to provide enough capital to meet the state's needs for this project, large sections of private capital were nationalised. Foreign loans, including funding from the USSR, provided another source of finance for projects such as the construction of the High Dam at Aswan. The period 1960–66 saw overall industrial production double in value. Other successes for the first Five Year Plan included the creation of a million new jobs and an annual rate of GDP growth of 6 percent.[32]

However, as Waterbury and Richards note, the 'Achilles heel' of Nasser's import-substitution policies quickly became apparent: Egypt's inability to earn enough foreign exchange to prevent a balance-of-payments crisis.[33] The second Five Year Plan was abandoned as the government failed to raise sufficient investment capital, and instead found itself having to negotiate with international lenders for loans to close the widening gap between imports and exports. Compensation agreements with foreign investors for the first wave of nationalisations in 1956 further drained foreign currency reserves. By the mid-1960s Nasser had already embarked on an austerity programme which forced down workers' wages and increased working hours. His successor,

Sadat, embarked on a series of reforms which aimed at opening the economy to Western investment.

Sadat's 'turn' from East to West was a pivotal moment in Egyptian history. The policy of *infitah* ('the opening') was a turn from a trajectory of state-capitalist development in partnership with the USSR towards a new set of economic and foreign policies which broadly followed the lead of the USA. At the level of practical policy, *infitah* was a set of measures that liberalised and partially re-privatised foreign trade, encouraged private-sector imports, initiated steps towards multiple exchange rates, reformed the Egyptian banking sector, reorganised the public sector and extended privileges to the Egyptian private sector.[34] The goal of these policies was to attract external finance to Egypt, primarily from the Gulf and the West. However, although the language of *infitah's* supporters still echoed the rhetoric of the previous era, the logic of their reorientation marked a more profound change. The conditions attached to Sadat's application for a junior partnership with the US ruling class and its allies would be set by the global shift in economic policy prompted by the end of the long boom of the 1960s and the crisis of state-led development, which in turn precipitated the abandonment of Keynesianism in favour of the neoclassical and neoliberal schools of economic thought.

The new economic orthodoxy held that retrenchment and austerity would not be enough to restore profitability. Cutting wages, enforcing longer working hours, slashing spending on welfare: all of these mechanisms for making the poor pay for the crisis had a role to play. However, they were to be supplemented by a concerted effort to reconfigure the balance between the extractive and redistributive functions of the state for the benefit of a new coalition of state and private capitalists. *Infitah* necessarily involved a rebalancing of the relative economic and political weight of different sections of the ruling class, and therefore it was likely there would be winners and losers. There was thus intense debate and occasional conflict within the ruling class about tactics, despite the general and long-lasting consensus that there was no other viable strategy. Crucially, *infitah* also ignited resistance from below in the form of protests and strikes. The seriousness of this threat was made obvious to Sadat in January 1977 with the explosion of the 'Bread Uprising', a spontaneous wave of mass protests and riots in response the removal of subsidies on some basic goods, including bread, at the urging of the International Monetary Fund (IMF). The protests erupted against a backdrop of rising social and political tension, including a rise in street demonstrations and strikes, including one by Cairo bus workers in 1976. *Infitah* was a thus a protracted process which proceeded through several stages. The ruling class sought to put off for as long as possible the need to 'bite the bullet' and risk further social explosions. Sadat therefore used Egypt's strategic value as leverage to gain access to massive US subsidies. This combination of limited liberalisation and the expansion of private and foreign capital, combined with a new subsidy regime, worked for a while but by the end of the 1980s Egypt was perilously close to defaulting on interest payments on the US loans agreed in the 1970s.[35]

The scale of the economic crisis facing the regime in the late 1980s is illustrated by headline economic indicators from the period. Rates of GDP growth declined continuously between 1985 and 1991, with the exception of 1990, which saw a very slight increase. The same period also witnessed high inflation rates, a rise in unemployment, and a series of explosive protests and strikes, including the 1986 revolt by conscripts in the Central Security Forces, a rail strike in 1986 and a sit-in strike by steel workers in Helwan in 1989.[36]

Once again, economic crisis and shifts in the geopolitical balance intersected. The Mubarak regime's support for the US-led assault on Iraq following the invasion of Kuwait in 1990 was essentially traded against a write-off of much of Egypt's

'Paris Club' debts. However, the aggressive assertion of US hegemony in the Middle East and the final collapse of the Soviet Union further narrowed the regime's space for manoeuvre, and lent the international lenders' insistence on the imposition of a programme of structural adjustment much greater force. The changed geopolitical circumstances were one factor behind the achievement of greater level of consensus within the ruling class about the need to impose economic reforms which were likely to ignite serious social discontent. In particular, the leadership of the Egyptian Trade Union Federation, sections of which had previously expressed opposition from within the regime to neoliberal economic reforms, supported the Economic Reform and Structural Adjustment Programme (ERSAP).[37]

Structural adjustment: the state withdraws from the Nasserist social contract

The first phase of the structural adjustment programme was ushered in with the passing of Law 203 of 1991. The law created a legal framework for privatisation by dividing the public sector into dozens of 'holding companies' which were granted the right to dispose of their affiliates through merger, liquidation, partition and sale. The public sector was thus transformed from an economic development project, whose success was judged by whether or not it met the social and political goals of the state, into an estate agent's inventory. One of the central purposes of the law was to break down the planned integration of the deeply interconnected public-sector industries in order to create openings for new partnerships between private and state capital at local, regional and transnational levels. Neoliberal reforms aimed to strip away the redistributive functions of the public sector, principally the state's commitment to provide secure employment for millions of workers and its acceptance of a central role in economic planning to ensure the provision of basic goods to its citizens. Law 203 did not, however, reduce the role of the public-sector bureaucracy, but rather made it the agent of its own privatisation. Article 3 of the law stipulated that the first boards of the holding companies and their subsidiaries would be composed of the existing directors and management boards of the public-sector companies from which they were formed.

Following its assault on the public sector, the state enacted legislation providing incentives to investors. Law 8 of 1997 (the 'Law of Investment Guarantees and Incentives') was one of the most important instruments of neoliberal economic transformation and a clear expression of the class bias of the state. The law prohibits the nationalisation or sequestration of companies and prevents any administrative authority from intervention in the pricing of products or to regulate profits. In addition it prohibits intervention by public authorities to cancel licenses or stop the use of licensed property except in cases where licence conditions have been violated and only with the express authorisation of the Prime Minister. The same law brought in corporate tax exemptions of between five and twenty years, and removed taxes from the authentication of company contracts, land registration and company registration. Similar exemptions were also applied to taxes on bond yields, securities and gains from mergers or divestments. Law 8 was only the first phase in the comprehensive restructuring of the taxation and tariff systems to the benefit of corporations and high earners: income and corporation taxes were slashed further by Ahmad Nazif's government and restrictions on imports were cut.[38] The new law set a tax rate of 20 per cent on incomes over LE40,000, only rising to 40 per cent on incomes above LE400,000. The combination of changes to the income tax system and exemptions granted to investors allowed a layer of big investors and senior government officials to amass vast fortunes. Eissa calculated that thirty-eight major companies headed by investors close to the government and state officials owed only 8 per cent of their LE31.5 billion profits in tax during 2007 and 2008.[39]

Once again, neoliberal reforms weakened or removed instruments that the state had previously used to achieve a limited redistribution of wealth from the rich to the poor. However, the process of tax reform was paired with an expansion of state investment in some areas of infrastructure, such as roads, ports, bridges and drainage systems and the electricity distribution network. Yet these were often projects which selectively benefited, and in effect subsidised private capital. One example is the aggressive reshaping of Egypt's urban landscapes through the construction of roads to luxury gated communities on the outskirts of Cairo.[40]

The third crucial element in the neoliberal programme was the enactment of a new Labour Law (Law 12 of 2003). Like the rest of the laws passed in the process of economic transformation, this legislation shows clearly the state's bias towards the interests of capital over the interests of workers. It undermined workers' rights to job stability and protection against unemployment by ensuring that temporary employment contracts would be the norm and not the exception. In contrast to previous laws, fixed-term contracts could now be renewed indefinitely without workers gaining extra protection for length of service, or their being converted into a permanent contract. The law also set strict limits on the right of workers to exercise the right to strike. Even the limited benefits apparently guaranteed to workers by the legislation remained unfulfilled. The law contains provisions for the formation of a National Council for Wages with the power to establish a rate for the minimum wage, to be reviewed every three years in accordance with the rising cost of living, for example. Yet it was not until after the revolution of 2011 that the Council was convened.

The World Bank identifies two phases in the privatisation programme between 1991 and 1999. The government sold or partially divested from fewer than 20 companies out of 314 between 1991 and 1995. Between 1996 and 1999 the privatisation process speeded up and the government also pursued other reforms more aggressively: the state sold its controlling interest in 65 companies and minority interest in a further 16.[41] Further privatisations between 1999 and 2004 raised the level of formal state divestment further to nearly 200 companies out of 314.[42] The government of Ahmad Nazif which took office in 2004 accelerated the privatisation programme once again, expanding its operation outside the framework of Law 203. Privatisation receipts accounted for 2.5 per cent and 1.9 per cent of GDP in FY 2005/6 and 2006/7, largely accounted for by the sale of a large state-owned bank, the Bank of Alexandria, and the part-privatisation of Telecom Egypt.[43]

The reduction of public-sector employment

One of the goals of the ERSAP programme was the reduction of the public-sector workforce, both in the sense of reducing the number of workers employed directly by the state and in the sense of degrading the conditions of that employment. As we explore below, the specific reforms that sought to cut the numbers of public-sector employees were part of a much wider process of restructuring which reshaped the Egyptian working class during the neoliberal era. However, for a number of reasons, these policies were very important in shaping that overall process. First, the number of workers affected by the Law 203 reforms was around 1 million, or slightly less than 20 per cent of the total government workforce of around 5.5 million employees across the public-sector companies, local and national government and military-owned industries (but not the armed forces).[44] The state-employed workforce represented around 37 per cent of a total labour force of 15.2 million at the onset of privatisation. Second, the organisation of the public sector was highly centralised, and dominated by large workplaces: the process of privatisation was geared towards breaking these down into smaller parts that would be more attractive to private capital investment. Finally, a number of the large public-sector companies had accumulated long traditions of strike organisation and histories of militancy, particularly in the textile sector. The dispersal of the collective experience of workers in these companies compounded the sense of defeat and decline among these sections of the working class.

By 2001 the workforce employed by the state-owned enterprises targeted by Law 203 had been reduced by more than half, to 453,000. The state had deployed a variety of mechanisms in order to achieve this reduction, including restructuring prior to privatisation through an early retirement scheme (167,000 employees), divestiture to the private sector (222,000 employees) and not replacing workers who reached retirement age (148,000 employees).

Transfer of employment out of the public sector affected the workers concerned and their families negatively in a number of ways. In the mid-1990s real wages in the public and private sectors were approximately equal and continued to rise in a relatively synchronised fashion until 2000, when the gap began to widen. By 2005 the index of private-sector wages stood at 120 against a baseline of 100 in 1995, whereas the public-sector wage index had increased to 180.[45] Moreover, public-sector employment carries with it access to important non-wage benefits, including health benefits, retirement pensions and shorter working hours (which allow employees the time to take on a second job), as well as far greater job security.[46] Bassiouny notes the overall dramatic rise in job insecurity and declining access to social insurance across the workforce during the 1998–2006 period, correlating with the second and third accelerations in the privatisation programme. Between 1998 and 2006 the proportion of workers with an employment contract fell from 61.7 per cent to 42 per cent, while the proportion covered by social insurance dropped from 54.1 per cent to 42.26 per cent.[47]

In addition to the loss of wages and non-wage benefits to directly affected workers and their dependants, the neoliberal assault on the Nasserist systems of universal health care and education had a negative impact on far wider layers of the poor. Since the 1991 reforms, the cost to the poor of access to health and education has risen dramatically, and 'increased their vulnerability to exploitation by exposing them to a wide range of "hidden" and informal fees'.[48] Across both education and health sectors neoliberal reforms followed a similar pattern: policies of 'benign neglect of basic welfare programmes',[49] which led to a relative deterioration of publicly funded services; the imposition of cost-recovery mechanisms, which led to the institution of user fees or their increase; and various schemes introducing forms of direct privatisation. Expenditure on private education in an effort to offset the impact of the deteriorating quality of publicly funded education rose significantly during the 1990s, and the greatest share of this increase was among the poor. By 2000 poor families were reporting that nearly 20 per cent of total household spending was taken up by the costs of education.[50] Other elements in the neoliberal reform programme included the elimination of subsidies on some consumer goods, including sugar, cooking oil and dairy products.[51] The Egyptian government passed legislation in 1992 (delaying implementation until 1997) which removed restrictions on land ownership, thereby reversing the 1952 Land Reform, and worked systematically to undermine the rent control system which kept rents below market levels in around a third of Egypt's rental housing stock.[52]

A new amalgam of state and private capital

The experience of *infitah* and structural adjustment in Egypt undermines superficial claims that neoliberal reforms can be equated with the retreat or withdrawal of the state from the economy. Rather, it confirms the perspective that the role of the state cannot be measured simply against the scale of its ownership of the means of production and its direct involvement in delivering services. The structural adjustment programme initiated in 1992 consolidated a new amalgam of state and private capital in Egypt. State-run industries and services were forcibly opened up to private capital investment or allowed to fall into decay and neglect. Meanwhile, the state continued to act as a guarantor of the interests of capital in the enactment of legislation, as illustrated by the passage of the 1992 law liberalising agricultural rents. The state passed a law which benefited large agricultural landowners and removed protection from their small tenant farmers. Moreover, it ensured the implementation of this law through the violent intervention of the security forces, who carried out a campaign of arrests and repression against the opponents of the law and used all its powers to protect the owners and facilitate their seizure of lands which tenants had cultivated for generations.[53]

The key role played by the ruling National Democratic Party (NDP) in the process of reform is also important. Neoliberalism provided the opportunity for senior state officials to become major investors themselves, so that the men in power would not merely be managers of capital on behalf of the state, but owners who could profit directly and personally from their roles in business and government. The most grotesque example of this kind of convergence of political and economic power in the later stages of neoliberal reform was Ahmed Ezz's presidency of the Planning and Budgetary Committee of the People's Assembly. Ezz, who enjoyed near monopoly control of Egypt's iron and steel industry, therefore chaired the committee which decided the size of government investment in construction and public infrastructure, and thus determined the scale of demand for his own products. As the organisational secretary of the NDP, and the architect of plans to ensure the hereditary succession of Gamal Mubarak to his father's position as president, Ezz was a living embodiment of the intimate connection between the state and capital under neoliberalism.

However, he was not its *only* embodiment. The transformation of the Egyptian military's role in the economy during *infitah* and structural adjustment was an equally important expression of the same process. The relative decline of the public sector prompted the military leadership to expand the army's economic activities in several dimensions. As Robert Springborg details, under Mubarak's charismatic minister of defence, Mohamed Abdel-Halim Abu-Ghazala, the Armed Forces expanded its economic activities in three key areas after 1981: manufacturing (especially, but not exclusively in weapons production); agriculture and land reclamation; construction and service industries.[54] Under Abu-Ghazala, the leadership of the Armed Forces found a new role – as the directors of Egypt's most dynamic state capital. This period saw the creation of a massive manufacturing base for the military in the food industry, through the National Services Projects Organisation (Gihaz al-Khidma al-Wataniyya), which by 1986 was responsible for 18 per cent of the total value of food production in Egypt.[55] Abu-Ghazala also played a pivotal role in securing a deal with General Motors in 1986 which inaugurated a new era in car assembly in Egypt, apparently working closely with officials at the US embassy to win a $200 million subsidy for the project from the USAID budget for Egypt.[56] Blessed with access to subsidised manufacturing inputs, vast tracts of state land, a workforce consisting of conscripts or civilian workers under military discipline, and accounts which were completely outside the state's normal auditing procedures, the military was (and remains) an attractive partner for private capital.

As neoliberal reforms accelerated in the 1990s and 2000s, Abu-Ghazala's successors built on the foundations he had laid

to consolidate the military's role as a key player in the emerging neoliberal economy. As Marshall and Stacher document,
privatisation opened up unprecedented opportunities to develop
new partnerships with transnational capital (with Gulf capital
playing a leading role) in strategic areas such as energy, transport
and communications.[57] In such sectors, it was the military which
stepped in to 'buy out' other sections of state capital, as was the
case in the 'privatisation' of the Alexandria Shipyards, discussed
above. Meanwhile, retired generals continued to enjoy privileged
access to jobs in the rest of the civilian bureaucracy, including the
holding companies created by the structural adjustment reforms
of 1992, where they flooded into executive roles.[58]

It is of immense political importance to recognise the military
as one of the architects of neoliberalism in Egypt. First, it underscores the centrality of the state in the process of neoliberal reform
itself, and the mutual interdependence of state capitals, private
capitals and state institutions, historically enmeshed in (and now
increasingly transcending) Egypt's national boundaries. Second,
it gives the lie to the military's own claim – advanced for largely
self-serving reasons since 2011 – that it acted as the guardian of
the 'national interest' in protecting the public sector from the
depredations of Gamal Mubarak and his cronies.

The reconfiguration of the relationship between state and
private capital could appear to be an assault by some parts of
the state against itself. The asset-stripping of part of the public
sector and the degradation of much of the rest was considered
by the neoliberal reformers a price worth paying in order to
maintain overall levels of capital accumulation in the face of
economic crisis. Yet, as outlined above, there was actually a deep
and long-lasting consensus across the higher levels of the regime
around the trajectory of reform, and the military in particular
used the process of privatisation to entrench itself even more
deeply in the economy. The critical instability in the reform

process lay not in the potential explosion of tensions between different elements in the regime, and it is important to note that such tensions never did erupt in major political conflict at an elite level. Rather, it lay in the regime's failure to find new mechanisms to manage workers' discontent to replace the decaying structures of the old state trade-union federation, and the other corporatist institutions of the Nasserist state which had served so effectively in containing and stifling workers' protests in the early phases of *infitah*. In this respect, the neoliberal rhetoric against the public sector, and policymakers' public rejection of the basic tenets of the Nasserist social contract played a critical role in loosening the ideological grip of the institutions through which the ruling class had managed workers' discontent for the previous five decades. We explore this process in detail in Chapter 4 in relation to the Egyptian Trade Union Federation.

CHAPTER 2

The changing structure of the Egyptian working class in the neoliberal era

The resurgence of workers' struggles in Egypt after 2005 presents something of a paradox. The Egyptian working class at the turn of the new millennium was reeling from the impact of the neoliberal assault on its historic heartlands in public-sector manufacturing. As we saw in the previous chapter, hundreds of thousands of industrial workers had been forced out of the workforce through early retirement schemes and redundancy. New legislation removed obligations on employers to guarantee job security, safe working conditions and access to social insurance, which had provided at least minimum safeguards for two generations of workers. Meanwhile the neoliberal attack on the state's role as a provider of social welfare removed much of the 'safety net' that made the difference between living and survival for the working poor and their families. Moreover, the imposition of 'cost-recovery' mechanisms made public servants such as teachers and health workers the agents of marketisation at the expense of the poor. Yet, contrary to the expectations of many policymakers, academics and journalists, who had written organised workers as a social force out of history, Egyptian workplaces became laboratories for the rebirth of a new labour movement and a wave of strikes of unprecedented scale and duration. This chapter attempts to lay the basis for an explanation of the strike wave which recognises that Egyptian workers' capacity for collective resistance flows from the role they play in capitalist accumulation. Despite the changes in the social organisation of that process, the last three decades confirm the continued importance of wage labour to the Egyptian economy.

Workers' capacity to change the terms of their exploitation depends on two basic conditions: the fact that their labour remains indispensable to the creation of value, and that the labour process itself makes individual workers into a collective actor capable of confronting capitalists as a class. Central to our argument is a concept of the working class which is not limited to industrial workers, but encompasses the vast majority of wage workers in 'services', whether they work in manual or clerical occupations. However, the industrial working class in Egypt also went through a period of significant restructuring, which included the creation of new manufacturing zones. We will also briefly address the question of what workers' employment in micro-, small and medium-sized enterprises and the 'informalisation' of some forms of work in the neoliberal era have meant for workers' capacity to organise collective action.

'Where are the workers?'

Early in 2012 a stencilled graffiti image of a muscled man in a hard hat clutching a spanner began appearing on walls in downtown Cairo: 'Where are the workers?' the accompanying slogan demanded. While the combination of image and slogan reflected at one level the frustrations and hopes of young revolutionary activists searching for allies in their battle with Egypt's military rulers, at another level it connected with deeply embedded ideas about what it means to be a worker. Our understanding of how capitalism works and the experience of the post-2006 strike wave in Egypt both point to a definition of 'working class' that is much broader than male manual workers in factories. In the Egyptian context, it is no accident that the post-2006 strike wave was characterised by increasing numbers of strikes by clerical workers (*muwadhafin* in Arabic), and that the first independent union was founded by low-paid civil servants. However, as we also explore in detail below, far from disappearing, industrial workers have continued to play a central role in the Egyptian economy, with the creation of new centres of production outside the historic core of Nasserist-era industry.

Following Callinicos, the understanding of 'class' we propose here is defined by four distinctive features: it is a *relationship* defined by the *antagonism* between the direct producers and the minority ruling class which exploits them and thus is inseparable from *class struggle*. Finally, it is an *objective* relationship that is formed 'in the process of production'.

> Contrary to what those who define class in terms of status claim, a person's class position doesn't depend on subjective attitudes but on their actual place within the relations of production, independently of what he or she – or anyone else – may think. A car-worker who believes himself to be middle-class doesn't cease for that reason to be a wage-labourer exploited by capital.[1]

One of the central aims of this chapter is to demonstrate how the exploitation of wage labour provides the structure that defines the economy, society and the state in contemporary Egypt. More-over, the last thirty years have witnessed the increasing, although highly *uneven*, integration of Egypt into a global economy which is in turn shaped by the growth of the working class.[2] This does not mean, of course, that everyone in Egypt is either an exploited wage-worker or a capitalist exploiter. There are other classes of the poor who share broadly comparable living standards with the working class but whose income is derived from different kinds of economic relationships. Some of these are small craftsmen or the owners of small shops and businesses and other 'own-account' workers, as well as the declining numbers of small farmers in the countryside. Sources of income such as these may be more or less precarious, and will often be combined with some form of temporary waged work. There are also the social groups 'above' the working-class making up a highly heterogeneous 'middle class'. While there are many elements within the Egyptian middle class that have very little in common with workers or any of the poor, the combination of neoliberalism and dictatorship in the last years of Mubarak's rule increased pressure on others to identify with some of the social demands raised by workers and the urban poor, and even, in a minority of cases, such as junior doctors in the public health service, adopt workers' methods of struggle.

In estimating the overall size of the Egyptian working class, the data collected by the ILO from the Egyptian state statistics authority CAPMAS cannot provide more than a starting point. There are two primary reasons for this: first, the occupational classifications adopted by the ILO and other international bodies, and widely accepted by mainstream social science, are not very helpful when considering class from the perspective we outlined above. With the exception of category 1, 'Legislators, senior officials and managers', most of the other occupational categories include waged and own-account workers, and blur the distinction between workers who can exercise some degree of choice over how they spend their time and those who are forced to work under others' direction. The other way that the ILO organises its data is to specify the type of economic relationship that accounts for the income: waged labour, employing others, own-account working and so on. This, as we see below, gives a better overall framework from which to provide a rough estimation of the size of the waged working class. However, the comprehensiveness of the CAPMAS

TABLE 2.1 Waged employees and non-waged labour in the total labour force, 1980–2007 (million)

	1980	1984	1989	1992	1995	2000	2004	2007
Waged	5.6	6.4	7.3	7.9	8.7	10.3	10.6	12.7
Labour force	9.8	11.8	14.9	14.4	15.3	17.2	18.7	21.7
Waged as % of labour force	56.8	53.9	49.1	54.9	56.8	59.9	56.4	58.5

SOURCE ILO LABORSTA database, Tables 2A and 2E (total labour force excludes armed forces).

data has been called into question by some researchers. Sabry, for example, argues that CAPMAS's surveying practices are likely to generate a highly flawed picture of household income sources in the *ashwa'iyyat* (areas of 'informal' housing) which are home to millions in urban Egypt.[3]

The 2007 data on waged employment from CAPMAS gives a total waged workforce of 12,715,100, which represents 58.5 per cent of the total labour force. Taking this figure as a starting point, we assume that around 10 per cent of the employed labour force are not workers, but are managers or highly skilled professionals with a degree of control over their own work, which puts them outside the working class. This gives us a rough estimate of 11.43 million waged workers (including waged workers in the agricultural sector). If we make the relatively conservative assumption that these waged workers support on average four direct dependents each, including those below and above working age and the unemployed, this would mean that waged workers and their direct dependants accounted for around 60 per cent of Egypt's 76.5 million population in 2007.[4] As Table 2.1 and

FIGURE 2.1 Total employment by status in employment (million)

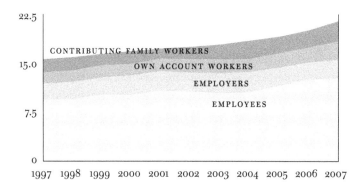

SOURCE ILO LABORSTA database, Table 2D.

Figure 2.1 illustrate, first, the absolute and relative weight of paid employment within the labour force as a whole has grown slightly since 1980. Second, the proportion of waged workers in paid employment (as opposed to own-account workers, unpaid family workers and employers) has also kept pace with the growth of the paid labour force as a whole.

It seems reasonable to assume that data from Egyptian government sources is likely to throw into sharpest relief those sections of the employed labour force which the state has the greatest incentive to map accurately: that is to say, sectors it employs directly, and those sectors that play a critical role in driving economic growth or produce commodities for important export markets. State officials can afford to have a relatively hazy idea of the exact numbers working as artisan furniture-makers, but more precision is at least likely in the case of workers employed in the petroleum and natural gas sector and on the Suez Canal. Does this mean that we can afford to do the same? The picture of the working class we will attempt to sketch here will naturally suffer many of the same defects as the picture drawn by the state's census-takers: the outline of the skeleton is likely to be relatively true, but the exact shape of muscles and flesh is unknown. Nor are we, in any case, rendering an image of the whole body; rather, we have focused on the impact of neoliberalism on the structure of the working class in specific sectors of the economy – manufacturing, transport and communications, and education. It is no accident, either, that the picture of the Egyptian working class drawn here is shaped so closely by the contours of the Egyptian state which guides much of its development (even in the private sector). In part this is simple polemic: Egyptian workers matter to Egyptian capitalists because without them no ships pass through the Suez Canal, no flights take off from Cairo International Airport, no trains run, no data flows through the stock exchanges, no taxes are collected, and neither gold nor natural gas finds its way to market. In part, the fact that the inner structure of the Egyptian working class remains very much defined by the Egyptian state simply reinforces the argument of the previous chapter: the neoliberal era brought about a new amalgam of state and private capital in which the state is no less important than during Nasser's time.

As our interest in the working class is not confined to describing it, but consists also in assessing its capacity for self-emancipation, this analysis will be directed towards two key questions. First, have the economic changes of the past three decades neutered Egyptian workers' collective disruptive power, that is to say their 'ability to take economically effective action', as Harman puts it?[5] In other words, if Egyptian workers stop working, do Egyptian capitalists suffer losses? The second perspective analyses how changes to the production and reproduction of capital in the neoliberal era affected workers' capacity to *use* their collective power. Here we are interested in factors such as alterations in patterns of employment concentration, centralisation and ownership, the 'spatial restructuring' of production and changes to workers' security in employment.[6]

This chapter cannot offer more than a preliminary sketch by way of an answer: we lack the space here to develop these points in depth, and in any case there is as yet very little empirical research to assist in constructing a more detailed argument. Nevertheless, the argument we present here is based on solid enough evidence to at least map out the terrain for future debate. Two objective conditions play a critical role in shaping Egyptian workers' capacity to act collectively. The first is that Egyptian capitalism continues to confer on Egyptian workers the *absolute* and *relative* advantages of concentration, despite its constant efforts to prevent workers from realising these advantages. Second, unlike other sections of the poor, workers in public-sector services and industry do not only experience the actions of the state as an external force, but also have the capacity to stop parts of it functioning from within. Three decades of neoliberal reforms may have increased the *unevenness* of the structure of the working class in several dimensions, but Egyptian capitalism continues to create the objective conditions for the realisation of the differentiated unity of the Egyptian working class. In the previous chapter we also discussed the *combination* of different phases in the social organisation of capitalist production, a process which fused state capitalist and neoliberal elements.[7] In the final section of this chapter we explore the effect of this process of combination on the structure of the working class, and argue that the specific features of this process helped to create the conditions for revolution in 2011.

Restructuring the Egyptian working class: global trends

While we will concentrate here on a single country case-study, it is important to note that Egypt has broadly followed a number of global trends of the past thirty years. The first of these is a decline

TABLE 2.2 The growing private sector, 1980–2004
(% of total labour capacity)

	Public sector	Private sector
1981/2	40	60
2003/4	32	68

Source: Al-Eissawi, 2007, p. 512.

in the proportion of the workforce deriving their living from the land. The second trend, which can be seen at work on a global scale, is the relative expansion of the proportion of employment in the 'service sector', and the corresponding relative contraction of employment in industry.[8] This should not be confused with each sector's contribution to GDP, as in the case of Egypt industry actually accounted for a higher proportion GDP in 2007 than in 1982. As Harman argues, this shift is a reflection of the long-term impact of technological development in both agriculture and, particularly, manufacturing, which means that far fewer workers are required to produce the same output.[9] This technological development is likewise at the root of the growth of much of the service sector. On the one hand, technological innovation in transport has made possible the expansion of production over ever-wider geographical areas and therefore new divisions of labour on a regional and global scale. Transport workers as a category of 'service' workers play an even more critical role in the continued production of value in industry and agriculture than ever before. On the other hand, the increasing level of skill required of the workers who operate new technologies in industry and agriculture has driven a global expansion of education, and therefore an expansion in the numbers of people providing education. A third area where Egypt follows global trends is

TABLE 2.3 Economic sectors: value added (% of GDP)

	Agriculture	Industry	Services
1982	20	32	48
1992	17	33	50
2002	16	34	49
2011	14	37	49

Source: World Bank Open Data, data.worldbank.org.

in the feminisation of the workforce. Although women form a lower percentage of the labour force than in other regions of the world economy, their participation rate has dramatically increased compared to the beginning of the 1970s.[10]

Since the early 1980s Egypt has seen a marked change in the relative contribution of the public and private sectors to the economy, with the private sector growing and the public sector shrinking. This trend is visible across three key indicators: share of GDP, percentage of the overall economically active population employed in each sector, and levels of investment.[11] The proportion of the labour force in each sector has also changed, although the shift has been far less dramatic.

Table 2.2 shows Al-Eissawi's tracking of the long-term shift in domestic investment between the public and private sectors over the past four decades: the public sector in the broad sense (government, state economic institutions and services, state sector and the 'public business sector' established under the structural adjustment regime) attracted 90 per cent of investment in 1974, falling to 65 per cent in 1990, then to 57 per cent in 2003/4. Over the same period domestic investment in the private sector rose from 10 per cent in 1974 to 35 per cent in 1990 and 43 per cent in 2003/4.[12]

Looking at the economy from a different perspective – the division between agriculture, industry and services – Table 2.3

TABLE 2.4 Non-agricultural paid employment as a proportion of total employment, 1980–2007

	1980	1990	2000	2007
Total paid employment (million)	5.5	8.0	10.3	12.7
Total non-agricultural paid employment (million)	4.1	6.9	9.3	11.3
Non-agricultural paid employment as % of total paid employment	73	87	90	89

SOURCE ILO LABORSTA database, Table 2E.

shows the development of another trend: the relative decline in the importance of agriculture compared to industry and services. The relative rise in the contribution of industry to GDP compared to services does not necessarily reflect the relative expansion of industrial *production*, however, as it includes extractive industries, such as natural gas, which have contributed an increasingly large share of Egypt's GDP in recent years. Natural gas rents peaked at 12.1 per cent of GDP in 2008, compared to 0.8 per cent of GDP in 1980, a rise that is in large part attributable to a surge in global natural gas prices.[13]

Table 2.4 shows, however, that the proportion of the waged workforce employed outside the agricultural sector rose from 74 per cent in 1980 to just below 90 per cent in 2007.

Neoliberal policies have also enforced restructuring within the agricultural sector as policymakers have pursued export-driven growth in horticultural commodities and cotton.[14] Legislation enacted in 1997 allowed landowners to charge market-based rents for land, undoing the Agrarian Reform Law of 1952, which had guaranteed tenants' rights and sought to limit the power of large landowners. Rents rose dramatically after 1997 and mass evictions followed changes to tenancy agreements allowing landowners to summarily dismiss tenants. The 200,000 smallholders with

TABLE 2.5 Economically active population relative to total population

	Total 15+ pop. (mn)	Economically active (mn)	M activity rate (%)	F activity rate (%)	Total activity rate (%)
1973	20.9	8.5	78.6	4.4	40.5
1983	26.4	12.6	77.5	17.1	47.5
1993	34.4	16.5	72.8	22.1	47.9
2005	44.0	21.8	75.2	23.1	49.5
2008	50.6	24.3	71.7	23.2	47.9

SOURCE ILO LABORSTA database, Table 1A.

less than 10 *feddan* and the 1 million landless *fellahin* and their dependants face an uncertain future. As Bush notes, it is unclear whether they will 'become wage workers in new desert irrigated estates or lumpen and landless unemployed readied for occasional work in the towns'.[15]

The relative feminization of the economically active population during the period 1973–2008 is another crucial axis of change. The activity rate for men dropped slightly over this 45-year period, but that for women rose dramatically, albeit from a very low base, representing a net gain in the overall activity rate of around 8 per cent.

Women made up nearly a quarter of the economically active population in 2008, and 17.4 per cent of all paid employment. Although by global standards Egyptian women's participation in the labour force is relatively low, these figures represent an enormous change from the early 1970s, when less than 5 per cent of women were economically active. The decade with the greatest rate of change was the 1970s, however, as between 1983 and 2008 women's participation in the economy only rose from 17.1 per cent to 23.2 per cent.

TABLE 2.6 Women as a proportion of the total employed workforce, selected sectors (%)

	Education	Public administration	Health and social care	Manufacturing
1999	39.9	20.8	52.8	15.0
2003	39.5	22.0	47.5	8.5
2007	43.9	23.0	55.6	7.0

SOURCE Calculated from ILO LABORSTA database, Table 2E.

Women's paid employment plays a key role in the Egyptian economy: the education and health systems, along with local and central government, would cease to function without their labour. In 2007, 75 per cent of women employees worked in education, public administration, and health and social care. Women also make up a large proportion of the total employed workforce in these sectors, as Table 2.6 illustrates.

Manufacturing, by contrast, was the largest sector of paid employment for men in 2006, followed by public administration, agriculture and construction. The hundreds of thousands of women employees are concentrated in the sectors of the economy with the lowest pay (Table 2.7).[16]

TABLE 2.7 Women's weekly wages in the lowest-paying sectors, 2007 (LE)

Education	94
Health and social work	96
Other community, social and personal services	118
Manufacturing	159

SOURCE ILO LABORSTA database, Table 5A.

Manufacturing: decline, renewal, relocation

Snapshots of Egyptian industry on the eve of the revolution presented a series of starkly contradictory images. On the one hand there were the massive decaying factories of the Nasserist era, situated in the old industrial heartlands of areas such as Shubra al-Khaima, Al-Mahalla al-Kubra and Helwan. They still employed a large proportion of the industrial workforce despite two decades of mass redundancies and early retirement schemes, but were starved of investment and inexorably losing ground to foreign competitors in the domestic market for their products. But in the new industrial cities, such as 6th of October, a new manufacturing workforce had been created to serve large factories producing cars from imported components and steel for export to Europe, the USA and China, as well as smaller firms in the engineering and pharmaceuticals sectors. Nor was all 'old' industry in decline: the privatisation of the state-owned cement industry began in 1994 and by 2011 foreign firms accounted for 80 per cent of production in this highly profitable sector.[17] Although the role of private capital in industry had grown enormously as a result of economic reforms and privatisation, sectors such as petroleum and natural gas, which were almost entirely state-owned, contributed an increasingly large proportion of both GDP and exports. The nature of capitals of the kind represented by Ahmed Ezz also demonstrates the need for caution in taking a narrowly legalistic view of what 'private' industrial capital means in contemporary Egypt. Ezz, steel monopolist and the owner of factories employing a workforce of around 6,300 and claiming a highly globally competitive output of 768 tons of steel per employee per year, was a central figure in the ruling party and deeply embedded in the state.[18] Yet, alongside the uneven growth of new capital-intensive industries, employing large concentrations of workers, the neoliberal era also saw informal micro- and small-scale manufacturing enterprises continue to flourish, particularly in garment and food production. National survey data from the mid-1990s found 233,845 micro-enterprises (employing 1–4 workers) and 43,315 small enterprises (employing 5–9 workers) in the manufacturing sector (authors' own calculations based on Ministry of Finance data).[19]

It is tempting to see the story of Egyptian industry in the neoliberal era through any one of these apparently counterposed perspectives: as a tale of either decline or growth; of ageing power looms in Al-Mahalla al-Kubra, or gleaming car assembly lines in 6th of October City or hand-powered knitting machines in a basement flat in Imbaba. Yet any one of these pictures will, if used alone, provide a faulty lens through which to view the restructuring of the Egyptian manufacturing working class over the last thirty years. Moreover, it is equally important to move beyond the static 'snapshot' or 'birds-eye view' of the manufacturing working class, towards an understanding that uneven and combined development has temporal as well as spatial dimensions. We will therefore highlight here two key trends: the partial decomposition of the vertically integrated Nasserist model of manufacturing and the spatial restructuring of class through the creation of the new industrial cities. However, these processes interacted to produce a third feature of the manufacturing working class: the combination of 'old' and 'new' in a complex and messy totality.

The pivot of our argument here is that the last thirty years have demonstrated that the industrial working class remains central to the strategy of accumulation pursued by the Egyptian ruling class in the neoliberal era. It is a working class that has been restructured, and suffered some heavy defeats in the process, but not a class that is in the process of disappearing. As Table 2.8 shows, relatively speaking there were fewer manufacturing workers, but their collective contribution to the economy was greater in 2007 than in 1983 in absolute, and not only relative, terms.

TABLE 2.8 Employment in manufacturing and value added, 1983–2007

	Total employees (million)	Total employees in manufacturing (million)	% of employees in manufacturing	Manufacturing value added (% of GDP)
1983	6.3	1.3	20.4	13
1993	8.2	1.6	18.9	17
2005	11.6	1.7	15.4	17
2007	12.7	1.8	14.5	16

SOURCE Calculated from ILO LABORSTA database, Table 2E, and World Bank Open Data, data.worldbank.org

Decomposition of the Nasserist model of manufacturing

The textile and clothing industry is of critical importance to the Egyptian economy. In 2008 the sector employed around 25 per cent of the entire industrial workforce, comprised around 20 per cent all industrial-sector firms, and accounted for 26.4 per cent of industrial production, resulting in total value-added of LE33.5 billion.[20] Large-scale, vertically integrated textile production was pioneered in Egypt in the 1930s by the industrialist Tala'at Harb. Under Nasser, this model was expanded to incorporate almost the entire textile sector in giant public-sector companies which brought together spinning, weaving, dyeing and garment production in factories employing tens of thousands of workers. The public-sector mills served two primary purposes in the state capitalist economy. First, they turned Egyptian cotton in state-owned mills into goods for sale at 'social' rather than market prices, to meet the needs of local consumers. Second, the textile industry played a critical role in producing goods for the global market, and textile products made up 50 per cent of Egypt's exports in the period from the 1950s to the 1970s.[21] A combination of factors undermined the viability of this model, leading to its partial decomposition. Improvements in global and local transport systems reduced the advantage of vertically integrated textile production, and created new competitors for Egyptian textiles, particularly in East Asia where wages were comparatively lower. Local pressures included declining yields and quality in Egyptian cotton production, which had a major impact on the public-sector mills, and declining state investment in the public sector following the onset of economic reforms. As a consequence, by the end of the 2000s local producers were being squeezed out of local markets.[22] Meanwhile, private-sector companies grew up to service global garment production chains which were disconnected from the old Nasserist model, assembling garments using fabric produced outside Egypt.[23]

Naguib's study of the old textile district of Shubra al-Khaima in the late 1990s illustrates a number of key features of the uneven and combined development of the textile sector in the neoliberal era which remain of wider relevance, more than a decade later. The town was dominated by the old ESCO mill, which, although a shadow of its former self, still employed 6,000 workers. By contrast, more than half (1,565) of the recorded establishments in the private-sector ready-made garment sector employed only one worker, and a further 724 employed only two. As for the unrecorded sector, small-scale production permeated the fabric of the city, but was statistically invisible, as the owners and workers in these small workshops were reluctant to even discuss their activities with a researcher for fear of discovery by the authorities. The gap between ESCO and these tiny workshops could not be used as a shorthand for the contrast between public and private sector, however. Private-sector weaving, which employed 21,000 people in the mid-1990s, was structured differently again: with four large factories employing over 1,000 workers each, followed by fifteen factories with over 100 workers. Less than 10 per cent of private-sector weaving establishments had only one worker.[24]

Ten years later, the working class in the wider textile sector exhibited many of the same characteristics. It was distributed in workplaces of extremely uneven size. The Nasserist model of totally vertically integrated textile production still survived, providing direct employment for 106,000 workers in 2006 in twenty-seven public-sector mills.[25] The largest of these was the giant Misr Spinning complex in Al-Mahalla al-Kubra, which employed 24,000. The private spinning and weaving sector included a number of employers, which, while not on the scale of the public sector mills, still brought together workers in large workplaces, such as the Abou el-Sibai'i group, which employed 3,000. There were also a mass of smaller companies – around 4,000 in 2006, according to one estimate – some of which were dependent on outputs from the public-sector mills and producing for the local market, while others were involved in garment assembly as part of global supply chains. In addition, a large number of garment producers and finishers were employed in micro-firms, similar to those found in Shubra al-Khaima.

A number of public-sector mills were sold to local and foreign investors in the mid-2000s, including Shibin al-Kom, which was bought by an Indonesian investor in 2005, and ESCO's mill in the Cairo suburb Shubra al-Khaima, which was bought by Hashem el-Deghri. The fate of ESCO's workforce haunted the public-sector textile industry: whittled down from 24,000 in the early 1980s to a rump of 3,500 by 2005, the sell-off triggered a four-month-long sit-in by workers in protest at the backdoor privatisation process and the new owner's failure to pay them benefits and bonuses. The plant, valued at LE60 million in 1999, had been sold to the investor for LE4 million. The strike resulted in the agreement of a compensation package, but workers were offered only 'seasonal contracts'.[26] The global economic crisis after 2008 further increased the pressures on workers in the textile sector. Haddad, in a survey conducted in 2009, found that production, domestic sales and exports had dropped by 21 per cent, 16 per cent and 22 per cent respectively since 2008, accompanied by large-scale job losses.[27]

Spatial restructuring: the growth of the new industrial cities

An important trend over the past thirty years has been the reduction of employment in the old industrial areas, which were dominated by large, state-owned enterprises, and the expansion of employment in new industrial cities characterised by smaller units of production and a new, better-educated workforce with a high proportion of graduates of technical institutes.[28] The first wave of these new developments included 10th of Ramadan City (established near Zaqaziq in al-Sharqiyya governorate in 1977) and 6th of October City (established on the edge of Giza in 1979). The relatively small size of new private-sector workplaces in these areas and the absorption of a new workforce, which lacked the traditions of militancy of the old industrial areas, raised the question as to whether this structural change could present an obstacle to workers in the new industrial cities organising collective action.[29] In the event, as we discuss in more detail later, the new industrial working class has not been immune from strike action and led the way in efforts to renew self-organisation as groups of workers in the new cities attempted to establish ETUF branches in their workplaces and faced fierce resistance from employers.

The range of industries established in the new cities was highly diverse, including specialised textiles, light engineering, chemical products, food and beverages, garment and textile production, plastics, toolmakers. Industrial sector A2 of 10th Ramadan City, an area 2.6 km by 1.1 km encompassing a range of small and medium-sized manufacturing units, for example, includes weaving, garment producers, power-supply equipment manufacturers, plastics manufacturers, pharmaceuticals, chemicals, detergents, light engineering, tea packing, electronics and cable manufacturers. The next-door plot, A3, is taken up by a group of large factories producing cables, steel and ceramics.[30]

Not all of the industries established in the new cities were small scale, as the example of car and truck production illustrates. Local car production began in Egypt in 1959 at the Al-Nasr factory as part of the strategy of import-substitution industrialisation promoted by Nasser. However, expansion in this sector took place in the 1980s following a new model in which the state no longer acted as direct producer, but structured local market conditions and provided an infrastructure in order to attract foreign manufacturers. High import duties on automobiles were maintained to encourage foreign car manufacturers to assemble their vehicles locally in order to reach the potentially large Egyptian market. Thanks to the energetic intervention of Mubarak's chief of staff, Abd-al-Halim Abu-Ghazala, a plant assembling cars for General Motors was established in 6th of October City in 1983 and production began in 1985.[31] Other international car manufacturers followed: the Seoudi Group established an assembly plant for Suzuki Motors in 6th of October City in 1988, followed by another factory assembling Nissan cars in the same location in 1996.[32] Daewoo's Speranza range has been assembled by the Aboul Fotouh group in a factory based in 6th of October City since 2006.[33] The 1990s saw rapid expansion in the industry, and by the end of the decade around 100,000 were employed in the sector.[34] The domestic economic crisis of the early 2000s led to rapid falls in demand for passenger cars and light commercial vehicles, and the numbers employed in the sector were reported to be 46,000 in 2011.[35] Output was expanding again, however, with around 200,000 cars assembled in Egypt in 2010. Despite the impact of the 2011 revolution in depressing the consumer market for cars, major importers remained confident of continued growth in car ownership. In early 2012, Ghabbour announced a new partnership to import CKD (completely knocked down) car kits from Geely, a car-maker based in Hangzhou, China, which bought Volvo in 2010.[36]

Workers in the new cities are, nevertheless, largely employed in smaller establishments compared to their colleagues in the bigger industrial production units of the Nasserist era, which were part of combines employing tens of thousands of workers. In order to visualise themselves as part of a wider collective, they would have to think in geographical rather than sectoral or institutional terms, and this would mean overcoming the subjective barriers to joint action posed by the difficulties of establishing unifying demands across a wide range of companies. Yet, both the earlier history of the Egyptian textile industry and the development of strike action after 2006 demonstrate that workers can realise the advantages of geographical concentration, even where the average units of production are relatively small in scale. During the 1940s, the centre of militancy in the Egyptian textile industry, and a leading centre of development in the workers' movement, was Shubra al-Khaima, which was dominated by foreign-owned small and medium-sized spinning and weaving firms, not the giant Egyptian-owned Misr Spinning plant in Al-Mahalla al-Kubra.[37]

Transport and communications

The transport and communications sector illustrates in different ways many of the same processes that have reconfigured Egyptian manufacturing over the past three decades. This should be no surprise: transport and communications have increased in importance in the neoliberal era, as competition has intensified between businesses across the globe. As with the textile sector, Egyptians whose living depends on the transport and communications sector work in an enormous variety of establishments and under a huge range of different conditions. 'Transport worker' describes an employee of Dubai World's container port in Ain Sokhna, a bus driver with the Public Transport Authority in Cairo, and a bullied teenage tuk-tuk (motorised rickshaw) driver in the back streets of Giza. On the surface they appear to have little in common: the first is employed by a highly profitable multinational, the second by an ailing and underfunded state institution, while the third scrapes a living from the owner of the tuk-tuk while perhaps dreaming of escape by buying his own vehicle one day. Yet the neoliberal restructuring of the transport sector shapes their working lives, and continues to bind their fates to the that of the wider working class even while it fragments and weakens old ties and solidarities.

As in other sectors of the economy, the statistics required to build more than a crude picture of the working class in the transport sector are either deficient or missing. According to the data provided by the Egyptian government to the ILO in 2007, the total employed in transport and communications was 1.03 million. According to the Labour Force Sample Survey of 2009, informal employment accounted for 77 per cent of total employment in the transportation sector. In other words, nearly four out of five workers in this sector were working in unregistered enterprises, self-employed, or employed on a casual basis without access to social security or other employment benefits.[38] From the perspective of ownership, both transport and communications sectors went through significant changes in the decades that preceded the revolution of 2011. Some state-owned transport services, including road freight, inter-city bus services and maritime transport services, were organised into two holding companies under Law 203 of 1991, employing 57,663 workers between them. By 2001, further restructuring had created a single holding company for maritime and inland transport, employing 30,216 workers.[39] As the privatisation programme accelerated following the appointment of Nazif's cabinet in 2004, the Egyptian government also offered concessionary agreements in the form of public–private partnerships (PPPs) to international and regional investors in the transport sector, launching PPP initiatives to build roads and upgrade railway lines and stations. By 2009 Egypt was considered one of the 'leaders in the PPP field' in the MENA region, with the unit overseeing the PPP programme at the Ministry of Finance winning the 'PPP 2009 Award' for being the 'best performing government organisation in Africa'.[40]

Critical sections of both the passenger and the freight transport systems, including Egyptian National Railways, the Suez Canal Authority, the Public Transport Authority bus service in Cairo and Alexandria, and EgyptAir, remained under direct state ownership. At the other end of the transport system, the neoliberal era has seen the explosive growth of new mass forms of unregulated passenger transport. From the mid-2000s three-wheeled motorised rickshaws, or tuk-tuks, have become a common sight. Able to navigate through the narrow and badly maintained alleyways of Egypt's urban sprawl better than the fleets of microbuses, which until then had been the main alternative to taxis and buses for the poor, numbers of tuk-tuks grew rapidly, reaching 500,000 with 750,000 workers according to one estimate from 2012.[41]

A different aspect of the interdependence of 'services' and 'industry' is well illustrated by changes in the Egyptian transport sector during the neoliberal era. The relative deterioration of the public transport infrastructure and the lack of investment in mass passenger transport systems accessible to the majority of Egyptians encouraged new, unregulated transport services, such as tuk-tuks, to flourish. The hundreds of thousands of tuk-tuks that appeared on Egypt's roads did not spring into existence by magic, however. They are imported by Ghabbour Auto, the biggest independent car assembler in the Middle East. In 2011,

Ghabbour's thriving tuk-tuk business was worth £287 million. The manufacture and transport of tuk-tuks from factory in India to the back streets of urban Egypt knit together thousands of workers in an international production chain: factory workers, dockers, shipping clerks, assembly workers, lorry drivers, distributors and sales agents. Keeping the half a million or so tuk-tuks on the road also calls into being systems to supply spare parts and provide mechanics to service the vehicles. Some parts of this system are more informal (in the sense of unregulated) than others: tuk-tuk owners and drivers were unable to obtain even legal licences to operate until 2010.[42] Nevertheless, their highly informal and often micro-scale businesses are embedded in much wider formal networks of production and distribution.

The increasing mobility of people and goods in the neoliberal era has enhanced the potential disruptive power of workers in the transport sector across several dimensions. Their capacity to directly interrupt the production and distribution of goods has been increased by the uneven transformation of some manufacturing sectors from the vertically integrated Nasserist model of production to a neoliberal model of partial integration into circuits of global production. As we saw in the case of the textile and clothing industry, national and international transport connections play even more important roles at different stages of the production process than they did in the previous era of capitalist development. The expansion of a private-sector garment industry that depends on the *import* of partially prepared clothing for assembly in Egypt and its *re-export* as finished garments to Europe and North America is one example. Likewise, the car assembly industry is completely dependent on the import of CKD kits from outside Egypt.

The acceleration of Egypt's integration into global production and trade can be crudely demonstrated by the dramatic increase in the value of both exports and imports in the decade

TABLE 2.9 Increase in goods exports and imports, 1980–2010 (BoP current US$ billion)

Year	Exports	Imports
1980	3.85	6.81
1990	3.92	10.30
2000	7.06	15.38
2010	25.02	45.14

SOURCE World Bank Open Data, data.worldbank.org.

immediately before the revolution. As Table 2.9 shows, it took twenty years for the value of exports to almost double in value between 1980 and 2000, but half the time for that figure to more than triple between 2000 and 2010.

Evidently the potential disruptive power of workers concentrated at Egypt's international connections has increased rather than decreased under neoliberalism. Suez Canal traffic and toll receipts peaked in 2008, and then fell back, probably under the combined impact of global economic crisis and the 2011 revolution. However, as Table 2.10 indicates, the net tonnage and the toll receipts in 2013 remained at more than twice their 2000 level.

TABLE 2.10 Suez Canal: brief yearly statistics, 2000–2013

Year	Number of vessels	Net tonnage (million tons)	Tolls (US$ billion)
2000	14,142	439.04	1.93
2005	18,224	671.95	3.45
2010	17,993	846.39	4.77
2013	16,596	915.47	5.11

SOURCE Suez Canal Authority, 2013.

TABLE 2.11 Egypt: number of inbound tourism arrivals and receipts

Year	International tourism arrivals	International tourism receipts (current US$ billion)
1995	2,871,000	3.0
2000	5,116,000	4.7
2005	8,244,000	7.2
2010	14,051,000	13.6

SOURCE World Bank Open Data, data.worldbank.org.

Dockers, port workers, airport staff, employees of the Suez Canal Company play an even more important role today in the economy than they did three decades ago.[43]

The potential disruptive power of workers in the passenger transport sector has likewise increased. If they stop work, this may indirectly affect production by preventing or hampering workers from reaching their workplaces or goods from reaching markets. In addition, passenger transport strikes also affect increasing numbers of travellers making journeys for other reasons. Numbers of international tourists arriving in Egypt rose almost fivefold between 1995 and 2010, for example (Table 2.11).

As in the logistics sector, the passenger transport workers whose power is most visible are those who form the backbone of Egypt's mass transport infrastructure: the railway workers, who can halt the movement of trains across a network carrying 1.2 million passengers daily with a well-located sit-in on the tracks at Ramsis Station in Cairo; the air-traffic controllers at Cairo Airport, who can ground flights bringing in 1,200 passengers per hour. However, transport workers in the informal sector can also potentially exercise great disruptive power by blocking or congesting roads or suspending services. Despite the obstacles to

TABLE 2.12 State-employed transport and communications workers

Institution	No. of direct employees
Cairo Metro	6,000
Suez Canal	14,000
EgyptAir	33,000
Cairo Public Transport Authority	42,000
Telecom Egypt	48,000
Egyptian Postal Service	52,000
Egyptian National Railways	86,000
Total	281,000

SOURCE Cairo Metro, 2014; Suez Canal Authority, 2014; Anadolu News Agency, 2013; Ahram Online, 24 February 2014; Riyyan, 2012; Zaidan, 2014; Al-Araby, 2012.

organisation in this sector, collective action by microbus drivers increased dramatically after the revolution of 2011: Cairo microbus drivers took strike action three times in the space of a month during September and October 2012, for example.[44]

Despite the effects of over two decades of privatisation, the core of Egypt's transport and communications systems still depends largely on workers employed directly by the state in large regional or national institutions. As we have demonstrated above, these workers play a critical role in the economy; however, even in numerical terms they represent a significant proportion of workers in the transport sector. The employees of the seven institutions listed in Table 2.12 alone account for 25–30 per cent of the total workforce in transport and communications.

'Core' institutions such as these are not hermetically sealed from the rest of the economy, but rely on the labour of workers in a wide variety of employment relationships who they may not employ directly, and are increasingly likely to be outsourced to the private sector. The Suez Canal Authority, in addition to its directly employed workforce of 14,000, relies on the labour of thousands of workers in nine subsidiary companies responsible for maintenance. The security guards on the entrances and exits of the Cairo Metro have been employed by multinational security firm G4S since 2008.[45] Outsourcing does create real barriers to collective organisation and common action between workers who may have previously worked for the same employer and who now may experience different terms and conditions as a result. The potential disruptive power of outsourced workers may, however, be as great as, if not greater than, that of workers still employed in-house.

In other cases, public-sector employment has shrunk, while private-sector employment has grown in companies providing services that replace those provided by the state. In the rapidly evolving telecommunications sector, this process has been interwoven with dramatic technological change. The state telecommunications operator was turned into a joint stock company, Telecom Egypt (TE), in 1998, while its previous role as a regulator was devolved to a new body.[46] Private-sector operators offering mobile, payphone, Internet, data and satellite services have been licensed and TE's monopoly over fixed-line domestic and international telephone services was ended by legislation passed in 2003. However, although telecommunications *services* are offered now by a more diverse array of private and public provides, TE's 48,000 employees remain the backbone of Egypt's telecommunications infrastructure. TE owns a 45 per cent stake in Vodafone Egypt, and was granted a mobile phone operator licence of its own in December 2012. While other mobile phone operators will be able to offer fixed-line services in future, they will use TE's infrastructure.[47] Parts of this infrastructure play a critical role in maintaining the Internet connectivity between Europe and Asia.[48] The Gulf States' links to global financial markets, for example, are dependent on access to Egypt's fibre-optic corridor.[49]

The expansion and proletarianisation of the white-collar public sector: the example of education workers

Contrary to the claims of neoliberal doctrine, the economic reforms in Egypt since the 1990s did not lead to an overall reduction in the number or proportion of state employees. The same period that witnessed the transfer of hundreds of thousands of workers out of the public sector in manufacturing also saw enormous growth in employment in the civil service, health service and state education system. The education system in particular was transformed into a sector of mass, low-paid employment, which by 2007 was in absolute and relative terms the largest single sector of the employed labour market. The expansion of the education system in the neoliberal era has taken place under very different conditions to the previous phase of growth during the construction of the welfare state under Nasser, and this has in turn shaped education workers' perceptions of their relationship to the working class in contradictory ways.

The development of the Egyptian education system under neoliberalism has put immense pressure on teachers to deepen the process of privatisation by turning them into private 'service providers' who supplement their declining salaries by giving private lessons and compensate for the lack of resources in schools by either buying their own or insisting that their pupils' parents pay for books and equipment. This option is not available equally to all education workers: teachers provide a service which is capable of privatisation at an individual level; administrators and school caretakers do not. Egyptian teachers have also experienced increasing control and regimentation by management, with the imposition of tighter professional standards and moves towards performance-related pay and incentive structures with the adoption of a new national pay and grading framework in 2007. The dual-faced nature of the restructuring of work in the service

TABLE 2.13 Economic sectors employing the largest proportion of employees (as % of the total number of employees in the labour force)

	1999	2003	2007
Education	17.1	18.7	16.2
Agriculture	10.4	9.3	10.8
Construction	9.9	9.6	11.6
Public administration	15.9	19.2	15.4
Manufacturing	17.2	14.3	14.5

SOURCE ILO LABORSTA database, Table 2E.

sector in the neoliberal era appears clearly in this context: on the one hand service workers are subject to more factory-like discipline and management control in order to counterbalance their greater disruptive power, while, on the other, new policies attempt to entrench competition between workers and conceal their common interests in collective resistance. Nevertheless, teachers and other workers in the public education system do retain a number of significant organisational advantages over their colleagues in the private sector, flowing from the state's need to intervene in and organise education on a national basis. The infrastructure of the state education system creates connections between education workers at local, regional and national levels which can stimulate the development of workers' organisation, as the subsequent experience of strike action by teachers and other education workers demonstrates.

The importance of the education system as a source of employment is illustrated by Table 2.13. A number of trends should be noted. First, levels of enrolment in all levels of education have dramatically increased, as have the overall completion rates in primary education. Enrolment in primary school, for example,

FIGURE 2.2 Weekly wages in selected economic sectors, 1999–2007 (LE)

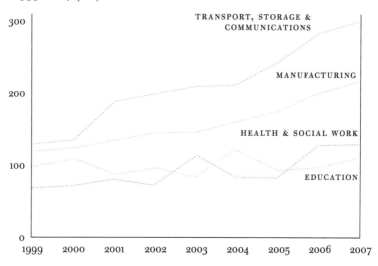

SOURCE ILO LABORSTA database, Table 5A.

rose from 67 percent of the eligible age group in 1980 to 112 per cent in 2012.[50] However, employment in education has grown much faster than the expansion in pupil numbers. Between 1984/5 and 2007 the number of pupils grew from 9.6 million to 17 million, an increase of 177 per cent, while the number of teachers grew from 155,000 to 821,000 during the same period, an increase of 530 per cent. In terms of the average ratio of pupils to teachers this translates into a drop from 62 pupils for each teacher in 1984/5 to around 20 per teacher in 2007. This does not mean, of course, that all Egyptian children are taught in classes that are a third the size of those in previous generations. Teachers in state schools which serve the poor commonly teach classes of up to eighty children and many of these schools still operate a 'shift system' of shortened school days of four hours in order to work at double capacity.[51] This helps to explain why adult literacy

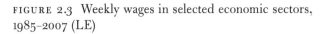

FIGURE 2.3 Weekly wages in selected economic sectors,
1985–2007 (LE)

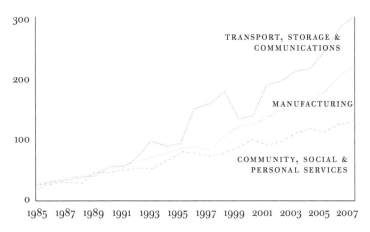

SOURCE ILO LABORSTA database, Table 5A.

rates are still relatively low: by 2006 only 66 per cent of the adult
population could read and write, according to the World Bank,
underlining the fact that improvement in the quality of education,
particularly for the poor, cannot be measured simply in terms of
school enrolments, and points to the continued importance of
Egyptian schools as 'warehouses' for poor children, rather than
spaces for genuine learning.

The growth of education and other public services as sectors
of mass low-paid employment is also a noticeable feature of the
last three decades. In 2007 education had the lowest-paid average
weekly wage, which was only 84 per cent of the average wage in
the next lowest-paid sector, health and social care.

Figure 2.2 illustrates the growing differentiation between
low-paid workers in two key predominantly 'white collar'
service sectors, education and health, and two of the key areas

of 'blue-collar' working-class employment: manufacturing and transport. Between them by 2007 these sectors of the economy employed 5.4 million workers or 43 per cent of the entire employed workforce. Data from a longer historical time span (Figure 2.3) demonstrates that these are long-term trends (data on wages in education and health was not collected separately until 1996, so the figures after this date represent an average across three sectors of 'services').

The assault on teachers' job security and pay has come from many different directions. In the public school system, Ministry of Education newly qualified teachers have found it difficult to obtain permanent contracts.[52] Tens of thousands are employed in hourly paid work as supply teachers, or teach classes in public schools for no pay at all, in order to be allowed the chance to compete in giving private lessons to the same children after the school day has ended.[53] Even teachers on permanent contracts are paid so badly that they regularly supplement their income through private tuition, or by other part-time work. In major cities, fee-paying lessons are largely institutionalised and essentially compulsory, taking place after the 'free' school day has ended in the same classrooms with the same teachers, with the school administration and the Ministry of Education taking a cut of the profits.[54] In the countryside, poverty is so entrenched that parents cannot afford to supplement teachers' salaries in this way, forcing them to take on other work such as painting and decorating, driving taxis or selling vegetables.[55] However, the example of the teachers' strikes since the revolution – which consistently linked demands to improve teachers' pay and conditions to calls for the banning of private lessons – demonstrates that this process is not an insurmountable obstacle to collective action. More importantly, in the process of taking collective action, the teachers transformed themselves from agents of the market into a powerful force leading the fight for an education system for all.

Precarious workers, informal economy?

The process of 'informalisation' in employment, in particular the development of new forms of 'precarious' working, has been hotly debated in recent years.[56] In the Egyptian context, it is important to distinguish between different measures and trajectories of 'informality', and to recognise that 'informal' is not simply a synonym for 'precarious', any more than it is a synonym for self-employment or employment in a micro-enterprise. Simplistic models of the economy propose a neat division into formal and informal sectors – with employment in the first regulated by formal contracts and access to social security benefits, in contrast to the informal sector where workers typically have neither of these things. More sophisticated versions of this approach argue that a shrinking 'core' of the working class enjoys stable, relatively well protected employment, at the expense of a growing, marginalised 'periphery'. In contrast to the mechanical dualism of formal and informal *sectors*, the concept of core and periphery can be applied within as well as between enterprises, as new workers are hired on different terms and conditions to their predecessors or work is outsourced.

The restructuring of employment in manufacturing, transport and public services, described above, provides examples of several different trajectories towards greater 'informality'. As we observed in Chapter 1, a central feature of the neoliberal reform process in Egypt was a frontal assault on job security, epitomised by the passage of Law 12 of 2003, which gave employers greater flexibility in hiring and firing workers, making it far easier to employ workers without a contract at all. 'Informalisation' in this sense is therefore a deliberate attack on legal employment protection, carried out by the state in order to provide the most advantageous conditions for capital accumulation. Yet the Egyptian economy has also witnessed a different process of 'informalisation' with the development or expansion of 'informal' employment in micro- and small enterprises or self-employment in parallel with (or parasitic on) the 'formal' economy. We can see both of these trends at work in the transport sector: in the transfer of tens of thousands of workers from direct state employment on the inter-city bus services to relatively more precarious employment in the semi-privatised holding companies and in the expansion of highly informal jobs in micro-enterprises run by tuk-tuk owners.

In modern mass transport systems, the 'informality' of employment for workers on whose labour the system depends could be thought of as more of a subjective rather than an objective condition. In other words, while it is in transport employers' interests to be able to exercise control over their workforce and demand 'flexibility' from them, there are limits to their ability simply to replace such workers at will: these limits vary, but are shaped by the size of the pool of suitably skilled labour from which they can recruit, and the costs of replacing and retraining workers, all of which has to be added to the calculation of losses caused by strike action or other forms of workers' collective action during a dispute. In such cases the imposition of more 'informal' or 'precarious' conditions of work is perhaps better understood as a defeat or setback which can potentially be reversed, rather than as a structural shift in how capitalism works.

The second type of 'informalisation' that has occurred during the neoliberal era raises more complex questions in assessing its impact on workers' ability to realise their collective social power, including the relative weight of workers in formal or secure employment compared to those in precarious or informal employment in terms of the value they create and their numbers. Another critical question, which is raised by advocates of a 'core and periphery' model, is whether workers in the 'core' have any common interest or even shared life experiences with workers in the periphery which can form the basis of collective action. As explored above, the development of Egyptian capitalism under neoliberalism has been characterised in part by the 'informalisation' of parts of the service sector, including services provided directly by the state, not only in the sense of the assault on job security for workers in those sectors but also in the creation of new consumer and labour markets characterised by relative increases in the levels of informality. This process is a mechanism for making the poor subsidize the poor: by topping up the low pay of service workers despite the declining quality of the service itself. Tuks-tuks and microbus services save the state having to provide mass transport systems for the poor, just as private lessons are primarily a subsidy from working-class and poor parents to make up for teachers' low pay. Neoliberalism attempts to entrench competition between the poor in more and more areas of life.

Yet, at the same time, the working class combines across generations, within its living spaces and in its shared experiences of exploitation and oppression. Using household survey data from a major study of Soweto in South Africa, Claire Ceruti presents a compelling argument for seeing the Sowetan 'reserve army of labour' of unemployed and 'precarious' workers as bound in a 'community of fate' with workers in more stable employment. The Soweto survey showed that workers in permanent and formal employment frequently supported members of the same household who were unemployed, part-time or working in temporary jobs.[57] While there has been no comparable study of existing Egyptian household survey data, Jackline Wahba's assessment of the impact of the 2003 Labour Law on employment security suggests that similar patterns of combined stable and precarious employment are likely to be found in Egypt.[58] Wahba found that the 2003 Labour Law intensified the generational effect of 'informalisation', with new entrants to the labour market gaining employment on more precarious terms than ever before. The proportion of workers employed in their first job without a contract rose from around 20 per cent in the 1970s to 69 per cent in 1998.[59] Other, more recent studies suggest a transition from informal employment to public-sector employment after age 24, with large numbers of workers 'queuing' in informal employment until formal employment becomes available.[60]

Conclusion: unevenness and combination

The examples we have explored in this chapter attest to the deepening unevenness of Egypt's economic development in the neoliberal era. A few sectors of the economy – extractive industries, parts of the garment, cement and steel industries, automobile assembly – are more deeply connected to the global economy than ever before. Workers in these sectors are, on the one hand, more vulnerable to global fluctuations in trade and production, but, on the other, the withdrawal of their labour is also potentially disruptive at a transnational scale. Likewise, workers in transport, logisitics and communications, play an enhanced role in the overall process of production: the state still guarantees the backbone of these systems and facilitates selective investment in an effort to improve conditions for accumulation, rather than to meet social needs. Services show similar unevenness: despite large government and foreign donor investments in the education system, millions of children are still taught in crumbling schools by teachers on poverty-level pay. While private universities claiming state-of-the-art facilities for technical education have sprung up by the dozen, overall literacy rates actually dropped in the mid-2000s.

However, we have also sought to show how an Egyptian working class is *objectively* formed by the needs of Egyptian capitalism across the divide between public and private sectors, and through the interpenetration of 'formal' and 'informal', 'precarious' and 'stable', labour relations in large parts of the economy. Egyptian capitalists' relative competitive advantage as they seek to carve out a niche for themselves in global markets, both in terms of producing goods and services for export, and in terms of attracting foreign investment, depends in large part on access to a critical mass of reasonably skilled but low-paid workers in a wide range of sectors, including mass transport systems such as road freight, railways and ports, as well as electricity distribution, sanitation and telecommunications. Health and education services for the millions employed in these sectors are provided in turn by other low-paid workers. It has proved advantageous to Egyptian capitalists to offload as much as possible of the burden of providing these services onto the poor themselves, but that does not mean that they can dispense with them altogether. Egyptian capitalists' need for the labour of workers whose levels of skill and strategic location in the process of production makes them indispensable to the process of accumulation, as well as the lower-paid, sometimes less skilled workers whose labour reduces the overall social cost of production, is a factor which knits together the apparently disparate parts of the working class into a variegated whole. Moreover, workers and their families are consumers of goods and users of both public and private services. This is a factor which binds together workers across different sectors of the economy: they have a common interest in reversing, or at least halting, the drive towards greater fragmentation of public services both as workers and as users. It is not the case that workers in 'core' jobs are offered benefits and services which are qualitatively different to the rest of the poor. Such services represent precisely the kind of 'soft tissue' of the Nasserist social contract that neoliberal policies first attacked: slashing the 'fringe benefits' attached to employment in the public sector in an effort to cut costs.

The examples outlined here demonstrate that the combination of state-capitalist and neoliberal features in the Egyptian economy needs to be explored as a *process*. The assault on the giant public-sector combines comprises one trajectory in class formation, while the concentration of industrial workers in new manufacturing zones comprises another. The timing and intersection of these processes was, as we will explore in subsequent chapters, of great significance for the rediscovery of workers' self-confidence and willingness to organise collective action. The transformative impact of the Misr Spinning workers' strike of December 2006, for example, was a reflection of both objective and subjective aspects of combined development. The strike halted the largest factory in the Middle East, and the social weight behind this blow was increased by the growing gap in size between Misr Spinning and other industrial workplaces following the restructuring of manufacturing. However, when the strike wave leapt from Mahalla to Kafr al-Dawwar and Shibin al-Kom, it followed a path mapped out by the old institutional structures of the public-sector textile industry – despite the privatisation of Shibin al-Kom two years previously. The timing of the Mahalla strike in relation to the internal processes of restructuring was also important: ESCO workers fought a courageous, but ultimately hopeless, rearguard action to defend their jobs after losing almost the entire workforce, while Misr Spinning workers went into battle still at full strength. Yet the Mahalla strike exploded into a context also shaped by the rising self-confidence and anger of workers in the private sector, both in the new industrial cities and elsewhere. It also intersected with the tightening grip of neoliberal policies on workers in the service sector and government bureaucracy. The most important aspect of the Misr Spinning strike was of course that it represented an unequivocal victory on scale Egyptian workers had not experienced for decades. In the following chapter, we explore the transformative impact of this victory on the workers' movement.

CHAPTER 3

Strikes, protests and the development of a revolutionary crisis

A decade and a half passed between the adoption of the Economic Reform and Structural Adjustment Programme and the eruption of a major strike wave. An initial flurry of workers' protests, including a major protest and a factory sit-in by workers at the public-sector mills in Kafr al-Dawwar in 1994, was contained by the regime. A report on Egypt's economic prospects after ten years of structural adjustment by the Operations Evaluation Department of the World Bank sounded a cautious note of satisfaction, congratulating the Egyptian government on its 'major achievement' in 'undertaking these reforms without significant social unrest'.[1] The optimism of the World Bank officials was misplaced. Before the end of the decade, Egypt would be in the grip of the biggest wave of strikes and workers' protests since the 1940s, unleashing a process of reciprocal action[2] between 'political' and 'economic' struggles which proved impossible to tame within the existing political regime.

The central argument in the previous chapter was that the working class was restructured under neoliberalism, but not weakened to the point where it could no longer deploy its collective social power. The sheer scale of strike activity from the mid-2000s onwards dramatically confirms this analysis. Further-more, the dynamics of the strike wave reflected key features of uneven and combined economic development that we highlighted in Chapter 2. The precursors of the revival of workers' collective agency emerged in the rash of workers' protests and attempts to establish unions in the new industrial cities in 2004–05, but the turning point was the December 2006 strike by 24,000 textile workers at Misr Spinning in Al-Mahalla al-Kubra, the heart of the state-capitalist industrial project; from there strikes spread among civil servants and teachers, who were the first to turn their strike committees into independent unions. The strike wave breached barriers between public and private sectors, leapt from large to small workplaces and back again, and demonstrated that workers in all these places could adopt the same tactics, raise similar demands, and learn from each other, even without organisations of their own to communicate those lessons directly. This experience underscores the important role played by the non-state media, particularly independent newspapers, whose industrial correspondents toured the country reporting on strikes.

However, we also argue that the recovery of workers' agency had both political and economic dimensions and that the strike wave must be understood in the context of the generalisation of a wider 'culture of protest'.[3] From the student-led protests in solidarity with the al-Aqsa Intifada in Palestine in 2000 to the demonstrations over the invasion of Iraq in 2003 which liberated Tahrir Square for the people for the first time in a generation, to the stirrings of a new kind of activism in late 2004 aimed at denying Mubarak the opportunity to bequeath political power to his son Gamal, to the rebellion of the judges in 2006, the first half of the decade was already rich in the experience of popular protest.

Nevertheless, the intervention of a sustained wave of strikes and workers' protests transformed the dynamic of opposition to the regime in three dimensions. First, it decisively set the pendulum swinging between waves of political and social collective action from below after a long period in which protests of any kind had appeared largely as isolated explosions of anger. Second, it transformed the character of resistance to the regime: in the aggregate the numbers of participants in all forms of workers' protests dwarfed the relatively modest numbers of activists who were mobilised by the political protests over regional issues such as Iraq and Palestine or the campaigns around democratic reform. Individual strikes and protests by workers were still generally small-scale (numbering in the hundreds or occasionally thousands); however, this chapter argues that their dispersal across almost every sector of the economy and wide areas of the country carried elements of the developing culture of protest into every corner of Egypt, turning thousands of workplaces into temporary laboratories for democratic self-organisation. The dispersed character of this resistance made it extremely difficult to repress, but was nevertheless effective in disorganising and confusing the regime, in particular by paralysing one of its key organs of popular political control, the Egyptian Trade Union Federation. This theme is explored in more detail in Chapter 4.

The pendulum's motion between waves of political and social protest also created the conditions for their integration. The eruption of strikes protected the democratic opposition movement, providing it with a 'breathing space' to regroup and arise anew after a period in which the regime had regained the initiative in suppressing street protests. This chapter argues that, although this process of integration was uneven and limited, the points of connection between the social and political aspects of resistance to the regime played a pivotal role in shaping the overall trajectory of struggle, illustrated by the coalescence of a coalition of democratic activists around the call for a strike by textile workers in Al-Mahalla al-Kubra on 6 April 2008. The events of the 'Mahalla

Uprising', which were the consequence of the security forces' intervention to stop the strike, played out in many respects as a 'dress rehearsal' for the uprising of January 2011.

A distinctive feature in the evolution of workers' protest tactics during the decade before the revolution of 2011 was the rediscovery of the strike. This chapter argues that the change from forms of protest such as a 'sit-in' (*itisam*) without stopping production, to the organised withdrawal of labour during a strike, was made possible by the reconfiguration of the relationship between the state, capital and labour during the long crisis of the Nassserist state. However, they also were a direct counterattack against the neoliberal policies of the ruling-class reformers who championed the strategic turn to the market. Unlike other forms of popular protest, strikes targeted both Nasserist and neoliberal elements in the unstable and complex amalgam which was the Mubarak-era Egyptian state. It is revealing that the most important points of connection between the political and social aspects of resistance to Mubarak were centred around strikes: in particular the strikes by the textile workers in Al-Mahalla al-Kubra and the national strike by employees in the property tax collection agency.

The pressures that generated the organic process of reciprocal action between political and social struggles are easy to identify: the repressive behaviour of the state, which criminalised both 'economic' strikes and 'political' protests; the crisis in the state apparatus itself, faced with the rise of popular resistance which encouraged further mobilisations and an escalation of demands; the interaction between global and local economic crisis, which manifested itself particularly in food price inflation and accelerated economic struggles. However, there were also counter-pressures driving economic and political protests apart. It is important to recognise that these counter-pressures had many sources, which were expressed in gaps, unevenness and contradictions in what Luxemburg describes as the 'interlacing' of the social and political aspects of the class struggle.[4] One source of counter-pressure was the regime, which mobilised its ideological and physical resources to enforce separation between economic and political resistance from below. Senior figures in the ruling party repeated insistently that the strikes were 'not about politics', while surveillance and harassment by the security forces of opposition activists raised barriers to deepening the interaction between the organisers of economic and political protests. Although the events of early 2008 showed that it was possible for activists in the wider political movement against Mubarak and in the workers' movement to pose the question of common action in such a way that it won wide support in both constituencies, the opposition to Mubarak lacked organisations that were rooted in the workplaces and that had a political perspective capable of uniting the social and the political.

The Misr Spinning strike of December 2006: a turning point

The strike at Misr Spinning and Weaving Company in the Delta town of Al-Mahalla al-Kubra, which began on 4 December 2006, played a transformative role in several dimensions. The Mahalla workers' victory, as we explore below, both transformed workers' perceptions of what could be achieved through self-organised collective action and played a critical role in shaping the overall trajectory of popular opposition to Mubarak. The protest began with the organised refusal of workers to cash their pay cheques in order to demand the payment of a profit-sharing bonus equivalent to two months' pay which the government had decreed would be payable in state enterprises that had managed to reduce their losses. The Misr Co. management had refused to pay the bonus, claiming that the decree applied only to the public-sector companies, and not to companies in the public business sector. The workers gave the company three days to respond to their demands, after which they would begin a strike and sit-in in the factory. The protest came at a sensitive time, as union elections had taken place at the end of November, some ten days before. When management refused to meet their demands, workers declared a strike beginning on 7 December, and gathered for the sit-in in the main courtyard of the factory. Women workers in the company's garment factory began the strike with the chant that became famous: 'Here are the women, where are the men?' Around 5,000 of the total workforce of 24,000 gathered in the courtyard.

The position of the trade union was clear from the first moment: the official union representatives took the position that workers had no cause for grievance and that the losing candidates in the union elections had exploited a misunderstanding. The factory union committee, the General Union of Textiles Workers and the Egyptian Trade Union Federation all opposed the strike. The strike took place on 7 and 8 December; on the third day Ai'sha Abd-al-Hadi, the minister of labour, announced that the workers' demands would be met and that the strike days would be considered a paid holiday.

The strike can be considered a turning point in the development of the strike wave and the workers' movement in Egypt, so that it is possible to talk about 'before' and 'after' the strike. This is not because of the scale of the strike, nor because of its impact on the media, or even the fact that it triggered the largest and deepest strike wave since the 1940s, but because the strikes after the Mahalla strike carried the features of this strike, which differed significantly from those in the previous period. The first feature of the Mahalla strike, which we explore in more detail below, was the fact that it was a *strike* rather than a 'work-in', in contrast to the general pattern of workers' collective action in previous decades. The second distinguishing feature was the duration of the strike, as it set a trend towards a pattern of collective action where events were played out over several days or even weeks. Again, this was in sharp contrast to the experience of the 1980s and 1990s, when workers' protests rarely lasted more than twenty-four hours. The relatively long duration of the Mahalla strike relates to a third distinguishing feature: the fact that it ended peacefully by direct negotiation rather than through the violent intervention of the security forces.

A new culture of protest

As we have already indicated, the upsurge in strikes in 2007, driven initially by workers in the large public-sector textile mills, had a wide range of causes. The revolt by workers in Kafr al-Dawwar in 1994 had erupted in a political and social landscape that was significantly different, and this helps to explain both why the authorities opted for concessions in 2006, in contrast to their violent response to the earlier strike, and the transformative impact of the Mahalla victory on workers' self-organisation and consciousness across wide sections of Egyptian industry. We explored previously how neoliberal reforms revoked the 'Nasserist social contract' which had promised workers a minimum standard of living in return for their social and political quiescence. However, it was equally important that, unlike in 1994, the rising tide of workers' protests engulfed a society already shaped by the emergence of what Rabab El-Mahdi has termed a new 'culture of protest'.[5]

The outbreak of the second Palestinian intifada in September 2000 in response to Ariel Sharon's visit to the Haram al-Sharif was the trigger for the demonstrations that opened this period. Islamist activists on the university campuses have generally been credited with mobilising the first protests: around 6,000 students demonstrated in Alexandria University on 30 September, followed by protests on the university campuses in Zagazig and al-Minufiyya. By Monday, 2 October, Nasserist and socialist activists at Ain Shams University in Cairo had organised a demonstration of around 500 people, while a protest was also held at the American University in Cairo. The following day 2,000 students rallied at Cairo University, and were joined by around 5,000 protestors from the Muslim Brotherhood.[6] So far the security forces were able to keep protests contained on the campuses, although at Cairo University a demonstration on 4 October nearly succeeded in reaching the Israeli embassy, a few streets away from the main campus.[7] The Israeli offensive of March–April 2002 against Palestinians in the West Bank, which included the destruction of much of Jenin refugee camp, again provided the spark for a round of protests. This time, however, the demonstrations were larger, and had more success at breaching the security cordons around the university campuses. Once again, students at Alexandria University organised the most militant protests.

In comparison to the events of April 2002, protests in March 2003 triggered by the US-led invasion of Iraq saw demonstrators temporarily take control of other spaces in central Cairo, including Tahrir Square. Not only did demonstrators 'cross the line' from the zones of tolerated dissent in the university campuses and mosques into the streets, but the protests were for the first time in decades large enough to fill some of the most important spaces in Cairo's urban landscape. Anti-war activists had called a protest to begin at 1.00 p.m. on the day external military intervention in Iraq began. The scale of the response to this call overwhelmed the security forces. According to one eyewitness account:

> What happened yesterday was something which Cairo did not see in decades, maybe since 1972. A crack [appeared] in the dreadful wall of dictatorship. In an hour the square was filled by people shouting slogans against America, Blair and Mubarak. Tens of thousands joined and the square was totally freed and occupied by the growing crowds. From the Nile to the People's

Assembly in Qasr al-Ainy [Street] people practised their political freedom for the first time since years. You could feel the joy, the anger and feeling powerful by being together. I cannot tell you about the initiatives people made. Our banners were held all the time by ordinary people. People [were] distributing water and food. Americans from the American University in Cairo joined [in] and were taken to the front of the demonstration. … The demo continued and turned to a real carnival in Tahrir Square. [People were] singing [in] circles. [There were] people holding candles, people drawing on the ground anti war and anti government slogans.[8]

Meanwhile, on the southern edge of the square protestors battled with the police as they tried to reach the American embassy in nearby Garden City. The Central Security Forces used water cannon, tear gas, electric batons and dogs against the crowds.

December 2004 saw another important evolution in the protest movement: the public launch of a campaign for democratic reform which targeted Hosni Mubarak himself. Until this date, while calls for democratic reform in the abstract and public criticism of corruption at lower levels of the state were tolerated by the regime, direct attacks on Mubarak's role were extremely rare. The loose coalition of Islamist, Nasserist and left-wing activists which coalesced under the slogan *Kifaya* (Enough) also adopted new tactics in relation to street protests, interspersing attempts to mobilise in the heavily policed areas of central Cairo with 'flash-mob'-style gatherings in the poorer suburbs. *Kifaya*'s protests focused on exposing the preparation of Mubarak's son Gamal for a key role in the regime on his father's retirement or death, challenging the continuation of the Emergency Laws, and calling for the extension or application of basic civil and democratic rights. The confrontation between sections of the judiciary and the regime in May 2006 took up similar issues. An attempt by the Court of Cassation to discipline two of its members, Hisham al-Bastawisi and Mahmud Mekki, was widely perceived as an act of retaliation for their role in issuing a report highlighting fraud and intimidation during the 2005 elections. Protests by their supporters inside and outside the judiciary triggered a violent response from the security forces. The sight of judges in their regalia facing riot police in the streets of the capital reinforced the sense of political crisis.[9]

However, although these protests marked a dramatic shift from the experience of the previous decade in terms of their willingness to confront the regime directly and in terms of their ability to draw in hundreds, and sometimes thousands, of activists, they remained relatively small and were largely concentrated in Cairo and Alexandria. The biggest mobilisations took place around the Palestinian intifada and the invasion of Iraq, while *Kifaya*'s actions, although symbolically highly significant, generally involved hundreds, not thousands, of protesters. Moreover, the violent response of the security forces was, by the time of the judges' protests in 2006, beginning to exhaust the relatively thin ranks of the groups from which *Kifaya* and similar campaigns drew their core activists.

The transformation of workers' collective action

The strike wave that emerged in the mid-2000s marked a qualitative shift from the patterns of collective action during previous decades. This shift can be observed in several dimensions; taken together these help to explain why the strike wave itself had such a transformative effect. Three of these dimensions can be represented to a certain extent statistically and graphically: the scale of the strike wave (measured in terms of the frequency of workers' protests and the numbers of participants); its geographical distribution; and finally the way in which workers' demands and tactics were replicated across multiple divisions within the economy (between the public and the private sector, large and small workplaces, manufacturing and services). The lack of accurate statistics means that this picture will naturally only show the basic contours of the landscape, but the enormous upward leap in the volume and quality of reports about strike action in the media and through activist networks provides us with enough usable data to attempt an analysis. Below we discuss in more detail dimensions of the strike wave which do not lend themselves so easily to statistical representation: the shift in workers' organisational tactics and strategy, and the altered responses of the state to workers' collective action. Our argument is underpinned by the contention that understanding the relationships between these complex phenomena requires the location of the strike wave at the intersection of two processes: the reconfiguration of the relationships between the state, capital and labour under neoliberalism; and the rise of a new culture of popular protest, which was driven at first by events at the regional level, such as the second Palestinian intifada and the occupation of Iraq.

As Table 3.1 demonstrates, changes in the frequency, scale and tactics of workers' collective action can form the basis for a rough division of the decade before the revolution into three periods.[10] The first period from 1998 to mid-2004 saw a wave of strikes and protests; these peaked in 1999 and then tailed off slowly during the following years, probably reflecting the dampening effect of intensifying economic crisis and rising unemployment on workers' confidence. The aggressive reassertion of the neoliberal economic agenda by the Ahmad Nazif cabinet of 2004 was reflected in a marked upswing in the tempo of workers' collective action, with overall numbers of all forms of collective action tripling in comparison with the previous year. However, a much more significant transformative shift came after 2006 in two crucial dimensions. First, the number of episodes of collective action more than doubled again; second, this transmitted an experience

TABLE 3.1 Episodes and forms of workers' collective action,
1998–2010

	Sit-in	Strike	Demo	Other	Total
1998	18	40	14	43	115
1999					164
2000					135
2001					138
2002					96
2003					86
2004	90	43	46	87	266
2005	59	46	16	81	202
2006	81	47	25	69	222
2007	197	110	43	264	614
2008	253	122	60	253	609
2009	126	84	42	180	432
2010	209	135	80	106	530

SOURCE Fouad, 2004; Beinin, 2010, p. 16; Awlad al-Ard, 2010. 'Other includes 'gatherings' and 'static rallies' and forms of protest not otherwise specified.

of strike action to far larger groups of workers. As we explore in more detail later, the adoption of strikes as a tactic in contrast to the use of the *itisam*, or sit-in, which usually did not involve the interruption of production by the workers, was a crucial marker of workers' changing consciousness of their own social power and an indicator of the declining grip of Nasserist ideology within the workers' movement.

The shifting geography of the strike wave points to another dimension of change: the failure of the state's earlier strategies of spatial and sectoral containment. During the 1980s and 1990s, collective action by workers in large workplaces was met with extreme repression. Strikes by textile workers in Kafr al-Dawwar

FIGURE 3.1 Episodes of workers' collective action, 1998–2010
(yearly averages)

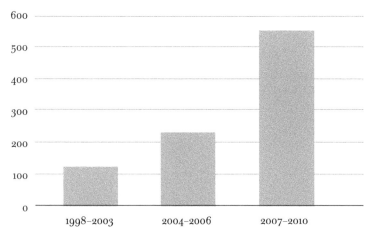

SOURCE Fouad, 2004; Beinin, 2010, p. 16; Awlad al-Ard, 2010, averages by the authors.

in 1984, the railway workers in 1986, Mahalla in 1986, light
transport workers in 1986, the Egyptian Iron and Steel Company
(EISC) workers in 1989 and ESCO workers in 1986 were all
ended by the violent intervention of the security forces. The last
mass workers' sit-in that the state broke up by force was at the
Spinning Company in Kafr al-Dawwar in 1994. The security
forces' intervention to break up workers' protests was, however,
accompanied in most cases by the implementation of the workers'
demands, while granting them in many cases paid leave to calm
the situation, sometimes restricted on a geographical basis to
the affected plants.[11] The tactics adopted by the security forces
demonstrate the importance to the state of containing strikes
within a limited geographical area: in the case of workers' protests
in large public-sector manufacturing workplaces, such as the
textile mills and EISC, the plants were physically isolated by
large numbers of troops which mobilised for an all-out assault

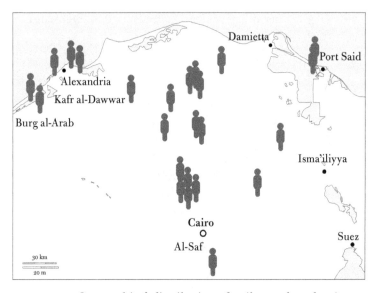

FIGURE 3.2 Geographical distribution of strikes and workers' protests, February 2007

SOURCE Egyptian Trade Union and Workers Watch, 1 March 2007.

on the factory under the cover of an almost complete information blackout in the state-controlled media. In the case of the EISC strike, armoured cars and live ammunition were used during the storming of the plant. The ferocity of the state's response to the EISC strike can be seen as reflecting a desire to forcibly contain dynamics of collective action which had begun to spawn processes of reciprocal action between economic and political struggles perceived as deeply threatening to the existing political order, the most worrying instance of which from the perspective of the state was the rebellion by Central Security Forces troops in 1986. The storming of the Kafr al-Dawwar mills that broke the 1994 strike played a crucial role in maintaining the policy of geographical containment.

The report on workers' collective action compiled by Egyptian Trade Union and Workers' Watch (ETUWW) for February 2007[12] illustrates the rapid geographical diffusion of strikes through the weaving and spinning sector, followed by a rash of strikes and protests in other industries.[13] As Figure 3.2 shows, strikes were spread out across the Delta, from Burg al-Arab near Alexandria in the west to Port Said in the east, and as far south as Al-Saf. Thirteen separate strikes or protests were recorded in weaving and spinning, almost all in the first half of the month. The trigger for this wave of action was the week-long strike by workers at Indorama (formerly Ghazl Shibin al-Kom) on 30 January, followed on 3 February by Misr Fine Spinning in Kafr al-Dawwar. The following day workers at Delta Spinning in Zifta walked out, triggering a copycat strike by workers at their sister plant in Tanta, and further solidarity action by the Zifta workers on 7 February. Meanwhile Industrial Silk Co. workers in Kafr al-Dawwar had also taken strike action on 5 February. Nor was it only public-sector mills that were affected: workers in private-sector mills in 10th of Ramadan City, Al-Salihiyya and Burg al-Arab joined the strikes. Beyond the textile sector, there were also strikes, demonstrations and protests by workers in the Sinai Manganese mines, the Giza Education Directorate, Cairo Poultry Group, municipal cleaning in Giza, the Port Said shipyards, river transport in Imbaba and bus station supervisors in Mahalla.

Over the following months, new workplaces were drawn into the strike wave, such as the 2,700 workers in the privately owned Makarem Group factories in Sadat City and the privately owned Arab Polvara in Alexandria in April 2007.[14] Garment workers, despite the problems of organising collective action in an industry characterised by low pay, job insecurity and a largely unskilled, female workforce, carried the strikes into sectors with weak traditions of collective action.[15] The workers at the Mansura-Espana garment factory occupied their plant and slept over on the shopfloor in order to prevent its closure.[16] A report on strike activity for the last two weeks in October 2007 provides a vivid picture of the further expansion of workers' collective action, with strikes in textiles and garment production, telephone manufacturing, electrical goods, building, light and heavy engineering, and general contracting (including cement and brick-making), along with transport (including port workers employed by the Suez Canal Company and Cairo Metro train drivers), energy, food production, hotels, commercial establishments, hospitals, schools and civil servants (including a national strike by property tax collectors).[17] Few areas of the Egyptian economy proved impenetrable to the strike wave, which would even reach military-owned factories operating under martial law.[18]

Repression of strikes during the 1980s and 1990s was not only an attempt to geographically isolate the contagion of workers' protests, but also served an exemplary purpose. The slaughter of workers in front of their colleagues during protests deterred others from taking action. The spectre of the storming of EISC in Helwan in 1989 and the killing of Abd-al-Hayy Sayyid by the bullets of the security forces hung over the workers' movement there for years afterwards, while the memory of the violence experienced by the workers in Kafr al-Dawwar in 1994 was still fresh even during their strike of 2007. This pattern also changed after the Mahalla strike of December 2006. Despite threatening and pressurizing the workers, the security forces did not end the 2006 Mahalla strike by force. At the time this was considered an exception, but it became the rule. Although 2007 was unusual in the number of strikes, interventions by the security forces were largely restricted to psychological threats and pressure. Moreover, the rare cases of direct repression did not affect the overall dynamic of the strike wave.

The changing tactics of the security forces in relation to strikes were clearly not a result of any kind of democratic transformation of the political system, as the same regime was in power in the 1980s and in 2007. However, there were changes in the objective circumstances which made it difficult to repress striking workers in the same violent manner as in the past. The first of these was the economic changes that the regime had carried out itself, such as the structural adjustment programme, which aimed as one of its aspects to prioritise the economic dimension of the process of production and distribution over the political and security dimension in order to realise profits either through the privatisation of state owned enterprises, or by restructuring to stop losses and thus realise profits. This approach was in contradiction with the complex way in which the state used to handle workers' protests: the storming of the factory while conceding workers' demands and giving them paid leave. This method preserved the security of the regime and protected its hegemony, but prioritised the political management of these conflicts over their economic costs. By contrast, during 2007 the state's attitude towards strikes in the public sector was closer to that of an employer, who, when confronted by a strike, makes decisions based on a comparison between the cost of the strike (whether directly calculated in terms of lost production, or indirectly in terms of how it will strengthen workers' situation in the future) and the cost of meeting workers' demands. Other factors preventing the state using the security forces to crush strikes, such as the fear of international criticism, particularly given the development of the media, and the reduced ability of the state to conceal events also played a role.

Rediscovery of the strike

For a long period the workers' movement relied on the weapon of the sit-in, or *itisam*, in its protests, which meant that workers stayed in the workplace after the end of working hours without stopping or affecting production. This was for a long time the most prominent form of workers' protest, particularly in light of labour relations in the public sector. Official propaganda circulated by the regime generalised the idea that the public sector was the property of the people, and that increased production would lead to increased welfare and that workers were partners in the public sector. This culture raised a barrier between workers and their principal weapon of protest, the strike. Ironically, during many workers' sit-ins during the 1970s and 1980s, rates of production actually rose, as was the case during the August 1989 Helwan steel workers' sit-in, where the rate of production rose 15 per cent during the workers' protest. Rapid intervention by the state to end workers' protests also contributed to the predominance of sit-ins over strikes, as there was often no time for the action to develop from a sit-in to a strike. It was often the state, rather than workers themselves, which terminated production, whether by cutting off water, electricity or gas supplies to the affected workplace, as happened during the 1989 steelworkers strike, and the textile workers' strikes in Kafr al-Dawwar in 1984 and 1994, or by granting workers paid holidays after the end of the protest. There were still episodes of strike action, such as the 1986 railway strike and a strike by workers in the Public Transport Authority in 1976; however, the prevailing form of collective action was the sit-in.

There was already a discernible shift from the use of sit-ins towards strikes in larger workplaces in particular before the Mahalla strike; however, this trend emerged most strongly after it had ended. The strike began with workers' organised refusal to cash their pay cheques for three days; they set the fourth day for the beginning of the strike. The adoption of strike action as a tactic was an important development for the labour movement, as it highlighted workers' economic power. In addition to the political, propaganda and security pressure that a sit-in causes, a strike causes direct economic losses for the employer as a result of stopped production, and forces the employer – whether a private company or the state, to weigh up the relative costs of conceding workers' demands or rejecting them and suffering the loss of production. Workers' consciousness of their economic weight and their willingness to use this are expressed in their tactic of timing strikes to cause the greatest economic losses to the company, as demonstrated by the timing of a strike by workers in the Integrated Oil Company in Suez in May 2007, who set a strike date to coincide with the arrival of an oil shipment in order to cause large losses. The immediate stoppage of work in certain industrial facilities without prior technical preparation may result in severe damage to equipment. Workers in refineries and in production processes using furnaces have usually been keen to avoid inflicting damage to equipment and facilities in order to preserve the peaceful nature of their protests. Cement production falls into this category of workplace; however, the cement workers in Tura, Helwan and Suez were able exercise economic pressure on the employers by organising a protest sit-in and shutting the gates of the plants, thereby preventing the movement of cement shipments until production stopped automatically.

The launch of the policies of structural adjustment, privatisation and early retirement, and those granting greater freedom for business and employers, have had dire consequences for workers and on labour relations; nevertheless they have also dispelled many illusions in the public sector and liberated the power of workers' anger, pitting them face to face with their enemy and allowing them to recover their most important weapon, the strike.

'These are liberated territories'[19]

The short duration of workers' collective action was a notable feature of the labour movement. Frequently, the first reports on protests were those bringing news of their suppression. This is logical when a large number of protests last less than twenty-four

hours, such as the 1989 Helwan steel strike, which began at
noon and ended at dawn, or the railway strike in 1986. The
heavy-handed intervention of the security forces is one factor
that ensures a swift end to workers' protests before they can
spread, particularly in large industrial areas such as Helwan, Kafr
al-Dawwar, Mahalla and Shubra. The extremely short duration
of the protest naturally curtails the development of the movement
in terms of consciousness and organisation, but also prevents the
emergence or development of attitudes of solidarity and the spread
of action to workplaces with similar demands or similar circumstances. The strike wave of 2007 was noticeable for the number
of strikes that lasted days, sometimes weeks, and in exceptional
circumstances months. The Mahalla strike of 7 December 2006
began with a three-day pay-cheque strike, followed by three days
of work stoppage. The second Mahalla strike on 23 September
2007 lasted six days. The strike in Kafr al-Dawwar in February
2007 took nine days, while the strike at Abu Makaram in Sadat
City lasted three weeks. Dozens of other strikes during 2007 were
characterised by relatively longer duration.

The continuation of a strike for several days opened up wide
possibilities for the workers' movement to develop on several
levels. On the one hand, the length of the strike, which is usually
accompanied by the overnight occupation of the workplace,
demands the organisation of mechanisms to regulate the sleep
and daily subsistence of the strikers, as well as protect equipment
and facilities so that workers are not accused of sabotage, and a
rota for participation in the sit-in so as to prolong the action and
to ensure large numbers. All of this becomes a real test of the
workers' readiness to organise, and a measure of the evolution
of consciousness of the movement. The fact is that none of the
workers' protests and strikes witnessed incidents of sabotage or
violence or internal conflicts between workers, or acute crises in
the organisation of subsistence and accommodation. This does

not necessarily mean that the workers' movement passed the tests of consciousness and organisation. If there are no unified mechanisms for workers' internal organisation during strikes, and if these mechanisms do not appear in a direct and explicit manner except through the presence of several thousand people in a single place for several days or weeks, this confirms that the mechanisms of self-organisation have grown and inevitably evolved among workers. Perhaps the simple and unequivocal answer that is most convincing is that given by the workers themselves to the question of internal organisation in the strike: during many strikes the workers responded to the question 'How do you organise yourselves in such large numbers, without major crises?' by simply saying 'We organise ourselves during the process of production, which is more difficult?' This answer does not explain the exact and effective mechanisms of self-organisation but it provides a cogent response to the constant allegations from official quarters about the presence of agitators and troublemakers among the workers. In relation to consciousness and organisation, which are produced by and are expressions of the duration of the strike, there are two other consequences of the length of the strike. The first is solidarity, which will be discussed in detail later. Here it is important to note that one of the most important factors in the emergence of solidarity with workers' strikes is the length of the action, which accounts for the degree of media coverage of the strike, and for information about what is really happening to get out, along with news of the workers' demands, as well as allowing those concerned with the strike to take positions of solidarity, as we saw during the strikes of 2007. The other feature that is a consequence of the length of the strike is the scale of its influence and reach; for the participation of workers in a strike lasting for days on end, and the raising of their demands stimulates the raising of the same, or even different, demands among other sections of workers. This is what occurred after the Mahalla strike of 2006, as the entire textile sector took the same position as the Mahalla workers, and even raised the same demands (although this happened in a sequential manner and not in one go), a process that stimulated the demands of strikers in other sectors.

Mahalla: towards the 2008 uprising

The December 2006 strike unleashed a series of events and a process of radicalisation both inside and outside the mill itself which played a pivotal role in the development of a revolutionary crisis during the last days of Mubarak's rule. As discussed above, the December 2006 victory was the spark for a wave of strikes across the textile sector in early 2007 which opened the door to a massive spike in strike activity in other sectors. Within the factory itself, activists who had led the strike launched a campaign to collect signatures for the withdrawal of confidence from the Factory Union Committee because it had opposed the action. By February 2007 more than 12,000 signatures had been collected, which were delivered by a delegation of workers to the General Union of Textile Workers' head office in Cairo. The delegation, which included some seventy workers from the company, met the president of the union, Sa'id al-Gawhary, and presented him with the signatures, asking him to change the factory union committee in response to the wishes of more than half its general assembly. Al-Gawhary asked for time to review the signatures and confirmed that he would respond to the workers within a few weeks. When the response failed to materialise, they began to send in their resignations and demands to stop union subscriptions being deducted from their pay. Although the number of resignations reached around 3,000, the union continued to ignore the workers.

In September 2007 workers returned to strike action, demanding a profit-sharing bonus as laid down by law, and improvements in pay and incentives. Although the strike took place during the month of Ramadan, it appeared stronger and more cohesive. The action lasted for six days with around 12,000 of the company's workers participating in the sit-in. The strikers formed groups to protect the company and equipment so that they could not be accused of sabotage. The workers continued to operate the factory water and power plant and the company transport garage on humanitarian grounds, as the water and power from the factory also supply homes belonging to company workers and the company hospital; the garage provides ambulances and transport for schoolchildren. The strike was very well organised and showed a very high degree of integration and cooperation among the company's workers.

The most important features of the strike are connected to the fact that it ended through negotiations. On the sixth day, an official delegation came to Mahalla to negotiate with the workers to end the strike. The negotiators included Mohsin al-Gaylani, head of the holding company for Spinning and Weaving; Hussein Megawer, president of ETUF; and Sa'id al-Gawhary, president of the GUTW; and some of the Mahalla leadership of the ruling National Democratic Party. It was curious that the heads of the ETUF and GUTW were part of the delegation negotiating on behalf of the employer, while the strikers' negotiators comprised twenty-five workers' leaders, not one of whom was a member of the executive of the Factory Union Committee (FUC). The head of the FUC was Sadiq Siyam, who had tried to convince some of the workers to return to work on the first day of the strike. The negotiations lasted five hours. Megawer had insisted that no journalists or media should attend the meeting. It ended with the implementation of most of the workers' demands, including a promise to dismiss the head of the company, Mahmoud al-Gibali, whom the workers accused of deliberately damaging the company. The strike was a model of the ability of workers to organise themselves – in this case, for six days in huge numbers and under different kinds of pressure – and to conduct successful negotiations.

The September strike raised the morale of the Mahalla workers and also pushed them to take an entirely new step in the workers' movement, from raising demands restricted to their own workplace to raising demands on behalf of workers at the national level. The National Council for Wages was scheduled to meet in February 2008, so the Mahalla workers organised a demonstration on the 17th. After work had ended for the day, around 12,000 workers joined a demonstration to demand a rise in the minimum wage to the level of the internationally recognised poverty line of $2 a day for a family of four, or LE1,200 a month. After this demonstration, 6 April 2008 was set as the date for a strike in protest at the failure to meet the demands as agreed by Hussein Megawer.

For the first time in decades, the demands raised by workers over their local or sectional grievances provided the starting point for a chain reaction which detonated a national political mobilisation against the regime. The call for a general strike in solidarity with the Mahalla workers' demands was taken up enthusiastically by some in the networks of activists who had been at the heart of the recent campaigns for democratic rights, but who quickly found a much wider audience. A Facebook group calling for a general strike on 6 April 2008 attracted nearly 70,000 members, demonstrating broad support for the Mahalla workers' demands beyond the existing networks of left, Nasserist and Islamist opposition groups. With consternation rising in official quarters, Hussein Megawer attempted to break the connection between the preparations for the strike and the growing calls for protests outside Misr Spinning. On 30 March he called a group of seven leading workers from the factory to his office at the ETUF headquarters in Cairo and forced them to sign pledges promising not to strike and to try to stop the strike taking place. Five signed the pledges and two refused, one of whom, Kamal al-Fayyoumi, was later arrested and detained for two months. Meanwhile, on 6 April, security forces dealt decisively with the strike, entering the plant before the workers started work and preventing them from gathering. They also sent the first shift home early so that workers would not gather at the gates when the next shift came in. That afternoon demonstrations erupted in the town. The security forces reacted with brutal violence: at least one person was shot dead and dozens were injured and hundreds arrested. For several days, the town was in a state of near insurrection: protesters cut the railway line to Cairo and tore down and trampled Mubarak's portrait. Outside Mahalla, there were significant protests on university campuses in solidarity with the strike call, while small street demonstrations in Cairo were broken up by riot police. Mass arrests of Mahalla residents followed the crushing of the localised uprising, coupled with a wave of repression against opposition activists who had supported the 6 April strike call.[20]

Nevertheless, workers returned to protest in October 2008 upon the publication of the annual accounts of the company, which included losses of LE140 million. The workers saw this as a threat to the future of the company and organised a protest in which more than 10,000 participated. Although the demonstration was after working hours, the management moved to punish those involved, which saw two women and three male workers transferred to new jobs, a reduction in bonuses for two others and investigations into a further 150.

Conclusion

Strikes by the Misr Spinning workers were the driving force behind events that took Mahalla to the brink of insurrection, prefiguring the development of a revolutionary crisis on a national scale. A process of what Luxemburg has labelled 'reciprocal action' between political and economic struggles could be seen strongly at work.[21] Strikes driven by 'economic' demands – generally motivated by sectional grievances over pay, conditions and management bullying – achieved significant political results by deepening the crisis of the regime, which in turn further encouraged and radicalised the economic struggle. The demonstration organised by workers in Mahalla on 17 February 2008 demanding a rise in the national minimum wage illustrated their growing consciousness of the importance of taking up issues of general relevance beyond the gates of their own factory. The development of the Misr Spinning workers' movement took place side by side with a battle of equal importance in the Property Tax Agency, which, as we explore in detail in Chapter 5, quickly brought organised workers into head-on confrontation with the state, and resulted in the formation of the first independent union for fifty years.

With the uprising in Mahalla on 6 April 2008, the popular movement crossed an important threshold. It was the first time since 1977 that the regime had faced social and political protest of this nature. In December 2004 a gathering of a few hundred leftist, Islamist and liberal opposition activists had held their breath nervously on the steps of the High Court in Cairo as they raised their placards in the first public protest to directly target Mubarak. In Mahalla, less than four years later, thousands chanted against the dictator, tore down his picture and stamped it to the ground. Organised workers not only *indirectly* created the space for democratic activism to revive after the repression of protests in 2006, but *directly* provided leadership for the revived democratic movement by proposing unifying slogans and setting the date for protests on a national scale. The revival of the democratic movement around the April 2008 events also took place at a higher level than the previous round of protests: participation was more broadly based, with the emergence of layers of new youth activists, more widely dispersed throughout the country.

However, the momentum of reciprocal action was never a smooth or continuous process, and the drama of the 2008 uprising also showed the work of forces driving economic and political struggles apart. The most obvious of these was the action of the regime itself, which mobilised its repressive institutions with the specific intention of separating striking workers from young Facebook activists, and disconnecting anger over rising prices from calls for democratic reform. The regime also mobilised politically, using the ETUF leadership to pressurise some of the leading activists at Misr Spinning to sign a no-strike agreement just before the planned action on 6 April. Their compromise pointed to a deeper political debate about whether workers' best hope of winning their demands rested on consolidating their movement around economic issues or in building stronger bridges with the wider opposition. A year after the 2008 uprising, in preparation for a visit to Misr Spinning, US embassy officials met Kamal Abbas, a former steelworker and director of the Centre for Trade Union and Workers' Services (CTUWS), which had played an influential role in supporting the Misr Spinning workers' movement. According to a classified cable released by Wikileaks, Abbas apparently expressed his frustration and anger with 'the Facebook activists who called for a nation-wide strike in support of the workers', complaining that they were '"intent on regime change", and had "hijacked" the Mahalla workers' apolitical campaign for higher food allowances, and "put the workers in front of the GoE's (Government of Egypt's) guns".'[22] While the idea that workers' protests were being appropriated by other activists for their own ends was mistaken, mistrust of the motives of the opposition was fed by the opportunistic way in which some politicians related to the 6 April strike call. At the Cairo Conference of 2008, a large gathering of opposition groups and international anti-war activists, meeting days before the planned strike, the representative of the Textile Workers'

League from Misr Spinning spoke to a half-empty hall at the tail end of the opening rally due to the fact that he had been preceded by a litany of speeches by opposition politicians.

The Misr Spinning workers' lack of a political voice was also – perhaps more surprisingly – mirrored by the failure to create an independent trade union, despite the depth and breadth of self-organisation required to organise the strikes of 2006 and 2007, and the campaign of collective resignations from membership of the General Federation of Textile Workers. As we explore in the following two chapters, the battle over organisation in the workplace, which the Mahalla workers had played such a key role in initiating, was just beginning.

Organisation in the workplace before the revolution: the Nasserist model in crisis

Three meetings frame our discussion of the crisis of the Egyptian Trade Union Federation (ETUF) in the last years of Mubarak's rule. All took place within just over a year, September 2007–December 2008, and all were ostensibly encounters between organised labour and senior officials in the state and ruling party at which the two sides were expected to bargain and strike a deal. Our interest in these events lies not in the content of the discussion or the individuals sat around the table, but in the way that they can be seen as an expression of a wider process of renegotiation of the relationship between workers and the state, which the explosion of self-organised strike activity in the workplaces made possible.

In December 2008, Gamal Mubarak, eldest son of the president and secretary of the NDP Policy Committee, called a meeting with the ETUF executive and members of the cabinet to discuss proposals for the management of state-owned assets. Around the table were the presidents of the ETUF general unions and Hussein Megawer, ETUF president and former leader of the NDP's parliamentary bloc. All the general union presidents, except one, were stalwart members of the ruling party. What on the surface appeared to be an encounter between representatives of organised labour and senior state officials was simply one of many routine meetings between members of the same apparatus of power.

Yet, even as they strove to maintain the illusion that nothing had changed, many of the participants in the December 2008 meeting must have known that the ground was beginning to shift beneath their feet. Signs of this shift could be seen clearly in a very different meeting, convened just over a year before in September 2007. It provided a more honest lens with which to view the relationship between the ETUF bureaucracy and the regime. Elected delegates representing tens of thousands of striking workers at Misr Spinning in Al-Mahalla al-Kubra sat on one side of the table. Facing them were representatives of the various agencies of the state with a stake in settling the week-long strike: the company's negotiators, the local governor, officials from the Ministry of Labour, state security agents, the president of the General Union of Textile Workers and the ETUF president.

A few months later, in December 2007, another meeting took place which showed even more clearly that the foundations of the ETUF's structures of control were being undermined. In one sense it was a replay of the drama of the Mahalla meeting: on one side sat the minister of finance, Youssef Boutros Ghali, and officials from the Property Tax Agency; facing them were the Property Tax Collectors' Higher Strike Committee, elected delegates representing tens of thousands of low-paid civil servants who had paralysed the Agency with a nationwide strike and brought 10,000 strikers to a sit-in on the steps of the Cabinet Office for ten days. In this case, however, there was a striking absence on the government side. Officials from the ETUF-affiliated General Union of Finance and Banking Workers had attempted to join the negotiations, but were ejected at the request of the Higher Strike Committee. As strikers and the minister wrangled for hours over the terms of a deal which would eventually provide the tax collectors with a pay rise of over 300 per cent and see the government's complete capitulation to the strike demands, the ETUF bureaucrats stood morosely in the street outside. As waiting journalists leapt to capture pictures of Kamal Abu Aita, president of the Higher Strike Committee, carried shoulder-high by his cheering colleagues, the ETUF officials quietly slunk away.

For more than fifty years the institutions that the Nasserist state created to monopolise associational life in the workplace – the labour and professional unions – had survived largely intact. Long after the turn towards neoliberalism signalled the state's withdrawal from the Nasserist social contract, the corporatist structures which had enforced its acceptance in the workplace remained a central pillar of the regime. This chapter explores the partial breakdown of the Nasserist model of 'trade unionism' through the decline and paralysis of the Egyptian Trade Union Federation, the sole legal trade union prior to the revolution of 2011. This process has to be understood as the combination of pressure from above with the explosion of resistance from below. Neoliberal reforms and changes in state policy undermined the ETUF's capacity to monopolise the management of workers' discontent on behalf of the state while workers' self-organisation in the strike wave began to create alternative structures of representation in the workplace. The following chapter will analyse the further transformation of these temporary structures into the first independent unions. We also consider briefly how similar pressures within one of the most important professional associations, the Doctors' Union, disrupted coexistence between the ruling party and the Muslim Brotherhood and opened the door to an alternative practice of trade unionism among junior doctors which advocated the tactics of agitation and strike action adopted by many other public-sector workers. Where the ETUF combined political and economic subservience to the state, the Muslim Brotherhood's approach within the Doctors' Union combined political opposition with accommodation to the regime's economic policies.

The Egyptian Trade Union Federation: from hegemony to paralysis

A central theme of this chapter is the argument that the ETUF is best understood as an extension of the bureaucracy of the ruling party rather than as a trade union. As the meeting in December 2008 illustrates, encounters between the ETUF's leadership and state officials were meetings between party colleagues with responsibilities in different state institutions, rather than between representatives of organised labour and the state. The ETUF's purpose was not to aggregate workers' demands and transmit them upwards, but rather to alternately mobilise and control workers from above. As we discuss in detail below, the ETUF's structures were designed to block any pressures from the base reaching the upper layers of the bureaucracy. Moreover, while organising strikes *outside* the federation could, theoretically speaking, have provided a mechanism for workers to force the ETUF leadership to bargain on their behalf with the state, this did not happen in practice. Rather, the ETUF bureaucracy actually tightened its control over the base of the unions during the final years of Mubarak's rule. We argue here that one of the principal reasons for this was the central political role that the ETUF played in the periodic reproduction of the ruling party's hegemony at the ballot box.

The meeting in Mahalla is representative of many such encounters at the negotiations that ended large numbers of the strikes after 2006. The location of the ETUF officials on the state's side of the negotiating table merely made visible a relationship of which many workers were already acutely aware. Yet, as we explored in the previous chapter, the fact that state officials were prepared to negotiate directly with delegates elected by striking workers was a dramatic shift. It was a reflection both of the overall transformation of labour relations that the state itself had initiated through neoliberal reforms, and of the rise of workers' self-organisation in the workplace in the course of the strike wave.

We discuss in detail below how neoliberal reforms had weakened the ETUF, despite the significant material resources at its disposal and the continuing deployment of the state's coercive and persuasive power to protect its organisational monopoly in the workplace. Structural blockages between the base of the ETUF unions and the leadership, reflecting the federation's core purpose as a means to control workers from above, did not diminish under pressure from below. Meanwhile, although the federation retained an organisational presence in some public-sector workplaces, a large proportion of the ETUF's claimed membership was organised in large, geographical 'branches' which essentially existed only on paper. Moreover, the strongholds of ETUF organisation were in precisely those areas of the public sector that had borne the brunt of the privatisation programme, and the federation had taken no serious steps to compensate for this loss by expanding into the largely unorganised private sector.

The triumph of the Property Tax Collectors Higher Strike Committee over the minister of finance while ETUF officials kicked their heels in the street outside raised the possibility of a further transformation: the founding of independent unions capable of maintaining organisation between strikes and completely excluding the ETUF from the process of collective bargaining. As we explore in the following chapter, this transformation was not an inevitable outcome of the strike wave: its success depended on sufficiently large numbers of workplace activists becoming convinced of the need to confront the state in order to break the ETUF's monopoly of workplace organisation. It was a political act which represented the most significant challenge by organised workers to the regime's hegemony over the workplace for more than half a century.

The origins and form of the ETUF

There is no space here for a thorough discussion of the relationship between the ETUF and the rich history of trade-union organising in Egypt before 1957.[1] However, some preliminary remarks are necessary in order to clarify the nature of the ETUF. We argue that the intervention of the state in the formation of the ETUF, and its development during a period in which the Nasserist state bureaucracy was in formation, were the factors which determined the nature of the federation and the role it was to play in later years. This analysis contrasts with that advanced by Marsha Pripstein Posusney in the most serious academic work on the ETUF's recent history, and with the arguments put forward for the best part of sixty years by the dominant section of the Egyptian left to justify a strategy of pursuing change from within the regime.[2]

Our conclusions are based not only on the evidence of the control of the ETUF's structures by the ruling party at every stage in its history, but also by the actions of the ETUF bureaucracy in response to the adoption of neoliberalism by the Egyptian ruling class. Rather than providing the left with increased opportunities to seize the initiative from below within the ETUF, and force the upper layers of the bureaucracy to mobilise the federation's resources in defence of workers' rights, in the context of neo-liberalism the NDP's control of the ETUF hardened and the federation became a *more* hostile environment for workplace activists attempting to support their colleagues' strikes and protests.[3]

The establishment of the ETUF was a political decision taken in 1957 at the highest level of the state. The centralisation of trade-union organisation was an aspect of the centralised political structure of the one-party state, and the trade-union bureaucracy was one part of a wider bureaucratic apparatus which laid claim to manage almost all aspects of political, economic and social life. It was the state's self-proclaimed role as guarantor of the right to work and its provision of social welfare which concealed the emptiness of these 'trade union' structures. Characterising the ETUF as an extension of the state bureaucracy and its creation as an action taken by the regime for its own benefit does not mean that we fail to recognise that trade-union activists before 1957 were deeply involved in efforts to create a unified trade-union federation independent of the state, in the face of fierce opposition from the governments of the day.[4] The fundamental problem lies in assuming that because the aims of trade unionists and state officials appeared to coincide, that organisational structures created by and for the state could be used by trade unionists for their own purposes.

The ruling party's machine

The ETUF's role in maintaining the hegemony of the ruling party developed early in the federation's history. After 1962 membership of trade unions and nomination for election to union executive committees were conditional on membership of the sole legal political party, the Arab Socialist Union. The regime's adoption of a very limited form of political pluralism in 1978 did not, however, introduce any great variety into the political allegiances of ETUF officials. The upper levels of the ETUF bureaucracy continued to be dominated by the ruling party, and moreover increasingly became the preserve of a narrow group of NDP officials who continued in post long after reaching the normal age of retirement. The boundaries between the ETUF and the Ministry of Labour were also blurred. Until the mid-1980s the minister of labour was in fact the president of the ETUF, and, although the posts were formally separated, after that the ministerial portfolio continued to be given as a reward to senior trade union leaders.

The ETUF's structures and internal regulations underscore the federation's role as a mechanism to mobilise workers from

above in the interests of the regime. The executive committee of each general union must be composed of between 11 and
21 members. The executive is elected by the general assembly
(annual conference) of the union, which is in turn composed
of representatives of the union committees, who are themselves
chosen by the executive committee. The top level of the ETUF
structure is the federation executive itself, which is composed
of twenty-three members, based on a single representative per
general union. The general assembly of the ETUF is composed
of representatives of the general unions.

According to the Labour Law 12 of 2003 and the Trade Union
Law 35 of 1976, the general unions enjoy full rights to conclude
collective agreements, conduct collective bargaining and manage
the activities of the lower-level union committees. The 2003
Labour Law also permitted general unions to organise strikes
with the approval of a two-thirds majority of the executive committee. The workplace union committees are unable to conclude
a collective agreement, or call or organise a strike. According to
Article 12 of Law 35 of 1976 on trade-union organisation their
role is restricted to expressing opinions on the regulations or
settling individual and collective disputes, and preparing reports
on their own activities and sending them to the general union.
It is clear, therefore, that the organisational level that is elected
from the rank and file of the unions has the least authority to act
as a trade union. The primary function of the union committees
in the ETUF structures is to act as an electoral college for the
reproduction of the upper layers of the bureaucracy. And, as we
discuss further below, despite gaining the *theoretical* capacity to
act as a trade union through the Labour Law of 2003, the ETUF
bureaucracy did not, in fact, utilise any of its powers to call
strikes or even win gains for its members through negotiations or
campaigns over the issues that were mobilising tens of thousands
of workers.

The ETUF bureaucracy's resistance to pressure from below is not just a reflection of the conservatism of a trade-union bureaucracy attempting to preserve its own privileges, but rather a sign of the continued importance of the federation as one of the regime's last remaining institutions for popular mobilisation, managing elections and creating the appearance of support for its policies. It is not surprising, therefore, that as the regime issued policies that changed the nature of labour relations, which ought to have entailed a different approach to trade-union practice and organisation, it also amended the trade-union legislation in 1995 to confirm the dominance of the bureaucracy over the federation. The reforms allowed candidates to stand for higher office without having to pass through the lower levels of ETUF, extended the period between trade-union elections, and allowed those above the age of retirement to stand for office.[5]

The ETUF as gatekeeper to the electoral arena

Under Mubarak, the ETUF's party-political role was not merely that of a state institution which needed to be managed by NDP cadres. Rather, it was an extremely important instrument for the reproduction of NDP hegemony at the ballot box. Presidential elections were one arena where the ETUF's party-political role was particularly apparent. The ETUF would declare its support for the president and its unconditional allegiance to him, on behalf of all Egyptian workers, even those outside the ranks of the federation. It was also visible in the direct financial support from the ETUF for trade-union candidates standing for the ruling party in the legislative elections. Moreover, the ETUF was given a privileged role as gatekeeper for candidacy in up to 50 per cent of the seats in parliament through its validation of prospective candidates' occupational credentials in the 'workers and farmers' seats. Article 49 of the 1964 constitution instituted an occupational quota, to ensure that at least 50 per cent of the membership of the National Assembly were workers or small farmers.[6]

The quota operated by creating two-member parliamentary constituencies ensured the election of at least one worker or farmer by excluding other candidates from the run-offs if no worker or farmer received an absolute majority in the first round. The National Congress of the ruling Arab Socialist Union in June 1968 defined 'worker' as someone 'engaged in manual or intellectual work', dependent on this work for his livelihood, and neither entitled to membership of one of the professional associations nor holder of a university or higher education diploma. Nasser's successors, Sadat and Mubarak, maintained the quota, even as they moved away from the corporatist political institutions of the state-capitalist era, towards an appearance of Western-style liberal democracy with competing political parties and regular elections. The ruling party completely monopolised the electoral arena throughout the period of these reforms, averaging just over 83 per cent of seats in all parliamentary elections between 1979 and 2010. This figure would be even higher but for the exception of 2005 when Muslim Brotherhood supporters were briefly allowed to win a substantial minority of seats for the first time, reducing the percentage of NDP-held seats to 69.9.[7]

The application of the quota system was overseen by the Egyptian Trade Union Federation, which provided the documentation workers needed to supply in order to qualify for nomination in the workers' seats.[8] The ETUF bureaucracy actively intervened to ensure the election of worker candidates who supported the regime and prevent the victory of their rivals. Even the timing of the application process for the certificate of trade-union membership was geared to the needs of the ruling party. In September 2010, the ETUF president Hussein Megawer explained to the press that those wishing to apply for a certificate in order to stand as a parliamentary candidate as an independent or for

one of the opposition parties would have wait until after the
3,500 members of the National Democratic Party who wanted to
stand in the ruling party's selection meetings had received their
documents.[9] Moreover, the actual social class background of the
'workers' elected to parliament in the 'workers' seats reflected
the interpenetration of the ETUF bureaucracy and the wider
public-sector bureaucracy.

The NDP's domination of the workers' seats saw no significant challenge until the 2005 elections, where electoral success
for the Muslim Brotherhood brought the greatest ever number
of non-NDP members into parliament. By contrast, the legal
secular left party, the National Progressive Unionist Assembly
(al-Tagammu), was reduced to a token presence in parliament by
this date.[10] The 2005 elections were the first occasion that the
regime had relaxed its authoritarian grip on the electoral process
to allow even a muted echo of the extra-parliamentary opposition
find expression. Although officially banned, the Muslim Brotherhood won 88 seats, 34 of them under the workers' quota. The
concentration of Brotherhood MPs in the workers' seats was
greatest in the biggest urban centres. Seven out of nine of the
Brotherhood's seats in Cairo, and four out of eight in Alexandria
were held by candidates elected as workers.[11]

A closer look at the Brotherhood candidates for the workers'
seats in the 2005 elections underlines, however, that while
working-class voters were being offered a political alternative to
the ruling party, the space within the Brotherhood for worker
activists to pursue a political project expressing their class interests was very limited. In fact, the Brotherhood's 'worker' MPs
tended to mirror the career paths of their NDP rivals, as they
were frequently drawn into the middle levels of the public-sector
bureaucracy by similar routes, serving on the executive committees of local trade-union committees, and from there winning
a seat as worker representative on the management board of

public-sector institutions. Ali Fath-al-Bab, who served as an MP representing one of the Helwan constituencies from 1995 to 2005, followed precisely this route within the Egyptian Iron and Steel Company where he worked.[12] Mustafa Mohamed Mustafa, MP for the workers' seat in Montaza constituency in Alexandria, was deputy director of the state-owned Petrogas company.[13]

The deepening political crisis of the regime during its final years prompted a dramatic reassertion of the NDP's domination of the electoral arena in the legislative elections of 2010. The Brotherhood withdrew its candidates from the run-offs, complaining of systematic fraud and intimidation after its candidates failed to win a single seat in the first round of voting. It is also important to note that Brotherhood supporters were never permitted to penetrate the upper reaches of the ETUF bureaucracy, in contrast to their success in winning high office in a large number of Egypt's professional associations before the revolution.

The ETUF's response to neoliberalism

The most compelling evidence for an analysis that locates the ETUF within the structures of the Mubarak regime lies in the collective response of federation officials to the neoliberal turn in state policy. The organic relationship between the ETUF leadership and the state required that the federation act as the first defender of government policies regardless of their impact on rank-and-file workers. More tellingly, it meant that the ETUF officials placed the overall interests of the state above their sectional interests, even when the state was pursuing policies which damaged their own organisational base and weakened their own position within the state apparatus.

Posusney is correct to identify resistance from ETUF officials to structural adjustment as a factor that is likely to have slowed down the implementation of economic reforms during the 1980s.[14]

However, this was not because they were subject to pressure from rank-and-file workers below, who also opposed privatisation and the running down of the public sector. Rather, it reflected the fact that the argument that 'there was no alternative' (in the words of Margaret Thatcher) to neoliberal reforms had not yet been won within the Egyptian ruling class. The intersection of geopolitical and domestic crises in the late 1980s and early 1990s (including economic stagnation, the debt crisis over US loans, a sharp rise in popular protests 1986–89, the 1991 US invasion of Iraq and the demise of the Soviet Union) produced a new ruling-class consensus to which the ETUF leadership wholeheartedly subscribed, as their subsequent behaviour demonstrates.

At the launch of the Economic Reform and Structural Adjustment Programme, which included the privatisation of state-owned enterprises, the closure of some of these, and the implementation of a programme of forced early retirement affecting hundreds of thousands of workers, the ETUF declared its unconditional support for these policies and issued a joint statement with the Egyptian Confederation of Industry backing privatisation. It was among the first supporters of the law on the public business sector (Law 203 of 1991), which was the beginning of the privatisation programme, without even making any real efforts to negotiate over the conditions of privatisation or reduce its impact on workers.[15] The only example where an ETUF-affiliated union took a real initiative in relation to the terms and conditions of employment is the case of the call by the General Union for Mining and Quarrying Workers for a national strike to demand special legislation to govern their working conditions in recognition of the arduous nature of their profession.[16]

The attitude of ETUF officials towards Law 12 of 2003 (the Labour Law) is particularly revealing. As discussed in Chapter 1, the government's rhetoric concerning the new legislation was framed around the idea that it represented a trade-off between employers' and workers' rights. Specifically, the right to strike was apparently offered in exchange for granting employers greater rights to fire workers. ETUF officials were quick to proclaim their support for the proposals: when worker activists demonstrated in front of parliament in 2003 during the discussion of the law, the ETUF organised a counter-demonstration the following day calling for the speeding up of the passage of the bill. Nor did they make use of their new powers to authorise strike action following the implementation of the law. Out of the hundreds of episodes of strike action between 2006 and the fall of Mubarak, only one temporarily gained official ETUF support: the long-running dispute between the workforce at Tanta Flax Company and the Saudi investor who bought the company in 2005.[17]

The Labour Law also contained other provisions, which the ETUF chose to ignore, despite their potential to benefit workers. The law stipulated the formation of a National Council for Wages (NCW) to determine the minimum wage and to periodically revise its level. However, over the following five years the ETUF did not call for the convention of the NCW. In 2008, the NCW did meet, but failed to reach a decision, and discussion of the issue was suddenly halted by the presidential decree on 1 May which promised a 30 per cent bonus for workers, paid for, as we have seen, by increases in fuel prices and that of basic goods, and which most private-sector companies refused to distribute. The ETUF welcomed the decree and the price rises while refusing to discuss further the issue of the minimum wage. Nor did the ETUF take any serious steps in opposition to the government's absorption of workers' social insurance funds, which worker activists considered an attack on workers' savings to the benefit of the state Treasury.[18] ETUF officials could not claim that workers were indifferent to these issues: as we saw in the previous chapter, the call for a rise in the national minimum wage was championed by workers at Misr Spinning in Mahalla, around 10,000 of whom joined a demonstration on 17 February 2008 as the NCW met. It was also one of the demands of the proposed strike on 6 April 2008.

Workplace union committees: an exception?

The lowest levels of the ETUF structures, the workplace union committees closest to the rank-and-file membership, need to be considered in a different light to the upper levels of the federation bureaucracy. Even in the final years of the Mubarak era, some workplace union committees contained individual activists who were genuinely responsive to demands raised from the rank and file. Some individual members of union committees and a small number of whole committees supported strikes and even oc-casionally helped to organise them. Kamal Abu Aita, who would go on to play a leading role in the property tax collectors' strike of 2007, was a member of an ETUF workplace union committee until 2006. Two prominent examples of workplace union commit-tees which took consistent positions in support of demands raised by the rank and file include the ETUF factory union committee in Turah Cement works, and that in Tanta Flax.

Despite this, with the exception of the Tanta Flax dispute, union committee members who supported rank-and-file demands and stood with their colleagues during strikes and protests proved completely unable to mobilise any of the resources of the fed-eration on their behalf. On the contrary, the upper levels of the ETUF bureaucracy frequently victimised union committee members who backed strikes, accusing them of 'incitement' and imposing disciplinary sanctions on some of them. For example, Ai'sha Abd-al-Aziz Abu Samada, a member of the factory union committee in the Hennawi Tobacco Company in Damanhour, had her union membership frozen, and then was sacked by the company in 2008 because she adopted the workers' demands for inclusion of the social allowance in workers' basic pay and played a central role in organising a strike. Fatma Ramadan, who received the highest number of votes for the union committee in the Ministry of Labour in Giza, was also suspended from union membership for 'inciting' her colleagues, because she campaigned for the equalisation of pay and conditions for Ministry of Labour employees in provincial offices and the Ministry following the success of the property tax collectors in achieving this with the Property Tax Agency.

The case of the ETUF's attitude to the Tanta Flax dispute is revealing precisely because it was so exceptional. However, it is likely that the fact that this was a strike where the employer was a private foreign investor, rather than the state, was a significant factor in encouraging the ETUF leadership to take an opportunistic stance in support of rank-and-file demands. Calling for support for the strike could safely be framed in nationalist terms in such circumstances. Yet the ETUF's backing for the strikers was short-lived, leading to accusations from the workers and their supporters of betrayal by the federation.[19] Moreover, the experiment was not repeated elsewhere, despite the continuation of a number of similar disputes with private foreign investors, such as the long-running battle between workers and the Indonesian owner of Shibin al-Kom Spinning.

In addition to victimising union committee members who backed rank-and-file protests, the ETUF bureaucracy mobilised systematically to prevent candidates who might have proved susceptible to pressure from below from reaching the ballot paper for the union committee elections. The process of standing for election was dependent on receiving a document from the federation proving union membership. Proof of payment of union dues through the wage slip was not acceptable. These certificates were only available to prospective candidates from the general unions' main offices, meaning that residents in remote provinces could not get them from a branch closer to them. This mechanism was used extensively in the 2006 trade union elections to disqualify potential candidates, according to the CTUWS report on violations in the elections.[20] The violations during 2006 were not exceptions: the report issued by the Coordinating Committee for the Rights and Freedoms of Association in the trade union elections of 2001 noted similar practices, including the intervention of the administrative authorities in the electoral process from the announcement of the date, and in the procedure for nomination, voting, counting and announcement of the result, as well as intervention by the security services in the candidate screening process. A number of leading workplace activists who failed to make it onto the ballot paper, including Kamal Abu-Aita, complained that the vote was rigged against them.[21]

ETUF workplace union committees were in fact the primary targets of organised attempts by the rank and file to change ETUF structures from below. The initial efforts were spearheaded by the Misr Spinning strikers, who collected 12,000 signatures on a petition to the leadership of the General Union of Textile Workers. As we saw in the previous chapter, they demanded the re-election of the factory union committee (FUC) in the plant after it failed to support the December 2006 strike. When this failed to produce a result, there followed by a campaign of mass resignations from the union in the factory. Other groups of strikers also frequently demanded the dissolution of their existing workplace union committee: in February 2007, for example, half the workforce in Shibin al-Kom signed a petition calling for the dissolution of their union committee during their strike, as did workers in Kafr al-Dawwar. During the same month, workers at the Daqhiliyya Company for Spinning and Weaving in Mit Ghamr likewise demanded fresh elections for their union committee during an abortive strike attempt. Nor were these demands raised only in the textile sector. Later the same month river transport workers in Imbaba also withdrew confidence from their committee during a strike, while workers at the Hennawi Tobacco plant in Damanhour collected dozens of signatures calling for new union elections.[22]

The manoeuvres of the ETUF bureaucracy over the factory union committee in Misr Spinnning were – like its intervention in the Tanta Flax dispute – an important exception to a general rule. Faced with an organised campaign for the withdrawal of confidence in the FUC in February 2007, followed by mass collective resignations from the General Union of Textile Workers, ETUF officials offered a compromise in the shape of 'delegates' committees' (*ligan mandubin*) composed of elected lay members which would play a role in 'linking' the FUC to the mass of rank-and-file workers.[23] The tradition of forming elected rank-and-file committees which could either play a role in monitoring the performance of the official union apparatus on behalf of members, or in some cases act independently of the union officials as an alternative union leadership, in case of their arrest or incapacity, goes back to the 1940s in Egypt. Textile worker activists Taha Sa'ad Uthman and Fathallah Mahrus have both noted that these elected committees were the backbone of the 1940s' textile unions, and provided 'day-to-day leadership' in the mills.[24] In this case, however, it was clear that ETUF officials hoped to channel angry members' energies away from the more threatening alternative of establishing organisation completely outside the union structures, and direct them into a cul-de-sac.

The failure of sustained pressure from below to shift or fracture the ETUF bureaucracy contrasts with the experience of the Tunisian trade-union federation, the UGTT. Both in the late 1970s and in 2011 mobilisation from below *within* the federation as well as outside it propelled the UGTT leadership into direct conflict with the state. As Bellin notes, in the late 1970s the old UGTT leadership responded to the rise of a new generation of militant activists by attempting to embrace them for fear of drifting into irrelevance or falling victim to an internal putsch by the 'young Turks' clustered in the white collar unions. Consequently, the older leadership endorsed an increasing number of strikes mounted by the rank and file. They also invited militant leftists to join the union central and take control of the union paper, Al-Sha'b. By the late 1970s, political ambition led union militants to propose that the UGTT form an independent political party to advance the interests of the working class.[25]

The outcome of this shift was a head-on conflict with the Bourguiba regime, which saw the UGTT leadership call a general strike against the state's attempts to force new trade-union elections, followed by the jailing of the UGTT leadership and widespread repression. In 2011, the UGTT leadership was again propelled into confrontation with the state, this time with catastrophic results for Ben Ali, who fled Tunisia on the day of a nationwide general strike. UGTT support for the revolutionary wave spreading across the country over the previous weeks grew from the rank and file upwards: the federation's leadership was supportive of Ben Ali during the early years of his regime, when he courted the trade unions as a potential base of secular opposition to his Islamist opponents. As UGTT regional official Mohamed Sghaeir Saihi commented after the revolution, the hegemony of the upper layers of the UGTT officials was broken by a determined campaign from within the federation to support the emerging protests by unemployed and youth activists in late 2010.

> We broke the control of the bureaucracy by working with the youth groups, the school and college students and the large numbers of unemployed. They didn't have unions of their own, so we opened the union offices to them. This was the opposite of what the bureaucracy wanted. The union leaders were telling us to close the doors of our offices and not to get involved in 'politics' inside the union buildings.[26]

The contrast with the situation in Egypt highlights the powerlessness of the ETUF workplace union committees: the scale and intensity of workplace-based strike activity in Egypt was probably greater than in Tunisia, yet it could not break through to the upper levels of the ETUF bureaucracy. Fundamentally this was because, unlike the UGTT, which preceded and helped to create the post-independence Tunisian state, the ETUF was not a trade union but an extension of the state bureaucracy.

The state of the federation during Mubarak's last years

During the final years of the Mubarak regime, the ETUF's organisation was characterised by hollowness, a rank and file which was largely passive but in some workplaces actively hostile to the bureaucracy, and declining overall membership as a result of the very neoliberal policies championed by the ETUF leadership. ETUF's structures can be considered *hollow* in the sense that, behind the facade of apparently still impressive mass membership, large sections of that membership were organised in loose 'professional committees' which brought together workers in the same trade or profession across a geographical area. Although professional committees accounted for 255 of the 2006–11 union committees, as opposed to 1,554 workplace committees, they comprised around a third of the federation's total membership. According to data from 2005, the membership of the professional committees was just under 1.5 million, while the workplace committees covered 2.8 million members.[27] In a number of professions, there was a large degree of compulsion driving workers' membership of the ETUF professional committees. Taxi drivers, for example, were unable to gain or renew a driving licence without producing their membership card for the General Land Transport Union, which is conditional on their membership of the appropriate geographical ETUF professional committee. Another example is agricultural workers, who cannot benefit from agricultural co-operatives without membership of the ETUF General Union of Agricultural Workers.

We have already indicated how the ETUF's structures were designed to induce passivity in the membership and among lower levels of the elected bureaucracy, and concentrate decision-making powers at the top. This resulted in increasing numbers of uncontested elections at the upper levels of the federation. Overall the percentage of union committees elected unopposed in 2006–11 across the federation was 44 per cent, while the same source indicates that in the results for the national executive committees in the general unions, 14 out of 23 were also uncontested; in the remaining 9, elections were held with 258 candidates competing for only 69 more seats than were available.[28] This means that the proportion of uncontested seats in the executives of the general unions was more than 60 per cent, and thus the degree of real competition was very limited. In 2006–11 the highest proportion of uncontested elections was in the General Union of Agricultural Workers (74 per cent) and the General Union of Land Transport Workers (73 per cent), while the lowest was in Communications (6 per cent) and Military Production (11 per cent).[29]

Moreover, in the public sector union membership was automatic, as workers completed union membership forms when they applied for jobs. While this involved no direct coercion, the absence of alternatives meant there was no choice. And while there was no legal mechanism for enforced union membership, the actual practice of the ETUF unions when faced with direct demands by workers to cancel their membership bears out the analysis that membership was in effect compulsory. For when around 2,000 members of the General Union of Textile Workers at Misr Spinning attempted to resign in 2007, they were ignored.

According to statistics from the Central Agency for Population Mobilisation and Statistics, across the public, public-business and

FIGURE 4.1 ETUF membership decline in a context of workforce growth, 2003–2011 (selected years)

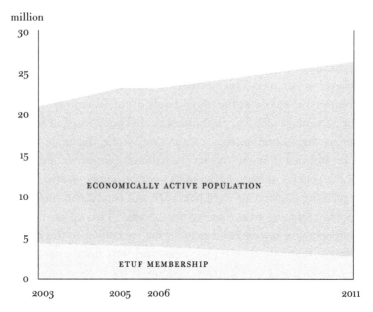

million

SOURCE Bassiouny, 2009; ITUC, 2011; ILO LABORSTA database, Table 1A.

private sectors in 2006 the combined number of workplaces was 16,578, of which 3,481 were in the public and public-business sectors, and 13,097 in the private sector. Given a figure of 1,554 union workplace committees, this means that less than 10 per cent of all workplaces had a committee, and union organisation was absent in 90 per cent of them. The absence of trade-union organisation was therefore the rule and not the exception. The sector that suffered most severely from the absence of union organisation was the private sector. In 2002 there were 2,116 private-sector workplaces in the 'new towns' and only twenty-five union committees.[30] Despite the growth of the private sector, the presence of union organisation did not improve. Private-sector workers suffer from strong resistance by employers to their attempts to set up union committees. Employers have customarily greeted attempts to found unions by their workers by sacking the leaders and visiting collective punishment on the workforce. Examples include the sacking of workers from Ayyad Sons Steel Co. in Helwan in 2005, and of workers from Samuli Co. for Spinning and Weaving in Mahalla in 2003, the dismissal of a worker from the National Co. for Steel in 6th of October City in 2004, and Eldorado Ceramics Co. preventing workers forming a union committee in 2006.

Despite these difficulties, workers in the private sector did attempt to unionise through the formation of new ETUF committees, such as those founded at Suez Fertilisers, Aytal Steel, Eldorado, the National Steel Company and others. The demand for the formation of a union committee was raised by rank-and-file workers more widely, either on its own or in conjunction with other economic demands, as was the case in Eldorado Ceramics in Suez, Swiss Cables in 10th of Ramadan City, Electrometer Co. and National Steel Co. in 6th of October City, Aytal Steel in Suez, and Ayyad Sons in Suez and Helwan. However, as with the new forms of organisation growing in public-sector workplaces, the drive towards forming new union committees in the private sector was an initiative from below, rather than a reflection of any conscious policy by the ETUF bureaucracy.

The ETUF's waning influence within the state

For more than five decades, the ETUF bureaucracy claimed to be the sole legitimate representative of Egyptian workers. The meeting between the minister of finance and the Property Tax Collectors' Higher Strike Committee, with which we began this chapter, illustrates that this monopoly was threatened from two directions. We explore in more detail in the next chapter how workers' self-organisation created new structures of representation which excluded the ETUF. However, it is also important to recognise that the relative weight and political influence of the ETUF bureaucracy within the wider state bureaucracy was weakened by the neoliberal turn. The shifting balance of forces between and within the different state institutions tasked with managing relations with workers was reflected in the willingness on the part of some state officials to negotiate directly with striking workers and thus contribute to ETUF's marginalisation.

As discussed previously, the ETUF's function within the state bureaucracy was intimately connected to the pivotal role of the public sector in the version of state capitalism adopted by the Egyptian ruling class in the Nasserist era. It was primarily the mechanism through which workers expressed their political allegiance to the state, both at the ballot box and through mobilisation to meet production goals within the workplace. In return, the state guaranteed minimum standards of living, basic standards of universal health care and education, and job security in a large public sector which was the heart of the economy. The ETUF was largely an instrument of political mobilisation and control, but this depended on a symbiotic relationship with the bureaucracy of the public sector. It was also, as we have seen, a direct mechanism for the incorporation of a layer of working-class activists into the state, as its integration with the Ministry of Labour offered the promise of a route from the factory floor to the Cabinet Office.

The neoliberal assault on the public sector therefore threatened ETUF in several dimensions. As we saw above, the large public-sector enterprises were the bastions of the federation's industrial organisation; hence the loss of hundreds of thousands of ETUF's members to early retirement and unemployment was a severe blow. Just as significantly, the ideological offensive against the public sector that the structural adjustment programme represented directly attacked the ETUF bureaucracy's claims to represent workers. The potential for growth of union membership within the private sector was not exploited, because, as explained above, this would have required the ETUF to behave like a trade union rather than an arm of the state, by taking up workers' demands and confronting employers. Essentially, the ETUF officials' loyalty to the regime overrode their desire for self-preservation, forcing them to participate in slow-motion organisational suicide. As outlined above, the ETUF bureaucracy was not completely paralysed. It proposed compromises in the face of the Mahalla workers' mobilisation, supported the Tanta Flax dispute in an effort to control it from above, and – as we explore in the following chapter – induced a leading figure from the Property Tax Collectors' Higher Strike Committee to break with the embryonic independent union and return to the ETUF fold.

However, these efforts were not enough to halt the progressive weakening of the ETUF's position. Three signs of the ETUF's declining status were clearly visible during Mubarak's last years. First, there was a systematic shift by both striking workers and other state officials to bypass the ETUF, or at least sideline the federation's role, during negotiations to end workers' collective action. It is vital to recognise that this shift was initiated by workers, and that it was prompted by the abject failure of the state's efforts to prevent workers from exercising their right to strike. The state was often not even capable of forcing workers to take unpaid holidays for strike days and conceded full pay for days on strike. However, there was clearly also a policy shift by officials at the Ministry of Labour and other ministries in the face of the upsurge in strike action in early 2007. In a meeting with a US embassy official, a senior figure at the Ministry of Labour acknowledged that ministry officials were consciously experimenting with direct intervention in order to settle disputes. In a cable to the US Department of State, the embassy reported on the Ministry's novel case-by-case approach:

'If after our intervention the workers strike again', the official told us, 'then we will realize it was not successful. But if there are no strikes, then they must be satisfied.'

Concerned by this complacency and armed with warnings from the International Labour Organization that this 'fire-fighting' technique was actually encouraging more strikes, the cable author added a blunt title to the report: 'GoE (Government of Egypt) approach unsuccessful in stemming protests'.[31]

Another highly suggestive illustration of the ETUF's decline can be tracked in the changing attitude of major US funders towards the federation. The institutions of the Egyptian state have, since the consummation of Sadat's neoliberal policies, been profoundly shaped by their role in the preservation of US regional hegemony. The AFL–CIO's Solidarity Center received funding from USAID between 2001 and 2003 for a major programme of assistance to ETUF focusing on eradicating child labour, gender-equality, vocational and trade-union training. Within a few years, however, the Solidarity Center's work was openly supportive of the drive towards independent unions.[32] The fact that the Solidarity Center and its US government funders were prepared to abruptly abandon what the authors of the report on the 2001–03 programme called '30 years of productive partnership' with ETUF, which included decades of funding for the ETUF's Workers' University, in favour of a new approach, provides a striking illustration of the changing balance of forces within the Egyptian state as a result of the deepening of neoliberal reforms (which were, of course, themselves promoted by the US government).[33]

Political opposition, economic accommodation and the rise of an alternative from below

In contrast to the industrial unions, over which the ruling party continued to exercise almost complete internal control until the revolution, Egypt's professional unions became an important political space for the expression of opposition to Mubarak. We have already outlined above how supporters of the Muslim Brotherhood were able, in a small number of workplaces, to win elected positions in the lower levels of the ETUF structures, and use these as stepping stones to success in the parliamentary elections, without this disturbing the NDP's complete hegemony over the ETUF bureaucracy itself. In the case of the professional associations, the fracturing of the ruling party's control of organisations such as the Bar Association, the Journalists' Union, the Doctors' Union and the Engineers' Union decades before the revolution gave opposition groups access to resources and spaces which they were able to use to project their voices to wider audiences within Egypt and even internationally. This process was at times bitterly contested by the regime, but at other times the ruling party was prepared to reach an implicit compromise with some of the opposition forces, particularly the Muslim Brotherhood.

Large sections of the membership of the professional unions in Egypt would not generally be considered to be part of the working class; the label 'professional union' (*niqaba mahaniyya*) covers organisations representing members in a wide variety of employment relationships, large numbers of whom have little in common with white- and blue-collar workers. The specific case we will discuss here, that of the Doctors' Union, provides, however, an important example of the emergence of an organised challenge from below *within* a professional union, led by activists who won support for a kind of trade unionism which was diametrically opposed to the existing practice of both the ruling party and the Muslim Brotherhood. As we discuss in more detail below, the significance of this development could be seen after the revolution, in the national doctors' strikes of May 2011, which were the first examples of nationally coordinated strike action after the removal of Mubarak, and the deepening radicalisation of a layer of doctors through their participation in the 'field hospitals' of Tahrir Square and the mass street protests. The example of the Doctors' Union is also important because it highlights how the Brotherhood combined political opposition to the regime with accommodation to its economic policies, while demonstrating that the relentless pressure of neoliberal policies on the public health service opened opportunities for left-wing activists to begin building a political alternative to Islamism within the union. Following Shafiq,[34] we will argue here that the Brotherhood successfully counterposed a new 'service-oriented' model of trade unionism to the corporatist model of the Nasserist era, but that this in turn began to lose credibility among sections of the union's membership as it failed to address their grievances in the workplace.

Like the pre-1952 trade unions, Egypt's professional associations were incorporated into the state's mechanisms of corporatist control from above during the Nasserist era. During the 1980s, however, the ruling party's hegemony within the professional associations fractured. The career of Essam al-Erian, who would become vice chairman of the Brotherhood's Freedom and Justice Party, illustrates this process neatly. Al-Erian, a student activist during the 1980s, was first elected to the Doctors' Union general council in 1986, later serving as the union's vice president and then treasurer.[35] According to Shafiq, the Brotherhood articulated an alternative form of trade unionism to the Nasserist model:

> The Brotherhood's idea was to turn the Doctors' Union into a service-oriented union. From the 1970s, under President Anwar Sadat, the state began withdrawing from public services with the beginning of the era of neoliberalism. So the Brotherhood proposed to fill the gap. The union began to organise exhibitions and shows. It offered hire-purchase schemes to buy commodities, and provided treatment projects. It began to take on some of the state's duties in terms of social support which Nasser had initiated but the state had abandoned.[36]

The Brotherhood's accommodation to the neoliberalism of the regime was combined, however, with its use of the Doctors' Union as a political platform. As in other professional associations, the Muslim Brotherhood activists within the Doctors' Union organised campaigns over issues such as support for the Palestinian cause and against political repression in Egypt. While the idea that a combination of charity and private provision could fill the gap left by the weakening of the state's role as health-care provider was attractive to some doctors, after 2001 a layer of junior doctors in the public hospitals began to look for an alternative to the Brotherhood's model of trade unionism. Declining opportunities to work abroad as a result of increased competition in key labour markets such as the Gulf and the tightening of restrictions on work in Europe closed off personal escape routes from the relentless deterioration of pay and conditions in the public hospitals.

It was in this context that Doctors Without Rights was born. It is a group of trade unionists which offers a different conception of trade union activism: defending the interests of union members, including their material interests, and their social and economic rights. It began as a small group of a few dozen people, standing on the steps in front of the union headquarters, outside this huge organisation with money and a vast membership. It began to agitate and cause problems, and had some real successes, for example stopping one of the laws privatising part of the health service, and successfully fighting for an increase in the health budget.[37]

Doctors Without Rights activists were key to the attempt to organise a national doctors' strike in 2008. Emboldened by teachers' success in winning a national pay and grading framework, a layer of junior doctors in public hospitals began to agitate for strike action. Despite winning a vote in the union's general assembly for a strike, the combination of pressure from the security forces, lack of support by the union's general council for the strike, and a well-targeted concession from the government undermined the mobilisation. Nevertheless, the networks that were first tested in 2008 would re-emerge and expand at the heart of the mobilisation which organised the national strikes of May 2011.

Conclusion

The crisis of the Nasserist model of workplace organisation had two main sources. First, as indicated in Chapter 1, the adoption of neoliberal policies in Egypt has to be understood as a policy shift which entailed a rebalancing within the ruling class – and there were relative winners and losers as a result of that shift. The ETUF bureaucracy was one of the losers because it was organically bound up with the public sector. The hollowness of its claim to represent workers' interests was concealed by its interpenetration with the wider public-sector bureaucracy and its integration into the ruling party. Its complicity in the neoliberal assault on the public sector was ideological suicide: once the state withdrew from the Nasserist social contract, its role as 'representative' of workers' interests within the regime no longer held the same appeal as in previous decades, when the ETUF could channel significant material and political benefits to mollify workers' frustrations. Acquiescence to the economic reform programme could also be seen as a kind of organisational suicide – as we have seen, the vast bulk of the ETUF's membership was concentrated in those sectors of the economy hardest hit by neoliberal reforms. The federation not only refused to defend the interests of its existing members, but failed to make any efforts to unionise the expanding private sector.

The second, and far more important, root of the ETUF's crisis was the reawakening of workers' self-activity and self-organisation in the explosion of strike activity in the mid-2000s, and particularly after the Mahalla strike of December 2006. As explored in detail above, it was workers' collective action, organised almost entirely outside and against the official trade-union structures, which forced other state officials to negotiate directly with strikers' representatives, thereby deepening and intensifying the crisis in the ETUF. The complete failure of this ferment of activity from below, despite the opportunity afforded by the relative decline of ETUF's position within the state bureaucracy, to break through the structural blockages preventing pressure from the rank and file from reaching the upper levels of the federation is testament, however, to the fact that the ETUF remained to Mubarak's last hours in power an instrument of state control over Egyptian workers and not a 'trade union' in the genuine sense of the term.

The ETUF's critical role in the reproduction of the regime's hegemony at the ballot box was, we have argued here, a central reason why control over the upper reaches of the ETUF bureaucracy remained so important to the ruling party, even as the federation's monopoly in representing workers in the workplace began to disintegrate. In contrast to the professional associations, which became to a certain extent zones of tolerated dissent for the Islamist opposition as early as the 1980s, the ETUF's upper levels were not penetrated at all by the Muslim Brotherhood until after the 2011 revolution. Moreover, the Brotherhood's political opposition to the regime was combined with accommodation to its economic policies, whose effects it sought to alleviate not by workers' collective organisation but by the expansion of charitable works to fill the void left by decaying public services.

The final result of the ETUF's crisis in the pre-revolutionary era was, as we examine in more detail in Chapter 7, its paralysis in Mubarak's final hour of need. It was to ETUF president Hussein Megawer that Mubarak turned after Interior Ministry troops had been forced to withdraw from the streets in disarray after the protests of the 'Day of Rage' on 28 January 2011. Yet Megawer had no army of counter-demonstrators to mobilise against the hundreds of thousands in Tahrir Square: the ETUF's organisation was hollow, its membership hostile or indifferent to Megawer's last-ditch appeal to save Mubarak from his own people in revolt.

CHAPTER 5

From strike committee
to independent union

On 7 April 2007, encouraged by the liberal opposition figure Saad
Eddin Ibrahim, director of the Ibn Khaldun Centre, US embassy
officials met Ali El Badry, a leading activist with the Generation
Party (*hizb al-gil*), a small opposition group, to discuss his plans
for the formation of an independent union federation outside the
ETUF, and his request for US government funding for the project.
According to a cable released by WikiLeaks, the officials came
away with 'serious doubts about the seriousness and credibility
of El Badry and his "free union" movement'.[1] These concerns
were reinforced by El Badry's performance at a public meeting
a few weeks later, when he declared that the new union would
be unveiled at simultaneous protests in Cairo and provincial
capitals.[2] The contrast between El Badry's opportunist press
stunt and the actual experience of building the first successful
independent union, which began to develop in embryo in the
epic strikes by civil servants in the Property Tax Agency in the
Autumn of 2007, could not be greater.

In a very direct sense the Independent General Union of
Property Tax Agency Workers grew out of the 2007 strikes:
the organisation of the strike and that of the new union shared

a core group of the same leaders, whose relationships with each other and the networks of activists who formed the backbone of the new union's organisation were largely forged in the course of the strike. The independent union was the extension and expansion of the Higher Strike Committee, and was formed with the purpose of overseeing and guaranteeing the implementation of the negotiated agreement that ended the strike. The space within which it developed had been punched open by the sheer force of the strike: the blow it struck against the Ministry of Finance caused panic and paralysis within the relevant institutions of the state, which were unable to agree an effective strategy for defusing the situation except by acceding to the tax collectors' demands. Of course this was not a blow struck alone, but one which has to be understood in the context of whole evolution of the strike wave, and in particular the role of the Mahalla strikes of 2006 and 2007.

We will argue here that the relationship between the 2007 strike and the successful launch of the independent union has also to be understood at a deeper level in two crucial respects. First, the engine that drove the strike was a model of democratic organising in which delegates and negotiators were accountable to mass meetings of the strikers, and leadership was predicated on the self-activity of the rank and file. Moreover, the strike organisers, at least in the best-organised areas, made a serious attempt to gain a democratic mandate to speak on behalf of *all* the employees of the Property Tax Authority by winning a majority for taking action. Thus in Daqhiliyya, as we explore in more detail below, participation in the December 2007 sit-in was not concentrated in a small number of tax offices, but spread out across the province. The founders of the new union attempted to carry both of these principles forward into the union's structures and the practice of its officials. It was the fact that they partially succeeded in doing this during the critical first year after the strike that gave the organisation the resilience it needed to withstand mounting pressure from the state from mid-2009.

The second vital connection between the strike and the project of building an independent union lies in their shared political dimensions: both constituted an explicit and successful challenge to the authority of the state. The tax collectors did not only win a pay rise, they humiliated the minister of finance, won the right to protest outside the Cabinet Office, forced the state to change its administrative structures to the benefit of tens of thousands of low-paid civil servants, and broke the monopoly of 'trade union organisation' enjoyed by the ETUF bureaucracy for more than half a century. The political aspects were not incidental but integral to the success of the strike and the foundation of the union. The sit-in outside the Cabinet Office brought the strike wave 'home' to the highest institutions of the state in a way which no other action by organised workers, even the Mahalla workers' epic strikes of 2006 and 2007, had yet achieved. The degree of confusion and paralysis it temporarily created in the state, and therefore the consequent gains that were achieved by the tax collectors in the agreement which ended the strike, reflect the political audacity of their tactics.

The democratic and political aspects of the strike were inextricably interlaced. The means by which the tax collectors triumphed over the state – the mass sit-in outside the Cabinet Office between 3 and 12 December 2007 – was also the democratic forum where the rank and file asserted their authority over their own leaders. The breakthrough in negotiations with the minister of finance followed directly on from a decision to escalate the strike taken at a mass meeting in the sit-in after rejection of an offer from the government which some of the tax collectors' negotiators thought was sufficient to justify an end to the sit-in.

Sustaining the interlacing between democratic self-organisation and political challenge to the regime proved much more difficult after the strike had ended. This chapter is therefore also an exploration of how and to what extent it came undone. In part this was a consequence of the inevitable pressure towards bureaucratisation inherent in the project of building a trade union.[3] We argue, however, that in the case of the tax collectors there were a number of factors which intensified and accelerated that process. The first and most important of these was the fact that there were no further strikes in the Property Tax Authority which achieved the same degree of self-organisation from below as did the campaign in 2007. The second factor was the growing influence on the leaders of the new union of a bureaucratic model of independent trade unionism shaped by their interactions with labour NGOs and the international trade-union bureaucracy. Over time these two factors reinforced each other: without strike action that demanded the re-creation of the democratic forums in which they could be challenged and held to account from below, the autonomy of the union's leaders increased.

The chapter therefore also explores another important element in the creation of the independent unions: the role played in their development by political and civil society activists based outside the workplaces. We will analyse the role of labour NGOs in supporting independent trade unionists, and argue that a culture of NGO activists 'servicing' the new unions increased pressures towards the bureaucratisation of their leadership. We will also explore the differences in political perspective which emerged over the central question of whether and how the 'economic' struggle of workers could become a weapon in the struggle against the state, and who Egyptian independent trade unionists' principal allies should be. These debates about the structures, practices and politics of trade unionism took place within a context shaped by the fracturing of the previous political consensus which had dominated the left's relationship with the workers' movement and the state, including the abandonment by a layer of left reformists within the ETUF of the perspective of 'reform from within' and the emergence of a 'new left' outside this tradition. Moreover, the 'anti-political' discourse of independent trade unionism reflected workers' rejection both of the state's claim to speak on their behalf, and of the opportunistic claims of political activists like Ali El Badry. The development of these trends before the revolution profoundly shaped the organisational landscape of the workers' movement after the revolution. In particular, even before the revolution the workers' movement had forced open a new space for reformist practice outside the corporatist structures of the ETUF.

The property tax collectors' strike[4]

The dispute in the Property Tax Agency (PTA) had its origins in a decision by then prime minister Abd-al-Aziz al-Higazy in 1974 (Directive 136 of 1974) to attach the Agency's 50,000 employees to the provincial adminstration both administratively and financially, rather than to the Ministry of Finance. This meant a huge reduction in their income in comparison with those employed by the Property Tax Authority centrally and in the Ministry of Finance. For example, PTA workers employed by the provincial administrations were eligible for a 25 per cent incentive payment, whereas those in the central administration were eligible for a 350 per cent incentive.[5] Despite ongoing demands by employees for parity with the central administration the government ignored their demands.

The protests which set in motion a qualitative shift in workplace organisation and changed the dynamics of the resistance to the Mubarak regime began outside the Property Tax Authority headquarters in the government services complex in Giza on 11 September 2007. Several thousand men and women working in the PTA responded to a call from activists in the Giza PTA directorate to join the demonstration demanding a return to the Ministry of Finance and equal pay with their colleagues in the central administration of the Property Tax Authority. Kamal Abu Aita, a well-known activist in the left Nasserist Karama (Dignity) Party, and until the previous year president of the Giza union committee in the ETUF-affiliated Banking and Insurance Workers Union (BIWU), was one of the leaders of the protest. The serving Giza committee president, Al-Sayyid Badawi, addressed the crowd, hoping to end the demonstration, and promised to organise a meeting with minister of labour Ai'sha Abd-al-Hadi in the ETUF headquarters in order to 'solve the problems' of the property tax collectors.[6]

Badawi's intervention failed to halt the spread of protest to other PTA offices in the provinces. The Giza demonstration featured prominently in news coverage on 11 September, including a report on the widely viewed *10 O'Clock* programme anchored by Mona el-Shazly. Soon other provincial directorates were mobilising in solidarity with the demands raised first in Giza. Makram Labib, Gamal Uwayda and other members of the BIWU committee in Daqhaliyya called for a sit-in in front of the PTA directorate in Al-Mansoura: around 1,000 demonstrators gathered on 24 September, surprising shoppers in the nearby market with their banners and chants.[7] Six days later, the quiet of the government offices in the Salah Salem residential district of Beni Sueif was shattered by a demonstration outside the PTA provincial headquarters, followed by protests in other provincial centres.[8]

The large numbers joining the provincial protests spurred on contacts between the organisers of the first two sit-ins in Giza and Daqhaliyya. It was agreed to call a nationwide mobilisation for a protest outside the Ministry of Finance headquarters in the Cairo suburb of Madinat Nasr on 21 October. In Daqhaliyya province the organisers of the al-Mansoura sit-in systematically contacted colleagues in all twenty-two district offices, setting a meeting point on the ring road near Salka village. The convoy of buses arrived at noon in front the Ministry of Finance to find some 4,000 of their colleagues from around the country already gathered. Negotiators came back empty-handed: the minister was on a visit to the USA, and in any case responsibility for the matter lies with the prime minister, officials told them.[9] After a short discussion, the protest voted to march to the Cabinet Office in the centre of Cairo, carrying Kamal Abu Aita on their shoulders. For five hours, the street outside the Cabinet Office off Qasr al-Aini Street was filled with the tax collectors' chants and banners. However, believing that officials from the Ministry of Finance had agreed to meet their negotiators, the protesters agreed to pack up and return home at around 9 p.m.[10]

When the eleven-member negotiating committee arrived at the Ministry of Finance on 11 November, they were met only by the head of security. The minister was in a meeting with officials from the International Monetary Fund, the negotiators were told. Infuriated, the committee took the decision to escalate. It was agreed to bring forward the date planned for the next sit-in and strike from 3 December to 13 November, and to target the leadership of the ETUF. On 13 November, delegations of property tax collectors from Giza, Daqhaliyya, Qalyubiyya, Menufiyya, Beni Sueif, Gharbiyya, Al-Fayyum, Al-Minya, Assyut and Al-Sharqiyya arrived at the ETUF headquarters on al-Gala'a Street. Hussein Megawer, the ETUF president, offered soothing promises, which became more desperate as the hours lengthened and the tax collectors refused to move. Megawer began to bluster, promising to speak to the minister, and even to organise a sit-in himself if his intervention failed to resolve the dispute. 'We'll stay here while you negotiate', retorted Kamal Abu Aita and Makram Labib.[11] After two days of sleeping on the steps and pavement outside ETUF, committee and protesters decided to withdraw in order to prepare for a new mass mobilisation and strike while waiting for the outcome of negotiations with the authorities, which Megawer promised would take place.

The activists returned to Daqhaliyya and drew up battle plans for the expected showdown on 3 December. On 24 November, thirty-two activists from eleven different offices across the province and a representative from neighbouring Damietta met to divide up responsibilities. Each member of the mobilising committee committed to contact a group of offices and a rota was drawn up to ensure that the numbers participating in the Cairo sit-in would remain at around 600. Early on the morning of 3 December, Gamal Uwayda and colleagues from the central directorate in Al-Mansoura crammed into six buses and set off for Cairo. Other buses from Dikirnis, Sanbaliyun and Mit Ghamr joined them en route, so that by the time they reached Kafr Shukr the convoy was twenty-two buses long.[12] He describes vividly the scene that met the 600-strong delegation from Daqhaliyya as they arrived in Husssein Hegazy Street outside the Cabinet Office a few hours later.

> We were greeted with open arms and cheers, by smiling, laughing, cheerful faces as if we had known them for years. The place itself was no stranger to us either, as we had walked there the 25 km from the Ministry of Finance ... The drums, tambourines and megaphones, the joy and the shouting: some people cannot believe that the numbers on that day were more than ten thousand. And everywhere you heard the beautiful chant: 'a decision, a decision ... we're not going home without a decision'.[13]

The days that followed were filled with drama as the striking tax collectors met the minister's indifference with escalation, outmanoeuvred the ETUF officials and pressed home their advantage as panic set in at the higher levels of the state. They proved adept at managing the media circus around them, maintained good relations with local residents who provided food for the strikers and allowed them to use their bathrooms, and most importantly continued to draw on reservoirs of support, which ran deep into the provinces. On several occasions, Faruq Shahata, president of BIWU, appeared at the sit-in, but the tax workers shouted and chanted at him, forcing him to leave.

The sit-in developed its own organisation, which broadened the leadership of the strike beyond the eleven-member Higher Strike Committee. Four committees organised provisions, relations with the media, chants and slogans – the general organisation of the sit-in. Women played a prominent role, sleeping in the street alongside their male colleagues. Uwayda lists the names of twenty-seven women activists who were central to the organisation of the Daqhaliyya delegation.

The first major test came on 9 December. The Property Tax Agency's estimated losses had reached LE300 million, but minister of finance Youssef Boutros Ghali was refusing to negotiate and the strikers rebuffed further attempts by ETUF officials, including Megawer, to mediate. According to Uwayda the mood in the sit-in was turning sour and the tax collectors were beginning to debate whether the tactics of the strike committee were correct, when the news broke that Boutros Ghali had agreed to direct talks. The negotiators, led by Kamal Abu Aita and Makram Labib, emerged with the outlines of a deal which would have ended the sit-in in return for the equalisation of pay and conditions with the central property tax administration. The proposals were to be implemented in stages, with full equalisation deferred until after discussion in parliament of the new law regulating property tax collection.[14] When this was put to the mass meeting of the strikers opinion was divided, so it was decided to set a deadline for consultation of the morning of the following day and then to vote on whether to continue the strike or end it. The vote the following day was that the action should to continue, and all respected the result.

At a hastily convened press conference that night on the fringes of the annual Socialist Days event organised by the Centre for Socialist Studies, members of the Higher Strike Committee fielded questions from some 200 journalists.[15] Meanwhile, across the country, the mobilising committees were organising to reinforce the sit-in in response to the call from the strike committee for an escalation to all-out strike. New delegations arrived, carrying with them the keys of the provincial property tax authority offices, which they had left locked and bolted behind them. Four strikers were taken to hospital suffering from suffocation as the crush in Hussein Hegazy Street increased. Harassment from the security forces and riot police surrounding the area intensified.

In the end, the government blinked first. Boutros Ghali finally agreed to the strikers' demands in principle during the course of marathon negotiations, which ended at 4 a.m. on 12 December. The strikers decided to end their sit-in. On 31 December 2007 the minister of finance and the director of the Property Tax Authority met the strike committee in the PTA headquarters in Cairo and agreed to implement the demands, beginning with a pay rise for employees. BIWU president Faruq Shahata attempted to join the negotiations, but the strike committee refused to allow this and insisted he leave.

From strike committee to independent union

Victory brought immediate and substantial material gains for the property tax collectors: in effect a pay rise of around 300 per cent. The success of the strike posed challenging questions to its organisers: should they disband their committees and return to their workplaces? What would be the justification for the continuation of the strike committee beyond the end of the strike? If it continued, what form should the committee take? After intense discussions and calls from the workers, the strike committee decided to continue with the aim of founding a union for Property Tax Agency workers outside the ETUF. According to the account of the foundation of the union presented by Abd-al-Qadir Nada, manager of Al-Warraq office in Giza and a member of the strike committee, in the new union's newspaper in May 2009, the vote to continue was taken on 1 March 2008, and followed by a campaign of meetings across the country to sign up new members in preparation for a founding conference. Kamal Abu Aita, in an article published in October 2008, explained the motivation and the process by which the strike organisation became the core of an independent union. The primary goal, he argued, was to protect and extend the gains made during the strike:

> If we lose our committee, we will lose a weapon which we sweated and struggled to create, and it will give the state and management a chance to attack us again.[16]

It was not enough to maintain the organisation that had developed to lead the strike, so the strike committee was relaunched as the 'Permanent Committee to Defend the Rights of the Property Tax Collectors'. However, this was not simply a matter of re-labelling the old committee with a new name: 'the new committee had to be the property of tens of thousands of property tax collectors, they would build it themselves, so that they would defend it, and be ready to protect it.' If the committee was constituted 'from above' by a small number of leaders announcing it, Abu Aita argued, then it could easily be struck down 'from above' by the state. The permanent committee was composed of three delegates per province, elected by the regional strike committees.

> So we strove to create it from the bottom to the top, by encouraging the creation of delegates' committees in every governorate and directorate. Committees were elected or chosen by some method or other, with the condition that this was a democratic method and expressed the will of all the employees.[17]

The committee's aims were to oversee the implementation of the deal agreed with Boutros Ghali in December 2007 and to continue negotiations until equalisation of the property tax collectors' pay and conditions with tax collectors employed directly by the Ministry of Finance. A new goal was also agreed: to campaign for the establishment of a social fund for the property tax collectors which would be independent of the control of the ETUF-affiliated union. Abu Aita was among a number of leading activists in the permanent committee who were now beginning to articulate arguments in public for the formation of an independent union. The success of the attempt would be conditional on continued efforts to expand the organisation at the base, he cautioned.

> The goals of the National Permanent Committee to Defend the Rights of the Property Tax Collectors will not be achieved overnight. This will be a long process which will include the formation of delegates committees in the provinces, whose members must win the confidence of their colleagues everywhere. Only then will we be able to say that we are founding an independent union.[18]

By December 2008 the Permanent Committee had recruited a membership of nearly 30,000 across all twenty-six provinces, around a third of them women. On 20 December a conference took place in the Journalists' Union, which was attended by 4,000 to commemorate the first anniversary of the strike. This was considered the founding conference of the new union, RETAU, during which elections took place for a secretariat with representation from all the provinces, as well as the completion of the procedures of founding the union, the adoption of a constitution, and consideration given to membership of international and regional unions.

The picture of the new union's internal structures that appears in the union newspaper, *Nubat Sahiyan*, published in May 2009, reveals the depth of the roots that had grown out of the previous year's strike organisation. The union claimed membership in

TABLE 5.1 Provincial committees of the independent union of
workers in the property tax authority, December 2008

Governorate	Delegates on governorate secretariat	Offices or departments represented by delegates	Total membership
Cairo	35	32	2,450
Assyut	15	14	2,352
Al-Daqhaliyya	25	19	2,307
Sohag	19	13	2,060
Al-Sharqiyya	21	12	1,873
Minufiyya	19	14	1,749
Gharbiyya	17	n/a	1,623
North Sinai	11	5	1,623
Beni Sueif	11	9	1,563
Minya	21	13	1,443
Al-Baheira	19	n/a	1,300
Qena	25	12	1,247
Isma'iliyya	21	n/a	978
Al-Qalyubiyya	17	11	841
Giza	17	10	724
Damietta	17	9	618
Red Sea	13	4	437
Suez	9	3	434
Aswan	13	8	420
Al-Fayyum	17	11	405
6th of October	11	8	342
Helwan	13	6	334
Luxor	7	4	226
Kafr al-Shaikh	14	n/a	142
Marsa Matruh	11	10	117
Alexandria	13	7	77
TOTAL	431	234	27,685

SOURCE *Nubat Sahiyan* 4 (May 2009), pp. 12–15.

every province, from Aswan in the far south to the western coastal province of Marsa Matruh. The network of elected members on the provincial committees provided the union with named representatives in at least 234 offices or departments across the property tax authority. The organisation of the sit-in outside the Cabinet Office the previous year had been dominated by activists from Giza and Daqhaliyya, who formed the membership of the sit-in's Organisation Committee and accounted for five out of the eleven members of the Higher Strike Committee.[19] By December 2008 there was strong growth in a number of other provinces, with Cairo, Sohag and Assyut also claiming more than 2,000 members each.

The distribution of elected representatives in the provincial offices (Table 5.1) suggests that the methods used by activists in Daqhaliyya to build a strike organisation by creating a network with roots in as many of the PTA's small, local offices as possible were replicated in large areas of the country. The main PTA directorates (*al-mudiriyya*) located in the provincial capitals were generally well represented in the new union's regional committees; however, the vast majority of members came from offices serving local areas, many of them small rural towns. The 2,060 members of the union in Sohag, 450 km from Cairo, for example, were represented by a nineteen-member provincial committee, composed of delegates representing thirteen different offices. Five delegates came from the provincial headquarters of the property tax authority, located behind the Governorate Buildings in the province's capital, but the other fourteen represented offices covering the outlying districts.

The union's 43-member General Secretariat included five members of the original Higher Strike Committee. A number of the women activists who had played a key role in the organisation of the sit-in were elected to the General Secretariat, including Fatima al-Nabawiyya, Karima al-Guma'a and Mervat Qasim from the Giza directorate. Altogether there were eleven women members of the General Secretariat. The process of building the independent union's structures went hand in hand with collective resignations from the ETUF-affiliated union BIWU. Kamal Abu Aita's resignation from BIWU was reported in the January 2009 issue of *Nubat Sahiyan*, while the May 2009 issue covered the mass resignations from BIWU's Daqhaliyya committee.[20]

One name was conspicuously absent from the list of resignations from the BIWU committee in Daqhaliyya: that of its president, Makram Labib. Despite playing a key role in the protests and strikes of 2007, Labib would go on to lead an attempt to break the independent union by organising a return to the ETUF. On 5 September Hussein Megawer, the ETUF president, announced the formation of a committee tasked with creating a twenty-fourth member union of the federation, representing employees of the Ministry of Finance, including the Property Tax Authority, the General Tax Authority, the Sales Tax Authority and the Customs Authority. The committee was chaired by the ETUF's deputy general secretary and included a number of senior figures in BIWU, Makram Labib and Azzat Sa'ad, the general secretary of the BIWU committee in Giza. Labib's public break with his former colleagues came in the midst of a campaign of physical and legal harassment of the independent union's leadership orchestrated by ETUF officials. In a letter to the International Trade Union Confederation (ITUC) in June 2009, Kamal Abu Aita detailed a series of incidents, including physical attacks by BIWU officials on the chairs of the independent union committees in Gharbiyya and Sharqiyya governorates. Tareq Mustafa Ka'eb, the union's treasurer and chair of the Qalyubiyya committee, and leading activists in the Beni Sueif, Assyut, Qena and Aswan governorate committees were facing proceedings in the administrative courts or legal investigation by the Property Tax Authority as a result of their trade-union activities. Meanwhile, despite having resigned from BIWU, the ETUF-affiliated union's subscriptions were still being deducted from the salaries of the independent union's members. The Ministry of Finance had retreated from cooperation with the independent union's officials and, Abu Aita explained, was refusing to implement the agreement negotiated at the end of the 2007 strike.

In August 2009, Faruq Shahata, BIWU president, lodged a legal complaint against Abu Aita himself, arguing that he had violated Law 35 (1976) by founding a union outside the ETUF structure. However, the independent union's leadership could also point out that the same law violated several ILO conventions that Egypt had signed. Moreover, when they had lodged registration documents with Ai'sha Abd-al-Hadi, minister of labour, on 22 April 2009, she had not raised any objections, which they took as a sign of de facto state recognition.[21] The attempt by ETUF officials and Labib to break the independent union did not succeed in its primary objective: the collapse of RETAU and the demonstrative defeat of the project of independent trade unionism. Even in Daqhaliyya, where Labib's personal standing might have been expected to win over some of his colleagues to return with him to the ETUF fold, other local leading activists in the independent union, such as Gamal Uwayda, rejected the path he had chosen. Despite the difficulties, on the eve of the 2011 revolution much of RETAU's network of provincial committees was still functioning, as was evidenced by the leading role played by the union's activists in efforts to build a regional structure for the Egyptian Federation of Independent Trade Unions, and the visibility of RETAU activists in the street protests that marked the early phase of the revolution.

The development of other independent union networks

RETAU's consolidation sharply posed a further question: was the experience of the Property Tax Collectors replicable in other sectors? Makram Labib, who, as we saw above, abandoned the project of building an independent union to return to the ETUF fold, thought not. In a meeting with US embassy officials on 30 September 2009, he attacked Kamal Abu Aita for using RETAU as a vehicle for his 'political' aims, opining that workers in other sectors might 'threaten to form independent unions, but as soon as they achieve their immediate economic objectives, they will lose interest'.[22]

This assessment was wrong on a number of different levels, although it pointed to the powerful ideological pull of the idea that 'proper trade unionism' required the separation of economic and political struggles (although in Labib's case this meant in reality capitulation to the politics of the regime). The networks of activists in the Property Tax Authority which organised the 2007 strike were neither isolated nor exceptional. The reactions between the elements that produced the conditions for RETAU's birth were, independently of events there, sparking similar processes in other sectors. Embryonic forms of independent union organisation began to develop in the postal service, the Public Transport Authority, among school teachers, as well as within professional and technical grades of health workers.

The postal workers' movement in 2009 began with the implementation of regulations on the annual appraisal system which gave management greater scope to dismiss workers. There are around 52,000 postal workers in Egypt spread across the country, earning salaries between LE200 and LE800 per month. Postal workers organised protests in a number of governorates, the biggest of which was in Kafr al-Sheikh involving more than 2,000 male and female postal workers. The sit-in on 7 May 2009 is considered the beginning of the movement and launched preparations for a new round of protests. But the postal workers found themselves under attack from all quarters. The General Union of Postal Workers strongly criticised the workers and accused them of fomenting riots. It supported the General Postal Authority's refusal to meet their demands, and suspended from union membership Ahmed Allam, a member of the union committee in Kafr al-Sheikh, who was elected by the workers. The security services arrested a postal worker in Kafr al-Sheikh and accused him of incitement to strike, while the intelligence officers of State Security at the Ministry of the Interior followed a large number of workers in order to intimidate them and threatened them with arrest. The Postal Authority referred a large number of postal worker activists for investigation and brought disciplinary proceedings against them, and transferred a large number to faraway offices. This victimisation did not deter the postal workers, who organised another sit-in on 17 May, which was stronger than the first and lasted for six days. With support from the Freedoms Committee at the Journalists' Union they organised two enthusiastic conferences to publicise their demands. These were: the cancellation of the regulations allowing annual appraisals to lead to sacking; parity with colleagues in Egypt Telecom, which came under the same ministry; permanent contracts for temporary workers, who numbered more than 5,000, as recognised in law. Spurred on by the hostile attitude of ETUF officials to their demands, postal workers began to establish a committee of delegates from different provinces to organise the dispute.

The form of the postal workers' Higher Strike Committee took direct inspiration from the example of the Property Tax Collectors' Higher Strike Committee. It held many of its early meetings in the Centre for Socialist Studies (CSS) in Giza, whose activists also worked closely with RETAU's leaders. Kamal Abu Aita, in an article for the CSS newspaper *Al-Ishtaraki*, published on 1 July 2009 at the height of the sit-ins, directly addressed the postal worker activists, summing up the organisational lessons of RETAU's experience. He argued strongly for 'the creation of a committee in every governorate, composed of one or more representatives from every post office or workplace, which should choose one or more delegates to represent all the postal workers on the Higher Strike Committee at a national level'. This committee should be responsible for negotiations and 'take decisions in consultation with the regional committees'. In this way, Abu Aita concluded that 'the reins of your movement will be in your own hands.'[23] The postal workers should be wary of the ETUF unions, Abu Aita argued, even though their strike committees included a number of members of the ETUF-affiliated General Union of Postal Workers.

> Do not trust the official trade union organisations, do not allow them to take decisions for you, because they will sell you out at the first opportunity ... refuse to pay your subscriptions, deny them the honour of representing you, resign from their unions and do not believe their lies.[24]

Like the postal workers, teachers were spurred to action by changes to their working conditions at a national level – in this case a far-reaching restructuring of their pay and grading system which imposed new professional standards and performance-related pay.[25] The laws creating this new 'cadre' for teachers were promulgated in June 2007, stimulating grassroots opposition to the reforms from teachers across country. As Hala Talaat, a teacher from Giza and one of the founders of the Egyptian Teachers' Federation after the revolution, explains, opposition to the Teachers' Cadre played a critical role in winning a wider audience to activism. However, the agitation over the Cadre was often led by activists who were part of existing networks, such as the Teachers' Leagues (*rawabit*).

> A league [rabita] was a group of teachers in a governorate or a locality, who got active to demand teachers' rights. But there was no coordination between us and other governorates. Co-ordination began to develop over issues like the Teachers' Cadre, which led to a crisis between the teachers and the Ministry.[26]

In Giza, the activists who set up the league were members
of Tagammu, the sole legal left-wing opposition party. Talaat
recalls how frustration with the party's failure to relate to the
teachers' problems prompted them to turn towards organising
in and between workplaces:

> We set up an irregular publication which talked about the
> problems of education and the problems for teachers and our
> crisis in the educational process, as well as the activities we were
> organising. After that we moved on from the idea that this was a
> party activity, and began to think of ourselves as teachers, first
> and foremost, and began to mobilise ourselves around develop-
> ment of education, and relating to teachers, away from party
> activities. This was because Tagammu at that time was just a
> 'cardboard party', there was no effective work taking place on
> the ground, and it used just to demoralise anyone who wanted
> to do genuine work.[27]

As in the Property Tax Authority, teacher activists were frustrated by the ossified bureaucracy of the existing unions, which
was firmly in the grip of the ruling party. The president of the
Union of Education Professions served as speaker of the Shura
Council, the upper house of parliament between 1989 and 2004;
he was first elected in 1980, holding the post continuously between
1989 and 2008.[28] The union's internal democratic mechanisms
were extremely weak: the general secretary presided over a series
of indirectly elected national and regional committees, with each
layer forming the electoral college for the layer above. Teacher
activists also felt that the union, which represented 'educational
professionals' rather than only teachers, was failing to represent
their professional interests effectively, and turned towards agitation around the Cadre as a way of mobilising around what they
felt were issues specific to teachers.[29] As discussed in Chapter 2,
the restructuring of education during the neoliberal era dramatically increased pressure on teachers' salaries and raised tensions
between them and parents over the issue of private tuition.

The protests and rallies against the Cadre attracted new activists to these small networks and stimulated connections between them. A Federation of Teachers' Leagues was set up by activists in Giza, and there were also leagues active in Dahaqaliyya, Al-Sharqiyya, Damietta, Beni Sueif and Alexandria. The first independent union for teachers, the Independent School Teachers Union, was founded in 2010, while Talaat and her colleagues would later go on to play a leading role in forming the second of the independent teachers' unions, the Egyptian Teachers' Federation, in 2011. The founding committee of Independent School Teachers' Union, led by activists such as Ayman al-Bialy and Abdul-Hafiz al-Tayyal, presented registration papers to the Ministry of Labour. After these were rejected, they announced the foundation of the union on 15 July 2010, publicising the high-level support from officials of the International Trade Union Confederation (ITUC), who had met with the founding committee.[30]

Ahmed el-Sayyed, president of the Health Technicians Union (HTU, *al-niqaba mustaqilla lil fananin al-sahiyyin*), which was founded in December 2010, relates a story that illustrates a number of similar features, including frustration over the lack of 'professional' representation within the ETUF union structures and poor pay and working conditions across the public and private health systems. Like the Property Tax Collectors in RETAU, the HTU was built up systematically on a national scale before the holding of a founding general assembly which brought together around 1,000 activists. Unlike RETAU, however, the HTU did not rely on the energy generated by strike organisation to start the process of organising, as the union's leading activists rejected strike action as a method of collective action, arguing that this would damage patients' interests.

The HTU's constituency is the 200,000 or so graduates of the Egyptian Health Technicians' Academy, which provides a two-year tertiary professional qualification for a range of technical professionals in the health service, including radiologists, laboratory assistants, dental technicians, medical equipment repair specialists, anaesthetists and specialist nursing roles such as post-operative care.

> Across history from the time that the Academy was first founded in 1927 until now, they have had no one to represent them, and no one to speak about them. There were 'semi-unions', not real unions, but associations, to which small numbers belonged; however, these associations were not real unions, because, as you know, they didn't defend our pay; they were just supposed to provide limited social services.[31]

Like the activists around the Teachers' Leagues, el-Sayyed describes a relatively lengthy process of crystallisation of a small network of activists 'who loved [the] profession, who wanted to develop it, to win a decent wage'. This initial group had already attempted to interest politicians in the project of setting up a union to represent health technicians, arranging numerous meetings with MPs and digging out draft legislation from the 1980s as a possible model for a new union within the ETUF structure. Now they turned to another tactic, directly organising among their colleagues around the country by calling regional meetings to discuss setting up an independent union.

> When we felt that the mobilisation was gathering pace in the governorates, we starting sending out delegations to the provinces to organise meetings. Seven or eight would go to a particular place and organise a big conference which would bring together 350–400 people, according to the numbers who were able to come. Of course everywhere we faced the intervention of the Security Forces. ... It was never easy. We'd gather people and propose the idea to them 'Why don't we set up a union to demand our rights.'[32]

The founding General Assembly of the HTU was held on 10 December 2010, largely in the street outside the RETAU offices off Faisal Street near the pyramids, as hundreds of delegates from around the country spilled out onto the pavement. RETAU not only provided the venue for the conference, but inspired the HTU's constitution, with its emphasis on the sovereignty of the General Assembly's delegates and their power to directly elect the general secretary.[33]

Another significant group of workers whose prehistory of collective organisation played a critical role in the rapid emergence of an independent union in the wake of the 2011 revolution were the Cairo Public Transport Authority workers. The September 2009 bus strike, and the network of activists spanning garages across the city which led the action, played a critical role in forging what became the leadership for the new union. It is also important to recognise that even where new forms of independent organisation did not crystallise before the revolution, there were still many workers watching the strikes and protests with growing sympathy, which they would translate into action only after the fall of Mubarak. As Namaat Gaber, an activist in the Independent Union of Workers in EgyptAir Maintenance and Technical Company at Cairo International Airport, put it in an interview after the revolution:

> I always used to talk about politics in my workplace, and I was always opposed to the old regime. And of course I saw the companies being privatised, and I saw the demonstrations by the journalists and lawyers, by the textile workers and the tax collectors, and I was angry about what was going on in the country.[34]

The process of union formation from strike action was naturally highly uneven, and there were many significant strikes which did not result in the same kind of concrete steps towards the formation of new unions as the examples of the Property Tax Collectors, the postal workers and the PTA workers. Independent union organisation did not crystallise at Misr Spinning in Mahalla, despite the Mahalla workers' mass campaign of resignations from the ETUF-affiliated General Union of Textile Workers. In an article published in May 2009, Hisham Fouad argues that the leaders of the 2007 strikes missed the opportunity of utilising the momentum which built up when workers' confidence was rising before the repression of the 2008 uprising set organising within the mill back and made it more difficult to convince workers of the need for independent association.[35]

The contradictions of trade unionism

A specific combination of circumstances – mass strikes and division within the state regarding how to deal with the revival of workers' protests – created a space in which the first independent union, RETAU, was able to develop. Its creation was, as outlined above, not a *spontaneous* eruption from the strike wave, but the transformation and development of strike organisation into something new. The significance of RETAU's survival is clear on a number of different levels: the new union fractured the regime's monopoly within the workplace, and brought experience of collective self-organisation to tens of thousands of civil servants, in hundreds of towns and cities across the country. RETAU's organisational culture represented a dramatic shift away from the bureaucratic model of leadership that dominated within ETUF towards a more democratic, accountable and open form of leadership.[36] This was all the more remarkable an achievement given how few resources the new union's activists could draw on beyond their own efforts. As we explore in more detail below, the very small forces of the revolutionary left did play a crucial practical and political role in initiating and sustaining the project of building an independent union. Labour NGOs, in particular CTUWS, also shaped the development of RETAU, acting as a conduit for the influence of the international trade-union bureaucracy on the new union's leadership.

RETAU's triumph against the odds revealed the continuing importance of a problem that has haunted workers' movements since the birth of capitalism: how to sustain mass, democratic participation once the fires of strike activity have cooled, and how to counteract the establishment of a bureaucratic leadership primarily concerned with perpetuating its own role. As discussed in the Introduction, the trade-union bureaucracy's dual role as a mediating layer between workers, on the one hand, and their bosses and the state, on the other, leads union officials inevitably in the direction of compromise and conciliation whenever possible. However, leading figures in RETAU, such as Kamal Abu Aita, Tareq Mustafa Ka'eb and Abd-al-Qadir Nada, openly articulated the need to build organisation which would prevent, or at least restrict, the development of a new bureaucracy mirroring that within the ETUF trade unions whose embrace they were fighting to escape. They condemned not only the ETUF officials for their failure to defend rank-and-file union members' interests and pursue their demands for better pay and conditions, but also the undemocratic and unaccountable *practices* of leadership in the ETUF unions. Yet, despite numerous constitutional safeguards, such as reducing the term of office of elected officials from five to two years, pressures towards bureaucratisation quickly emerged. In particular, the dislocation of some of the union's elected officials from the workplace and their consequent ability to act autonomously of the rank and file, damaged the mechanisms of democratic accountability which were so important to the success of the 2007 strike. As we will see, after the revolution of 2011 the dislocation of union leadership from workplace organisation re-emerged as an even greater problem within the Egyptian Federation of Independent Trade Unions, in which RETAU leaders such as Kamal Abu Aita played a pivotal role.

The opening for the development of a new bureaucracy in the leadership of the independent unions was also contingent on the willingness of sections of the state to create a space in which this kind of reformism could operate, by granting at least de facto recognition to the new union, and engaging its officials in meaningful negotiations. However, this was precisely what happened. Despite the ongoing harassment of union officials by parts of the state apparatus, including a vicious campaign of intimidation and legal harassment instigated by the ETUF leadership against union leaders, other parts of the state were prepared to engage the independent union in negotiations over wages, and minister of labour Ai'sha Abd-al-Hadi did not oppose the union's attempt to register legally. Ironically, the crushing victory over the Ministry of Finance in the 2007–08 strike may have been a factor in expanding the union leadership's room to manoeuvre as it also reduced the immediate pressure from below to defend and extend the gains made in the strike. Levels of strike activity by property tax collectors dropped dramatically after 2008, which meant that the union leaders were not forced to constantly renew their democratic mandate from below in the active way they had done during the strike. While the exertions of the mass mobilisation for the 2007 strike meant that a lull in collective action immediately afterwards was highly likely, the property tax collectors were also almost entirely absent from the waves of strikes in 2011 and 2012. The union's internal democracy also appeared to have decayed: the second conference was postponed several times and levels of participation were significantly lower than at the founding conference. In any other circumstance this would have not been surprising, but in the context of the ferment of organisation after February 2011 it pointed to a deeper problem.

Beyond the workplace: opportunities and problems

The development of the independent unions beyond RETAU, and the consolidation of RETAU itself, would not have happened in the way it did without deep-rooted cooperation between workplace activists and political and civil society groups. The relationship between the emerging networks of independent trade unionists and the revolutionary left, on the one hand, and activists in labour NGOs, on the other, will be explored here. The two major 'external' organisations that influenced the development of the independent unions under discussion here were the Revolutionary Socialists (RS), an underground Marxist opposition group, and the Centre for Trade Union and Workers' Services (CTUWS), an NGO dedicated to supporting labour movement development. To focus on these two organisations is not to deny that independent trade unionists had relationships with other political groups, or that other NGOs also played an important role. Kamal Abu Aita, for example, was a long-standing political activist and a close collaborator of Nasserist opposition figure Hamdeen Sabahi. The Egyptian Centre for Economic and Social Rights (ECESR), another NGO with a track record of working with labour movement activists, also played an influential and supportive role as the independent unions were in formation: organising meetings and workshops and providing legal advice for labour movement activists.

However, we focus on the RS and CTUWS because leading figures in the two organisations began to articulate contrasting political perspectives on issues such as the relationship between the independent trade unions and the international trade-union bureaucracy; internal democracy within the new unions; and where 'independent trade unionism' should situate itself in the complex interlacings between 'economic' and 'political' struggles. The differences between these approaches were not always articulated openly, and both organisations had to navigate in a political environment which required maximum public unity between supporters of the independent unions in order to avoid providing the regime with opportunities to exploit divisions and weaken the new movement.

As discussed above, the RS supported the development of independent unions in a number of different ways. This was in one way an extension of the group's efforts to mobilise solidarity campaigns for striking workers – it was not an accident that the Property Tax Collectors' Higher Strike Committee made its dramatic announcement of the escalation to an all-out strike at a meeting on the fringes of the annual public conference organised by the RS. However, leading activists in the RS also formulated a political perspective which emphasised not only the theoretical desirability of forming independent unions, but the practical possibility of achieving this. This perspective was articulated systematically in the group's publications, on its website and in countless meetings in which leading independent trade unionists participated. In addition, the RS offered practical support in other ways: by facilitating the generalisation of lessons from one sector to another through publications and events; by providing rooms for organising meetings; and by helping to ensure sympathetic press coverage through the intervention of RS activists who worked in the media.

The CTUWS provided support for the independent unions through similar kinds of activities within Egypt, and in addition was the main conduit through which connections flowed between RETAU, and later the Independent School Teachers' Union, and the International Trade Union Confederation (ITUC) and its affiliates such as the US union federation AFL–CIO. Both the leadership of the ITUC and the AFL–CIO displayed considerable interest in the formation of RETAU. Kamal Abu Aita, RETAU's president, was invited by the ITUC to attend its second congress in Vancouver in June 2010.[37] The AFL–CIO awarded the 2009 George Meany–Lane Kirkland Human Rights Prize, an annual award named after the organisation's first two presidents, to RETAU and the Centre for Trade Union and Workers' Services (CTUWS) on behalf of 'all Egyptian workers' in 2010.[38] Unlike the newly founded union, CTUWS already had a long history of engagement with international bodies, and counts among its objectives 'building bridges with the labour and trade union movements at a global level and developing mechanisms for co-operation and joint action'.[39] The Centre received funding from the international development NGO Oxfam in 1993, a human rights prize from the French government in 1999, followed by other international awards and funding, including from the British trade union UNISON, through its international development fund.[40] The US-based Solidarity Center, which is affiliated to the AFL–CIO, counts CTUWS as a partner organisation; it worked closely with the Centre for at least six years before the 2011 revolution.[41]

At one level, engaging the ILO, international trade union bodies such as the ITUC and the global federation of public service unions in support of RETAU's attempts to force the Egyptian state to concede legal recognition of the independent unions was a tactical decision, motivated by the need to find and mobilise external allies in the face of repression. The ILO and ITUC exerted pressure on the Egyptian government over the lack of trade-union freedoms through official protests and public campaigns. The tactics of RETAU activists were shaped by their perception that such external pressure was effective: the presentation of RETAU's registration papers to the Ministry of Labour was deliberately timed to coincide with the visit of an ILO delegation to Egypt. The acceptance of RETAU's member-ship application by Public Services International (PSI), despite protests and complaints from ETUF, was justifiably celebrated by RETAU activists as a victory over their adversaries, arguing that membership of the PSI provided confirmation of the independent union's legitimacy and standing in the global workers' movement.

However, at other levels, the time and effort spent deepening relationships with international organisations was costly. Trips

abroad or attendance at conferences and workshops with NGO activists, international trade-union and government officials removed
leading activists from the workplace and from relating directly to
the concerns of rank-and-file union members. Even if these visits
were for a short period, the huge gap between the lifestyle associated with international travel paid for by foreign funders (whether
trade unions or NGOs) and the everyday life of union activists is
likely to have intensified this sense of disconnection. Moreover,
many of the trade unionists whom RETAU activists are likely to
have met at these events were also full-time officials in far larger
and wealthier – and therefore more bureaucratic – organisations
than RETAU itself. The model of trade unionism that will have
commonly been presented on these occasions stood in sharp
contrast to that on which RETAU was built. Another set of
bureaucratising pressures are introduced into the picture by the
mediating role of an NGO. Just as the trade-union bureaucracy's
primary collective concern is its own self-perpetuation, the same
can be said about the employees of NGOs. This does not mean
that individuals working for NGOs that rely on foreign funding
are motivated only by self-interest, but rather that, as a whole,
NGO employees have to ensure continuous funding in order to
carry on playing their professional roles.

However, in comparison to even the most bureaucratic trade
unions, employees of labour NGOs enjoy a qualitatively different
relationship to workers compared to that between trade-union
officials and the rank and file. They have far greater autonomy,
as they do not depend on union members' dues to pay their
salaries and maintain the bureaucratic apparatus itself. They
are rarely subject to any kind of democratic control from below.
Most NGOs are not mass membership organisations, but small
groups of professionals offering specialised services. There are
no formal democratic mechanisms by which the groups they
interact with (and whose interests they often claim to represent)

can exert any authority over what the NGO employees do and say. By contrast, as we saw in the case of Tunisia, the democratic structures within even highly bureaucratic unions can become a battleground where rank-and-file struggles can set limits on the bureaucracy's autonomy. The ability of the rank and file to impose those limits is linked directly to the overall balance of forces between the working class, on the one hand, and the employers and the state, on the other. For the reasons outlined above, the democratic structures of trade unions never *guarantee* control from below over the bureaucracy, but their presence is an expression of the bureaucracy's unique role as a mediating layer formed in the space between labour and capital, and dependent on both for its existence. These conditions do not apply to NGO employees, even if they come to play similar professional roles to the trade-union bureaucracy in relation to the workers' movement. In fact, as we discuss in more detail in Chapter 7, the relationship between leading officials in RETAU, including Kamal Abu Aita, and the CTUWS broke down over precisely this point, when in the wake of the revolution Abu Aita claimed that CTUWS employees were attempting to insert themselves into the democratic decision-making structures of the emerging Egyptian Federation of Independent Trade Unions on an equal footing with elected union officials.

On the other hand, the role played by the RS in supporting the development of the independent unions also raised complex questions about the relationship between economic and political struggles, and specifically the question of whether revolutionaries could collaborate in a project to build reformist organisations (trade unions) without either compromising their own principles or turning the new unions into adjuncts of the revolutionary organisation itself and thereby excluding the mass of non-revolutionary workers from membership. The key elements of a model of trade union practice which provided the best hope of protecting the independent unions from these problems could, however, be found in the experience of democratic self-organisation exemplified by the Property Tax Collectors' strike and the transformation of the Higher Strike Committee into RETAU. From this perspective, the critical meaning of 'independence' in the practice of independent trade unionism was not legal independence from the state in a formalistic sense, but building the independent capacity of rank-and-file members of the new unions to organise themselves and hold their elected leaders to account. Putting into practice this understanding of 'independence' would require revolutionary activists to maintain their independence of and critical attitude to the new union leaders and prevent the emergence of a 'revolutionary leadership' in the unions which was dislocated from the base. The independent unions in the pre-revolutionary period owed a large part of their success, we believe, to the application of some of these principles, as it was the sustained involvement of tens of thousands of new workplace activists in the democratic process of building unions like RETAU and the HTU that created the critical mass needed to create viable new organisations in very difficult circumstances.

Conclusion

In this chapter we have proposed a model for explaining the emergence of the first independent union, RETAU, as an *extension* of the highly democratic and participatory forms of strike organisation that played a key role in the success of the Property Tax Collectors' strike in 2007. However, equally importantly, RETAU was also a *transformation* of strike organisation: a project which had significant political implications as it struck at the heart of the regime's continuing claim to 'represent' workers through the ETUF structures. The intertwined participatory and political aspects of the Property Tax Collectors' strike and the activities that built RETAU were integral to the success of both projects, we have argued here. Despite access to vastly superior resources and the willing connivance of the state security apparatus, which persecuted his rivals, Makram Labib, who defected from RETAU to build a Property Tax Collectors' union within the ETUF structure, failed to win the majority of RETAU's membership away from the independent union. The fact that enough rank-and-file activists in the new union preferred to accept the risks associated with building an organisation outside the ETUF to allow the independent union to consolidate, despite the offer of an alternative acceptable to the regime, was in itself an indication of the weakening of the dictatorship's grip. Moreover, the failure of ETUF officials to crush RETAU intensified divisions and confusion within the regime itself about how to relate to the workers' movement's new-found self-confidence. Minister of Labour Ai'sha Abd-al-Hadi pursued a policy of de facto recognition of RETAU, in contrast to the ETUF bureaucracy's attempts to use the courts and physical harassment of RETAU activists to smash the new union.

Yet the pre-revolutionary experience of RETAU also illustrated the pull towards the bureaucratisation of the union's leadership, and the weakening of its democratic mandate. The union's highly democratic structure and the mass participation of workplace activists in its creation were a reflection of the immense energy of thousands of workers in the tax authority whose self-activity and self-organisation were the key to victory over the Ministry of Finance. Yet, despite this, as the union leadership attempted to build stable organisation and take on a role representing their members in routine negotiations with the state, they faced intense pressures to accommodate to a bureaucratic role in the emerging union apparatus. Some of these pressures related to the routinisation of aspects of trade-union work, such as engagement in wage negotiations. These pressures were important, even though the margin within which RETAU could operate as a 'normal' trade union was extremely narrow, and bitterly contested within the state itself. They were intensified by the interaction between RETAU officials and the international trade-union bureaucracy, mediated through the CTUWS.

Nevertheless, not only did RETAU survive, but the union's consolidation played an important part in the crystallisation of other independent unions and proto-union networks. Other unions were able to emerge in embryo in other places for a range of reasons. In a number of sectors, activists' frustrations with existing forms of workplace and political organisation coincided with attacks on working conditions, demanding a nationally co-ordinated response such as the imposition of the Teachers' Cadre and the new appraisal system in the Post Office. The visibility of workers' strikes and protests in general stimulated a ferment of questions in the workplaces, but RETAU's consolidation set in motion a mutually reinforcing dynamic as activists in different sectors attempted to assimilate the lessons of the property tax collectors' experience and apply them to their own situations. In this sense, the property tax collectors provided a 'model', but it was widely accessible because similar conditions existed in a large number of workplaces. In most cases there was a direct connection between union formation and strike organising, although the Health Technicians' Union provides an example where activists applied the formula of a slow build-up of regional mass meetings and the systematic creation of networks on a national scale without strike action.

The Health Technicians' conference took place in the context of a deepening political crisis for the regime. The parliamentary elections had ended with a crushing victory for the ruling party, while opposition groups withdrew in protest at vote-rigging and intimidation. Simmering resentment over the ability of the police to torture with impunity was becoming visible in the tens of thousands of 'likes' for the 'We are all Khaled Sa'id' Facebook page – set up to highlight the murder of a young man in an Alexandrian café in June 2010. Yet it was not in Egypt at all, but in the provincial town of Sidi Bouzid in Tunisia that the next moves in the deepening revolutionary crisis would take place. On 17 December 2010, street vendor Mohamed Bouazizi set himself alight in protest at being humiliated by municipal officials. His act of despair set in motion processes which transformed crisis into revolution: within two months the leaders who had ruled Tunisia and Egypt for decades were gone.

CHAPTER 6

The revolution's social soul: workers and the January Revolution

The revolution of 25 January 2011 represented, on the one hand, a continuation and deepening of the patterns of social and political protest of the previous decade, and, on the other, a profound rupture with them. To a certain extent, the initial sequence of events replayed the story of 2000–2011, compressed into eighteen dramatic days and nights. The initiators of the street protests that began on 25 January were a loose coalition of opposition groups and activists, many of whom had found common cause in the Palestine solidarity movement after 2000 and the anti-war protests of 2003, demonstrated for change and constitutional reform in 2004–06, mobilised in solidarity with the call for a national minimum wage by the Mahalla workers in 2008, and organised protests against torture in the wake of Khaled Sa'id's murder in 2010. The rupture with the pre-revolutionary period lies in the fact that the magnitude and intensity of popular mobilisation during the '18 Days' uprising against Mubarak forced one part of the state – its highest military commanders – to sacrifice the president and his immediate entourage in an attempt to preserve the integrity of the whole. These two actions – the one signalling that, as Lenin once famously put it, the 'lower classes' did not want 'to live in the old way',[1] and the other that the ruling class was equally unable to continue as before – triggered a revolutionary process on a scale not seen in the region for decades.

It was not only the scale of popular mobilisation that transformed the regime's crisis, but its character. Workers participated in huge numbers in the demonstrations, at first as citizens, rather than as workers. However, it was not until workers began to move *as workers*, through strike action, that Mubarak's fate was sealed. The wave of strikes which began around 6 February not only ensured his swift departure; they carried revolution into the body of the state itself, paralysing large parts of the government apparatus and public sector as strikers replayed the overthrow of the dictator by unseating their bosses, who were frequently senior figures within the ruling party. The call for the cleansing (*tathir*) of state and public-sector institutions was one of the main demands of the strikes after the fall of Mubarak, and continued to mobilise hundreds of thousands of workers in collective action throughout the two years that followed.

At a broader level, the eruption of the strike wave in February 2011, and the increasing scale and intensity of strike action after Mubarak's departure, had a profound impact. Through their self-organised collective action, workers asserted the centrality of the social aspect of the revolution, in confrontation with the reformist political forces such as the Muslim Brotherhood, who hoped to restrict its scope to a limited democratic transition. This continuation of the workers' revolt was the key factor in the destabilisation of the post-Mubarak political settlement between the Brotherhood and the generals of the old regime. In this chapter we trace the development of the strikes, exploring the patterns of collective action in terms of numbers of participants, geographical dispersion, timing and demands. Workers' mobilisation over social demands not only directly affected the functioning of the state and made the recovery of its internal cohesion more difficult; it enlarged the space in which all those political forces striving to continue the battle to implement the goals of the revolution could develop.

Yet, as we will also explore here, there remained limits to the process of integration between social and political struggles. Between February 2011 and June 2013, workers did not deploy their collective social power in order to resolve the political crisis of the ruling class in their favour, as the conjuncture of strikes and mass protests had achieved during the 18 Days uprising against Mubarak. Nor were the sit-ins and protests in the streets between November 2011 and January 2012 capable of imposing the demands of the revolutionary movement on the state. An attempt to reconnect the political and social souls of the revolution in a general strike on 11 February 2012 failed largely because the revolutionary movement lacked real roots in the workplaces where the arguments about strike action were won and lost. Meanwhile, the institutions at the core of the old regime – in particular the army, police and security services – partially recovered from the blows they had sustained in January 2011. The Supreme Council of the Armed Forces began to organise openly for a counter-revolution, backing the electoral campaign of Mubarak's last prime minister, Ahmad Shafiq, in the presidential elections of 2012. However, the scale and continued resilience of social and political protests forced the openly counter-revolutionary elements of the old regime to retreat in favour of a compromise which would allow the Muslim Brotherhood to come to power in the hope of containing and absorbing the revolutionary mobilisation from below. The Brotherhood, in its turn, would face the same unresolved contradiction that destabilised the generals' rule: between workers' expectations of real social change, their undiminished capacity to organise collectively to fight for their demands, and the stunted version of neoliberal democracy on offer 'from above'.

Dynamics of the uprising:
workers and the Republic of Tahrir

The 'Republic of Tahrir' has been described well in many accounts by participants as an alternative Egypt in embryo – characterised by highly democratic forms of self-organisation, free from sectarian and sexual violence, its citizens organised for self-defence but committed to mass, peaceful protest.[2] Although organised workers were not, in general, a large visible presence in the Square during the 18 Days, we will argue here that they played numerous roles in the uprising which were critical to the creation of the 'Republic of Tahrir' and the revolution's success in forcing the removal of Mubarak. As we explore in more detail below, the key battles of the first phase of the uprising were fought not in Tahrir but in the suburbs of the capital as the Interior Ministry troops attempted to crush the protests. Manual and clerical workers took part in these protests as citizens, rather than as an organised force, forming the greatest proportion of the dead and injured. During the first week of the uprising a sweeping curfew was in force and large numbers of workplaces were shut. Ironically it was the regime's failed attempt to reassert the familiar patterns of normal life, by reopening government institutions and workplaces after 6 February, which provided the decisive opportunity for workers to use their power *as* workers by joining strikes, sit-ins and protests on an enormous scale. This strike wave, which continued long after the fall of Mubarak, was likely a crucial factor in forcing the hand of the military leadership against the president.

Finally, it was not simply by their *presence* that workers contributed to the defence of the 'Republic of Tahrir', but also by their *absence* from the desperate attempts made by the bureaucracy of the Egyptian Trade Union Federation to mobilise support for Mubarak during his final, embattled days. In many ways, the dynamics of 'the 18 Days' uprising thus represented a more perfect fusion of the political and the social than was to be achieved by the revolutionary movement in the subsequent three years. Yet it also revealed a striking gap between the vital role workers were playing both as citizens and in their workplaces, and their relative invisibility in the Square itself. The deepening contradiction between workers' social strength and their political invisibility was to play an increasingly central role in the revolutionary process in the years to come.

The uprising began with protests called by a broad coalition of opposition activists to mark National Police Day on 25 January 2011. Although directly inspired by the example of the Tunisian Revolution of 14 January, the organisers' goals were initially modest. But the unexpected size of the demonstrations, not only in Cairo but in dozens of towns and cities nationwide, exhilarated the crowds and sent the authorities into a panic. Opposition forces called for a 'Day of Rage' after Friday prayers on 28 January. It was the events of this day in Cairo's suburban streets which transformed the uprising into a popular revolution. For Sayed Abd-al-Rahman, an activist with the Revolutionary Socialists, the day began with frustration. The imam of his local mosque in Dar-al-Salam, a lower-middle-class and working-class area in the south of Cairo, flatly refused to end his sermon with a call for protests, and worshippers drifted away. Abd-al-Rahman and his friends took the Metro to the industrial town of Helwan, which lay further south. They found a crowd of 5,000–6,000 had already gathered to attack the police station:

> We'd already seen them direct their anger at the local headquarters of Mubarak's National Democratic Party, and they'd torn down the sign on the building. And people had attacked the police station. The police were firing in the air and throwing tear gas at the demonstrators. As a political activist and member of the Revolutionary Socialists, I felt that this wasn't going to

make a revolution, and it wasn't going to help people in Tahrir. All I was focused on was that we needed to get most of the people to Tahrir.³

The mobile phone network and the Internet had already been disabled by the authorities, leaving activists like Abd-al-Rahman complete cut off from information about what was happening in other parts of the city. Undeterred, he and a group of friends managed to persuade the march, which had by this time swelled to around 20,000 people, to march to the centre of Cairo, 50 km distant. Throughout the evening they walked, constantly expecting an attack from the Central Security Forces. Numbers dwindled, but a hard core of 3,000 finally arrived in the Square at around 1 a.m.

> We got to Tahrir expecting to find a huge battle going on and that we'd pitch right in. We weren't thinking about a revolution; we just were thinking of how to reinforce the numbers of demonstrators. But actually we found that the state had collapsed. We went into the square and found tanks with 'Down with Mubarak' written on them. It was an amazing scene. We didn't have a clue what was happening. Tanks with 'Down with Mubarak' on them! ... I walked around Tahrir and the surrounding area and couldn't find any police cars except ones which had been destroyed. Of course we found out from the TV later that there'd been huge battles. A war.⁴

The brutality of the 'war' that the state unleashed on its citizens on 28 January can be traced in the data compiled by activists and lawyers on the dead and injured of the revolution. Although it is still difficult to obtain complete data, what is available clearly shows that it was workers and the poor who paid the greatest price in loss of life and injury on 28 January and afterwards. The Arab Network for Human Rights compiled a list of 841 dead, but there was no systematic recording of data. However, the occupations listed detail many working-class jobs, including a welder, a plumber, a mechanic in a cement factory, an assistant cook in a hotel, and a laundryman, alongside school and university students, teachers and doctors.[5] Another list, compiled by the Egyptian Journalists' Union gives details of 279 dead, with occupational data on 120.[6] Of these, 74 were workers, and the rest students or professionals. Data on place of residence also indicates that the majority of those killed were from poor areas. The data on the injured in the revolution confirms the same picture and is easier to obtain. According to information collected by the Society of the Heroes and Victims of the Revolution, which recorded 4,500 injured, 70 per cent were workers without educational qualifications, 12 per cent were workers with intermediate qualifications, 11 per cent were school students, and 7 per cent held higher qualifications.

The professions of 45 of the dead from Cairo are recorded in the data collected by the Journalists' Union. They represent a wide range of trades, including a stonemason, a shoemaker, a microbus driver, a glass factory worker, a mechanic, a house-wife, café workers, chefs, taxi drivers, a worker in the customs administration, an army conscript, a metal worker and a seller of *galabiyyas*. The occupations of those who fell in Alexandria included a railworker, an assistant chef, a worker in a glass shop, a carpenter, a printworker, a former barber, a pizza chef, an air conditioner repairman, a furniture-maker and an army conscript.

In Cairo, the greatest concentrations of dead and injured were among residents of northern and southern suburbs. The crowded working-class district of Zawiya al-Hamra in the north of the city counted 5 dead and 63 injured, for example. Among the southern suburbs housing workers, artisans and the lower middle class, Dar al-Salam lost 8 killed and counted 28 injured, while from neigh-bouring Basatin there were 4 dead and 10 injured. Even when the dead and injured came from more middle-class or wealthy areas, they were still largely composed of white- and blue-collar workers.

Hada'iq al-Qubba, a formerly elegant northern suburb, counted 16 dead and 12 injured, who included a chef, a bus driver, a worker in an educational centre who had a second job working in a café in the afternoon, a carpenter, a taxi driver and a plasterer.

The 8 dead and 12 injured from Ma'adi, a southern suburb which includes some very wealthy areas, were drawn from a similar mix of professions, including a café worker, an electrician, a shop assistant, a car mechanic, an English teacher, a carpenter and a laundryman. When Abd-al-Rahman and his friends returned to Ma'adi they found the area in shock. The security forces had opened fire in the middle of Ahmad Zaki street, a busy route which bisects Basatin and Dar al-Salam. An 11-year-old girl was reported to be among the dead, killed on her balcony after the police opened fire, while friends and neighbours who rushed to help the wounded had also been cut down.[7]

The presence of workers and wider layers of the urban poor and lower middle class as insurgent citizens in the streets had dramatically shifted the balance of forces in the battle between the people and the regime. But now workers in the public sector heard a different appeal: the Egyptian Trade Union Federation called for protests in support of the regime at the same time as the security forces and ruling party officials gathered thugs to attack the protesters camping in Tahrir Square with rocks, live ammunition and Molotov cocktails in a confrontation later named 'the Battle of the Camel'. The plan was simple: a counter-revolutionary mobilisation would smash resistance in the Square while Megawer and his officials would provide cheering crowds of loyal workers to show that 'the people' backed Mubarak, just as they had done at election time for the past three decades. Both tactics failed. Tahrir Square's defenders – a medley of opposition activists from the youth of the Muslim Brotherhood, Liberals, Nasserists and Revolutionary Socialists, and tens of thousands who had joined them in the wake of the 'Day of Rage' – held the front line at hastily assembled barricades.[8] The ETUF bureaucrats, for their part, found that workers would not answer their call. In its darkest hour, the Mubarak regime turned back to the last remaining mechanisms for 'mass mobilisation' that Nasser had created, and found that the combination of neoliberal reform from above and workers' rebellion from below had paralysed them.

However, it was not until strike action changed the dynamic of the uprising during the last week before Mubarak's fall that the popular revolution became unstoppable. The curfew and closure of public enterprises and many other workplaces had made strikes almost impossible. But the regime's response to defeat at the 'Battle of the Camel' was to attempt to co-opt representatives of the opposition (including notably the Muslim Brotherhood) with a series of consultative meetings, while trying to restore normality outside the boundaries of the Square. So the curfew eased and workplaces opened again, turning the initial murmur of workers' protests into a real storm.

The first strikes to be reported took place on 6 and 7 February. By the end of the week they had spread across the country, bringing out around 300,000 workers. It was a seismic shift in strike activity. According to figures compiled by the NGO Awlad al-Ard, there were forty-two workers' protests in January 2011, while considerably more than that took place between 7 and 11 February alone. In the days immediately following Mubarak's fall there were between forty and sixty strikes per day, and overall February 2011 saw almost as many episodes of strike action as the entire previous year.[9]

The areas where the workers' movement had been strongest in the pre-revolutionary period led the way, such as Suez, Mahalla, Alexandria and Cairo. Suez fertilizer and steel workers went on strike and occupied their workplaces in support of the revolution. More than a dozen companies in the city joined the strike wave, including four subsidiary companies working on the Suez Canal and Lafarge Cement. Municipal cleaners in Giza began a sit-in strike and cut off one of the main streets in the area, while workers at the privately owned Abu al-Siba'i Company for Spinning and Weaving in Mahalla walked out.[10]

The first wave of workers' protests was followed by another, stronger one. Telecom workers demonstrated in front of many telephone exchanges in Cairo and the provinces. Workers in the railway workshops went on strike, while workers at the Public Transport Authority joined the battle, with employees at three garages going on strike, followed by their colleagues in other garages. Workers' protests erupted in the petroleum sector and in the textile plants in Helwan and Kafr al-Dawwar. Nor was the health sector excluded, with sit-ins taking place in hospitals in Assyut, Kafr al-Zayyat, Qasr al-Aini, the Heart Institute and elsewhere. The military-run factories of Helwan, where workers faced courts martial for insubordination, were in revolt, with nine out on strike by the end of the week. The uprising reached into the state-run media: printers and administrators at *Rose el-Youssef* magazine seized control of the building, and refused to let the editor in chief and the president of the board of directors, both of whom were close to Mubarak, enter. The ETUF-affiliated Workers' University was in a state of ferment as tutors and administrators organised a sit-in and locked up the University's president, who was vice president of the ETUF and a senior member of the NDP.

These represent only a small sample of the workers' protests and strikes during the week before Mubarak's downfall. Not all of them raised support for the revolution directly, although it could be argued that all expressed tacit backing for the protests against Mubarak, by raising their demands in the face of a huge propaganda campaign by the regime for calm and stability. Some strikes did, moreover, raise slogans in support of the popular revolution, as workers took up revolutionary chants against the regime in their own strikes and sit-ins.

The social and the political during 'the 18 Days'

The strikes played a number of critical roles in the downfall of Mubarak. First, they dispersed the revolution back outwards from the major public squares into new spaces across the cities. The insurrection had not begun in Tahrir; it was born in the suburbs and was carried inwards, towards the heart of the cities on the 'Day of Rage', with the marches which fought through ranks of police to seize the major public squares. Strikes created a new urban geography of revolution. In the case of Helwan, a major centre of heavy industry south of Cairo, we have already seen how the events of the 'Day of Rage' unfolded with spontaneous protests in the city centre, followed by an epic march on Tahrir. The strikes which erupted after 6 February brought back revolution to Helwan in a different form as it entered the military factories, the silk mills and other workplaces.

The revolution's escape from Tahrir and the other public squares punctured the isolation which the regime hoped to impose on the protesters, having failed in its first attempts to crush them by force. The growing wave of strikes ruptured the facade the regime hoped to construct around the protests by carrying what Rosa Luxemburg called 'the sultry air of revolution' into the workplaces.

This process did not simply disperse the revolution into new spaces, it opened an entirely new front in the battle. Crucially, strikes carried the revolution into the body of the state itself. Strikes by public transport workers, doctors in government hospitals, refuse workers, postal workers, and workers in state-owned enterprises had a dual effect: according to the function of the workers involved they directly paralysed parts of the machinery of government, industry and services. Some of these were in sectors of the economy of critical importance to the regime: one of the earliest strikes, reported on 8 February, was by 6,000 workers servicing the Suez Canal. However, as the immediate target of the strikes was often the NDP's functionaries, the corrupt managers and petty tyrants who could be found in the director's office of almost all public institutions and many private ones, they also paralysed the ruling party, preventing it from deploying its still considerable resources and organisation.

These first two points are valid regardless of whether the strikers raised 'political' demands specifically in solidarity with Tahrir. However, the small numbers of strikes which directly proclaimed their support for the revolution reinforced and reinvigorated the protestors, and broke down the regime's claim that they were isolated. The strike by the Public Transport Authority workers was particularly important in this respect because Public Transport activists went to Tahrir and distributed a statement announcing their decision to strike on 9 February.

It is important to understand the character of the strike wave, and the relationship between spontaneity and organisation within it. It was not a 'general strike' organised by revolutionary activists and independent trade unionists, or on their behalf, even if some of them called and agitated for it. Yet, in its timing, scale and intensity, it had many of the same effects that such a general strike would have had. It reflected both the high level of pre-revolutionary strike organisation and the small scale of pre-revolutionary independent union organisation.

The strike wave was 'spontaneous' in the sense that it was mostly organic strike organisation within the workplace. On one level it was an instinctive reaction by hundreds of thousands of workers to the opening of an opportunity to settle accounts with their bosses and win concessions in the workplace as a result of the crisis of the regime. However, as discussed earlier, for residents of many working-class and poor neighbourhoods, the revolution had started on their doorsteps in bloody battles fought with the police between 25 and 28 January. In other words, strike action was not just an opportunistic response to a crisis created by others, but a replaying of the drama of the revolution within the workplace. This particular dynamic became even more apparent after 12 February, but even in the days before Mubarak fell some strikes were already raising demands for the removal of corrupt managers and not merely improved pay or working conditions, as the uprising at the Workers' University illustrates.

Nevertheless, the organised agitation for strikes by activists from the revolutionary left and the independent unions who were in Tahrir and the other public squares had a significant impact. The newly founded independent union federation, which put out a call for a general strike, was a small, but visible, presence in Tahrir. Activists from the revolutionary left and the independent unions directly contacted workers' leaders in a number of key workplaces to argue that they should mobilise before the first strikes were reported. These organised interventions were important in shaping the political character of some of the strikes such as that by the Public Transport Authority workers.

The Egyptian revolution between Mubarak and Morsi

The two and a half years between the fall of Mubarak in February 2011 and the fall of Mohamed Morsi in July 2013 can be divided into two phases, marked by Morsi's assumption of power in June 2012. Morsi's taking power marked an alteration in the terms of the tactical alliance between the leaders of the core institutions of the old regime, with the Armed Forces at their head, and the reformist organisation with the greatest popular base, the Muslim Brotherhood. During the first phase, the military ruled directly through the Supreme Council of the Armed Forces, but permitted the expansion of Islamist influence at the ballot box and in the legislative arena, with the convention of a parliament dominated by the Muslim Brotherhood's Freedom and Justice Party and the

Salafist Nour Party in January 2012. In some ways, this division of labour represented simply an extension of the experience of the 2005 parliamentary elections. Thanks to the force of the January 2011 uprising the Brotherhood had elbowed its way into discussions about a new political settlement at an elite level, but this was conditional on the containment of the revolution within the doors of parliament, thus protecting the core institutions of the regime from further popular assaults.

This arrangement was destabilised from two directions. From one side, by spring 2012 there was growing confidence among some in the counter-revolutionary camp that an open restoration of the old regime was possible under the presidency of Ahmed Shafiq, Mubarak's last prime minister. From the other, the continuing vitality of street protests and strikes posed a serious challenge to reformists and counter-revolutionaries alike, despite their lack of national leadership and the deepening disconnection between political and social protests. This is probably why within the army leadership the view prevailed in June 2012 that an immediate restoration of the old order was too dangerous to the long-term interests of the ruling class. Thus the terms of the compromise between the old regime and the Brotherhood were rewritten and the top rank of Mubarak's commanders replaced by their immediate subordinates by the newly elected civilian president. Abdel-Fattah al-Sisi, the new minister of defence, would overthrow Morsi by means of a military coup just under a year later on 3 July 2013.

The same two basic destabilising factors could be seen at work during Morsi's period in office. The continuing ferment in the workplaces and local neighbourhoods created a rising tide of social protests, fuelled in part by frustration at the Brotherhood's failure to meet the expectations of social and political change on which it had surged to electoral victory. Meanwhile, behind the scenes of power the key institutions of the old regime were regrouping their forces and exerting every possible effort to rebuild their political credibility. The disjuncture between the social and political dynamics of the revolutionary process became increasingly apparent during the last months of Morsi's presidency. For, despite the rising tide of social protests, the domination of the opposition to Morsi by Liberals and Nasserists determined to ally themselves with elements of the old regime created a political context far riper for political intervention by the military than had been the case in June 2012.

There were other important elements of continuity across both phases. The first, and most important, of these was the contradiction between the relative lack of change in the apparatus of the state after Mubarak's fall and the continuation of extremely high levels of social and political protest. The purge of supporters of the old regime from the state administration moved glacially slowly at the upper levels, even while state employees were taking matters into their own hands below, and mobilising hundreds of protests and strikes calling for the 'cleansing' of public institutions. At the same time, repeated street protests demanded justice for the dead and injured of the revolution through a purge of the Ministry of the Interior. As we discuss in more detail in Chapter 9, Morsi's period in office *was* marked by efforts by the Brotherhood to insert its own supporters into parts of the state apparatus. However, this change of personnel did not, we will argue, signal any real change in the form or content of state power. At the same time as attempting to promote Muslim Brotherhood cadres within state institutions, Morsi took concrete steps to ensure the continuation of the military's political and economic privileges, protected the police from reform, and even strove to maintain the old trade-union federation's domination of workplace organisation.

The second major element of continuity across the two phases was the alternating partnership between the core institutions of the old regime – with the leadership of the army forming the vanguard, but also including the Ministry of the Interior and elements of the judiciary and the state media – and the major Islamist and secular reformist currents. This was never a partnership of equals: the military always enjoyed a decisive advantage in terms of its resources, organisation and, above all, monopoly of legitimate armed force. It was driven by the recognition on the part of the old regime that without a buffer which could absorb the anger and energy of the mass protests from below, the revolution might spill over into a process threatening the integrity of the state itself. As we explore in detail in Chapter 9, the strikes demanding the 'cleansing' of the state apparatus, as they raised the prospect of new forms of democratic control over the existing state institutions from below, were particularly threatening to the interests of the old regime, precisely because they fused both political and social demands with workers' social power. The military oscillated between flirtation with the major Islamist parties (led by the Muslim Brotherhood) and their secular rivals (principally liberal forces, such as Mohamed ElBaradei's Constitution Party, and the Nasserists, represented by Hamdeen Sabahi and the Popular Current). Yet it never sought more than a temporary tactical marriage of convenience with either of the reformist currents. From the moment that the minister of defence, Field Marshal Mohamed Tantawi signed off the order deposing Mubarak, the strategic aim of Egypt's military leadership has remained the same: the restoration of the old order and bloody revenge for its humiliation at the hands of the people.

An important difference between the crises of June 2012 and June 2013 lies, however, in al-Sisi's success in enabling the emergence of a counter-movement against the Brotherhood which appeared to re-create the loose, popular revolutionary coalition of 2011. The fact that the vast majority of the publicly recognised leaders of this movement acquiesced not only in Morsi's removal but also in al-Sisi's rapid moves towards consolidating his own power while unleashing the security state against his opponents demonstrates that such similarities were only skin-deep. By contrast, in June 2012 when Tantawi moved to dissolve the Islamist-dominated parliament in a series of moves which seemed to threaten an attempt to restore the old regime by force, no crowds filled the streets cheering for the military police or urging the army to act against the Brotherhood.

Some further comments are necessary here. The mutual relationships between counter-revolutionaries, reformists and the popular revolutionary movement cannot be understood from a static perspective. Their organisational and ideological coherence changed in absolute terms and in relation to each other during the period of our analysis. In July 2013 Abdel-Fattah al-Sisi was not in the same position as his predecessor Mohamed Tantawi had been in February 2011. Al-Sisi enjoyed widespread confidence in his political leadership among the Armed Forces, in contrast to Tantawi, who was acting, at least in part, to stave off the looming threat of a fracture between the lower and upper ranks of the officer corps. Moreover, the Ministry of the Interior in July 2013 was not reeling from defeat at the hands of the people, as it was in February 2011, but had seen much of its institutional capacity for repression restored over the preceding two and half years. Likewise, the relative strength of the Islamist and secular reformist currents altered as the secular reformists benefited from growing disillusionment with the Islamist project, once it had been tested by a spell in power, as we explore in more detail in Chapter 8.

Strikes undermine the military-Islamist consensus

We noted above how the 'political settlement' between the military leadership and their principal reformist opponents in the wake of Mubarak's fall represented an attempt to contain the revolution by expanding the Islamists' access to the parliamentary arena while preserving the core of the regime intact. The dynamics of strike action between February and October 2011 played a crucial role in undermining this consensus between the military and the Islamist parties. The scale of the strike wave frustrated all efforts to sap workers' energies and divert their hopes for change into the relatively safer channels of electoral politics. Workers in large numbers of industries were often relatively successful in using direct action to improve wages, rein in abusive managers and secure recognition for their elected workplace representatives during the first year after Mubarak's fall. Yet the expectations raised in the course of the revolution were much higher than these modest gains, as can be seen from the large numbers of strikes where the demands pointed towards a desire for a genuine shift away from the neoliberal policies of the previous decade. Demands for an end to casual labour, for the redistribution of wealth through the application of a minimum and maximum wage, for the return of privatised companies to the state, for massive investment in health and education, and, most worrying of all, for the complete 'cleansing' (*tathir*) of the state apparatus, were profoundly threatening to both the generals and the Brotherhood.

Between February and early March 2011 the revolution entered the workplaces on a mass scale. Although a whole range of demands were raised during this period, the motive force behind many of the strikes was the demand for *tathir* – in other words the removal of managers and foremen associated with the ruling party. In Mansoura, for example, on 13 February, the first working day after Mubarak's removal on the 11th, one newspaper report alone details strikes and protests demanding the removal of senior officials by employees in two of the city's local authorities, the First Criminal Court, the Mansoura International Hospital, the Mansoura General Hospital, and a demonstration by workers in the province's central administration demanding the sacking of the provincial governor for corruption.[11] A wave of struggles also engulfed the university campuses, with students and staff seizing control of the offices of the hated secret police and organising massive protests against the heads of universities appointed by Mubarak.[12] Government ministries, hospitals, the postal service, and the big public-sector workplaces such as the massive spinning and weaving plant in Al-Mahalla al-Kubra went through similar protests and strikes.[13] The NGO Awlad al-Ard recorded just under 500 separate episodes of strike action or other forms of collective protest by workers during February 2011.[14]

From March the number of workers' strikes and protests dropped in comparison to the explosion of February, and steadied at roughly 65,000 participants per month in all forms of workers' protests (see Table 6.1 for more detail). This period coincided with a rapid expansion of organisation and the rapid spread of independent unions, as we discuss further in Chapter 7. September's strike wave marked a definite shift upwards in terms of independent organisation and consciousness among Egyptian workers. Up to 500,000 workers participated in strikes and protests that month alone, a figure significantly higher than the entire previous six months. The significance of September's strikes lay in the qualitative shift towards coordinated national and sector-wide action, most importantly in the national teachers' strike. These were mass strikes articulating generalised social demands with a greater degree of common purpose than had been evident in previous months. The teachers' strike, which mobilised hundreds of thousands of strikers, demanded the resignation of the minister of education, a Mubarak appointee, and other strikes, such as the Cairo Public Transport Authority workers' strike, began to raise similar demands.[15]

Compared to the pre-revolutionary strike wave, September 2011 also marks a dramatic shift, as Table 6.1 shows.[16] Around the same number of workers took part in collective action that

TABLE 6.1 The growing wave of collective action in 2011

	Estimated number of workers involved
March	82,000
April	65,000
May	95,000
June	57,000
July	33,000
August	65,000
September	up to 500,000

SOURCE Estimates calculated by the authors from Awlad al-Ard monthly reports on workers' collective action, March–September 2011, and other press reports on strike action.

month as did during the whole of 2008.[17] Coordination of strikes and protests also sharply increased in September compared not only to previous months, but also to the pre-revolutionary strike wave. The overall number of episodes was significantly fewer, but the increased numbers participating points to the consolidation of the strike wave into fewer, better coordinated disputes.

A week after the fall of Mubarak, around forty leading worker activists from twenty-six different workplaces met at the Centre for Socialist Studies in Giza and agreed a joint statement, which was later published under the title 'Demands of the Workers in the Revolution'. The programme of radical reforms outlined in the document included raising the minimum wage and imposing a maximum wage of no more than fifteen times the minimum; freedom to organise trade unions, protests and strike; the complete abolition of casual contracts; renationalisation of all privatised enterprises; the removal of corrupt managers; improvement of health care; and the dissolution of the Mubarak-era trade-union federation.[18] An analysis of the demands raised in over 700 separate episodes of workers' collective action between March and

TABLE 6.2 Analysis of patterns of workers' demands,
March–September 2011

	Mar	Apr	May	Jun	Jul	Aug	Sept
Contracts	39	43	38	40	37	28	38
Working conditions	16	22	29	10	15	16	28
Tathir	29	13	15	6	11	23	21
Wages	48	37	47	37	28	49	62
Management and ownership	19	20	13	8	17	16	9
Trade union organisation	10	4	6	4	4	3	2
Political demands	<1	2	2	3	1	1	5
Solidarity	<1	1	0	0	0	2	3
Other	6	7	15	13	5	8	19
Total no. of protests	123	90	103	95	75	89	58

SOURCE Based on Awlad al-Ard monthly reports on workers' collective action, March–September 2011. Figures show % of episodes of collective action in which each demand was raised.

September 2011 shows how the activists' programme accurately captured the mood in thousands of workplaces.

The demands raised by striking workers in the wake of Mubarak's fall had many elements of continuity with the demands of strikes during the pre-revolutionary era. As Table 6.2 shows, the largest category of demands concerned wages, followed by permanent contracts. Poor working conditions and bullying management were also issues which drove many workers' protests. However, the demand to cleanse workplaces of corruption and the remnants of the Mubarak regime was also raised in a significant proportion of strikes. This was a break with the experience of the pre-revolutionary period: while battles over allegations of corruption and mismanagement had played a role in many significant disputes, for example at Tanta Flax, Misr Spinning

TABLE 6.3 The rise in demands for *tathir*, March–September 2011

	Mar	Apr	May	Jun	Jul	Aug	Sept	Total
Total no. of protests	123	90	103	95	75	89	58	633
Protests demanding *tathir*	36	12	15	6	9	21	12	111
Estimated no. of workers demanding *tathir* (1,000s)	15.8	9.4	53.5	0.7	1.3	17.7	39.6	493.6

SOURCE Based on Awlad al-Ard monthly reports on workers' collective action, March–September 2011.

in Mahalla, and Indorama in Shibin al-Kom, the call to remove managers because they were associated with the old ruling party was, evidently, a new and revolutionary demand, which, as we saw above, was already being raised in some workplaces in early February 2011, before the fall of Mubarak.

Workers' demands in the aggregate did not remain static, but evolved in response to changing circumstances. The strikes of September 2011, for example, showed a marked shift in the articulation of workers' demands. Rather than being raised in countless individual workplaces, the larger strikes, and in particular the teachers' strike, brought together the same key elements, but this time reinforced them with the force of half a million organised workers. Demands raised by striking teachers began with the sacking of the Mubarak-appointed minister of education, but also included investment in public education, a minimum wage for teachers of LE1,200 per month, the building of new schools, and the extension of permanent contracts for fixed-term and supply teachers.[19] Public transport workers demanded wage rises, an end to corruption in the Public Transport Authority and investment in the ageing bus fleet. Textile workers in the giant Misr Spinning plant in Al-Mahalla al-Kubra threatened to strike in early September and forced the government to open negotiations. These ended with an agreement by the government to improve pay and conditions across the textile sector, and to direct investment in the public-sector textile mills.[20]

The strike wave of September 2011 was also notable for the return of mass strikes for *tathir*. As Table 6.3 demonstrates, the numbers involved in strikes demanding the cleansing of state institutions and workplaces was greater in this month by a long way than in any month since February 2011.

The major problem facing worker activists was that while specific, localised demands for improved pay and conditions were often met, they made little progress in forcing either the state or employers to address the general demands indicated above. In fact, the pattern of strike demands in the wake of Mubarak's fall reflects the lack of progress towards meeting any of the main demands that workers had raised over long years of protests: permanent contracts and job security, the right to organise unions independent of the state, and a fair minimum wage sufficient for a decent life. After the revolution, in terms of job security, for example, far from making progress, the position of most workers deteriorated. The proportion of workers with permanent contracts decreased by 3.5 per cent in the private sector within enterprises between 2010 and 2011, while the proportion of private-sector workers outside enterprises with permanent contracts decreased by 3.8 per cent. The proportion of government employees with permanent contracts did increase marginally – by 0.5 per cent – between 2010 and 2011, but this has to be set against an overall expansion in the government workforce by 2.3 per cent during the same period. Strikes did bring some results in terms of wages. The average weekly wage for workers in the private sector rose from LE299 in 2010 to LE397 in 2011, while the average weekly wage for workers in the public sector and the public business sector rose from 542 to 657 in the same period.[21] Rising living costs ate up much of these increases, however.

As discussed in Chapter 3, the adoption of the demand for a rise in the minimum wage to LE1,200 per month by sections of the workers' movement in 2008 was a turning point in the evolution of workers' political consciousness, as it marked the shift from purely localised demands to more general issues concerning the working class as a whole. The demand for a minimum wage was linked to the call for a maximum wage in order to reduce massive income inequality, and to provide adequate resources to implement the minimum wage. After the fall of Mubarak the minimum wage of workers employed by the state rose to LE700 per month. However, the new level of minimum wage was implemented in relation to total pay (including bonuses), rather the much lower rate of basic pay. Despite the issuing of Decree 242 of 2011 on maximum income, linking it to the minimum wage, the implementation regulations for the law were not issued until 2012, by Kamal al-Ganzouri's government, and these had still not been implemented by mid-2013. It is noteworthy that the figure agreed by the government was much less than that campaigned for by workers. Its application was limited to raising variable pay, and it only applied to state employees, thereby excluding around three-quarters of wage earners. Even the implementation of the original demand of LE1,200, given the level of inflation since 2008, would have constituted a retreat from the 2008 demands.

The battle for the streets

The ebbs and flows of workers' action and the evolution of their demands cannot be understood in isolation from the peaks and troughs of popular street mobilisations. As indicated above, the relationship between the two strands of collective action from below was complex and during the first period of military rule they tended to interlace, rather than merge. After the fall of Mubarak, the February 2011 peak of workers' action came at a time when the streets were empty, and calls for protest did not mobilise significant numbers again until April and May. More than in the workplaces, the question of *tathir*, and specifically the issue of cleansing the Ministry of the Interior in order to obtain justice for the revolution's dead, was the dominant issue. It was under this slogan that tens of thousands rallied in Tahrir Square on 8 April, although SCAF was able to enforce the curfew, sweeping away a relatively small sit-in, which was significant because it included a number of junior army officers in uniform. It was not until 27 May, however, that the street mobilisations began to make a national impact, with protests reported across Egypt that day. An attack on families of the dead during an event at the Balloon Theatre in late June sparked escalating clashes between protesters and the police, paving the way for the first wave of sit-ins on a scale comparable with the mobilisations of the 18 Days. These began with a month-long sit-in in Tahrir Square on 1 July. The July protests by and large coincided with a relative lull in workers' protests, but stimulated the revival and transformation of strikes on an even bigger scale in September and early October 2011, as discussed above.[22]

The combined effect of these interlaced social and political protests can be seen at work in the crisis of November 2011, which many revolutionary activists initially hoped would rerun the events of the January uprising but this time with SCAF as the target. In fact the outcome of the street mobilisations of November was quite different: the military managed to ride out the crisis through a combination of concessions on the issue that had provided the trigger for the protests. This was the so-called 'Selmi Document', a proposal from SCAF which gave the military leadership 'supra-constitutional powers' to intervene in drafting the new constitution. This was strongly opposed by the Muslim Brotherhood.[23] Another factor was missing from the ingredients of the November 2011 crisis: there was no repeat of the strike wave which had played such a crucial role in Mubarak's downfall. Although activists from the independent unions were involved in the protests throughout, and attempted to mobilise workers as an organised presence in Tahrir, their numbers were too small either to make an impact on the overall character of the protests or to provide a pole of attraction strong enough to win political arguments at a workplace level in favour of strike action.

The failure of the call by revolutionary activists for a general strike on 11 February 2012, a year after Mubarak's fall, underscored the difficulties in achieving genuine fusion between social and political struggles. In the wake of mass street mobilisations on the anniversary of 25 January, a call by student activists for a national student strike on 11 February was enthusiastically adopted by wider sections of the revolutionary movement and extended to a demand for a general strike against SCAF. It was endorsed by the leadership of the two major federations of independent trade unions, but when it came to winning arguments at the factory gates the combination of counter-propaganda from the authorities and a determined mobilisation against the strike call by Islamist activists on the ground tipped the balance against the revolutionaries.[24]

The outcome of the crisis of November 2011 suggested that an unstable equilibrium had been achieved. The popular movement from below (of which continuing strikes and protests by workers was one of the strongest components) was too powerful to be crushed by force and could not be appeased without either more change in the state and deeper social reform than SCAF was prepared to concede. But this 'movement' lacked organisation and coherence, and in particular the organised forces seeking to unite the social and political struggles were very small. The lack of roots of any political forces in the working class (except the Brotherhood, which was implacably hostile to strikes, and which, although it had large numbers of working-class members and supporters, had only a very small presence in the emerging workers' movement) entrenched the gap between social and political movements. In these circumstances, the unevenness of the revolutionary process risked deepening the gulf between the vanguard and the sections of society just beginning to mobilise, as could be seen in the widespread calls for election boycotts among some groups of revolutionary activists.

The instability of this equilibrium was underlined by the resurgence of confidence on the part of the counter-revolutionary forces. The first major test of the street movement's resilience came on 9 October 2011 outside the State TV building in Maspero, when a protest by Coptic Christians was attacked by the Armed Forces, outside the television buildings, leading to the deaths of at least twenty-five demonstrators.[25] The deaths of seventy-four football fans at the end of a match between Al-Ahly and Port Sa'id at the beginning of February 2012 were also regarded by many in the revolutionary movement as a massacre orchestrated by the military, in revenge for the prominent role played by the Ahly Ultras movement in street protests since January 2011. During April and May 2012, the remnants of the old ruling party began to coalesce around the electoral campaign for Ahmad Shafiq, Mubarak's last prime minister and the counter-revolution's choice for president. Despite its public protestations that the revolution had found its final home in parliament, the Muslim Brotherhood's leadership was gripped with panic, as they saw cracks appearing in the marriage of convenience they had negotiated with the military. Perhaps fearing that their domination of parliament would not be enough to counterbalance the growing confidence of the old regime, they decided – contrary to previous promises – to field a candidate for president in order to give them more leverage within the institutions of the state.

A surge of social protest
against the Brotherhood in power

We will return to the specific sequence of events between June and August 2012 which marked the moment of transition between the first two phases of the revolution in more detail in Chapter 8. Here we are concerned largely with mapping the major dynamics of the revolutionary process, particularly in relation to the relationship between the revolution's social and political aspects. The first important point to emphasize here is that, far from improving, even the official statistics indicate a decline in key indicators of many workers' living standards during 2012–13. Overall unemployment rose from 12 per cent in the last quarter of 2011 to 13.2 per cent in the first quarter of 2013.[26]

The deterioration in workers' conditions was not limited to rising unemployment: wages were also reflective of the same trend. The *Annual Bulletin on Employment, Wages and Hours of Work* for the year 2012 indicates an increase in the average worker's wage in the public sector of LE657 per week in 2011 to LE845 per week in 2012 but records the wages of workers in the private sector as falling from LE397 in 2011 to LE395 in 2012. As previously explained, private-sector workers represent the bulk of wage earners. Rapid price rises accompanied workers' deteriorating wage packets as the *Monthly Bulletin of Indices of Consumer Prices* for the month of April 2013 indicates. The overall accumulated inflation on consumer prices since January 2010 stood at 36 per cent. Inflation in food and drink prices underwent an even steeper rise of 53 per cent rise for the same period. This increased already severe pressures on living standards for millions of working-class families, who spent 30 per cent of their total annual expenditure on food and drink, according to data from 2010/11 issued by the Central Agency for Public Mobilization and Statistics.[27] Nor did changes in taxation policies provide any relief for workers and the poor. The limit for tax exemption was revised upwards from LE9,000 to LE12,000 per year in the state budget for 2013–14, but the new figure had been set in 2011 and failed to take into account rising inflation and stagnant or declining wages. At the same time the budget aimed to increase the proceeds of sales taxes to LE15 billion.

As we discuss in more detail in Chapter 7, activists in the workers' movement, particularly the independent trade unions, had further specific reasons for feeling anger towards the Muslim Brotherhood-led government, including dozens of victimisations of trade-union activists followed by an escalation in the level of repression, such as the use of police dogs to attack a peaceful sit-in by Portland Cement workers in Alexandria in April 2013, leading to the injury of a number of workers. Moreover, there was also procrastination over the issuing of the trade-union freedoms law. These conditions stood in sharp contrast to the pledges made by Morsi during his presidential election campaign. We return to the Brotherhood's failure to live up to workers' expectations of social reform, or at least to deliver the stabilisation of their declining living standards, in Chapter 8.

The combination of declining living standards, unmet promises and raised expectations of change in 2012–13 took place in extraordinary circumstances. As we have discussed in previous chapters, Egyptians had already, even before the eruption of revolution in 2011, lived through the biggest upsurge of workers' protest in their history. This workers' movement has been characterised by the length of its duration, from December 2006 to 2013; by its geographical and sectoral distribution, which covered all sectors of wage workers, from government and public-sector workers to the public business sector, and the private sector, and

TABLE 6.4 Analysis of protests, February–May 2013

	Feb	Mar	Apr	May
Workers' protests	359	334	461	450
Economic and social protests	113	350	312	369
Total no. of protests	864	1,345	1,462	1,300

SOURCE Adil, February–May 2013.

even spreading to unorganised/informal sector workers. Over this period, the different means of protest, such as strikes, sit-ins, demonstrations and rallies, were transformed into an integral part of working-class culture. And it was to these methods that workers turned in response to either partial success or partial failure.

A report by the Egyptian Center for Economic and Social Rights documenting labour and social protests in Egypt in 2012 reveals a marked increase in the rates of social protest, especially labour protests. The report counts 3,817 social protests in 2012, a figure greater than the 3,313 social protests in Egypt reported by ECESR during the period from 2000 to 2010. According to the ECESR report, there were 1,969 protests by workers during 2012, accounting for more than half of all social protests. Other reports suggest that the first half of 2013 saw a further marked rise in the frequency of social protests. According to a report by the Democracy Index issued by the Centre for International Development in June 2013, 5,544 protests took place in the period from January to May 2013. Not all of these were labour protests but, according to the monthly reports to the same source, these occupied a leading place in the total number of social protests. As illustrated in Table 6.4, January 2013's report from the IDC gives a total of 864 protests. According to the IDC's data, 54 per cent of these were protests raising economic and social demands, but not organised by workers, whereas a further 33 per cent were directly workers' protests. This rising tide of social anger found little echo in the mainstream media, however, which focused on directly political protests and the conflict between the Muslim Brotherhood-led government and its opponents.

Taking these figures at face value is problematic for a number of reasons. There is no accurate inventory of social protests, many of which are not organised or announced in advance. The principal source of the data analysed by the IDC and ECESR is media reports on protests, and there are many reasons why these sources may fail to report some protests, and report inaccurately on others. The numbers of participants are also very difficult to ascertain, and this is evidently a critical question when attempting to assess the importance of particular strikes or protests. As we saw in relation to the analysis of strike data from 2011, there can be enormous leaps in overall numbers of participants while the incidence of strike action falls, as was the case in September 2011. Furthermore, these figures give no sense of the duration of strike action, which is an important indicator of the evolution of the labour movement as it reflects its organizational capacity, its awareness and the cohesion of its leadership.

Nevertheless, it is reasonable to conclude that the overall trends indicated by these figures are correct, and that the frequency of social protest dramatically rose during Morsi's presidency. As we explore in more detail in subsequent chapters, the further upsurge in social protest during the second and third years of the revolution was a reflection of workers' sense of betrayal as the demands that they had raised over the preceding years remained unmet, despite the fall of Mubarak and the ascension to power of the chief reformist party opposing him. As we have argued above, the Egyptian working class played a key role in preparing the ground for the January revolution. It was an active partner in the revolution, playing an important role in tipping the balance of forces against Mubarak, leading to his removal from power.

Yet workers saw no fundamental or even partial shift in social and economic policies thereafter, and living conditions steadily worsened as a result of the growing economic crisis.

On the surface, the wave of strikes and social protests against Morsi that erupted thus appeared to be deepening the revolutionary process. However, the very different outcome to the street mobilisations against the Brotherhood poses the question, was at least some of the ferment of social protest also in part a response to convulsions at the top of the state, as workers looked for opportunities to impose their demands on a weakening government? Moreover, a fatal obstacle to the realisation of the revolutionary potential of the social struggle lay in the absence of organisations capable of translating the anger of the poor into a programme of political demands independent of those raised by secular reformists allied with the military. As we explore in the next chapter, the massive growth of workers' self-organisation in the wake of Mubarak's fall did not overcome this obstacle.

CHAPTER 7

Workers' organisations since the revolution

The rich experience of workers' self-organisation in Egypt since the revolution of 2011 needs to be viewed from multiple perspectives in order to analyse the most important patterns of development. The first of these is the view 'from below', by which we mean an attempt to understand the impact of the revolution on workers' organisation in the workplace or institution. We discussed in the previous chapter how the grievances of workers within their workplaces have remained powerful engines of strike action in the period since the revolution. Below we explore the organisational consequences of this tendency. This does not mean, however, that the perspective 'from below' remains narrowly focused on forms of organisation which have emerged within individual workplaces. On the contrary, the revolution heralded a period of intense growth outwards and upwards from workplace-based organisations.

The second perspective views the organisations of the workers' movement 'from above' – that is to say, from the viewpoint of the state and of the political parties which gained a foothold there after the revolution. As we argue in detail below, the actions of state officials, the judiciary and politicians played important roles in shaping the new wave of workers' organisations. Their ability to determine the forms and capacities of workers' organisations was badly shaken in the early days of the revolution, but they slowly regained confidence over the subsequent two years. This had not, as the second anniversary of the revolution approached, resulted in attempts to dissolve or repress the independent unions, but employers and the state appeared to be acting in concert to restrict their role. Moreover, state officials and leading figures in the Muslim Brotherhood collaborated in the revival of the Egyptian Trade Union Federation, thus ensuring the survival of a powerful competitor.

The emergence and consolidation of a small layer of union and federation officials in the independent unions who have begun to take on many of the classic attributes of a trade-union bureaucracy is a reminder, however, that a simplistic combination of 'below' and 'above' perspectives is inadequate. Unlike ETUF officials, the new bureaucracy was not an extension of the state bureaucracy, but was composed largely of workplace activists whose role in leading strikes and forming independent unions led them to create new trade-union structures at regional, sectoral and national levels. Partially disconnected from their own workplaces and daily pressure from their own union members, and thrown into more or less regular contact with state officials, politicians, the media and international trade-union officials, they were subject to intense pressure to act as mediators between workers, employers and the state.

The most important perspective from which to view the development of workers' organisations since 2011 is to locate them *within* the revolutionary process. As we discussed in the previous chapter, this process was itself being shaped *through*, although not directed *by*, workers' collective action on an immense scale. Nor were the ebbs and flows of battles between labour, capital and the state the only expression of this process. The changing balance of forces in the struggle between the emerging revolutionary movement, the remnants of the old regime inside and outside the state, and Islamist and secular reformists altered the environment within which workers' organisations developed. While it is never enough to 'read' the potential of any specific organisation from its structures or form alone, this is especially true during moments of revolutionary crisis. However, structures and forms of organisation do, even in circumstances of enormously heightened class struggle, make particular patterns of events more or less likely. They also test people's capacities – both individually and collectively – in different dimensions.

In this chapter we explore workers' organisation through three different lenses. First, we examine strike organisation, looking at the rank-and-file organisation of the Cairo Public Transport Authority workers' strikes of 2011 and 2012, the national teachers' strike of 2011, and the 2011 and 2012 national doctors' strikes. Strike organisation, as all of these examples illustrate, has to be considered separately from the question of independent union organisation. Strike organisation in the first two of these cases was broader than the membership of the independent unions, or, in the case of the doctors' strikes, operated partially independently of and partially within the official structures of the union. Our second lens will view the huge expansion in the independent unions since 2011, reviewing the challenges of consolidation and strategy and the problem of the emergence of competing new union bureaucracies. Third, we analyse the achievements and limitations of experiments in workers' control within the workplace. We also analyse the impact on workers' organisations of the revival of the Egyptian Trade Union Federation under the guidance of the Muslim Brotherhood and the governments of the period of military rule.

Despite enormous gains in terms of organisation, the workers' movement has faced a number of serious challenges. While many within the leadership of the independent unions would agree that there is enormous unevenness within the workers' movement, we will argue here that the problems are not only organisational but also political. The independent unions, in particular, and the workers' movement more generally, have not been able deploy their potential collective power to full effect on either the industrial or the political level. While strikes have often won economic gains within individual workplaces, the workers' movement has been much less successful in imposing any of its general demands on the state. As discussed in the previous chapter, the rise in the national minimum wage which was finally agreed was set at a much lower level than the LE1,200 demanded by activists in 2008. There has also been little progress since the first weeks of the revolution in winning battles for *tathir* within the workplace, although the demand to remove corrupt managers is constantly raised by striking workers. Nor has the workers' movement been able to assert itself on the national political arena, whether over the national minimum wage or in consolidating concessions made by the state towards the full legal recognition of the independent unions and the right to strike. In fact, the period of military rule and the first phase of civilian rule after the election of the Muslim Brotherhood's Mohamed Morsi as president in June 2012 have been marked by an escalating offensive by the state and the employers against both the independent unions and strike organisers.

In conclusion, we attempt to draw up a provisional balance sheet on the organisational experience of the workers' movement during the first two years of the revolution. The following chapter addresses the problem of the silence of workers' voices in the key arenas of mainstream politics, and the difficulties faced by the new organisations of the workers' movement in confronting this challenge.

Strike organisation since the revolution

In the previous chapter we discussed patterns of strike action
and the demands raised by striking workers during the first two
years of the revolution. The thousands of separate episodes of
collective action over this period compelled millions of workers
to organise themselves on a scale not seen for generations. We will
argue here that strike organisation was not simply interchangeable
with the emerging independent unions: it was usually broader
(involving large numbers of workers who had not formally signed
up to the new unions), deeper (claiming greater authority over the
workplace than was usually possible for any trade union outside
of the conditions of the strike) and more transient. As we saw in
Chapters 4 and 5, these features of strike organisation were present
in the pre-revolutionary period, and the Property Tax Collectors'
Union represented the first successful attempt to consolidate and
develop strike organisation into a permanent presence. The altered
conditions of the revolutionary period, such as the expansion of
the legal space for independent unions and workers' own increased
self-confidence, did not mean that strike organisation ceased to
have a life of its own. For two primary reasons, strike organisation
remained distinct from union organisation in a large number of
workplaces. First, where independent union members were a minority of the workforce, effective strike organising required its own
structures, which could draw in enough of their colleagues to win
the dispute. Second, the heightened activism of the strike naturally
mobilised larger numbers of workers than routine trade unionism.
However, as we discuss in detail below, it is utterly mistaken to
conclude that there is no relationship between strike organisation
and independent union organisation, or that the two could even be
easily separated during the period of our study. Rather, in many
of the most important strikes independent union organisation
played a catalysing role in several dimensions, particularly in the

transition from localised grievances to institution- or sector-wide action. The challenge for the leaders of the independent unions, as we explore below, lay in consolidating their organisation out of the strikes using the sediment left behind by successive waves of mobilisation from below, rather than letting it wash away again as the energy of the strike ebbed.

Workers in the Cairo Public Transport Authority played an important role in the uprising against Mubarak. Over the following two years they organised a series of highly politically charged strikes demanding improvements in their pay and conditions, investment in the bus fleet, and action against corruption in the management of the Authority. The Independent Union of PT Workers was founded in May 2011 and recruited around 16,000 workers out of a total workforce of 42,000 over the following months. The independent union leadership was the driving force behind the strikes in September 2011, March 2012 and September 2012. However, as Ahmad Mahmoud Ahmad, the president of the new union's strike committee, explained in an interview in April 2012, the fact that independent union members made up a minority of the workforce demanded forms of organisation which were open to any striking worker.

> We elect a Negotiation Committee of 10, a Strike Committee of 10 and a Security Committee of 10 because the police might set the buses on fire. The committees are not only union members. I will take any workers who are on strike. We say 'welcome' to them. I want them to feel part of the strike, to encourage them to be part of it. They are angry, they want us to win.[1]

For Ahmad, the sovereignty of the mass meetings at the garages from which the strike committees are elected and to which they are meant to report back is an absolute principle.

> In any strike, the negotiators must be an elected committee of strikers. If you have an appointed committee it won't get the workers their rights. If it is an appointed committee of salaried

officials its job will be to stop the strike. The goal of an unelected committee of negotiators is to stop the action.[2]

During the September 2011 strike, these mass meetings of
striking workers were able to assert the authority of rank-and-file
workers over their elected representatives. An attempt by Ali
Fattouh, the independent union's first president, to settle the
strike was rejected at mass meetings and Adil Shazly was elected
to replace him as union president.

Mass gatherings of striking workers did not necessarily always
impose their views on their representatives by formal means, but
sometimes nominated negotiators by acclaim. This was the case
in the PT workers' sit-in outside parliament during the March
2012 strike. Strike organisation formed a bridge by which Tareq
el-Beheiry, a former official in the ETUF-affiliated Land Transport Union, rose to a leading position in the independent union.
El-Beheiry's narrative of the strikes is rather different to Ahmad's.
In contrast to Ahmad's view of the ultimate sovereignty of the
rank and file, he suggested that the officials' authority derived
from their ability to wrest concessions from management, not on
their democratic mandate from below.[3]

The September 2011 nationwide teachers' strike provides
another example of strike organisation that stretched far beyond
the ranks of the independent teaching unions. Hala Talaat, vice
president of the Giza Committee of the Egyptian Teachers' Federation, describes how 'spontaneous', locally organised protests
by teachers in the first half of 2011 coalesced into national strike
action at the beginning of the new school year.

> Groups of teachers would organise a protest in front of the local
> branch of the official teaching professions union demanding
> their rights, calling for permanent contracts and so on. Or they'd
> go to the Ministry of Education with these demands. There
> were sit-ins and protests, and we, the activists, would go and
> join them. This was happening constantly but the numbers were

not very large. Then the numbers started building up from two to three hundred, then five hundred and a thousand, until by the end of August there was a big protest in front of the Cabinet Office with four thousand teachers.[4]

The first steps in organisation had been taken by teachers at a local level; often the most active groups were supply teachers and young teachers who were denied permanent contracts. However, the intervention of the independent unions was critical to the qualitative shift that took place between late August and mid-September:

> Then we really started to get organised, and set up a co-ordinating committee across the different governorates which brought together the Egyptian Teachers' Federation and the Independent Teachers' Union and other independent teachers' groups. We started to meet and to coordinate regularly and we set the date for 10 September as a big protest and agreed we'd go for a strike at the beginning of the school year.[5]

Around 40,000 teachers from across Egypt protested on 10 September, and between 250,000 and 500,000 took part in the strike which began the following week. The coordinating committee remained in place at the national level. It conducted negotiations with the Ministry of Education, and represented the leadership of the strike to the media and the public. However, strike organisation mushroomed underneath as thousands of school-based strike committees were set up. In some areas, new forms of coordination emerged, such as in Al-Arish, where delegates from different school strike committees met as a 'Conference of the Teachers' Strike Committees'.[6] Facebook was a particularly important mechanism for coordination between local teachers' groups, and may have also accelerated the rise of the movement.[7]

The leadership of the independent teachers' unions were able to ride the rising movement, and steer its development and direction, but as the mobilisation from below began to ebb it was hard not to be swept back. The government offered concessions which led a majority on the Coordinating Committee to argue for suspending the strike, a move which appears to have been broadly supported by striking teachers. The government then reneged on most of the deal. However, the independent union leaders found it hard to revive the mood for action in the face of frustration and demoralisation among the large numbers of teachers.

The national doctors' strikes of 2011 and 2012 provide another extremely significant model of strike organisation, which differs from the experiences of manual workers and civil servants. In Chapter 4 we discussed the emergence of networks of activists within the Muslim Brotherhood-dominated Doctors' Union before the revolution. Doctors Without Rights (DWR), the movement that emerged in 2008 around an attempt to call a national doctors' strike, played the leading role in organising the 2011 and 2012 strikes. In contrast to the PT workers or the teachers, the doctors had to win a battle for strike organisation as members of the Doctors' Union, rather than by building their organisation from scratch.

However, this did not mean that they relied exclusively on the union's existing structures, but rather employed tactics which allowed them to work both inside and outside the union. The core of the strike leadership in 2011 and 2012 was the Doctors' Without Rights network, which could be characterised as a rank-and-file movement within the Doctors' Union. It was composed of Doctors' Union members, adhering to a specific political programme, but had its own structures and organisation, independent of the union. DWR intervened as an organised group within the main democratic forums of the union, attempting to win the backing of wider layers of union members for its tactics and policies. The road to strike action in both the May 2011 and October 2012 national strikes thus began with debates at Doctors' Union general assemblies, at which DWR and its allies won the debate among delegates for strike action against the opposition of the Muslim Brotherhood leadership of the union.

These general assemblies were mass meetings in the true sense of the word. The first took place on 25 March 2011 with around 3,000 delegates from across the country. It set a list of demands for the government to answer. Negotiations failed to produce any results, and at a tumultuous reconvened general assembly on 1 May DWR activists won the vote for strike action on 10 May. Knowing they would face massive opposition from the union leadership, which would do everything in its power to sabotage the strike, DWR activists argued for the creation of a Higher Strike Committee to coordinate the action at a national level. Beneath the Higher Strike Committee, regional and hospital strike committees were swiftly formed, drawing in doctors who were not supporters of DWR but were radicalised by the revolution and wanted the strike to succeed. A one-day national strike on 10 May was followed by open-ended action beginning on 17 May, which mobilised tens of thousands of doctors.[8]

The 2011 strikes did not result in an outright victory, but in relatively limited concessions by the government. The 2012 strike called for even greater levels of resilience and organisation. Once again, DWR and its allies won the debate for strike action at a union general assembly, despite the opposition of the union leadership. In the face of enormous hostility from the media and the Muslim Brotherhood-led government, they organised a partial national strike for over forty days, demanding a rise in doctors' basic pay to LE3,000 a month, and an increase in state spending on the health service to 15 per cent of GDP.

Strike organisation and union formation during the revolution

In Chapter 5 we discussed the development of the first independent union, the Property Tax Collectors union RETAU, out of the coordinating body that was created in the midst of their 2007 strike. Strike organisation continued to be distinct from union organisation, in that it mobilised wider layers of workers than the membership of the union, and generally exerted greater authority over the workplace for the duration of the strike. Yet, as in the pre-revolutionary era, many of the unions that were strongest in terms of the numbers they were capable of mobilising, and most effective in terms of winning concessions from the employers and the state, were transformed and expanded strike committees. However, new processes affecting union formation were at work also in the wake of Mubarak's fall. The first of these was the enormous impetus that the uprising of January 2011 gave to ordinary people's confidence in the possibilities of self-organisation. Moreover at this stage, the independent unions were emerging in a political landscape where workers' social demands found almost no expression, as main-stream reformist politicians rushed to condemn strikes as 'selfish'.

A second, critically important, process was the opening up of a legal space in which independent unions could operate for the first time. This was the result both of conscious strategy on the part of some state officials, notably Ahmad al-Borai, the minister of labour in Essam Sharaf's 2011 cabinet, and of the confusion and paralysis affecting those parts of the state apparatus, such as the top layers of the ETUF bureaucracy, which would have otherwise opposed it. The independent unions' legal standing remained ambiguous, as the laws governing trade-union formation such as Law 35 of 1976 and Law 12 of 2003 remained on the statute book, but Al-Borai's creation of a process of registration for independent unions gave impetus to the expansion of unions by bureaucratic methods, without the need for strikes or organisation from below. We discuss below the role in this process played by the emerging bureaucracies in the independent unions, channelling efforts in union formation towards fulfilling the criteria for legal recognition and at times engaged in fierce competition to claim the largest number of members even if these were passive or simply registered on paper.

We will argue here that the critical differentiating factor between unions was not which of the competing federations they joined, but whether they retained a living relationship to the day-to-day struggles in the workplace. The evidence that mere formation out of self-organised collective action was no guarantee against later bureaucratisation and passivity can be seen in the role played by RETAU officials in the development of the bureaucracy of the major independent union federation EFITU. Ironically, the incipient trends towards bureaucratisation which were visible in RETAU's leadership during 2009 and 2010 became much stronger during the revolution, even as hundreds of thousands of activists in other workplaces were repeating for themselves some of the Property Tax Collectors' experiences of 2007–08.

The other aspect of union formation and growth that needs emphasizing here is the extreme unevenness and complexity in the changing patterns of workplace organisation. The revolution was followed both by an enormous expansion of unions within single workplaces and by the development of union organisation between workplaces across state institutions, companies and, eventually, different sectors, such as transport, and geographical regions. This was not a static picture, of course: in sectors where the preparatory work had been done before the revolution, such as the Public Transport Authority in Cairo or among school teachers, the revolution created opportunities for the consolidation and transformation of existing networks. In many other workplaces, by contrast, the revolution provided the initial impetus for the formation of unions among workers who had no prior history of self-organisation.[9]

As discussed in Chapter 6, the independent unions played a marginal role in the success of the uprising against Mubarak. The existing four unions were simply too small to make much impact in shaping the street protests, and they did not represent workers in sectors where strike action would have a critical impact on the outcome of the uprising. Nevertheless, their visible presence in Tahrir Square was important, as it propagated the notion of working-class organisation to wide new audiences. Only a few days into the revolution, representatives from the four existing independent unions met in Tahrir Square and agreed to found the Egyptian Federation of Independent Trade Unions (EFITU).[10] While they formed only a small fraction of the huge crowds, activists from the tax collectors' union, with their banners and trademark blue baseball caps, were very visibly an organisation in the midst of a sea of individual protestors. Many of those individual protestors were quick to grasp the potential of independent union organisation. Interviewed at the founding conference of the independent rail workers' union in Bani Sueif on 4 May, one of the activists in the new union explained how he heard about independent unions first in Tahrir Square from workers in the Public Transport Authority.[11] Oil workers and teachers tell similar stories about their first encounter with the idea of independent trade unions.[12]

The rail-worker activists from Beni Sueif quickly found that the independent unions could become a rallying point for thousands of workers. The banners they hung up at railway stations brought hundreds flocking to join the new union, which organised all grades of railway staff. The union's founding conference on 4 May 2011 was reportedly attended by around 4,000 people, including large delegations of rail workers from outside the central section of the rail network where the founding activists were based.[13]

As discussed above, an important feature of the post-Mubarak strike waves was the adoption by other sections of society of strike tactics and other forms of collective action pioneered by the workers' movement. There are important examples of this process happening 'upwards', affecting sections of the highly educated but relatively precarious middle classes, such as doctors and university lecturers, as well as 'sideways' into sections of the urban and rural poor who, for both sociological and political reasons, have had little tradition of identification with the workers' movement, although their living standards are comparable to those of the urban workers at the core of the workers' movement. Hospital doctors, mosque imams, fishermen, microbus drivers, skilled craftsmen, intellectual property rights consultants, daily-paid labourers and the operators of the 'Scarab boats' which take tourists on Nile river trips were among those drawn into the orbit of the workers' movement, adopting forms of collective action and organisation shaped by the strike wave.

The meaning and impact of 'strikes' and 'independent unions' organised by these sections of the working class, middle class and urban poor naturally varied immensely from one situation to another. Self-employed skilled and semi-skilled craftsmen may have seen independent union organisation as primarily a means of creating a collective voice to put pressure on the authorities, rather than a mechanism to organise strikes. New organisations such the Union of Intellectual Property Consultants, representing a section of middle-class professionals, rejected strikes, but nevertheless applied to join the EFITU.

The first flush of revolutionary enthusiasm carried the idea of workers' self-organisation deep into thousands of workplaces. Strike organisation, union organisation and dramatic shifts in management's 'frontier of control', combined with the revolutionary dynamic of the struggle for *tathir*, created a ferment in the workplaces. As the months passed, however, the resolve of state institutions and employers in resisting workers' demands toughened. We have already discussed how the September 2011 strike wave provides an example of an organic process whereby strike organisation reaches out against the limits imposed by the individual workplace, logically pushing workers towards coordination between workplaces and therefore developing forms of organisation that express energy and anger from the base upwards. We have already discussed how this process can be seen concretely at work in the case of the national teachers' strike. Likewise the strike by postal workers which shut down around half of all post offices nationwide in early September began in the Kafr al-Sheikh and Alexandria offices but rapidly escalated into a national strike demanding improved pay and conditions and the 'cleansing' of the postal authority.[14] The strike that closed most of the public-sector sugar refineries in September 2011 was initially driven by a dispute at Armant sugar refinery near Luxor, but spread to the rest of the sector. In all three cases, organisation grew beyond individual workplaces, developing and strengthening pre-existing networks in the process of strike organisation. Moreover, the independent teachers' unions, the Postal Workers' Union and the 25 January Committee for Change, which had led the sugar workers' strike, continued in existence long after the end of the dispute.

The escalating confrontations between organised workers, on the one hand, and the state and employers, on the other, during Morsi's presidency demonstrated the urgent need for activists to find means to strengthen organisation and coordination between the workplaces as a concerted offensive by employers and the state aimed to roll back workers' gains of the previous two years. The success of this offensive was patchy – in some places workers' resistance won victories, or at least forced a stalemate. This was particularly apparent in strategically important sectors such as transport and shipping, where strike action caused immediate and significant economic disruption. Port workers employed by Dubai World at Ain Sokhna near Suez, for example, forced the return of laid-off workers to their jobs in October 2012 after a two-week strike paralysed operations in Egypt's main transit point for the Far East. A presidential adviser was appointed to the committee tasked with resolving the dispute.[15] A month or so later, workers on the Cairo Metro staged a highly effective strike and wrung significant concessions from management within a matter of hours.[16]

In manufacturing, a number of important disputes were triggered by management effectively withdrawing recognition from union committees that had won concessions the previous year. A lengthy and bitter battle at the Ideal Standard ceramics factory in 10th of Ramadan City during March–May 2013 ended in victory for management, and the resignation of most of the union committee, who had been victimised during the strike. May 2013 saw strikes at other major factories in the city, including Pyramid Ceramics, Deltapharm and Seoudi Cables. The dispute at Seoudi Cables was seen by local activists as an attempt by management to repeat the success of Ideal Standard's management in breaking union organisation within the factory, at least temporarily. In response, union organisers and local revolutionary activists had begun to try to create city-wide forums to coordinate action and solidarity. Hind Abdel-Gawad from the Revolutionary Socialists in nearby Zagazig helped to organise a large meeting as part of the May Day celebrations, at which delegations from a large number of local factories gathered to hear speeches and discuss ways of building coordination across the city.

> On 20 May we had a big meeting as part of the activities for May Day. This was a joint effort between the Revolutionary Socialists, the Popular Socialist Alliance, 6th of April, the Constitution Party and the independent unions. Ten factories sent delegations, including Ideal Standard, Venus, DeltaPharm, Kouta Steel, Jak, Seoudi Cables and Arna. We also had delegations from the Union of Administrators, the Electricity Workers' Union and the Building and Woodworkers' Union. Petroleum workers from outside 10th of Ramadan sent people as well. Altogether there were about 400 in the audience.[17]

Not all attempts by management to break the independent unions succeeded. In June 2013, some 600 workers at IFFCO, an edible oils manufacturer near Suez, were locked out after striking in protest at management's refusal to negotiate with their union committee. Unlike Ideal Standard, however, the IFFCO management backed down, reinstating the sacked workers and the union committee.[18]

The emergence of the national federations

In contrast to the forms of coordination between workplaces engaged in strike action described above, the national federations of independent unions were created without any direct relationship to the task of coordinating industrial action. Rather, as we explore below, the organisational drive behind them reflected the desire of sections of the emerging trade-union bureaucracy to consolidate their networks at a national level, in order to project their voice more strongly into the national political arena, and strengthen their relationships with the international trade-union bureaucracy. This lack of connection to the organising of industrial action shaped the character of the national federations, giving their leaders far more autonomy to speak on behalf of the workers' movement than would have been accorded to negotiators or members of a strike committee in many workplaces.

The Egyptian Federation of Independent Trade Unions was founded on 30 January 2011 in Tahrir Square, at a meeting between representatives of the four existing independent unions: the Property Tax Collectors' RETAU, the Health Technicians' Union, the Independent School Teachers' Union and the Pensioners' Union. At this stage the CTUWS was still a partner in the project of building a national federation. However, over the following months disagreements between Kamal Abu Aita of RETAU and Kamal Abbas of CTUWS about the role of CTUWS employees in the decision-making structures of the new federation escalated. On 28 June, at a meeting held in the RETAU offices off Faisal Street in Giza, representatives of fifteen unions agreed a statement of principles, which asserted that

The independent unions confirm that they only follow the wishes of the general assemblies of their members and that the principle of independence is a general principle which applies to all without exception. In the same vein, the independent unions assert that only elected representatives from the base of the unions have the right to speak on behalf of the trade unions and declare their positions, and that no outside parties have the right to do so, unless those positions have been agreed by the elected representatives of the independent unions.[19]

A few days later CTUWS officially withdrew from EFITU, and summarily ejected EFITU officials from the offices the organisations had shared on Qasr al-Aini Street. Initially Abu Aita and EFITU activists made the strongest headway as they raced to build up numbers of affiliates over the summer and autumn of 2011. By September they had secured new premises further down Qasr al-Aini Street, and by mid-October claimed over seventy affiliated unions, with a further forty in the process of completing registration as members. EFITU officials put the number of members in affiliated organisations at 1.4 million.[20]

Affiliated unions varied widely in size, from small unions of a few hundred members representing a single workplace or government institution, to well-established national unions such as RETAU (54,000 members), the Independent Teachers Union (40,000 members in May 2011) and the Health Technicians Union. Other powerful unions affiliated to EFITU included the Independent Union of Public Transport Authority workers, the Union of Workers in Egypt Telecommunications Company, the Independent Postal Workers' Union and the cluster of unions representing airport workers (including the Civil Aviation Pilots' Union, the Independent Union of Egypt Air Ground Staff, the General Independent Union of Airport Service Workers, the Union of Workers in the Egyptian Aviation Maintenance and Technical Work Company, the Independent Union of Security

TABLE 7.1 EFITU registered unions by sector, October 2011

Sector	No. of unions
Transport	15
Civil service and local government	10
Petroleum and gas	8
Manufacturing	7
Craftsmen	6
Food production and distribution	5
Agriculture and fishing	4
Tourism	4
Post and telecommunications	2
Construction	2
Education	2
Media	1
Banking	1
Health	1
Retail and wholesale trade	1
Electricity and water	1
Pensioners	1
Daily-paid labourers	1
Total	72

SOURCE Unpublished list of EFITU affiliates provided to the authors by EFITU officials, October 2011.

Workers in EgyptAir). The EFITU's founding congress was held on the first anniversary of the revolution, 28 January 2012, claiming the affiliation of 24 'general unions' (representing workers across an entire institution or several workplaces), 118 workplace unions, and 1 regional union federation (Alexandria). Ninety-four candidates were reported to be competing for the twenty places on the executive, but there was only candidate standing for the position of Federation president.[21] Regional federations of independent unions affiliated to the EFITU also began to develop in a number of provinces, including Suez (January 2012) and Daqahiliyya (May 2012).[22]

EFITU soon faced a number of rivals contending for the leadership of the independent unions, however. The first and largest of these was the Egyptian Democratic Labour Congress (EDLC), which Kamal Abbas and activists from CTUWS played a central role in founding. The EDLC's birth was announced in October 2011 with the affiliation of 149 founding unions.[23] However, the organisation's founding congress did not take place until April 2013, at which point the EDLC claimed an affiliated membership of 300 unions.[24] Like the EFITU, the Congress formed regional federations of independent unions, such as the federation in Gharbiyya province. A number of other, much smaller federations were also established during 2012 and 2013, including the Workers of Egypt National Union (*Al-itihad al-qawmi l-ummal masr*), and the General Federation of Egyptian Trade Unions (*Al-itihad al-am lil-niqabat al-ummaliyya al-misriyya*).[25] Although the EFITU remained the largest of the independent union federations, the emergence of a serious rival in the form of the EDLC was an unwelcome development for the Federation's leadership. The EFITU also faced difficulties in retaining the support of some of the important unions it had attracted at an early stage in its development: for example, the leadership of the powerful and well-organised Public Transport Authority Workers' Union distanced itself from the federation during 2012.[26]

Trade-union bureaucracy in the independent unions

It is important to distinguish between two concurrent and interwoven processes of union formation: one process connected intimately with the struggle from below, and another bureaucratic process driven by opportunities created from above and by competition between sections of the emerging trade-union bureaucracy. These developed together as, during the first year of the revolution, the explosive growth of unions at a workplace level and the creation of coordinating bodies between workplaces and across sectors took place alongside similarly rapid growth in the national union federations. They were interwoven because the spectacular growth of the EFITU and its rivals reflected the desire of worker activists to find a national voice for their demands, and because the emerging bureaucracy at the centre of the EFITU was composed largely of activists who were recognised as leaders in their own workplaces and sectors, even if some of the key players, such as Kamal Abu Aita of the Tax Collectors' Union, had long been detached from the rank and file.

Another critically important distinction between the two kinds of organisations (or two aspects of the same organisation), beyond their being formed in struggle or not, was whether their central role was the organisation and coordination of industrial action or something different – such as political campaigning, lobbying the government, projecting workers' demands to the media, encouraging solidarity between different groups of workers engaged in action, developing relationships with international trade unions. The second set of tasks are, of course, integral to the work that trade unions do, but they can also be carried out by other kinds of organisations from NGOs to political parties. Crucially, this work can be carried out on a day-to-day level by relatively small groups of people, and does not carry the same democratic imperative as the organisation of industrial action, which to be successful requires the active participation of much larger numbers.

As we will demonstrate here, the activities carried out by the national structures of the EFITU and EDLC almost entirely fell within the second set of tasks: the national federations did not become bodies where industrial action was initiated or co-ordinated;

their role was more like that of a campaigning group or an NGO. This does not mean that all the individual members of the EFITU executive, for example, were divorced from their own workplaces, or that they played no role in organising strike action. Rather, it means that the EFITU's structures were not the mechanisms through which that action was organised or coordinated.

Thus it is important to distinguish between two different layers of union officials, which remained relatively distinct. The first layer comprised the leaderships of individual independent unions, for whom the primary pressure towards bureaucratisation came from their role as mediators in negotiations with employers and the state, and generally only secondarily as a result of their disconnection from the workplace. There was also a very small layer of national officials in the two independent union federations where additional pressures featured strongly: in this case it was less their role as mediators and more their high degree of autonomy from union members and their public visibility as spokespersons for the wider independent union movement which were the primary factors in their bureaucratisation. Other factors encouraging the relative autonomy of the emerging bureaucracy included the prominence of NGO activists in some of the new union structures, and the intensifying interest of international trade unions and other international bodies in the Egyptian workers' movement.

The strategic vacuum at the heart of the workers' movement is not simply a matter of the lack of coordinating bodies, but reflects the nature of the trade-union bureaucracy that has developed within the independent unions. Some aspects of the problem are intrinsic to trade-union bureaucracies in general, but others are more specific to the Egyptian experience. At a general level, the creation of national structures for the EFITU tended to act as an escalator out of the workplace for a small layer of trade-union leaders, and propelled some of them into mediating roles with the minister of labour and other state officials. Kamal Abu Aita, then acting president of the EFITU, played just such a role in attempting to mediate between the minister of labour and the leaders and members of the Public Transport Authority Workers' Union in September 2011.

However, as strike negotiations continued to take place by and large between directly elected representatives of striking workers and the relevant authorities, the actual space in which federation officials could play out a mediating role was relatively limited. The problem of the bureaucracy took other forms: the phenomenon of the escalator was still a problem, but, rather than delivering workplace militants into mediating roles in which they were balanced between the rank-and-file union members, on the one hand, and the employers and the state, on the other, it deposited them into a form of organisation which at times behaved more like a campaign group or solidarity committee. Federation officials worked tirelessly to project the voices of the independent unions onto the stage of national politics: they lobbied state officials, spoke to the media, took up the cases of striking, locked-out or arrested workers, attempted to mobilise contacts with the unions internationally, and occasionally organised protests, rallies and meetings. And, as it turned out, this kind of structure proved to be an equally effective 'escalator', as was demonstrated in July 2013, when Kamal Abu Aita was appointed minister of labour in Hazem Beblawi's Cabinet following the fall of Morsi.

The revival of the ETUF

As discussed in Chapter 6, the initial successes of the revolution were an enormous blow to the Egyptian Trade Union Federation, whose leaders had acted as one of the last lines of defence of the old regime. The ETUF played an active and highly visible role in attempts to mobilise counter-revolutionary protests, and Hussein Megawer, ETUF president, was prosecuted after Mubarak's fall on charges of organising the infamous 'Battle of the Camel' on 1 February 2011, when armed thugs attacked protesters in Tahrir Square. The ETUF faced further blows with the decision of Ahmad al-Borai, minister of labour in Essam Sharaf's Cabinet, succeeded in creating a legal mechanism for independent unions to register with the Ministry of Labour, even though laws prohibiting the creation of unions outside the ETUF framework remained on the statute book. Then, in August 2011, Al-Borai agreed to implement a decision taken by the administrative courts to annul the ETUF elections of 2006, thus requiring the dissolution of the Federation executive. Leaders of the independent unions welcomed Al-Borai's decision. Kamal Abu Aita convened a triumphant meeting of the EFITU inside the ETUF headquarters, at which the Federation's founding committee was elected. He announced to journalists that this was a 'historic meeting at a headquarters which was built out of the blood of Egyptian workers' and that the clearing out of the remnants of the old regime was a 'sacred task'.[27] Yet independent unionists' jubilation proved to be premature: the mechanisms by which the state dissolved the Federation executive in fact led to the eventual revival of the state's labour arm, saving it from collapse.

The interim executive the government appointed included several trade-union leaders from the dissolved NDP who were all involved in its earlier work. The president of the interim executive was Ahmad Abd-al-Zahir, who organised a campaign in support of Mubarak when he was head of the Federation of Co-operatives, and was also among the leaders of the dissolved federation, and a member of the NDP. The rest of the interim executive seats were allocated, by way of a political quota system, to the Brotherhood, the Left, the Nationalists and the independents, who took up 18 seats.

Moreover, the dissolution of the ETUF's executive was only carried through at the top level of the Federation, and not at the middle level of the general unions, nor the workplace union committees. The dissolution of the Federation council, without any change to the general unions and factory union committees, did not therefore represent a genuine change in the ETUF's organisation and role. The alternation of individuals at the top of the bureaucracy, through direct appointment by the state, without dissolving the lower levels of the Federation (although this was implied in the court decision justifying Al-Borai's move), indicated the unwillingness of state officials to relinquish the ETUF as a means to intervene in the workplaces. There was strikingly little reaction by the independent unions to the dissolution, beyond Abu Aita's symbolic (and temporary) appropriation of the ETUF headquarters for an EFITU meeting. Some very limited calls were heard at workers' gatherings to implement the decision on the general unions and the workplace union committees and the rest of the trade-union organisation, but these found little echo, and the opportunity to seize the initiative from the state over the fate of the ETUF passed.

The following year saw the slow revival of the ETUF's fortunes. The Muslim Brotherhood proved to be both an important ally and a rival for the remainder of the ETUF bureaucracy in this respect. As discussed in Chapter 4, the Brotherhood had by the mid-2000s established a presence in the bottom layers of the ETUF bureaucracy in a small number of areas. The dissolution of the ETUF created opportunities for the insertion of a few more Brotherhood cadres into the top of the Federation, by appointment to the interim executive. Leading activists from the Brotherhood who took positions on the executive included Yosri Bayyoumi, who was appointed treasurer, and Khaled al-Azhary, a union official in the Petroleum Workers' Union, who later became minister of labour.[28] Membership of the ETUF interim executive gave the Brotherhood a platform to intervene directly in industrial disputes, and its members were soon claiming credit for negotiating solutions to workers' problems. Al-Azhary told the *Ikhwanonline* website in September 2011 that the interim executive's intervention was crucial in heading off a strike by workers in Misr Spinning which threatened to ignite a wave of industrial action across the textile sector by convincing the minister of labour to meet some of the Mahalla workers' key demands for increased bonuses and pay.[29] By late February 2012, Brotherhood MPs and ETUF officials were working together on draft legislation on trade-union freedoms and had proposed an initiative to parliament to 'solve workers' problems' by creating a special committee to negotiate with management on their behalf. As we explore in more detail in Chapter 8, the ETUF's crucially important role as gatekeeper to nominations for the 'workers' seats' in the parliamentary elections gave an added incentive to the Brotherhood's attempts to insert its cadres into the Federation's leadership.

The ETUF's revival was also aided greatly by the fact that the Federation continued to enjoy the benefits of its legal monopoly over workplace organisation, long after its dominance of union membership had been broken. More than a year after the revolution began, the ETUF was still taking subscriptions from workers' pay packets through an automatic 'check off' system, even where they had expressly opted out. The ETUF also controlled the social funds of its affiliated general unions, which provided access to pensions and other benefits for millions of workers.[30] The ETUF was, moreover, not merely a shell, inhabited at the top by the remnants of its old bureaucracy. A few unions affiliated to the ETUF still retained a base in the workplaces, such as the Land Transport Union, which was engaged in fierce competition with the new independent union in the Public Transport Authority in Cairo. The Land Transport Union played a key role in aborting attempts to win support for strike action on the buses in solidarity with the call for a general strike on 11 February 2012.

In other sectors, particularly the textile industry, the ETUF-affiliated union committees were not displaced by independent unions, but continued to function. As in the pre-revolutionary period, not all ETUF-affiliated workplace committees were hostile to workers' self-organisation and collective action, although the ETUF bureaucracy remained consistently opposed to strikes.

The Brotherhood's determination to facilitate the continuation of a bureaucratic model of trade unionism patterned precisely on the ETUF can be seen in the draft law on trade-union organisation drawn up in 2012. The threat that the provisions in the law posed to their existence provoked an unusual degree of unity across the two major independent union federations. Joining forces in a National Front to Defend Workers' Rights, they accused the Muslim Brotherhood of mounting a 'savage' attack on workers' rights.[31] Campaign leaflets prepared by the EFITU laid out the independent unionists' criticisms:

> The Brotherhood's draft law proposes trade-union structures in the form of a pyramid (workplace union committees – general unions – general federation). All authority is concentrated in the general federation, which the government or security forces can put under pressure, while the workplace union committees have no powers. We want unions, not the federation, to have full rights to negotiate and take the decision to strike. Workers themselves are the decision-makers. They must be able to elect their leaders freely and exercise authority over them.[32]

According to the draft, on leaving ETUF-affiliated general unions workers would lose access to their deposits in ETUF-administered social funds. The new law gave employers the right to prevent trade-union activities and elections, as these were only permitted 'if they do not affect the course of work in the institution'. Trade unionists convicted of 'spreading false information' could be fined LE10,000, while employers who victimised trade-union activists would only have to pay LE1,000.[33]

Conclusion: the limits of trade-unionism and the search for a political voice

Egyptian workers' revival of self-organisation before and during the revolution was, on many levels, an astonishing feat. With few resources and often in conditions of acute repression, factory and office workers created the workplace organisations that guarded and nurtured the revolution's 'social soul'. The independent unions represented one of the most impressive flowerings of popular organisation in the Arab world for decades. Yet, as we have outlined in this chapter, the workers' movement also suffered from significant weaknesses. In particular, as we explore in more depth in the following chapters, the experience of revolution demonstrated both the limits of the 'politics of trade unionism' and the problem of workers' subordination to the political agenda of other forces.

'Trade-unionist politics' dominated the practice of the leaders of many of the independent unions for much of the first two years of the revolution. As discussed here, this perspective was focused on developing industrial muscle in order to project workers' voices into the national political arena to win a specific set of fairly narrow demands: in particular full legal recognition for the independent unions. Yet the major independent union federations were unable to impose their demands on the state, and instead faced increasingly severe attacks on the small gains won in the aftermath of Mubarak's fall. The following chapters examine how key leaders of the independent unions, such as Kamal Abu Aita, despite their earlier protestations regarding the need to separate 'politics' from 'trade unionism', were pulled closer and closer into the orbit of the broad 'secular' coalition of the Muslim Brotherhood's opponents, and ultimately into coalition with the military.

CHAPTER 8

The crisis of representation: workers and elections

In October 2010, as Egypt prepared for parliamentary elections, Minister of Labour Ai'sha Abd-al-Hadi called a press conference at the Egyptian Trade Union Federation offices in Alexandria. There was no need for workers to worry about how they would be represented in the coming parliament, she told the assembled journalists: 'if we integrate our party and political work, we can well maintain the proportion of workers' seats.' The issue at stake was not about the 'quantity' of seats reserved for workers and peasants – at that time set at 50 per cent of parliament – but their 'quality'. 'We're right in the heart of the party,' she argued, 'no one is going to steal our seats from us.'[1] Sayyid Habib, a leading activist at Misr Spinning in Mahalla during the 2006–07 strikes, presented a very different view of the NDP's 'worker' MPs: 'Even when we took our protests and sit-ins to the street outside Parliament and the Shura Council, none of the members offered us solidarity', he told Al-Jazeera TV; 'this was a crisis in terms of the workers' representation in parliament.'[2]

The acute contradiction between formally very high levels of workers' representation in the mainstream political arena, particularly parliament, and the reality of a political system which silenced their voices while mobilising their votes in order to perpetuate dictatorship had, of course, already been apparent for several years. It was intensified by another contradiction – this time between workers' collective social power as demonstrated by the pre-revolutionary strike waves and their collective political weakness. This chapter will explore how the reforms of the electoral system after the revolution, far from resolving the 'crisis of representation' for workers, re-created it in a new form. During the first post-revolution elections, the parliamentary arena proved to be almost impenetrable by workers themselves, or even by political organisations articulating workers' social and political demands. The Muslim Brotherhood gained privileged access to the main mechanism of control over nominations for the workers' seats, through its post-Mubarak partnership with the old ruling party within the leadership of the Egyptian Trade Union Federation. It then proceeded to remove the quota of workers' seats from the 2012 Constitution, along with the state's formal commitment to a wide range of social and economic rights.

Yet, it would be a grave mistake, we argue here, to conclude that what happened in the electoral arena during the first two years of the revolution was as meaningless as elections under Mubarak. On the contrary, elections reflected, and in some cases condensed or intensified, social and political tensions to a degree that was previously impossible. This was at one level an expression of the temporary weakness of the leading institutions of the old regime, particularly the leadership of the Armed Forces, which was forced to partially relinquish control over the electoral process in order to create a space in which the enormous tensions and energies unleashed by the revolution could be absorbed by reformist political forces and channelled into the relatively safe passions of parliamentary democracy.

At another level, continued high levels of collective action outside the parliamentary arena shaped politics within it. The backwash from the repeated waves of street protests and strikes after the Brotherhood's success in the parliamentary elections helped to propel the left Nasserist Hamdeen Sabahy into third place in the initial round of the presidential elections with liberal Islamist Abd-al-Moneim Abu-al-Fotouh close behind. The significance of the votes for Sabahy and Abu-al-Fotouh lay in the fact that they represented an electoral alternative to the Brotherhood which drew its energy from the impatience of the large constituencies radicalised by the revolution at the slow pace of political and social change. The success of Sabahy was particularly important, as it ruptured the Islamist dominance of formal politics and demonstrated the potential of mass electoral support for a political project which provided an alternative to the Brotherhood's neoliberal economic agenda. However, Sabahy's role in forming a political alliance with the liberals and politicians from the old regime, such as Amr Moussa, against the Brotherhood confirmed the difficulties in translating the roar of workers' voices in their strikes and protests into votes for a genuine programme of social change at the ballot box. And we discuss in the next chapter how, in July 2013, Sabahy fell in behind the military, as Minister of Defence Abdel-Fattah al-Sisi turned events in a counter-revolutionary direction.

Moreover, although elections were an important gauge of the wider balance of forces in the revolutionary process, in comparison to other post-revolutionary societies Egypt's democratic experience was relatively shallow, characterised by declining levels of voter participation and growing disillusionment with parliamentary politics. We argue here that this reflected the inability of both Islamist and secular reformist currents to overcome either of the two main obstacles that blocked the road to serious social or political reforms: the lack of change within the state once the president and his immediate entourage were removed, and the lack of alternatives to neoliberalism and austerity on a global scale. These two factors combined to constrain the space in which reformist forces operated, pointing towards a deeper 'crisis of representation', resulting in the development of a shallow and transient parliamentarianism, drained of both real social and democratic content.

The reconfiguration of electoral politics after the fall of Mubarak

Before the revolution, the space for electoral politics was tightly constrained by the power of the regime's bureaucracy. We return to this problem in detail, and to the challenges raised by the specific character of the entanglement between officers and officials in Egypt's 'bureaucratic-military machine',[3] in Chapter 9. The ruling class did not use elections as a mechanism for thrashing out its own disagreements and contradictions, unlike its counterpart in Iran, for example, where competing sections of the elite use elections for this purpose.[4] Moreover, the opportunities for anyone outside the elite to use the electoral process to their advantage were minimal. As discussed in Chapter 4, the regime's control of the procedure for nomination and the institutional definition of the occupational quota meant that the presence of 'worker' MPs was never more than a mechanism for mobilising workers from above in order to better manage their discontent below. Its existence appeared to show that workers' concerns would be heard at the highest levels of the state, and made workers' support for the regime collectively visible.

After the fall of Mubarak, electoral politics, after decades when (with brief exceptions) the results were a mere formality and the process largely theatrical, took on new and different meanings. There was a much higher degree of competition between different political platforms, and the authorities were far more constrained regarding overt intervention than they had been before the revolution. Although politics in the streets, the workplaces and the electoral arena frequently appeared to be *disconnected*, particularly to activists in the workers' movement and the wider revolutionary movement, events during 2011–12 confirmed that the battle between political forces advocating counter-revolution, reform or further revolutionary change was also being played out at the ballot box, and that those results were shaping events in other domains of politics.

However, the very small degree of change in the core institutions of the state, and the increasingly bitter confrontations between protesters and the military leadership, led many to question whether it was worth engaging in electoral battles at all, if the military was able to overrule any elected body it chose. And even the reformed electoral landscape of the post-Mubarak era offered openings which benefited established political parties, such as the Brotherhood. Worker activists experienced not only the problems raised by a costly and cumbersome registration process for new political parties and individual candidates, but also the difficulties caused by the long-term absence of independent political organisation advocating a social and political programme which reflected their interests. Moreover, the route to nomination for the workers' parliamentary seats remained largely controlled by the Egyptian Trade Union Federation, which, as detailed in the last chapter, had opened partially to incorporate the Brotherhood, but not other political forces. Workers wanting to be accepted as candidates by the Brotherhood itself had to accommodate to the organisation's hostility to strikes and workers' protests.

In order to grasp the dynamics of the electoral process during the revolution, and the opportunities and challenges it presented to activists in the workers' movement, it is necessary to see beyond formal changes in procedure and transcend a mechanical understanding of the relationship between different political arenas. Electoral politics was shaped by the attempts of the military leadership and the Islamists to use it as a vehicle to contain political reforms within mutually acceptable limits, and forestall serious social reform which might threaten the neoliberal status quo. However, electoral politics was also shaped by the fact that these same political reforms had been wrested from the regime by a revolutionary uprising mobilising millions of people. The Islamist reformists who dominated the first post-Mubarak parliament therefore found themselves caught between competing pressures on either flank. On the one hand, the revival of the old regime constrained their capacity to satisfy voters' expectations of genuine reform, as their own gains were almost entirely within the legislature, leaving the basic structures of the state unchanged. On the other hand, hundreds of thousands of their working-class and poor voters refused to rely on the ballot box alone to complete their revolution, and continued to join street protests and strikes on a scale which ruled out a comfortable transition to a post-revolutionary order.

From the perspective of the majority of working-class voters the story of electoral politics in the first two years of the revolution was one of growing disillusion with the Muslim Brotherhood and the increasingly urgent search for an alternative. Activists in the workers' movement, while in many cases already identifying with the Brotherhood's competitors on the left, and in others with the Salafist movement, also faced the challenge of finding a political platform capable of projecting their voices onto the stage of national politics and breaking down the mainstream consensus that there was no alternative to neoliberalism, and no space for independent workers' organisations.

Workers in the 2011–12 parliamentary elections

The reform of the electoral system in the wake of Mubarak's overthrow was a controversial process. The military-authored draft electoral law presented in May 2011 was criticised by Islamist and secular liberal political forces alike, and went through a series of amendments, each of which dramatically reshaped the electoral system.[5] The amendments that were adopted in September 2011 created two parallel electoral systems, one based on individual candidates, the other on proportional representation lists. The country was divided into 83 two-member individual candidate constituencies, and 46 PR districts, which ranged in size from 12 to 4 seats.[6] The individual candidate constituencies operated the same rules for the occupational quota which had been in force during the 1990s and 2000s, ensuring that at least one worker/farmer would be elected. The PR lists were required to alternate worker/farmer and professional candidates, and the former would also be promoted up the PR district lists over higher-polling candidates in the professionals category to ensure the occupational quota was met for at least 249 seats out of 498.[7]

The electoral reforms instituted after the fall of Mubarak did not remove the principal obstacles impeding worker activists from standing in the parliamentary elections. In theory, the combination of PR for the election of two-thirds of parliamentary seats with the occupational quota should have created relatively favourable terrain for activists in the workers' movement to make an electoral impact. The reality was somewhat different. A number of factors combined to actively exclude many potential worker candidates from competing, and ensured that very few activists from the independent unions were elected. First, the large, multi-member constituencies favoured well-resourced parties with a national political profile, a status which none of the new revolutionary groups or independent trade unions enjoyed. Second, the certificate of trade-union membership, which remained essential to securing a nomination for a 'workers' seat, was still legally and practically in the gift of the Egyptian Trade Union Federation.

Following the dissolution of the ETUF executive in August 2011 (see Chapter 7), the Federation had been placed under the control of a caretaker executive which included former members of the NDP, the Muslim Brotherhood's leading trade unionists, and a small number of independent worker activists and left-wing political figures. The committee responsible for issuing certificates of trade-union membership for prospective electoral candidates was chaired by the ETUF's interim president, Ahmad Abd-al-Zafir, and included among its members leading Brother-hood trade unionists Yosri Bayyumi, the interim ETUF treasurer, and Khaled al-Azhary, later appointed minister of labour in Morsi's government in August 2012, alongside trade-union leaders under the old regime, such as president of the Health Service Workers' Union, Abd-al-Hamid Abd-al-Gawad.[8] The committee was reported to have endorsed membership certificates for 8,500 prospective candidates by 15 October 2011.[9]

The Egyptian Federation of Independent Trade Unions challenged the ETUF's monopoly on the issuing of trade-union membership certificates directly. Kamal Abu Aita, the EFITU's interim president, announced his candidacy for a workers' seat in Giza on 13 October 2011, affirming that he would present documentation from the EFITU, not the ETUF, as proof of status.[10] Overall, the EFITU issued at least 1,500 certificates of trade-union membership to prospective parliamentary candidates, Abu Aita claimed in mid-November.[11] The EFITU's move trig-gered battles in a number of district courts, where the committees overseeing the nomination process refused to accept certificates from the independent unions. The South Giza court rejected three electoral lists on these grounds at the end of October. Two were presented by the Revolution Continues Alliance list, which brought together a coalition spanning the left-wing Popular So-cialist Alliance Party, the Revolutionary Youth Coalition and the Egyptian Current Party founded by former youth activists of the Muslim Brotherhood. The third rejected list was that presented by the Egyptian Bloc, a secular liberal coalition dominated by the Free Egyptians Party founded by billionaire businessman Naguib Sawiris.[12]

Abu Aita told the press that his nomination papers had initially also been rejected, but that he had presented a letter from the minister of labour, confirming the EFITU's competence to issue trade-union membership certificates.[13] Abu Aita, a leading member of the left-Nasserist Karama (Dignity) Party went on to contest the election in Giza as the third candidate on the Democratic Alliance list led by the Muslim Brotherhood for the PR constituency of North Giza.[14] However, he was eventually elected in the 'professional' category, alongside Khaled al-Azhary, who had been able to secure nomination via ETUF, was elected to the first 'worker' seat in the constituency. Leading EFITU activists in Qalyubiyya faced similar hurdles to reach the ballot paper: nomination papers for Tareq Mustafa Ka'eb, treasurer of the property tax collectors' union RETAU, and Noha Muhammed Murshid, president of the union's media committee, were also rejected on the grounds that their trade-union membership certificates had been issued by the EFITU. However, on 15 November, the Qalyubiyya Administrative Court overruled the decision, allowing the two trade unionists to contest the elections for the North Qalyubiyya PR constituency on the Revolution Continues Alliance list.[15]

From parliament to the presidential palace

The overall results of the elections appeared at one level to signal a dramatic change in Egyptian political life. The main beneficiary of the revolution in the electoral arena was the major reformist organisation of the pre-revolutionary period: the Muslim Brotherhood. The Brotherhood-founded Freedom and Justice Party (FJP) took 235 seats, followed by the Salafist Al-Nour Party with 123. The Wafd and the secular liberal alliance the Egyptian Bloc won 38 and 34 seats respectively. Minor parties in parliament included Al-Wasat (10 seats), Reform and Development (9 seats) and the Revolution Continues Alliance (7 seats) and Karama (6 seats).[16] Independents accounted for 26 seats, while the remaining 18 directly elected seats were divided between a number of small parties.[17] The new parliament was inaugurated on 23 January 2012, two days before marches on the anniversary of the beginning of the revolution brought hundreds of thousands onto the streets. The Brotherhood and its Islamist allies made strenuous efforts to portray the parliament as the major gain of the revolution, and the sole legitimate arena for politics thereafter, a theme which was hotly debated in the media and in the streets over the following months.[18] Protesters who marched to parliament on the day of its inaugural sitting, demanding that their elected representatives challenge the ruling Military Council, found that the Muslim Brotherhood had mobilised its activists against them.

Many newly elected Brotherhood MPs were kept busy mediating between striking workers and their bosses, gaining promises from management in exchange for the suspension of the action, and telling workers they would also raise the matter in parliament. In the space of a single week in late February 2012, the Muslim Brotherhood's main website carried news of at least four separate strikes where the intervention of the Brotherhood's MPs apparently persuaded workers to suspend their protests, including a sit-in by petroleum workers in Alexandria,[19] a strike by 500 workers in a fertiliser factory in Aswan,[20] a road blockade by workers in a chemical factory in Fayyum[21] and a sit-in by workers in the Kom Ombo Valley company in Aswan.[22] However, when striking workers brought their complaints to the doors of parliament, organising sit-ins in the street outside, they faced harsh criticism from the Muslim Brotherhood MPs inside the building.

At the same time, the Brotherhood threw its organisational and ideological weight against efforts to quicken the pace of change within the state through mobilisations outside the parliamentary arena. It mounted a ferocious campaign against calls for a general strike against the Supreme Council of the Armed Forces on 11 February 2012. In hundreds of articles across its publications, the Brotherhood warned that plans for the strike and civil disobedience would lead to chaos and the collapse of the state.[23] It mobilised its activists in the workplaces to announce that, rather than joining the strike, they would be working an extra day 'for Egypt'. As discussed in Chapter 6, the calls for strike action found only minimal support in the workplaces, although there were large protests across the country on university campuses and by school students.[24]

The failure of the agitation for a general strike did not mean that the overall level of protests was subsiding: on the contrary, high levels of strikes continued into the spring. But it set the scene for the next round of the electoral drama: the presidential elections of June 2012. Overall, the elections pointed to the growing confidence of the counter-revolutionary camp and the growing alienation between the Muslim Brotherhood and candidates who were identified more strongly with the revolution, in particular the Nasserist Hamdeen Sabahy. The Muslim Brotherhood's campaign was beset with problems throughout. The organisation's first choice of candidate, Khairat al-Shatir, was disqualified on the grounds that he had served a prison sentence for belonging to a 'banned group' (the Muslim Brotherhood) under the former regime.[25] Mohamed Morsi, head of the Freedom and Justice Party, who eventually received the Brotherhood's nomination, was mocked by the media as a 'spare tyre', bolted onto the Brotherhood's electoral campaign wagon at the last minute. The Brotherhood's participation in the presidential elections was seen by many as a breach of a previous promise to limit itself to standing candidates in the parliamentary elections.[26]

Morsi narrowly won the first round of the elections, while Ahmad Shafiq, the former civil aviation minister, and Mubarak's last prime minister, took second place, followed closely by Nasserist Hamdeen Sabahy. Two candidates who did less well than expected, Abd-al-Moneim Abu-al-Fotouh and Amr Moussa, came fourth and fifth respectively. Abu-al-Fotouh and Moussa both – in different ways – represented a vision of compromise. Abu-al-Fotouh was expelled from the Muslim Brotherhood in 2011, ostensibly for announcing that he would stand for president, taking with him the support of a substantial section of the Brotherhood's youth organisation. He ran on a liberal Islamist, pro-revolution platform in the presidential elections.[27] Amr Moussa, by contrast, was a former senior figure in the ruling party, who had distanced himself from the regime somewhat even before the revolution and thus represented a compromise between counter-revolutionary and mainstream liberal currents.

Morsi and Shafiq went through to contest the second round of the elections, despite last-ditch attempts to block Shafiq's candidacy by a legal challenge and another round of large protests in Cairo and Alexandria which acclaimed Sabahy and Abou-al-Fotouh as the choice of the revolutionary movement. The numbers on the streets were swelled by hundreds of thousands after a court acquitted a number of senior figures in the Interior Ministry on charges of murdering protesters on 2 June. Although this was accompanied by a guilty verdict against Mubarak and Habib al-Adly, protesters argued that the acquittal of their subordinates undermined the basis for the conviction, opening the door to a successful appeal in the future. The mood on the protests was, however, also violently antagonistic to the Muslim Brotherhood, and many revolutionary activists raised calls for a boycott of the run-offs. The following two weeks saw the contradictions evident on 2 and 3 June intensify. The counter-revolutionary camp continued to gain in confidence both in the electoral arena and within the state apparatus. Shafiq, unperturbed by the anger in the streets, continued to stump the provinces, aided by the return to life of the old ruling party's electoral machine. On 14 June the courts once again moved into action on the counter-revolution's behalf: the Higher Constitutional Court not only ruled that the law of political isolation passed by parliament in April 2012 was unconstitutional, thus removing legal obstacles to Shafiq's candidacy; it also declared that the parliamentary election was itself invalid. The court argued that the rules governing candidate selection had been misapplied, giving the candidates of political parties an unfair advantage over those standing as independents.[28] The same day, the Ministry of Justice announced that the military police and military intelligence officers had been granted powers to arrest civilians, and by 15 June red-bereted military police troops could be seen setting up checkpoints around central Cairo.[29] In a triumphal press conference, Shafiq left his listeners in no doubt that his electoral victory would herald a crackdown on dissent: 'I promise to confront chaos and restore stability', he declared; 'Egypt needs leadership, and it needs manhood in leadership.'[30] Finally, as the polls closed on Sunday, 17 June, the Supreme Council of the Armed Forces announced sweeping restrictions on the powers of the newly elected president, reserving for itself the final say on legislation and seizing control of many executive powers.

The Muslim Brotherhood had already vowed to defy the decision to dissolve parliament and continue with Morsi's electoral campaign as planned. Some revolutionary activists marched alongside the Brotherhood against the military's 'constitutional coup', joining protests which began slowly to fill the streets again in the wake of the military's constitutional announcement. It was clear that others, such as the Popular Socialist Alliance's presidential candidate, Abu-al-Ezz al-Hariri, regarded the Islamists as a greater danger than Shafiq, even to the point where they were prepared to endorse an openly counter-revolutionary candidate in order to prevent Morsi's election. In the final tense days before Morsi's victory was officially announced on 24 June, all roads still seemed open. Would SCAF, under Tantawi and Anan's leadership, turn the 'soft coup' announced by the judges into a 'hard coup' backed up by military repression against the revolutionary forces? Or would the military step back from the brink of confrontation with the hundreds of thousands filling the streets again in order to give the Brotherhood its day in power? Would the Brotherhood continue to defy the judges on the streets and in parliament, or work out a new power-sharing arrangement?

In the end, the generals and the Brotherhood chose a combination of the second and third of these options. Just over a week after Morsi's inauguration he recoiled from confrontation with the Constitutional Court over the reinstatement of parliament, making it clear that he had no intention of fighting to implement a decision issued on 9 July, overturning the dissolution.[31] Within two weeks, Tantawi and Anan were gone, replaced by younger colleagues on SCAF, led by General Abdel-Fattah al-Sisi. Morsi was also able to annul the Supplementary Constitutional Declaration, not only restoring the presidential powers which had been seized by SCAF on 17 June but also taking over legislative authority in the absence of parliament, and granting himself the right to appoint a new Constituent Assembly.[32]

How did workers campaign and vote in the presidential elections?

Among the major candidates, the Nasserist Hamdeen Sabahy stood out as the most attractive to many activists in the independent unions for a number of reasons. Sabahy counted active supporters among the EFITU leadership, such as Kamal Abu Aita, the EFITU president and a founding member of Sabahy's Karama Party. Although Abu Aita accompanied Sabahy on the campaign trail,[33] he continued to distinguish between his

party-political activities and trade-union role, arguing against
the politicisation of the independent unions, in order to prevent
their capture by political interests. Other EFITU officials and
activists campaigned for Sabahy in their local areas: putting up
posters, handing out leaflets and encouraging their workmates
and neighbours to vote for him. Tarek Mostafa Ka'eb, treasurer
of the Tax Collectors' Union RETAU, mobilised on Sabahy's
behalf the networks he had used for his own electoral campaign
in the 2011 parliamentary elections, which were largely made up of
RETAU's local activists in Kafr al-Shaikh.[34] Support for Sabahy
united activists like Ka'eb and Abu Aita who had been divided
over electoral tactics during the parliamentary elections, with Abu
Aita following Karama's lead and standing on the Freedom and
Justice Party list, while Ka'eb stood for the left-wing Revolution
Continues Alliance. One of Sabahy's attractions to activists in
the workers' movement was his clear stance on many of the social
demands that mattered most to them. Sabahy campaigned for
the application of the minimum and maximum wage, expansion
of the public sector to create jobs, for the return of nationalised
companies to the state, and for a one-off 20 per cent tax on the
wealth of the richest 1 per cent of the population.[35] Although
other minor candidates, such as the left-wing activist Khaled Ali,
advocated similar or more radical ideas, only Sabahy brought the
'common-sense' social politics of the grassroots of the workers'
movement into the limelight of national politics.

Sabahy's vote in the first round of the presidential elections
confounded the expectations of many who had thought Amr
Moussa and Aboul-Fotouh more likely contenders for third place.
In fact, the margins of victory between Morsi, Shafiq and Sabahy
were incredibly narrow in many places, with Moussa and Aboul-
Fotouh making a relatively even five-way split in some districts.
In Matariyya electoral district in Cairo, Sabahy won the most
votes with 26.4 per cent, but Shafiq took 26.1 per cent and Morsi

came in third with 22.9 per cent.[36] A map of the first-round results in the Delta shows Sabahy's vote concentrated in urban Cairo and Giza and his home governorate of Kafr al-Sheikh. Pockets of Sabahy votes also appeared dotted across the Delta and the Canal Zone, corresponding to the industrial and urban centres including Qalyub, Tanta, Mahalla, Damanhour, Isma'iliyya, Port Sa'id and the whole of Alexandria, while the surrounding rural and semi-rural areas went to Shafiq in the heart of the Delta, and Morsi on the eastern and western flanks.[37]

As discussed above, Sabahy's elimination from the run-offs, and the looming contest between Morsi and Shafiq, created a difficult dilemma for voters looking for a candidate who would advance the agenda of the revolution, and particularly the demands for social justice. Shafiq clearly represented the choice of those who wanted a counter-revolutionary restoration, but he benefited from the animosity of revolutionary activists towards his rival, Morsi. Sabahy cried foul, demanding a recount and an investigation into alleged vote-rigging. Many of his supporters among the independent unions declared they would follow his lead and boycott the run-offs.

The Muslim Brotherhood, for its part, presented an electoral programme which aimed to win the votes of workers and the poor with promises appearing to offer a vision of 'social justice'. The 'Renaissance Project' made a number of promises that are likely to have boosted Morsi's appeal among working-class and poor voters, including the establishment of a national fund for unemployment benefit and 'restarting idle capacity' in the national economy.[38] He promised to 'reconsider the policy of privatisation' and protect 'successful public projects' from being sold off. Job creation was largely assumed to come through 'improv[ing] the investment climate', raising the level of national investment to 30 per cent of GDP, and the elimination of obstacles to private-sector development, but it was also envisaged that the promotion of health and education programmes would 'absorb large numbers of graduates'. A rather vague claim that Morsi would 'improve the conditions of workers and peasants' was expanded with a number of specific commitments, including the restructuring of wages so that the minimum wage would 'provide the opportunity for the Egyptian family to enjoy a decent life', with annual inflation-linked increases, in addition to 'determining the maximum wage'. The programme promised reform of the insurance funds legislation and reform of pension laws to extend coverage to all Egyptians.

There were even hints that trade unionists would benefit from the Muslim Brotherhood's ascension to power, through amendments to Law 12 of 2003 in order to 'create a fair balance between the interests of workers and employers', and amendments to Law 35 of 1976 and Law 12 of 1995 in order to 'increase the scope of trade-union freedoms without fragmenting trade-union organisation'. This last promise, as already discussed in Chapter 7, actually indicated the Brotherhood's commitment to a strategy of strengthening the ETUF as a counterweight to the independent unions. Another significant promise was the commitment to 'work towards permanent contracts for temporary workers or the provision of wages, conditions and contracts which give them security and equality with permanent workers'.

Careful reading of the policies of Morsi's 'Renaissance Project' revealed a different goal: the articulation of a neoliberal programme clothed in the rhetoric of reform. Most of the social reforms were vaguely defined: no figures were set for minimum and maximum wages, for example, and the commitment to job security was expressed in equally slippery rhetoric. And, as we have already seen in Chapter 6, the gap between the Brotherhood's electoral policies and the social crisis of his year in power was painfully large.

Nevertheless, Morsi could still count on the active support of some leading figures in the workers' movement, particularly those who, for reasons of personal religiosity and political conviction, inclined towards the Islamist currrent. Tareq el-Beheiry, a prominent figure in the Independent Public Transport Workers' Union in Cairo and a bus driver based at Imbaba Garage, mobilised, by his own account, around 14,000 votes for Morsi across the PTA. The PTA workers had been split between Sabahy and Morsi in the first round, but thanks, at least in part, to Tareq's energetic efforts, they swung towards Morsi in the second round, with senior management backing Shafiq. The Freedom and Justice Party intervened actively in the debates in the PTA, sending a delegation of high-ranking officials to visit Tareq and lead Friday prayers in the mosque at Imbaba Garage on 15 June.[39]

When it came to the second round of the presidential elections, comparison between voting patterns in a range of areas which share a high concentration of industrial workplaces reveals a complex picture.[40] Morsi won comfortably in the district of Mina al-Basl in Alexandria, which includes the naval shipyards, and scored an overwhelming victory in Al-Amiriyya and Borg al-Arab to the west of the city, which are home to a large number of factories (although the results for Al-Amiriyya also include the returns from the rural areas of the district). Like the rest of urban Alexandria, the district had been won by Sabahy in the first round.[41]

The town of Kafr al-Dawwar, dominated for decades by the public-sector textile industry, and scene of significant worker rebellions in 1952 and 1994, was taken by Morsi with 67 per cent of the vote, having voted for Aboul-Fotouh during the first round. Morsi also won the two most populous districts in Suez, a town also dominated by industry, including steel production and textiles, although by a smaller margin: 62 per cent in Al-Arba'in and 64 per cent in Faysal. He also took nearly 60 per cent of the vote in the two electoral districts in 10th of Ramadan, a 'new' industrial centre between Cairo and Zaqaziq housing dozens of factories. Although 10th of Ramadan's workforce includes a large number of commuters from Zaqaziq, neighbouring Bilbeis and the northern suburbs of Cairo, tens of thousands of workers live in the town itself. Morsi's comfortable victory in 10th of Ramadan went against the trend across Al-Sharqiyya governorate, where Shafiq took first place with 54 per cent of the vote.

It also ran counter to the trend in the working-class and lower-middle-class districts of Shubra al-Khaima on the northern border of Cairo. Shubra al-Khaima, an old industrial area with a large Christian population, is a historic centre for the textile industry, but is also home to other important industrial workplaces. Shafiq took the Shubra al-Khaima districts in both rounds of the presidential elections, although not by a large margin in district 2, where Morsi won 48 per cent of the vote. Shafiq won comfortably across all three electoral districts in the industrial town of Al-Mahalla al-Kubra, birthplace of the pre-revolutionary strike wave and home to the giant Misr Spinning complex. Hamdeen Sabahy had won the two urban districts of Mahalla in the first round, while the town's rural hinterland voted for Shafiq. Yet the industrial centre of Helwan, base of the Egyptian Iron and Steel Company and a large number of military-owned factories, gave Morsi 58 per cent of the vote, in contrast with Shafiq's overall success across the Cairo governorate.

Mahalla's disenchantment with Morsi during the presidential elections stands in sharp contrast to the Brotherhood's previous electoral success in the city. In 2005, Sa'd al-Husseiny, a local civil engineer and a leading figure in the Brotherhood, was elected to represent Mahalla in the workers' seat. The Brotherhood took 4 out 10 seats in the large multi-member PR constituency covering Mahalla during the parliamentary elections of 2011, while the Nour Party won 3 seats. Sa'd al-Husseiny was one of the FJP's 3 MPs elected out of 4 seats in the two majoritarian consituencies in Mahalla in the same elections. Shubra al-Khaima, too, had

voted for the Brotherhood in previous elections: Mohamed al-
Beltagi was elected MP for the 'professionals' seat in the city's
first electoral district in 2005.

A swift and bitter end to the Brotherhood's honeymoon

The stifling heat of summer makes Cairo hell for its poorest
inhabitants. As the rich turn up their air conditioners, in the
sprawling 'informal' neighbourhoods which ring the city hundreds of thousands suffer water shortages and power cuts. After
Morsi's election, the people of Saft al-Laban neighbourhood took
matters into their own hands. On 22 July, after weeks without
water, they stormed the Giza governorate buildings and locked
the gates. When this failed to solve the water crisis, on 11 August
they took their protests to the Ministry of Water and Sanitation.
Hundreds joined a demonstration outside the offices of the minister of water, Abdel Qawi al-Khalifa. At one point, protesters are
said to have cornered the minister himself, setting down a glass
of filthy brown water in front him. 'This is what you expect us to
give our children', they told him. 'Now it's your turn to drink it.'
Within hours of the protest, Morsi had rearranged his schedule
for an emergency meeting with al-Khalifa to discuss ways to
end the crisis. By the next morning, Water Ministry spokesman
Brigadier Muhyi Serafi was reassuring the media that a task force
had worked at immense speed to resolve the problems and get
the water flowing again in Saft al-Laban.

The forcible entry of Saft al-Laban's residents into the cor-
ridors of power came at the precise moment another drama was
unfolding – this time at the very apex of the state. As Morsi
listened to Al-Khalifa's excuses as to why the Water Ministry
had been unable to turn on the taps in Saft al-Laban, his mind
may well have been focused on other issues: in particular the
statement announcing Field Marshal Tantawi's resignation, which

his spokesman would read out to a stunned audience of journalists at a press conference the following day.

As the news of Tantawi's departure broke, the administrator of the 'Youth of Saft al-Laban Are One Hand' Facebook page, who, until the day before, had been focused on mobilising for the water protests, posted a comment: 'The decisions that President Morsi took are a "Night of the Long Knives" and the end of the army's state.' Another contributor was more cautious: 'These are decisions which all revolutionaries have been demanding. They are the first step towards Egypt's independence from military rule and the beginning of building a genuine civil democratic state. And I hope, god willing, we'll get rid of all the corrupt men.'[42]

While politicians and journalists digested the implications of Morsi's rearrangement of the military elite, discussions in Imbaba bus garage had turned back to one of the PTA workers' long-standing grievances. How could the bus drivers return to direct management by the Ministry of Transport, rather than by the local authorities in Cairo, who they blamed for corruption and mismanagement of the bus service? Tareq el-Beheiry was hopeful that the Islamist president he had helped to elect would intervene in the PTA workers' favour. Four previous rounds of negotiations had produced a draft law returning the PTA to the Ministry, but then the military had dissolved parliament. Undeterred, the union officials went to talk to the Public Transport Committee in the parliament's upper house, the Shura Council. Another agreement was thrashed out, this time making the PTA independent of both the Cairo governorate and the Ministry, but newly appointed prime minister Hisham Qandil refused to implement the deal. Tareq and his colleagues lost patience and called a strike to coincide with the first day of the new school year. To his fury and amazement, Tareq was denounced by the Muslim Brotherhood politicians he had brought to power, and arrested by the police along with several other striking workers. Months later he was still seething over the incident: 'I won't vote for the Muslim Brotherhood again; they want to make a new pharaoh and we won't let them do it', he said in October, 'I'll vote for the Salafists. They are religious, not political. They won't repress or betray anyone.'[43]

Even as early as August 2012, these unfolding dramas at the base and apex of the state revealed the constraints on the Brotherhood's room for manoeuvre. The bus workers' strike for decent conditions at work and investment in public transport marked the beginning of yet another battle pitting organised workers against a recalcitrant, neoliberal government, this time under the leadership of the Muslim Brotherhood. Likewise, Saft al-Laban's residents were only the first of many who would take to the streets in protest at water and electricity cuts, and shortages of cooking gas and petrol. As subsequent events were to prove, 12 August 2012 was not the 'end of the army's state', but merely marked a moment of transition from one generation of the high command to another.

The crisis over the constitution

The silence of workers' voices in the formal political arena became even more apparent during the first six months of Morsi's rule, as the Muslim Brotherhood's plans for the transition to a post-revolutionary era became clearer. Morsi's economic programme, the 'Renaissance Project', confirmed the Brotherhood's commitment to the neoliberal norms of the old regime. Rather than replenish depleted government reserves through progressive taxation, or confront the military's economic empire, the Brotherhood looked to negotiations with the International Monetary Fund for a way out of the escalating fiscal crisis.

The battle over the constitution was opened by the popular reaction to the deepening crisis in the relationship between the executive and the judiciary. On 22 November Morsi issued a new constitutional declaration, stating that presidential decisions taken since 30 June 2012 could not be challenged by any entity, appointing a new prosecutor-general, and protecting the Shura Council and Constituent Assembly from dissolution by the courts.[44] The declaration also reopened the prosecution of officials of the former regime 'in the cases of the murder, the attempted murder and the wounding of protesters as well as the crimes of terror committed against the revolutionaries'. Liberal, leftist and revolutionary youth groups called protests which brought hundreds of thousands onto the streets in protest, while the final votes on the draft constitution were rushed through the Constituent Assembly, by now lacking almost any representation from non-Islamist political forces. The Brotherhood, the major Salafist parties and other Islamist groups, mobilised tens of thousands in counter-protests in support of Morsi.

Many activists in the workers' movement threw themselves into the campaign against the constitutional declaration and the constitution. Although the Mubarak regime had used mechanisms such as the workers' and farmers' quota to control and silence workers' voices in the political arena, and the apparent obligation in the existing constitution on the state to guarantee social rights including to housing, free health care and education had been denuded by decades of neoliberal reforms, the 2012 Constitution either removed many of these provisions from the text altogether or couched the relevant clauses in ambiguous language and refused to specify any mechanisms for their implementation. Economist Ahmad al-Naggar's critique of the draft constitution highlights a number of issues which were of particular concern to activists in the workers' movement.[45] Article 14, for example, included the provision of a minimum and a maximum wage, but, like the 1971 Constitution, set no specific criteria for the relationship between minimum and maximum, and moreover allowed exceptions to the maximum wage, which was only applicable to state employees.

This article also linked wage levels to productivity rather than prices, a provocative step after years of inflationary pressure on the cost of living. Nor did the constitution offer much relief for the poor through the taxation system: Article 26 on taxation failed even to mention the principle of progressive taxation or capital gains taxes; nor did it provide for tax exemption for low-income citizens. Article 63 did not require the state to find jobs for citizens, nor to support the unemployed, nor to guarantee to provide social insurance. The wording of Article 66 was similarly mealy-mouthed, stating that 'the state will endeavour' rather than the 'state is obliged to' provide an adequate pension for workers and small farmers.

The constitution's failure to define and defend the social and economic rights of the poor was compounded by its hostile attitude towards the right to organise. Article 52 stated that the freedom to form trade unions, associations and co-operatives was guaranteed by law, but then permitted their dissolution by court order. As Al-Naggar and other critics pointed out, this represented a massive expansion of the powers of the courts to intervene in union affairs, as previously judges could only order the dissolution of a union executive, rather than the entire union. Article 53 banned the formation of more than one union per profession, thus contradicting the 'freedom' granted in Article 52, and reimposing a version of the centralised ETUF system. In terms of workers' representation in the legislature, many activists in workers' movement were angered by the removal of the occupation quota in the Shura Council (which was at the same time given expanded legislative powers), and by its retention for only one further electoral cycle in the People's Assembly.

The constitution's equivocation over Egyptian citizens' social and economic rights was noticeably absent from its attitude to the role of the military in the state. Far from reducing the Armed Forces' powers and their immunity from civilian oversight, the new constitution increased them.[46] Key concessions to the military included the explicit stipulation that the minister of defence must be a military officer, which was missing from the 1971 Constitution, even though the post has been held by serving officers since 1952, and the creation of a National Defence Council with a majority of senior military officers (Article 197).[47] The National Defence Council was to be consulted about draft laws 'related to the Armed Forces', and was declared 'responsible for matters pertaining to the methods of ensuring the safety and security of the country and to the budget of the Armed Forces' – in other words leaving both matters of national security and the oversight of the Armed Forces' vast economic empire outside civilian control.[48] Global and Egyptian human rights campaigners argued that Article 198 sanctioned the continued use of military trials for civilians, as it allowed their prosecution by the military courts 'for crimes that harm the Armed Forces'.[49] As the Egyptian campaigning group No Military Trials argued, the vagueness of the definition of these 'crimes' would allow the continued use of the Code of Military Justice against civilians. Under the Code, civilians may be brought before military courts if one of the parties involved in the case was a military officer or if the crime occurred in an area where the military was deployed.[50]

The process by which the constitution was drafted likewise demonstrated, once again, the Brotherhood's continued reliance on the Egyptian Trade Union Federation and the Ministry of Labour, which were the old regime's favourite mechanisms to engineer the presence of compliant workers' representatives. However, in contrast to the NDP's phalanxes of loyal 'worker' MPs, the 'workers' in the appointed Constituent Assembly were Khaled al-Azhary, the minister of labour, and a representative of ETUF. What emerged, then, in the 2012 Constitution was a recast version of the old regime, but one where the balance has tipped even further towards neoliberalism. Its hybrid character is camouflaged somewhat by rhetorical references to social justice and to the social provisions of the old constitution. In relation to the right to form unions independent of the state, it was the old Nasserist system that remained essentially intact, this time with a liberal covering.[51]

EFITU activists in the Federation's national leadership and in a number of independent unions made a concerted effort to mobilise a campaign for a 'No' vote which emphasized the constitution's failure to address workers' social demands. They distributed thousands of leaflets, helped to organise street protests and rallies, and set up a protest camp in Tahrir Square. Unions with a national network of branches, such as the Independent Teachers' Union and the property tax collectors' union RETAU, played an important role in mobilising protests by trade unionists in the provinces. Interviewed in Tahrir Square between the two rounds of voting in mid-December, Mervat Mahmoud, an activist from the Independent Property Tax Collectors' Union in 6th of October City, about 20 miles south of Cairo, explained how colleagues in the union were leading protests across the country:

> I came with a delegation at the beginning of the protests. Colleagues came from Suez, Port Sa'id, Dahaqiliyya, Alexandria, Giza, Cairo, Luxor, Aswan and Assiyut. Now they've returned home and are organising rallies and protests calling for the cancellation of the Constitutional Declaration and the Constituent Assembly.

Mahmoud's colleague Sherihan Sabry, an educational psychologist working in a Cairo primary school, reported a similar story:

> We've also done the same thing in the Independent Teachers' Union. Through the union we've organised in every governorate. We had protests in Alexandria and Port Sa'id for example. There were fantastic rallies and demonstrations and a lot of people took part in the provinces.

Teachers were furious that the constitution failed to clearly specify citizens' rights to education.

> We wanted to raise the general level of education and change the educational system and the curriculum completely. All the phrases about education in the Constitution are just rubber-stamp expressions. Even the part which mentioned free education was removed.

For Mohamed Hardan, vice president of the Independent Union of Water Company Workers, the link between social and political demands was vital:

> We've won a lot of support for our argument that wages must be linked to rising prices. Many workers are angry because they've heard that the constitution links wages to production. A few days before the new constitutional declaration price rises and taxes were announced, which the IMF is demanding as part of the conditions for the loan. Then the decision was delayed, but we are 100 per cent certain that after the referendum prices and taxes will rise.

Yet, although the battle over the constitution took place against the backdrop of large numbers of strikes and social protests – including a national strike led by junior doctors in public hospitals during October and November, strikes by port workers in Ain Sokhna, and successful action by thousands of workers on the Cairo Metro – the social crisis found only muted expression in the political arena. The major alliance that took shape among Morsi's opponents was the National Salvation Front, a coalition encompassing Nasserist Hamdeen Sabahy, liberal figures such as Mohamed ElBaradei, officials from the former regime who claimed to be promoting an agenda of liberal reforms, such as Amr Moussa, and sections of the far left, including the Popular Socialist Alliance. The very character of the National Salvation Front, as it was predicated on alliance with both elements of the old regime, and with mainstream liberals, precluded any serious orientation on social demands. It was only in the last week or so before the constitutional referendum that social demands began to percolate more widely, and even then these were only raised systematically by the revolutionary left and the independent unions.

Moreover, the ideological terrain on which the battle over the constitution was fought favoured those who wished to rehabilitate key elements of the old regime. The liberals and Nasserists focused on calls to respect the independence of the judiciary and the principle of the separation of powers. Morsi, by contrast, made concerted efforts to appeal to the Islamists' shrinking popular base by claiming to be carrying out the revolutionary task of purging the judiciary of supporters of the old regime. The problem with the first position was that it allowed some of Mubarak's most senior judges to clothe themselves in the popular legitimacy of the massive street protests against Morsi, and strengthened the idea that the institutions of the state should be protected from reform. The more radical elements in the National Salvation Front did not advance their own agenda for the 'cleansing' of the judiciary or present an alternative to Morsi's claims to be acting in the interests of 'revolutionary justice'.

The crisis of electoral legitimacy and the road to 30 June

Between March 2011 and December 2012, Egyptians went to the polls in four national elections: the referendum on the constitutional amendments in March 2011; the parliamentary elections, which were held in stages between November 2011 and January 2012; the presidential elections of June 2012; and finally the constitutional referendum of December 2012. Two major political cleavages shaped the electoral contests: the battle between revolutionary and counter-revolutionary forces, and that between Islamist and secular currents. These divisions did not map neatly onto each other, reflecting the shifting tactics of the counter-revolutionary forces, as they moved from alliance with different reformist currents in an effort to create a buffer between themselves and the continuing anger on the streets. So in the referendum of March 2011, the Supreme Council of the Armed Forces proposed the amendments and received the strong support of the Islamist current, which framed the vote as a battle between 'Islam' and 'secularism' in defence of Egypt's 'Islamic identity' as expressed in Article 2 of the constitution. By December 2012, as discussed above, counter-revolutionary forces were attempting to ride popular anger against the Muslim Brotherhood, and campaigning strongly against the new constitution. Both 'the Islamist vote' and overall electoral participation declined sharply during in the period 2011 to 2013. The constitutional referendum of March 2011 saw the 'Yes' camp, which was largely identified with the Islamists, win around 70 per cent of the vote. In the parliamentary elections the Islamist forces won around 30 million votes, yet in the presidential elections the Brotherhood's candidate only took about 6 million votes.

The outcome of the battle over the constitution showed the continuation of these trends, despite the Islamist camp organising an emotive campaign for a 'Yes' vote which mobilised religious language against the 'No' camp, while additionally accusing their opponents of being *feloul*, 'remnants' of the old regime. The overall turnout dropped to 32 per cent; the 'No' vote won in the capital city with 57 per cent and came close to a majority in Alexandria.[52] As in the presidential elections, the Islamist vote was shored up by large majorities in rural areas and in the south. Critically, a mere six months into his presidential term, Morsi was unable to project himself as being in any sense above partisan politics; nor was he able to use the authority of state office to disperse or repress protesters, resorting instead to mobilising the Brotherhood's own activist base to attack protesters outside Al-Ittihadiyya presidential palace. The referendum did take place according to the timescale dictated by Morsi. But the solid 'No' vote in many urban areas and the low turnout undermined Morsi's authority and provided graphic confirmation of the Islamists' narrowing electoral base.

Challenges to the Brotherhood's authority to govern thus came from many directions at once. The Islamists' electoral mandate weakened with each successive national election.[53] They had also clearly lost the support of the streets: despite being able to mobilise tens of thousands for their embattled president in each round of protests, the scale of popular mobilisation opposing Morsi was far larger, even if it is difficult to believe some of the largest figures claimed for the protests on 30 June. As the crisis deepened, so did the Brotherhood's reliance on the least representative institutions in the legislature, such as the Shura Council, which had been elected almost unnoticed in February 2012 on a turnout of less than 10 per cent,[54] and the Constituent Assembly, elected by the parliament which the Brotherhood stopped defending in July 2012, in return for partial access to the executive powers of the presidency. It preferred not to brave the certainty of censure by the electorate and the likelihood of having to work in coalition with other reformist forces by fighting to increase the sovereignty of the elected parts of the state over the non-elected.

At the same time, the Brotherhood made increasingly desperate attempts to win the loyalty of the police and army, by shoring up their repressive functions. The Shura Council on 27 January 2013, for example, voted in favour of a new public order law expanding the powers of the police to deal with 'riots and thuggery', while also giving the military the right to arrest civilians in Suez and Port Sa'id in the wake of protests and clashes between riot police and demonstrators.[55] On the occasions when the police refused to carry out Morsi's orders (for tactical reasons, and not out of any principled sympathy for the demonstrators, it must be emphasised), the Brotherhood turned increasingly to the activist base of the Islamist movement to act as 'police' – attacking demonstrators, and in some areas taking over functions of maintaining law and order.[56] These moves, which took place in the context of widespread police strikes in March 2013, inspired fears of both the collapse of public security and the emergence of a state of Islamist militias.

The crisis of electoral legitimacy was not, however, simply the result of the frustration and disenchantment of part of the Brotherhood's electoral base with reformists who had promised much and failed to deliver. Nor was it just a product of the clash between the rising tide of social struggles and the impatience of workers and the poor with parliamentary methods which compared unfavourably to their experience of the rapid impact of self-organised collective action. In retrospect it seems clear that Abdel-Fattah al-Sisi and the leadership of the Armed Forces also systematically undermined the authority of the elected presidency by reviving a form of populist authoritarianism which appealed simultaneously to sections of the middle and upper classes, who feared the disintegration of the state itself, and to a substantial constituency among workers and the poor who despaired of seeing even modest social reforms under the Brotherhood's rule. Even more disconcertingly, the secular reformists who worked with the army leadership against Morsi clothed the whole process in a rhetoric emphasising the revolutionary legitimacy of the movement in the streets. Yet, rather than counterposing an agenda of genuine social and political reforms to the Brotherhood's alliance with Mubarak's generals and policemen, they made their own marriage of convenience with sections of the judiciary who wanted to preserve at all costs their own privileged position in the state, and with politicians from the old order, who gained a gloss of 'revolutionary legitimacy' as a result. As events moved towards a climax in the final six months of Morsi's presidency, on the stage of national politics a mirror image of the Brotherhood's 'reformism' emerged as the dominant opposition force. The National Salvation Front strove to create an alliance with the military, police and judiciary to counterbalance the grip of its Islamist rivals on parts of the state apparatus, enabling all three to recover themselves and prepare for counter-revolution.

CHAPTER 9

Tathir: the struggle to cleanse the state

The Egyptian Revolution entered its third year still governed by the paradox that marked its birth. Participation in the revolution transformed millions of ordinary people from passive victims of history to its makers, but the state they confronted on 25 January 2011 remained essentially intact. Meanwhile, the legitimacy of the largest former Islamist opposition party, the Muslim Brotherhood, had already been badly damaged by the failure to achieve meaningful political and social reforms since its assumption of power six months previously. This deepening contradiction helps to explain why on 3 July 2013 the Armed Forces under the leadership of Abdel-Fattah al-Sisi, minister of defence, was able to intervene decisively and turn the Muslim Brotherhood's crisis in the face of an explosion of popular anger to the advantage of the core institutions of Mubarak's state.

For some commentators, the events of July 2013 confirmed their claim that the revolution of 2011 was a collective hallucination by millions of Egyptians who temporarily believed that the state which oppressed them could be changed for the better.[1] Our perspective is different. We concur that the central problem facing all those who had an interest in the continuation of the revolution after Mubarak's removal from power was the failure of the repressive institutions at the core of his state to fracture. We will explore here first the failure of the initial wave of *tathir*, the battle to cleanse the state of the old regime. Despite waves of strikes and protests demanding the ejection of Mubarak's supporters from positions of authority, the pace of change within the state during the first two years of the revolution was glacially slow. The principal reason for this, we will argue, is the resilience of the 'Officers' Republic', or the networks of patronage which enmesh the military and bureaucratic parts of the state machinery in an intimate embrace with sections of state and private capital.[2]

Where we disagree with pessimistic analyses which write the Egyptian Revolution out of history is in our assessment of the lessons of the struggle for *tathir*. Throughout this book we have argued that the Egyptian Revolution has been profoundly shaped from the outset by the role that workers have played as a self-organised force in both the development of the revolutionary crisis and the revolutionary process after the fall of Mubarak. 'Shaping' is not the same as 'leading' and we have also discussed the contradiction between Egyptian workers' evident collective social power and their collective political weakness. Yet, just as the strike waves were critical to the destabilisation and paralysis of Mubarak's regime before the revolution, so organised workers remain the section of the revolutionary movement with the greatest potential power to fracture the 'Officers' Republic'. This chapter will demonstrate how workers' collective action carried revolution deep into the institutions of the state itself, and in the process raised the spectre of a deeper process of social transformation which has the potential not merely to alter the existing state, but to break it and build a different kind of state in its place. In the final chapter we ask what kind of revolutionary organisation could prepare for this battle.

The Officers' Republic and the military's grip on the 'shallow state'

The failure of the Egyptian Revolution to fit neatly into the narratives of 'democratic transition' that have dominated academic analysis of the breakdown of versions of state-capitalist authoritarian regimes, from Latin America to the Soviet bloc,[3] needs to be explored from two perspectives. We discussed the first of these in the previous chapter: the lack of representation for the social demands of workers and the poor in the arena of formal democratic politics – an absence which, we will argue, was instrumental in creating the final crisis of Morsi's presidency in June 2013. The second, which is the primary subject of this chapter, sets the crisis of Mubarak's reformist opponents against the continued resilience of the old regime's core institutions, and in particular their failure to challenge the penetration of all layers of the state apparatus – and not merely the 'deep state' – by the military and police.

The prominent role played by the Egyptian state's 'special bodies of armed men'[4] in the wake of Mubarak's fall has often been labelled an assertion of the authority of the 'deep state', a term imported from the lexicon of Turkish politics.[5] However, it is not the case that would-be reformers in Egypt have only faced the challenge of confronting the state's buried core, which surfaces at times of stress. The problem lies also in the 'shallow state', where both military and police officers are embedded at almost every managerial level of the 'civilian' bureaucracy. As Sayigh and Abul-Magd document, the Egyptian Armed Forces provide a structured career path for those officers who wish to pursue roles in state administration.[6] Those who leave military service at the lower ranks of the officer corps are provided with opportunities to work their way up from middle-management roles within provincial or national administration or public-sector industry to Cabinet appointment: this was the route taken by Atif Helmi, minister of telecommunications appointed by Hisham Qandil in January 2013.[7] Officers who begin their administrative careers as the head of a local government unit, for example, may scale the bureaucratic ladder to senior positions in the provincial administration, and then possibly to a governorship and ministerial office. The provincial governors occupy a crucial place in the bureaucratic-military machine. This powerful role serves as the node of interchange between the civil and military wings of the bureaucracy. Although retired military and police officers have tended to predominate, governors are also drawn from the ranks of the civilian public-sector bureaucracy, heads of state universities and the judiciary. A provincial governorship is a common staging-post en route to a Cabinet appointment. However, a governorship is also an extremely powerful post in its own right, enjoying wide-ranging executive authority at provincial level. On the eve of the outbreak of revolution in 2011 fourteen out of twenty-nine governors were from a military background, and another six were police generals. The remaining nine included three lawyers, three engineers, an architect, and two senior academics. The Armed Forces generals had arrived in their roles as governors by a variety of routes. Some had worked their way up through the civilian bureaucracy to a governorship; others, such as the governors of Suez and Isma'iliyya, had risen through the ranks of the Armed Forces to command the Third and Second Field Armies respectively.

However, those officers who ascend to the higher ranks of the Armed Forces also benefit from direct appointment to equivalent levels of the civilian bureaucracy. At Cabinet level, a number of key posts have long been held by senior officers in the Armed Forces. Since September 1952, when the Free Officers first took control of the Cabinet two months after the overthrow of King Farouq, the post of minister of defence has been held by a senior army officer. It was widely seen as the second most powerful role in the state. When Mubarak forced Abd-al-Halim Abu Ghazala to resign as minister of defence in 1989, in the midst of a scandal about the transfer of restricted missile technology from the United States, this was interpreted by many as an attempt to reduce the influence of a powerful rival.[8] The Ministry of Civil Aviation, like the rest of the civil aviation sector, has long been within the purview of the Air Force.

The influence of the Armed Forces over the judiciary operates through distinct but complementary channels. The military judicial system has extensive powers over civilians, and was a key mechanism for policing political dissent during the pre-revolutionary period, through the use of military trials against civilian opposition leaders, such as Muslim Brotherhood deputy supreme guide Khairat al-Shater in 2008.[9] The use of military courts against civilians increased dramatically after the overthrow of Mubarak: between 28 January and 29 August 2011 a total of 11,879 civilians were tried in military courts. Articles 5 and 6 of the Code of Military Justice allow for the military trial of civilians for crimes under the penal code if the crime takes place in an area under military control or a military officer is one of the parties involved.[10] As we saw in Chapter 8, the privileges of the military judiciary were enhanced by the constitution of 2012. Moreover, the civilian and military judiciaries are not hermetically sealed; legal officials within the military judiciary can be appointed to high-level positions within the civilian judiciary. Faruq Sultan, the president of the Constitutional Court 2009–12, was a judge in the military and state security courts before being appointed president of the South Cairo Court in the civilian judicial system in 2006.[11]

Former and serving officers of the Interior Ministry forces are also woven into the fabric of the state bureaucracy. Police generals are to be found in mid-level roles in provincial administration, and are appointed to provincial governorships directly from senior positions within the state security apparatus. On the eve of the revolution, the governors of Beheira, Daqahiliyya, Sohag and Gharbiyya provinces were all police officers, having passed through a variety of roles in provincial security directorates, General Intelligence (*Mukhabarat*), and the Interior Ministry en route. As with their military colleagues, senior officials within the Interior Ministry can also count on a key Cabinet-level appointment to watch over their interests. The post of minister of the interior has been occupied by a long line of police officers since the 1970s.[12] Moreover, through their appointment to provincial governorships, police officers form part of the pool from which a large number of Cabinet appointments are routinely made. The selection of candidates for governorships is managed by the minister of local development. Before July 2011 the incumbent was General Mohsen al-Nu'mani, a former deputy head of the General Intelligence Department. He was followed by Mohamed Ahmed Attia, a former judge, who held the post until August 2012, when Morsi, perhaps in a gesture towards the military, picked Ahmed Abdeen, a retired general, to serve in Hisham Qandil's first Cabinet.[13] Abdeen was replaced by Mohamed Ali Bishr, a leading figure in the Freedom and Justice Party. Morsi's removal from power saw the return of the post to the Interior Ministry once again, however, with the appointment of Adel Labib, governor of Qena and a former state security officer: a clear indication of the reviving self-confidence of the Interior Ministry within the state apparatus.[14]

Cleansing the state: alternative perspectives

The 2011 uprising presented a profound challenge to those who had operated this machinery for decades. Protesters massed in the provinces, demanding the removal of incumbent provincial governors and decrying the appointment of replacements from the same stock.[15] As the protest movement in the streets revived in the late spring and early summer, successive Cabinets were buffeted by waves of demonstrations raising the call for a far-reaching purge, particularly of the Interior Ministry.[16] While the leaders of the Armed Forces fought to protect the core institutions of the state, sharply contrasting approaches to the demand for *tathir*, or cleansing, emerged among the reformist and revolutionary currents grouped loosely around the banner of the January Revolution. The first approach we will discuss here was implicit, but never fully articulated, in the battles fought by hundreds of thousands, and perhaps millions, of Egyptians to 'cleanse' the state from below. The struggles of public-sector workers to impose new forms of democratic control over their bosses, and to remove unelected generals from the lower levels of the state apparatus, pointed the way towards a mechanism to paralyse and ultimately fragment the 'Officers' Republic' from below. Yet this perspective found no echo among the main reformist currents on the stage of national politics.

Thus the second approach to the question of *tathir* was one largely shared by the Muslim Brotherhood and its secular rivals among the liberals and Nasserists. They agreed on the need to preserve the repressive core of the Mubarak regime largely unaltered, although they exhibited differing degrees of willingness to confront and change some of the personnel in other parts of the state. Furthermore, they both worked to fracture the unity of the political and social struggles that the January Revolution had briefly achieved. In particular they sought to separate the battle for democratic change from the struggle for bread and social justice, in order to better conceal their compromises with Mubarak's generals and policemen. As we saw in the previous chapter, the Brotherhood turned the 'revolution's parliament' into a weapon in the war against strikes and social protests by workers and the poor, while the liberals and Nasserists backed street protests cheering on the police and army and organised 'popular committees' to defend the repressive institutions of the state.

During the first year of the Egyptian Revolution, the process of *tathir* demonstrated the mutually reinforcing dynamic of reciprocal action between political and economic struggles, as identified by Luxemburg.[17] The removal of managers and state officials by popular protests and strikes dramatically shifted what Goodrich calls the 'frontier of control',[18] although on a temporary basis. In a small number of cases workers succeeded in imposing formal democratic control over their managers by choosing replacements to the purged officials of the old regime through elections. In other examples that we discuss in detail below, workers' action enforced the demilitarisation of sections of the state, such as parts of the civil aviation sector, challenging and disrupting the grip of the 'Officers' Republic' over the 'shallow state'. During the second and third years of the revolution, although some of these early struggles had been contained and their gains reversed, hundreds of thousands of workers within state institutions and across the public sector continued to raise demands for *tathir* in their strikes and protests.

Thus, despite its limitations, the experience of '*tathir* from below' is rich in ideological and practical lessons not only for the future of the revolution in Egypt itself, but for popular uprisings against other authoritarian regimes. These struggles remained relatively disjointed and isolated both from each other and from the popular revolutionary mobilisations in the streets, and thus were incapable, on their own, of enforcing the demands of their participants on the state as a whole. Nevertheless they opened up new ways of thinking for hundreds of thousands of Egyptians, who imagined and acted as if they could remake the state according to the principles of the popular revolution. It is no wonder that the organisers of counter-revolution were desperate to taint these dangerous ideas with the Brotherhood's unpopularity. Struggles for *tathir* from below were important precisely because they joined the social and political souls of the revolution, shifting the 'frontier of control' within state and public-sector workplaces, *and* attempting to impose workers' solutions on the state by their own methods: strikes and sit-ins. They showed the possibility that ordinary people could begin to 'think like a state', to impose the democracy they forged in collective action *in place of* the normal hierarchies of state institutions. In other words, they demonstrated in practice how workers' self-organised collective action could change the *content* of relationships within the state in ways far deeper than the Brotherhood, the liberals or the Nasserists ever dreamed.

It is important to emphasize that even if the struggles we will examine here had been better joined up, and more successful in effecting long-term change within state institutions, this would still not have been enough to alter the state as a whole. Numerous historical examples, from the outcome of the 1974 Portuguese Revolution,[19] to the battles for workers' control in the Iranian public sector after the Iranian Revolution of 1979,[20] to the more recent experience of the containment of the popular movements in Bolivia between 2000 and 2007,[21] demonstrate that the capitalist state cannot be transformed from within into an instrument of the exploited and oppressed. We return to what this means for the question of revolutionary organisation in the Egyptian context in the final chapter.

Re-imagining the public sector from below

As discussed in Chapter 6, demands for *tathir* were a consistent feature of workers' struggles during the first two years of the revolution. Across the public sector, from the bus garages of Cairo's public transport system to the university campuses and state-owned textile mills and sugar refineries, workers organised strikes and protests to demand the removal of representatives of the old ruling party from management. In a small number of cases, battles against the boss turned into much deeper struggles, raising questions about the organisation of work and the nature of the public sector itself.

The question of *tathir* was woven into many of the battles between the workers of the Public Transport Authority in Cairo and their management during 2011 and 2012. Through the independent union which was established in the wake of Mubarak's downfall, bus drivers organised strikes and protests in May 2011,[22] September 2011,[23] March 2012,[24] June 2012,[25] September 2012,[26] February 2013[27] and May 2013.[28] As discussed in Chapter 8, these raised a variety of different demands, ranging from raises in pay, bonuses and pensions, to improvements to and investment in the bus fleet, and the key demand of return to the Ministry of Transport. The question of *tathir* emerged largely within the framework of the bus workers' campaign against corruption in the PTA, and their demands for the removal and prosecution of its head and other senior figures, including the leaders of the ETUF-affiliated Land Transport Union, who were identified by striking bus workers as 'symbols of corruption' just like the PTA bosses. Telecom Egypt (TE) was the scene of similarly fierce battles between the largely state-owned company's insurgent workforce and management. Workers organised protests in July 2011, demanding the cleansing of the company, followed by a wave of sit-ins and strikes in October, triggered by the arrest of TE workers, who were accused of kidnapping the company's chief executive. Within hours of the arrests, thousands of TE workers were on strike, occupying their workplaces and threatening to cut off all services if their demands for the resignation of the board of directors and the release of their jailed colleagues were not met.[29] TE workers continued to organise themselves to demand *tathir* during the following year, with a large sit-in taking place during September 2012. Leaders of the TE workers' independent union welcomed the resignation of Aqil Bashir, the director of the company, and insisted that it was the pressure of their campaign that had pushed the Muslim Brotherhood-led government into action.[30]

The university campuses were another very important arena in which the struggle for *tathir* was played out. The battle over the public universities was a direct struggle with sections of the state bureaucracy. As discussed above, senior figures in university administrations form part of the pool from which high-ranking state officials, including the powerful provincial governors, are drawn. Appointments within university administrations were therefore subject to tight political control by the security forces, whose presence on campus was not meant merely to deter and prevent the development of student movements but also to keep watch on and police the staff.[31] The administrations of the new private universities, a number of which were formed as joint, profit-making ventures between Egyptian business and political leaders and foreign higher-education institutions, were less important as conduits to political office in the state bureaucracy, but many were equally full of Mubarak-era officials, such as Ibrahim al-Dimeery, a faculty dean at the German University in Cairo and a former minister of transport.[32]

Protests demanding the cleansing of the universities began as soon as the universities returned to life after the fall of Mubarak. Students from the faculties of Media and Communications; Economic and Political Sciences; and Commerce at Cairo University occupied their faculty buildings demanding a far-reaching purge of the university administration and other reforms.[33] September and October saw an even bigger wave of student protests, frequently combined with, or in parallel to, strike action by non-academic university staff. Hundreds of students at Mansoura

University protested in September demanding the resignation of the university's senior management.[34] Strikes and protests hit Cairo, Alexandria and Assiyut universities and many others. The following academic year saw an even bigger wave of strike action, this time led by non-academic university staff. Demands agreed by the Coalition of University Workers at a delegate meeting at Ain Shams University on 10 September called for the improvement of pay and conditions, as well as asserting that 'the right of all staff (academic, administrative and manual grades) to elect the heads of universities and departments is an absolute right' and insisting on the 'dismissal of all university presidents and new elections to be held, with the inclusion of non-academic staff'. Around twenty universities were reported to be on strike on 16 September 2012, including Cairo, Mansoura, Alexandria, Beni Sueif, Ain Shams, Tanta and Helwan.[35] Many of these battles were successful in forcing the resignation of deans of faculties and university presidents: at Ain Shams University the deans of all faculties and the president resigned in October 2011, as did the president of Assyut University.[36] The struggles to cleanse the university campuses continued right up to the final crisis of the Muslim Brotherhood regime in 2013: thousands of students at Ain Shams and Alexandria universities took part in protests in April calling for *tathir*.[37] It was no accident, surely, that the Engineering faculties of both these universities were in the forefront of a new wave of mass student protests in November and December 2013, this time in solidarity with colleagues jailed by the military regime that took power in July.

As discussed in Chapter 6, school teachers' strikes from 2011 onwards likewise raised demands for the 'cleansing' of the Education Ministry, beginning with the demand for the sacking of the minister of education, a Mubarak appointee; this was central to the September 2011 strike, which mobilised around 300,000 teachers. It was in the health sector, however, that examples of the most radical expressions of the process of *tathir* can be found. In the wake of Mubarak's fall, several public hospitals in Cairo, starting with Manshiyet al-Bakri in the northern suburbs, not only removed their Mubarak-era managers but instituted forms of democracy within the workplace which – at least temporarily – radically shifted the balance of power between workers and managers and transformed the service offered to patients. The key to these experiments was the establishment of independent unions of hospital staff. In the case of Manshiyet al-Bakri, the union cut across all professional boundaries within the hospital, from manual workers to admin staff, nurses and doctors. The initiative in this case was taken by Mohamed Shafiq, a junior doctor and a revolutionary socialist activist. However, as Fatma Zahra'a Abd-al-Hamid, representative for temporary admin staff on the union's council, explained, the union was internally highly democratic.

> After the revolution, we found that the issue of democracy and the legitimacy of the majority opinion became an 'open area' for everyone. The independent union knits everyone together. In the meetings of the union council, for example, the manual worker rep sits next to the doctors. There is equality. I've only been here a year, but the union gave me my rights, it made my voice louder, and raised the democratic will. That's why I joined the union.[38]

The union's first major campaign was to remove the director of the hospital, which was achieved by strikes and protests in March 2011. Union activists then organised an election for his replacement. Around 700 staff voted for their choice out of three candidates, who they had been able to hear speak at hustings before the election. The specially made ballot boxes, with glass sides to ensure transparency, were guarded by electoral observers from the Independent Union of PTA Workers. When Ministry of Health officials blustered that they could not appoint a director chosen in this matter, the union leaders threatened to call a strike, leading to a rapid retreat and the arrival of a fax with the official letter of appointment a few hours later. Other hospitals which attempted similar experiments included Zawiya al-Hamra, where junior doctors removed the existing senior management in the early months of the revolution, and formed their own committee in its place.[39]

In public-sector manufacturing, calls for *tathir* were raised in large numbers of strikes, aimed at both factory managements and the heads of the holding companies. The Sugar Workers' 25th January Front for Change was a network of activists in the public sugar refineries, with a strong base in Armant Refinery near Luxor. The Front, which evolved into an independent union during the autumn of 2011, led a sector-wide strike of 26,000 sugar workers in September 2011, which had as one of its key demands the removal of the head of the holding company.[40] The strike was suspended after some of the workers' demands over pay and bonuses were met, but the Front continued to agitate around the issue of *tathir*, publishing a daily countdown on its Facebook page to 1 January 2012, the date the Front's leaders had set for the resumption of strike action.[41] Workers at Armant again went into occupation on 1 January 2012, but this time the newly elected Islamist MPs from the Muslim Brotherhood's Freedom and Justice Party and the Salafist Nour Party successfully intervened in the strike, persuading the workers to end their action in return for promises that prime minister Kamal al-Ganzouri would investigate their complaints against senior management.[42]

Workers at Misr Spinning in Al-Mahalla al-Kubra also insistently raised demands for the cleansing of both the holding company and Misr Spinning itself. Activists at the company announced their participation in national protests on 8 July 2011, 'Cleansing Friday'.[43] Workers' leaders from the mill presented Ali Selmi, then deputy prime minister and minister for the public sector, with a memorandum on 15 October 2011 demanding the removal Mohsen al-Gilani, director of the board of the holding company for cotton, weaving and garments on the grounds that he was a 'remnant of the dissolved NDP'. They raised specific allegations of corruption, claiming that he passed information damaging the public-sector mills to their competitors in the private sector, in which Al-Gilani was himself an investor.[44] Demands for the removal of Al-Gilani were also raised by activists in the mills in April 2012 as they agitated for a strike on 7 May.[45] This strike was aborted in the midst of a crisis over protests at the Ministry of Defence in Cairo, but the same call for cleansing was one of the central demands of the July 2012 strike by Misr Spinning workers which greeted Mohamed Morsi within days of his taking office,[46] despite Al-Gilani's replacement by Fu'ad Abd-al-Alim at the end of May 2012.[47] Strenuous efforts on the part of the military regime that took power in July 2013 to prevent a resurgence of strikes could not prevent further walk-outs by workers at Misr Spinning in August 2013 and October 2013, again demanding Al-Alim's resignation, in addition to claims for bonus payments.[48]

Workers on the frontline of the battle against the Officers' Republic

The most significant struggles for *tathir* are those which have breached the bounds of the existing form of the state to demand changes that represent a profound challenge to the existing regime. In Egypt, the critical issue for the core institutions of the Mubarak regime has been defence of their current position embedded in both the 'deep' and the 'shallow state'. At the lowest levels of the state, workers and civil servants rejected the generals' claim to authority over the administrative apparatus. In a small number of cases, workers in these sectors launched an offensive against existing or new military appointments, while in others they fought to defend themselves against the military's encroachment on the workplace. Here we examine three examples of such struggles: a battle by local council workers in Alexandria's Western Quarter in July 2011 against the reappointment of figures from the old regime, which escalated into a challenge to the whole structure of unelected, militarised local government; the battle by workers in the civil aviation sector against military appointments during 2011–12; and the successful defensive action by rail workers and Metro workers to stop the conscription of striking train drivers in April 2013.

On 5 July 2011 the governor of Alexandria tried to transfer the secretary of the local council in the city's Western Quarter, Farag Sha'aban, and a colleague to new jobs, in a bid to stop them speaking out against plans to reinstate members of the old ruling party. Local government workers in the Western Quarter declared a strike and locked the head of the council, an unelected general, out of the building, chasing him away when he attempted to break his way in with a gang of thugs. A few days later, with huge protests and occupations flooding the streets across Egypt, the same local government workers announced another strike and joined the sit-in in Alexandria's Sa'ad Zaghlul Square in their hundreds. As well as demanding the resignation of the governor of Alexandria, they now added their voices to the hundreds of thousands calling for the downfall of the government. However, they also took another step, by democratically electing Farag Sha'aban as a replacement for their old boss as head of the council. A strike in defence of a whistle-blowing colleague suddenly became something much bigger: a means to remake a small part of the Egyptian state from below. 'We have to get things done' explained Sha'aban in a video interview, 'so we decided that the head of the quarter should be elected by the council workers to lead a campaign of reform and change in the neighbourhood.'[49] This rupture in the existing institutions of the state turned out to be only a temporary break, however. Within a few months, the council workers' rebellion had been contained. Eleven workers were handed sentences of six months' imprisonment after the courts ruled in favour of their boss's complaint that they had insulted him. The workers were later acquitted on appeal, but the trial's deterrent message was clear.[50]

Some of the most important and successful battles for the demilitarisation of state institutions from below have taken place in the civil aviation sector. March 2011 saw a national strike by 3,000 employees of the Civil Aviation Ministry and air traffic controllers, who occupied the air traffic control tower at Cairo Airport. The strikers demanded the resignation of the aviation and transport ministers, the formation of a new government and the prosecution of the ministers and senior Aviation Ministry officials for corruption.[51] Some 250 workers at Sharm al-Sheikh Airport held a sit-in during the same month raising similar demands.[52]

July 2011 saw the beginning of a battle over the post of minister of civil aviation and the management of Cairo Airport. Essam Sharaf's appointment in his Cabinet reshuffle of Air Force general Lutfi Mustafa Kamil as the new minister of civil aviation, prompted by the renewal of nationwide street protests and sit-ins at the beginning of the month, sparked a furious reaction from Cairo Airport workers. Hundreds walked out on strike, blockading the airport roads and demonstrating in the terminal buildings. Strikers demanded an end to military appointments in the Civil Aviation Ministry and called for the removal of the current director of the state-owned airports holding company, General Mohamed Fathi Fathallah.[53] Direct negotiations between the commander-in-chief of the Air Force, Air Marshal Rida Hafiz, and representatives of the strikers brought an end to the strike and the sacking of both the head of the holding company and the director of Cairo Airport company. While Fathallah was replaced by another Air Force general, Hassan Rashad, the appointment of Dr Ahmad Hafiz to the airport director's post marked the first time a civilian had taken up the role for fifty years.[54] Hafiz lasted a further seven months before being sacked following another round of workers' protests for wage rises and bonus payments in February 2012.[55] Further appointments of civilian directors followed, however, and in June 2013 leaders of the airport workers' unions still considered their struggle to demilitarise the top level of the airport management to have been a success.

Aviation workers also continued to challenge other military appointments in further strikes and protests. Some 700 air traffic controllers went on strike again in October 2011 in protest at the continued failure to appoint a civilian minister of civil aviation. The same month fifty workers at Aswan Airport staged a collective hunger strike over the lack of progress since the January Revolution in tackling financial and administrative fraud. Workers in the Egyptian Airports Company prevented the newly appointed director, an Air Force officer, from entering his office and again threatened strike action in January 2012 demanding the demilitarisation of management appointments.[56]

These strikes took place in a context of generally high levels of industrial action across the aviation sector. Other strikes and protests by aviation workers between 2011 and 2013 included a strike by maintenance workers at EgyptAir in November 2011 demanding higher wages and the payment of bonuses, and a strike by EgyptAir cabin crew in September 2012 which grounded some fifty international flights;[57] while in May 2013 an attempt by riot police to end a strike by baggage handlers at Cairo Airport Terminal 3 by force after negotiations failed led to fighting in the terminal.[58] There were also strikes by customs officials and National Airports Company workers in June 2013.[59]

The independent unions in the aviation sector also made a direct intervention in the June 2012 presidential elections, organising a public campaign against the candidacy of Ahmad Shafiq, the former minister of civil aviation. Thugs attacked and shut down a public meeting and press conference called by airport workers' independent unions during the second round of the presidential elections to expose corruption during Shafiq's tenure.[60] Despite this the Independent Union of Workers at the Maintenance and Technical Works Co. at Cairo Airport mobilised a protest by hundreds of civil aviation workers in the airport on 11 June against the ruling Supreme Council of the Armed Forces and Shafiq. Passengers and workers chanted together: 'They got rid of a pilot [Mubarak] and brought in another one [Shafiq] – Get out, Council of Shame'; 'Listen to the mother of the martyr – I want my rights and my children's rights!'[61]

In the civil aviation sector, Shafiq's role as the champion of military interests long pre-dated the revolution. He had determinedly pursued policies favouring the extension of military influence over civil aviation for around a decade prior to the revolution, for example by prioritising the appointment of pilots with over 4,000 hours flying time, a practice which disadvantaged those with only civilian experience.[62] It would be a mistake, however, to see the aviation workers' opposition to military appointments as being driven solely by concerns within the sector and lacking a wider political dimension. Rather, local and national grievances interacted to intensify and politicise further the struggle for *tathir*. It could be argued that in July 2011 the aviation workers' struggles were part of a generally rising tide of anti-military sentiment; activists from the independent unions in the sector worked to strengthen and develop the links between the protest movement in the streets and their own struggles. A delegation of aviation workers was prominent in the sit-in in Tahrir Square which began on 8 July 2011. However, the overall political situation was very different in June 2012, when the outcome of the presidential elections hung by a thread, and large sections of the revolutionary movement were refusing to mobilise against Shafiq, because of their criticisms of his Muslim Brotherhood opponent Mohamed Morsi. The aviation workers' own experiences in the bitter battles against Shafiq and his generation led them to intervene in the electoral debates with a degree of political clarity about what was at stake in the contest between Shafiq and Morsi, which contrasted sharply with the abstentionist stance of much of the rest of the leadership of the independent unions.

Organised workers also proved themselves capable of resisting attempts by the military to use its privileges within the state to break their strikes and protests. A strike by train drivers in April 2013 proved to be an important test of the ability of workers' self-organisation to withstand pressure from the state. On 7 April, train drivers launched the first national rail strike since 1986, raising a number of wage-related demands including the payment of bonuses, meal allowances, holiday pay, a rise in the per-kilometre allowance paid to drivers from 11 qirsh to 25 qirsh, and the implementation of a national pay scale for drivers as agreed by the government.[63] In contrast to previous attempts to break strikers' resolve through arrests by the civilian or military police and prosecutions on civil and criminal charges, the authorities initiated a new tactic: issuing hundreds of drivers with military conscription notices and assigning them to the Armed Forces Transport Directorate. Drivers who failed to report for duty after receiving their assignments would face a six-month jail term or a fine of LE5,000, or both.[64]

As activists from the independent unions, NGOs and revolutionary movements argued in a solidarity statement condemning the military's intervention, the use of conscription notices against striking workers was a significant escalation in the state's war against the workers' movement. Under the anti-strike legislation passed by the Military Council in March 2011, prosecutors could already impose fines and imprisonment on workers convicted of 'aggression against the right to work', a charge increasingly used against strikers.[65] The conscription of transport workers in peace-time, using decades-old legislation designed for general mobilisation in case of war, was a forceful reminder of the military's long reach within the state. Nor was this the unilateral action of the Armed Forces; it was a decision implemented by the Minister of Transport in the Muslim Brotherhood's government. The military's intervention was successful to the extent that it stopped the strike, but it was also forced to retreat from conscripting the drivers. Workers on the Cairo Metro threatened to strike in solidarity with their rail worker colleagues, prompting the rapid withdrawal of the conscription notices. Transport and military officials had good reason to be concerned about such a threat: a well-organised strike by thousands of Cairo Metro workers in December 2012 resulted in a victory for the strikers within hours.

The 'Brotherhoodisation' of the state?

On taking office in June 2012, Mohamed Morsi was faced with a state apparatus that was little changed from the Mubarak era in either form or content at its upper levels. The scale of mobilisation from below both in the streets and in the workplaces had circumscribed the old regime's room for manoeuvre, and several of its key institutions, including the Ministry of the Interior, the judiciary and the military leadership itself, remained to varying degrees besieged by an insurgent and self-confident people. Yet that popular mobilisation from below had also demonstrated its inability to cause another crisis at the top of the state apparatus without further development into an organised revolutionary movement capable of projecting the revolution's core demands onto the national political stage.

The Brotherhood's approach to this problem was to avoid confrontation with the old regime when possible, and to attempt to work with its leaders based on the continuation of the military's political and economic privileges. Later it would become clear that the exemption of the Interior Ministry from any serious reform or reconstruction was also a key component of the Brotherhood's increasingly desperate attempts to maintain their tactical alliance with the military. Morsi's choice for his new minister of the interior in January 2013 – police general Mohamed Ibrahim, who was previously in charge of Egypt's prison system – makes that particular point neatly.

In other institutions, the Brotherhood seemed happy to take over the whole architecture of control inherited from Mubarak. Morsi's decision to appoint a close political ally, fellow FJP activist Salah Abdel Maqsoud, to the post of minister of information alarmed many journalists and revolutionary activists. The revival of the Information Ministry, temporarily suspended during the period of military rule after Mubarak's fall, was an ominous sign of the Brotherhood's willingness to use the minister's editorial control of the state media to assert itself against its critics.[66] Only a few weeks before, FJP youth activists were still supporting calls for the abolition of the entire ministry alongside the 'cleansing' of the media, according to a statement signed by revolutionary youth groups and the FJP's youth section which was circulating online in early July.[67] Soon the first court cases of newspaper editors and journalists on charges of 'insulting the president' had begun, with the confiscation of the 11 August issue of *Al-Dostour* newspaper and the trial of its editor Islam Afify.[68] Morsi reformed the Supreme Press Council in September, again facing criticism for appointing Muslim Brotherhood members and other Islamists. Another decree transferred authority for the State Information Service to the presidency.[69] Meanwhile the legal architecture which Mubarak had used to repress media freedoms remained unchanged: a report by the Arab Network for Human Rights Information published in January 2013 counted seventy separate articles in eight different laws restricting freedom of expression.[70]

Yet the Brotherhood was forced to alter its tactics under the combined pressure of mobilisations from below raising social grievances and opposing the new constitution, and manoeuvres by elements of the old regime at the top of the state aimed at restricting the expansion of the Brotherhood's networks in the bureaucracy. As these struggles intensified during the autumn and winter of 2012, the Brotherhood attempted to change the institutions not only 'from above', relying largely on the authority of the presidency to push through new appointments and legislation, but also 'from outside', by mobilising or encouraging Islamist-led street protests calling for 'cleansing' of the institution. In December 2012, thousands of Islamist demonstrators picketed Media Production City in 6th of October City answering the call of former presidential candidate Hazem Abu-Ismail for a mass mobilisation to defend Morsi's 'legitimacy'.[71] Another series of protests targeted private satellite channels at Media Production City in March 2013. Muslim Brotherhood activists and other Islamists also launched hundreds of criminal defamation cases against individual journalists.[72]

The struggle over the judiciary took on particular significance for several reasons. First, it was the only area of the state bureaucracy where the Muslim Brotherhood managed to gain a significant foothold before the 2011 revolution. A number of senior judges were well-known sympathisers and supporters of the group. Judge Mahmoud Mekki, who was appointed vice president by Mohamed Morsi in August 2012, had been, along with Hisham al-Bastawisi, a rallying point for a judicial rebellion in 2006, when he was disciplined by the Court of Cassation for leading a campaign for judicial oversight of the electoral process in the face of stiff opposition by the government.[73] The fact that the regime's authority was more contested within the judiciary than within the other key institutions of the state may have been a factor motivating the Brotherhood to engage the judges in battle.

Or it may have been a pragmatic response to the fact that, at this stage, it was largely through judicial decisions – such as the Higher Constitutional Court ruling on the invalidity of the 2011 parliamentary elections – that the old regime sought to test the Brotherhood's resolve and impede its progress.

A key battleground in the struggle was the office of prosecutor-general, a post which was still held by one Mubarak's most important supporters within the judiciary, Abdel Meguid Mahmoud. After months of growing tension between the presidency and the prosecutor-general's office, which was raised by the acquittal of defendants in the 'Battle of the Camel' trial in October 2012, Morsi finally sacked Mahmoud on 22 November 2012. In order to replace Mahmoud, whose post was not at the time one appointed by the presidency, Morsi added that power to his role through the constitutional declaration. As we saw in Chapter 8, the focus then shifted to the battle over the constitution, which was approved by referendum in December 2012. The relatively narrow victory of the 'Yes' camp set the context for the next moves in Morsi's struggle with the judiciary. By 23 December he had already appointed the remaining ninety seats in the Shura Council; following the approval of the constitution, Morsi formally passed over legislative authority to the now-complete body, tasking it with the preparation of a new electoral law. Attempts by Morsi's opponents in several branches of the judiciary to block this process triggered another round of dramatic confrontations between the presidency and the judges. On 6 March the State Administrative Court rejected a decree by Morsi calling elections for the lower house of parliament in April, referring the case to the Higher Constitutional Court.

Morsi then counter-attacked on two fronts. On the one hand, the Brotherhood began to mobilise protests by the Islamist street calling for the 'cleansing' of the judiciary, which reached a peak in the week of 19 April just as the Supreme Administrative Court threw out the appeal against the suspension of the parliamentary elections. On the other hand, Morsi pushed ahead with the development of a Judicial Authority Law, which included a number of provisions specifically aimed at weakening the position of his opponents within the judiciary, such as the enforced resignation of large numbers of judges who had passed the legal age of retirement.[74]

The problem for Morsi and the Brotherhood was that the collateral damage sustained during these last few rounds of battle included many of the remaining supporters of his presidency beyond the ranks of the Brotherhood itself. The Salafist party Al-Nour, which had been the Brotherhood's key electoral ally during the 2011–12 parliamentary elections, winning the second largest number of seats, became increasingly alienated from Morsi. In February its leaders began talks with the opposition National Salvation Front.[75] Furthermore, although the former jihadist organisations such the Gama'a Islamiyya remained staunch backers of the Brotherhood, other more moderate Islamists were falling away. Even as the confrontation with the judiciary escalated, the Brotherhood was losing the backing of the very reformist judges it had invited to join Morsi's government. Protesters pinned a banner across the doors of the High Court on 19 April demanding the resignation of the minister of justice whom Morsi had himself appointed, Ahmed Mekki.[76] After protests continued the following day, Mekki resigned, issuing a curt statement which made clear that the demonstrations against him had been the last straw.

> Since you assigned me to take over the burden of the Ministry of Justice, the opposition has been urging me to resign in conformance with my previous positions. And yesterday, under the slogan of 'cleansing the judiciary' and the legislation for a new Judicial Authority Law, your supporters have united around the demand of my dismissal to achieve their noble goals. And thus, consensus has been achieved ... May God save you and save Egypt for your supporters and your opposition, and may God save you from both of them.[77]

Mekki's brother Mahmoud, who had served as Morsi's vice president, had already resigned in December 2012 during the crisis over the constitution. Mohamed Fouad Gadallah, Morsi's adviser for legal affairs, and considered to be the architect of the November 2012 constitutional declaration, also resigned at the same time as Ahmed Mekki, protesting at what he described as an 'attempt to assassinate the judiciary and undermine its independence',[78] bringing to twelve the number of presidential advisers to have quit their posts since Morsi took office.

Once again, Morsi's response to these challenges was to reach deeper into the Brotherhood's own, still-formidable organisational apparatus, to make senior appointments within the state. A Cabinet reshuffle on 7 May brought in three new ministers from the Brotherhood, and, as discussed above, the 17 June appointments of provincial governors also saw the insertion of more Brotherhood cadres into local administration. And by now it was becoming clear that, after a lull of five months, the popular mobilisation in the streets was gathering pace again with the explosive success of the *Tamarud* – 'Rebellion' – signature campaign, which we explore in more detail below.

Despite the fury that Morsi's appointments generated, it is important, nevertheless, to put claims of the 'Brotherhoodisation' of the state into historical and comparative perspective. For all that Morsi's failure to keep faith with even his closest allies demonstrated a political perspective narrowly focused on the interests of his own organisation, it did not change the fact that none of the political forces that had participated in the revolution had been able to make much headway in prying open the state 'from above' in order to force significant changes in personnel, let alone advance a genuine agenda of reform. Morsi was not in a similar position to Ruhollah Khomeini in Iran, for example, who in the wake of the Shah's downfall had 130,000 vacant posts in the state apparatus and industry to fill as a result of the revolutionary upheaval.[79] The critical question for revolutionary activists was not the superficial issue of how many new, bearded faces the Brotherhood could insert into the top layers of state institutions, but whether battles over their appointment were signs of commitment to genuine reform, or of tussles between parties to a marriage of convenience over who would gain the greater part of the spoils.

From 'Rebellion' to compromise: Nasserism 2.0

The most spectacular confirmation of Nasserism's continuing importance in Egyptian political life lies in the political fate of the Tamarud 'Rebel' campaign which began in April 2013 with an initiative by a small number of young activists who launched a petition calling for Morsi to step down in order to hold early presidential elections. The signature campaign quickly developed momentum, channelling the frustrations of millions with the Brotherhood's failures to deliver on their social and political promises into a movement focused on mobilising demonstrations on 30 June, the anniversary of Morsi's inauguration. However, in the context of the political crisis generated by the combination of mass mobilisation from below and the trench warfare within the institutions of the state between the Brotherhood and the core of the old regime, Tamarud changed from being a vehicle for the revival of the revolutionary movement into a vehicle for counter-revolution, abandoning its call for early elections, delegating political authority to the military and cheering on the brutal repression of Morsi's supporters in August 2013. For Hugh Roberts, writing shortly after the events of 30 June, the actions of Tamarud's leaders can be explained by reference to the influence of Nasserism on their political development, through their involvement in Kefaya in the pre-revolutionary period, in which long-standing Nasserist activists such as Abd-al-Halim Qandil also played a leading role. Roberts argues that all the revolutionary activists of 2011 (with the exception of the Revolutionary Socialists) can be seen as Kefaya's 'spiritual children'.[80]

Nasserism played a pivotal role within the axis of 'secular' politics that emerged as the organising principle across Morsi's opponents, from the Stalinist left to the *feloul* parties of the NDP fragments. Sabahy made a fateful political choice in the wake of Morsi's election to seek alliance with elements of the *feloul*, such as former foreign minister Amr Moussa. Sabahy and Moussa were (together with liberal politician Mohamed ElBaradei) the key personalities in the National Salvation Front (NSF), a coalition of parties that formed in November 2012 to campaign against Morsi's constitutional amendments. Increasingly, this political choice was justified by reference to the idea that Islamism posed an existential threat to Egyptian society, and should be understood as a form of fascism. As Phil Marfleet notes, this analysis was actually pioneered by the Stalinist left, which had a long history before the revolution of accommodation to the Mubarak regime on the grounds that it represented the last line of defence of 'progress' and 'modernity' against 'Islamic reaction'.[81] Ironically, the track record of Nasserist activists such as Sabahy and Abu Aita before the revolution was very different to that of leading Stalinist figures such as Rifa'at al-Sa'id, as they participated in joint activities with the Muslim Brotherhood such as the large anti-war Cairo Conferences. Sabahy's Karama Party, as discussed in Chapter 8, was part of the Muslim Brotherhood's electoral coalition in 2011, and Abu Aita was elected to parliament on the Freedom and Justice Party's slate for the Giza district. This underlines the point that 'Nasserism' is a broad current of opinion. Despite the historic antagonism between Nasser himself and the Muslim Brotherhood (whose deputy general guide he hanged in 1954), influential currents within it could justify alliance with Islamists on tactical grounds until late in 2011.

A further element within Nasserism which became important in the crisis of 30 June and after was the idealisation of a particular vision of 'the people' or 'the masses' as cover for specific practices of leadership within the state. This was a vision of 'the people' as a stage army which appeared at crucial moments in history to cheer and shout their adoration for the appropriate leader (whether in uniform or out of it). It was achieved in the 1950s by the appropriation of a genuine popular movement by the Nasserist state, which captured its energies within new paramilitary, political and labour institutions.[82] Despite the fundamental differences between his project and Nasser's, there is no doubt that Abdel-Fattah al-Sisi benefited from a similar confusion between 'the people' as a self-organised collective force *against* the state and 'the people' as cheering crowds mobilised *by* the state. The confusion arose in July 2013 not only because the state was divided against itself (with the Brotherhood embedded in parts of it), but also because most of Morsi's opponents made the political choice to give al-Sisi the cover of a popular 'mandate' (*tafwid*) to commit massacres against supporters of the Brotherhood.

It is important to set the revival of Nasserism as a force in mass politics within the context of the contradictions outlined above. It is also vital to understand that the counter-revolutionary appropriation of the popular mobilisation against Morsi was aided by the political and organisational failures of his opponents. Rather than hold to an independent position advocating a different programme of reform to both the Brotherhood and the *feloul*, key Nasserists, such as Sabahy, chose to ally themselves with the *feloul* and ultimately with the core institutions of the Mubarak regime. Rather than build a genuine organisational base of his own, Sabahy squandered the political opportunity provided by his mass vote in the presidential elections and was eventually upstaged by the unlikely combination of young 'revolutionary' activists working in concert with the military high command.

A final comment is necessary here about the disastrous political trajectory followed by Kamal Abu Aita during the final crisis of Morsi's rule. Abu Aita's acceptance of the post of minister of labour in Hazem Beblawi's government was an important factor in providing cover for the military's counter-revolutionary ambitions, as he toured television stations and newspaper offices promising to meet the long-standing social demands of the workers' movement at the very moment that al-Sisi was beginning his campaign for a 'mandate' to crush the Brotherhood. Abu Aita's insistence on separating 'politics' from 'economics' in his practice as a trade unionist morphed seamlessly into surrender to the politics of the counter-revolution.

Liberal leaders such as ElBaradei, whose Constitution Party did build a real base among revolutionary activists (despite being beset by perpetual internal conflict), also played an important role in cloaking the military's ambitions with 'revolutionary' legitimacy. ElBaradei did at least resign his post in protest at the massacres in August 2013, unlike the majority of liberal figures who hitched their star to the military's intervention against Morsi. However, we have concentrated more on Nasserism in our analysis here for two key reasons: first, because of the far more powerful pull of Nasserism as an ideology and practice of state power than liberalism; second, because of the specific role played by Nasserism within the Egyptian workers' movement.

It could be said that the National Salvation Front as a whole followed a trajectory similar to that of Sabahy – riding the crest of a wave of popular anger in November and December 2012, but losing momentum as the demonstrations subsided. It took an initiative from outside the NSF leadership, with the initiation of the Tamarud campaign, to propel the Front into a position where it could present an alternative to the Brotherhood, whereupon its leaders promptly collapsed into the arms of al-Sisi and gave away their political independence to a new military regime. The critical point that united Nasserists, liberals and *feloul* was the inviolacy of Mubarak's state, whether they justified this through rhetoric invoking the mythical union of people and army, or the doctrine of the separation of powers, or with the mantra of 'respect for the judiciary'. And it was not the more 'revolutionary' elements within the NSF – that is to say the opposition leaders such as Sabahy and ElBaradei who had been marginalised and persecuted by the old regime – which set the tone, but its most conservative sections, leading to its co-option by the counter-revolution.

Tathir from below: a provisional balance sheet

As outlined here, the 'cleansing' of corrupt officials, even when framed in terms that are squarely within a narrative of political reform, if it is carried out by means of collective self-organisation from below, has potentially profound implications in the social dimension. At the very least, the removal of a director through collective action from below overturns normal relations between workers and bosses. In the context of revolution, 'cleansing' has much greater potential to grow from being a largely political campaign (and one which can be taken up by a variety of political forces, not always those on the left, as the Muslim Brotherhood's adoption of the term illustrates) into a deep social process. The battle for 'cleansing' provided a model for social struggles, and vice versa, since both were carried out by the same means. The success of strikes and protests to remove corrupt bosses in February and March 2011 encouraged workers in different sectors to begin the same process in September and October, and stimulated the raising of wider social demands. A similar feedback loop was established in reverse in many workplaces, where collective action for social goals emboldened workers to demand changes in management, and then propelled them into confrontation with the state.

The struggle for *tathir* is, of course, fundamentally a strategy for the *reform* of the existing state. But, when carried out in conjunction with the social struggle, it opens new fronts in the war between the people and the state at both a practical and an ideological level. *Tathir* is one of the means by which ordinary people can begin to think differently about the state and their relationship to it, seeing themselves as active agents in the re-making of the state at every level, rather than its passive subjects. Taking this process *inside* the institutions of the state was also vitally important, as explored in Chapter 6, to prolonging and deepening their crisis, while giving time for a revolutionary movement to mature *outside* them. However, the relationship between the struggle for *tathir* and the fight for both bread and freedom cannot be seen as incidental: it is the integration of all three, which creates the widest possible space in which the fight to impose reforms on the existing state can grow into a struggle to replace it.

Moreover, in the Egyptian context, even the partial success of *tathir* as a strategy of reform was always contingent on its relationship to the social struggle. As seen in Chapter 6, it was the widening horizon of social protests that forced open the space in which the political demands of the mass movement could develop during the first period of military rule. The Muslim Brotherhood, alone of all the reformist forces that participated in the January Revolution, appeared to have a mass base capable of absorbing the energies of this mobilisation from below. This is precisely the quality that made it an attractive partner for the military, as it sought desperately to contain the revolution and divert it into safer channels.[83] The reformist political forces and the leading institutions of the old regime consciously pursued strategies to contain the massive pressures from below for *tathir* within a framework which could protect, rather than endanger, the existing state. Their interests converged entirely on this fundamental point, although the Islamist and secular parties diverged sharply over the question of the timing and extent of change within the administrative apparatus, and influential sections within the old regime's camp were committed to first halting and then rolling back the work of reconstruction in order to rebuild their power.

The counter-revolutionary camp benefited enormously from the mutual hostility and competition between the two principal reformist currents, and from the extreme weakness of revolutionary organisation. The leadership of the Armed Forces was able, from the early days of the revolution, to play off the secular and Islamist currents against each other, holding out the prospect of them joining the regime as junior partners. As discussed in Chapter 6, during the first period of military rule the Supreme Council of the Armed Forces under Tantawi's leadership sought to restrict this arrangement to a reworked version of the political settlement under Mubarak: opening a space in the legislature for the reformist forces, but retaining full control of the rest of the state apparatus while resisting as far as possible the pressure for *tathir*. Under the pressure of the mass movement in the streets and workplaces, this arrangement lost its attraction for the military. Some elements, such as Tantawi and Anan, wanted to dispense with making deals with the reformists altogether, and gamble on hostility to the Muslim Brotherhood allowing them to attempt a full-scale return to the old regime under Ahmad Shafiq's presidency. Others preferred to bide their time by letting the Muslim Brotherhood take power for a period, in the hope that they would absorb and divert anger from below.

Demands for *tathir* raised during the course of workers' strikes and protests opened up a Pandora's box of questions and debates. The ideological and institutional membranes separating 'regime' from 'state', which both reformist and counter-revolutionary camps were desperate to preserve at all costs, threatened to rupture. Even more dangerous was the vision it raised of reconnection between the revolution's political and social souls: where struggles to replace corrupt directors grew rapidly into a wider battle over whether the public sector could be remade in a democratic fashion from below, with the extension of workers' control over their own workplace acting as the motor for this potential transformation. These battles were profoundly political: if they had been translated upwards and outwards through the entire body of the state, even partial victories would have set in motion a deep transformation of Egyptian society.

For both secular and Islamist reformists, *tathir*, in the form understood by the workers and civil servants at the lowest levels of the state, posed a danger to the prospects of partnership with the institutions of the old regime, particularly the military. Both currents worked tirelessly in different ways to contain the pressure towards *tathir* within boundaries that the military would find acceptable. The word *tathir* all but disappeared from the vocabulary of the secular reformists after Morsi's election; as the battles over the Constitution and judicial reform intensified, the Brotherhood's liberal and Nasserist opponents were more often to be heard talking of protecting the institutions of the state, rather than purging them. In January 2013, the left-wing news website Al-Badil could write quite uncritically about how Ahmad Shafiq's pursuit of militarisation within the civil aviation sector would be a barrier to its 'Brotherhoodisation'.[84]

The Brotherhood, for its part, was resolutely opposed to *tathir* from below, particularly in the form of strikes. As we saw in the case of the sugar workers, in the early phases of the revolution, the Brotherhood sought to end workers' collective action for *tathir* with promises that the elected parliament would address their grievances. During the first few months of Morsi's rule, there were further promises of reform, while the police were regularly deployed to break strikes by force. Then, with pressure from below on Morsi's government rising, Islamist rhetoric in favour of *tathir* turned in a superficially more radical direction, even while the Muslim Brotherhood sought desperately to maintain its partnership with the military. Yet, as discussed above, in the two key areas where the Brotherhood was the most strident in calling for *tathir* – the media and the judiciary – it failed to present even an effective top-down agenda for reform, instead retaining the form and content of the Mubarak-era institutions, while simply proposing changes in personnel. For all the reformist forces – Islamist and secular alike – the greatest service they could render the old regime was to strip the concept and practice of *tathir* of its revolutionary implications at both political and social levels. The outcome of this process was that the repressive institutions of the state regained a degree of popular political legitimacy which they had not enjoyed for decades, despite remaining completely unreformed and even unpunished for their crimes.

In this chapter we have presented evidence for seeing the struggle for *tathir* as one of the fundamental processes of the popular revolution. We have also argued for distinguishing the practice of *tathir* from (and seeing that it is in contradiction with) the approach of both Islamist and 'secular' reformist currents, which have consistently sought alliances with the core institutions of the Mubarak regime, in particular the leadership of the Armed Forces. Moreover, as we explore in our final chapter, the terrain of the struggle for *tathir*, despite its limitations, is the most fertile ground for the fusion of the revolutionary practice of the masses themselves with theories that equip them for an assault on the state. But achieving that aim will depend largely on whether during its phase next the social and democratic souls of the Egyptian Revolution can be reunited in the struggle from below.

Beyond the Republic of Dreams: revolutionary organisation, democracy and the question of the state

We began this book in Tahrir Square's 'Republic of Dreams', with a powerful vision of 'the people' uniting Muslim and Christian, secular and Islamist activists against Mubarak's regime. The crowds which made the streets speak with one voice – 'The people want the downfall of the regime!' – appeared to be an intoxicating blend of unity in diversity. Yet, as traced in the closing chapters of this book, this vision of 'the people' was unsustainable beyond the end of the 18 Days uprising. In fact, during the years that followed at least three competing visions of 'the people' could be seen hovering like mirages above the crowds in Egypt's streets.

The Brotherhood's image of 'the people' was calculated to appeal to Western governments, the international financial institutions they dominate, and a section of the local and regional capitalist class. This version of 'the people' was meant to materialise only at election times, standing in line obediently to place a cross in the appropriate box before returning home. In between elections, however, they tighten their belts, put their shoulders to the wheel of production, and accept that sacrifices and cuts have to be made in an era of global crisis and austerity.

Another, older vision of 'the people' was resurrected during the protests of 30 June 2013, and grew in strength over the following year as Abdel-Fattah al-Sisi's political ambitions took shape. This version of 'the people' is steadfast in its loyalty to and appreciation of the army's role as protector of the nation. Its crowds wave pictures of Gamal Abdel-Nasser, or Abdel-Fattah al-Sisi, as they march to defend the national and secular character of the state against the Muslim Brotherhood's encroachment. Of course, in the original version of this drama there was a trade-off between the people and the state: a limited redistribution of wealth in return for the state's usurpation of the people's political voice. Now even the limited reforms of the Nasserist era are being undone by neoliberalism, so 'the people' now have no choice but to tighten their belts and keep the wheel of production turning. Meanwhile, al-Sisi's defenders castigate the Western media for failing to see that Egypt is being transformed into a 'representative, pluralistic democracy' which will welcome foreign investment.[1]

The third vision of 'the people' is quite different to the fantasies of the Islamists, liberals and Nasserists. 'The people' in this sense are the vast majority of Egyptians: the urban and rural poor; the small traders and artisans; industrial, transport and office workers; teachers and health workers. They are the heart and soul of the January Revolution. One of the key arguments advanced in this book has been that while the organised working class is not a majority of 'the people', it can form its strategic core. This vision of 'the people' would have been easily recognisable to Lenin, as it has many echoes of 'the people' he discusses in his 1917 pamphlet *The State and Revolution*.[2] 'The people' for Lenin in this case was not simply workers – a tiny minority in Russian society at the time – but workers and poor peasants combined, united by the fact that they are oppressed, crushed and exploited by the 'bureaucratic-military machine' of the state.

We have argued throughout this book that Egypt's impoverished majority faces a common enemy in a similar 'bureaucratic–military machine', which is seeking to consolidate a new amalgam of state and private capital in order to deepen processes of exploitation, allowing the Egyptian capitalist class to compete in regional and global markets.

More than this, as argued throughout this book, the third vision of 'the people' is more than a theoretical construct or the figment of a counter-historical imagination. Just as the working class makes itself,[3] 'the people' in the sense that Lenin meant can be seen taking shape in the moments when political and social struggles have fused. This vision of 'the people' is implicit in the embryonic beginnings of a workers' movement uniting 'Scarab boatmen', fishermen and street traders with rail workers, civil servants, steel workers and textile workers. It is implicit in the teachers' strikes demanding better working conditions and the abolition of private lessons as a tax on the children of the poor, in the halting steps towards democratic control over the delivery of health services in public hospitals like Manshiyet al-Bakri, and in the Cairo bus drivers' battles to win investment in public transport. It is implicit in the Metro workers' action to defend their colleagues on the railways from military conscription, in the airport workers' imposition of civilian management at Cairo Airport, and in the confident assertion by Alexandrian council workers that they would do a better job of running local government than some unelected general.

This is why from the earliest hours of the Egyptian Revolution a question was waiting to be asked: would the people remake the state in their image, or the state remake the people? The problem was that very few dared even to pose the question, let alone argue for a different kind of state, one capable of realising the demands of the January Revolution.

The problem of democracy

The experience of 2011–14 underscores the importance of exploring the specific challenges raised by the democratic aspect of the January Revolution. The way in which the military, under al-Sisi's leadership, was able to divert some of the energy of the mass protests against Morsi to give new life to an ideology of authoritarian populism which many thought had been buried with Gamal Abdel-Nasser demonstrates the urgency of addressing this issue. Although in terms of its social content, al-Sisi's regime is a recast version of Mubarak's, not Abdel-Nasser's, the powerful pull of this ideology on the revolutionary movement is undeniable, exemplified by the transformation of some of the Tamarud movement's founders into cheerleaders for al-Sisi's bid for the presidency.[4]

While it is important not to overstate the lessons about the resilience of populist authoritarianism that can be generalised from the Egyptian experience – given the specific resonance of Nasserism within the workers' movement there, for example – it also seems clear that broader questions of 'what democracy looks like' (to take up a slogan from the early days of the anti-capitalist movement which erupted after the 1999 protests in Seattle) are relevant far beyond Egypt. At a time when neoliberalism is draining the social content from bourgeois democracy in the core of the capitalist system while empowering and enhancing the power of different kinds of authoritarian regimes in much of the rest of the world, it is relevant to ask what kind of democratic demands future popular movements against neoliberalism and dictatorship can articulate.

The states of the Middle East throw this process into particularly sharp relief precisely because of the region's strategic importance on account of its natural resources and, more recently, the role of Gulf capital in accelerating the financialisation of capital.[5] As Adam Hanieh rightly emphasises, the authoritarian form of the state in the Middle East is not an accident or deformity; it is necessary for the dominance of both local and global capitalist ruling classes.[6] In the case of Egypt, it has always been a delusion on a grand scale (as Eberhard Kienle noted in relation to the reforms of the 1990s) to imagine that neoliberalism would really enhance or extend the content of bourgeois democracy.[7]

In Chapter 8 we analysed the weakness of parliamentarianism in practice in Egypt during 2011–13, while recognising its importance and resilience as an idea. Disenchantment with 'the revolution's parliament' took hold in a timescale which was brutally swift, to the extent that even the Brotherhood rapidly abandoned any pretence of defending it from dissolution by the military's judges. And the elected presidency of course suffered the same fate as the parliament almost exactly a year later. The problem was that very large numbers of Egyptians did appear to draw the conclusion from this process that they needed a *more* democratic form of government, one which was better able to deliver social justice for the poor, but that the only option was to acquiesce in the restoration of military-led authoritarianism which claimed to be able to offer 'stability' and held out the vague promise of social reform.

Hal Draper, writing about the evolution of Marx's thought during the 1848 revolutions, noted that one of the challenges facing emerging workers' organisations was how to 'sort out' the elements of democracy which benefited their bourgeois rivals from those which 'furthered the widest extension of popular control'.[8] Through the bitter experience of betrayal and defeat, they began to understand how the democratic forms that appeared to be the common goal of workers and their liberal allies were double-faced. From one perspective they were a 'swindle' and 'a safety valve for the effervescing passions of the country'.[9] The other perspective, however, saw 'the struggle to give the democratic forms social (class) content, above all by pushing them to the democratic extreme of popular control from below, which in turn entailed extending the application of democratic forms out of the merely political sphere into the organisation of the whole of society.'[10]

The experience of the Egyptian Revolution suggests that a similar process of 'sorting out' needs to take place in at least two dimensions. There is first the crucially important process of workers developing their own agenda for the *democratic reform* of the state, and developing the independent means to articulate and defend this programme against both the half-hearted liberal and the Islamist versions of democracy. And, as Marx argued in 1850, such a programme of reforms must constantly strive to 'breach the boundaries of bourgeois acceptability'[11] by demanding the expansion of popular control from below into as much of the social and political domains as possible. This cannot be simply a propagandistic exercise from the sidelines, however. Rather, it requires correctly identifying the specific demands where the organised working class *takes sides* in the wider political struggles of the day.

But, second, there is also the need to 'sort out' the experiences of the popular mobilisation from below which can be developed into democratic practices and institutions, and those which are less useful for this purpose. The presence of large numbers of people on the streets can be an expression of a democratic process of self-organisation from below, or it can express the influence of a particular practice of authoritarian rule which mobilises cheering crowds to applaud the existing order. The experience of Egypt 2011–14 confirms that democracy from below needs both practices and institutions of its own: democratic practices which revolutionary activists seek to apply wherever they can, and institutions which are the kernels of alternative organs of state power.

What would a provisional balance sheet of democracy from below during the Egyptian Revolution look like? We have argued in this book that it is the workplaces that have witnessed the richest experiences in democracy from below. In a significant minority of workplaces, workers gained experience of temporary direct democratic control over the workplace itself, and in a much wider layer of workplaces gained experience of direct democratic control over organisation. This is one of the greatest gains of the revolution and preceding years – an immensely powerful and rich experience involving hundreds of thousands of people. Its organic expression in workplace struggles has largely been based on the idea that workers' leaders should be elected delegates, not representatives; it fuses executive and legislative authority and breaches the separation between political and social struggles enforced by bourgeois democracy. We have not had space here to properly explore other kinds of democratic experiments, such as the experience of some of the popular committees set up in local neighbourhoods in the immediate wake of the 18 Days uprising. However, it is noticeable that this kind of democratic organising on a popular level faced difficulties in sustaining itself beyond the first few months of the revolution. Attempts to develop national networks of popular committees gained some traction early in 2011, but quickly lost momentum after that.[12] Similarly, the democratic experience of the street protests and occupations of public squares needs to be carefully examined, something we have been unable to do in this book. Yet we note that in the Egyptian case the 'democracy of the streets' has proved stubbornly resistant to taking institutional form, and its lack of institutional presence makes it susceptible to external pressures. In comparison with the democratic experiences of other street-based movements, Egypt's example seems less rich than, for example, that of the 15 May movement in Spain, or the popular assemblies of Argentina's anti-neoliberal revolt in 2000.[13]

In the face of an offensive by the resurgent security and military apparatus of Mubarak's state, it seems that it will be in the *combination* of social and democratic struggles that Egyptian revolutionaries will face their sharpest test. The experience of democratic organising at a workplace level, even aggregated across thousands of separate workplaces, is not the same as democracy *for* all the exploited and oppressed. And the Egyptian experience illustrates that turning the organic democracy *of* the workplaces into democracy *for* the people requires the generalisation of two processes. First, it requires winning an argument in the workplaces about why workers should take decisions there about politics. In other words, they should decide collectively in the workplace who represents them and how, what form the government should take, whether they support general political freedoms and stand against tyranny, and when and on what terms to support specific democratic initiatives and campaigns. Second, it requires taking these decisions *out* of the workplaces and into the wider struggle – through initiatives such as sending organised delegations to demonstrations, and delegates from workplaces to coordinate strike action and street protests with political allies, and the debating of democratic demands by congresses of strike committee delegates. Fighting for liberal democratic reforms by such 'proletarian methods' (as Trotsky once put it) can set the 'democracy of the workplaces' in watchful guardianship over those sent forth in the name of those workplaces to negotiate, to be elected to parliament, or as delegates to any other forum which operates by different democratic rules (or none).

However, the experience of 2011–14 also underlines the fact that democracy without a social soul is incapable of winning the kind of mass popular support necessary to overcome the current regime. As discussed in Chapter 8, the Brotherhood used its period in power to assert its neoliberal credentials. Right down to his last public speech, Morsi insisted that 'Egypt's revolution wasn't the revolution of the hungry.'[14] One of the bitter ironies of Morsi's year in power is that while the old regime mobilised under the cover of the impeccably liberal demand to respect the separation of powers, and the Brotherhood rallied its supporters to defend the legitimacy of an elected president, no one in national politics seemed able to articulate a set of demands which would undercut both, by breaking with neoliberalism and confronting the military at the same time, putting the social back into democracy from below.

Problems of revolutionary organisation

The phase of the Egyptian Revolution that unfolded between 2011 and 2014 was pregnant with unrealised possibilities for deeper social and political transformation. One of the great problems confronting organised workers, and the wider layers of the poor more generally, was their lack of organisations of their own. As we have traced throughout this book, despite the very rich experience in building independent unions to take forward struggles in the workplaces, workers lacked a political voice. Therefore we will briefly sketch out here five elements of an approach to building revolutionary organisation which seeks to address the specific challenges of the Egyptian context, while also being rooted in a broader tradition of revolutionary socialist politics.

Setting down roots for revolutionary organisation in the workplaces constitutes the first element. Its representatives would have to be organisers of a specific kind, striving at every opportunity to breach the current limited horizons of the organic democracy of the workplaces. Here we have already reached the second element: the transformation of the democracy of the workplaces into an instrument of alternative political authority *of* and *for* 'the people'. '*Of* the people' in the sense that these democratic practices and embryonic institutions will be created from below, by a section of Egypt's exploited and oppressed majority; '*for* the people' in the sense that this transformation can only be achieved by convincing workers not only to act for themselves, but to take up a role as 'revolutionary leaders of the people' against the capitalist class and its state. The third element is necessitated by the second: such a revolutionary organisation would need to be composed of women and men who consciously 'think like a state'. To a certain extent, any revolutionary minority has to think *like* the state it wants to defeat. It has to centralise its small forces, deploy its resources carefully, generalise lessons learnt across space and time. It has to consider how to use the balance of class forces to its advantage, make and break tactical alliances beyond the ranks of the working class. Above all it means building organisation which knits together people who are able to make the right arguments in enough places to shift the balance of forces in the wider class struggle.

But, and this brings us to the fourth element, they will also need to think *beyond* the state as it currently exists, to imagine a different state altogether – not *reformed* but *remade* according to the principles of the January uprising; a state of freedom, social justice and human dignity. As noted above, from the earliest hours of the Egyptian Revolution a question was waiting to be asked: would the people remake the state in their image, or would the state remake the people? Thus it is critically important to expand the numbers of those who can begin to think beyond the existing state and start to put flesh onto the bare bones of the imagined state-to-be which arises like a shimmering ghost out of Tahrir's 'Republic of Dreams' and the myriad struggles for *tathir* it unleashed.

The final element also involves thinking beyond the state, but in a different way. As discussed at the beginning of this book, the revolution of January 2011 was the result of the intersection of crises at national, regional and global levels. Nationalist and internationalist interpretations of the 18 Days uprising were both possible, and many demonstrators in Tahrir Square drew on both.

Yet the ubiquitous symbolism of the Egyptian flag – which in January 2011 was deployed in defiance of the Mubarak regime – was relatively easy for the military to reappropriate. Campaigns whipping up fear of 'foreigners', whether Western NGO workers and journalists or Syrian and Palestinian refugees, were just some of the most obvious manifestations of this process. The intersection between counter-revolution and xenophobic nationalism provides a compelling reason for Egyptian revolutionaries to adopt a conscious and active internationalism.

Notes

INTRODUCTION

1. Dina Hashmat, 'Ahlan Bikum Fi Midan Al-Tahrir ... Gumhuriyya Al-Ahlam Al-Mumkina', *Al-Akhbar* (Beirut), 8 February 2011, www.al-akhbar.com/node/3842 (accessed 25 April 2014).
2. Rassd Network, 'Abu-Al-Fotouh: Adly Mansour Wa Awanuhu Hawwalu Masr Li Gumhuriyat Al-Khawf', *Rassd*, 2014; Borzou Daragahi, 'Human Rights: Egypt's Black Holes', *Financial Times*, 22 April 2014, www.ft.com/cms/s/0/b0ac6ccc-c97e-11e3-99cc-00144feabdc0.html?siteedition=uk#axz z2zhAMLzqE (accessed 23 April 2014).
3. Karl Marx and Frederick Engels, 'Communist Manifesto', Chapter 1, in *The Manifesto of the Communist Party*, 1848, www.marxists.org/archive/marx/works/1848/communist-manifesto/ch01.htm (accessed 22 March 2014).
4. Nikolai Bukharin, *Imperialism and World Economy*, New York: H. Fertig, 1967; Alex Callinicos, *Marxism and the New Imperialism*, London and Chicago: Bookmarks, 1994; Alex Callinicos, *Imperialism and Global Political Economy*, Cambridge: Polity Press, 2009.
5. Colin Barker, 'The State as Capital', *International Socialism Journal*, vol. 2, no. 1, pp. 16–42.
6. Hazem Kandil, *Soldiers, Spies and Statesmen: Egypt's Road to Revolt*, London: Verso, 2012.
7. C. Barker, 'A Note on the Theory of Capitalist States', *Capital & Class* 2 (1978), pp. 118–26.
8. Leon Trotsky, *The History of the Russian Revolution*, New York: Pathfinder, 1992.
9. Wahdat al-Dirasat, 'Tahawwulat Al-Iqtisad Al-Misri (Muladhat Awliyya)', *Al-Tariq al-Ishtaraki*, 1999, pp. 5–51.
10. Sameh Naguib, *The Egyptian Revolution*, London: Bookmarks, 2011, p. 5.

11. Chris Harman, 'The State and Capitalism Today', *International Socialism Journal*, vol. 2, no. 51 (1991), pp. 3–54.
12. Hazem Beblawi and Giacomo Luciani, *The Rentier State*, London and New York: Croom Helm, 1987.
13. Adam Hanieh, *Capitalism and Class in the Gulf States*, Basingstoke: Palgrave Macmillan, 2011; Adam Hanieh, *Lineages of Revolt: Issues of Contemporary Capitalism in the Middle East*, Chicago: Haymarket Books, 2013.
14. Hanieh, *Lineages of Revolt*.
15. Neil Davidson, *How Revolutionary Were the Bourgeois Revolutions?* Chicago: Haymarket Books, 2012; Joseph Choonara, 'The Relevance of Permanent Revolution: A Reply to Neil Davidson', *International Socialism Journal*, 2011, www.isj.org.uk/?id=745.
16. Hal Draper, *Karl Marx's Theory of Revolution II, The Politics of Social Classes*, New York: Monthly Review Press, 1978, p. 17.
17. Ibid., p. 18.
18. US Embassy in Cairo, 'Supporting Egypt's Democratic Transition', 2012, http://egypt.usembassy.gov/democracy.html (accessed 5 May 2014).
19. Vladimir Lenin, *The State and Revolution* (1917), ch. 1, www.marxists.org/archive/lenin/works/1917/staterev/ch01.htm, p. 46.
20. Rosa Luxemburg, *The Mass Strike, the Political Party and the Trade Unions* (1906), trans. *Patrick Lavin*, London: Merlin Press, 1964.
21. Yezid Sayigh, *Above the State: The Officers' Republic in Egypt*, Carnegie Endowment for International Peace, August 2012, www.carnegieendowment.org/files/officers_republic1.pdf (accessed 30 September 2012).
22. Gilbert Achcar, *The People Want: A Radical Exploration of the Arab Uprising*, London: Verso, 2013, p. 119.
23. Ibid., p. 121.
24. Fred Halliday, *Islam and the Myth of Confrontation: Religion and Politics in the Middle East*, London: I.B. Tauris, 1996; Fred Halliday, 'The Left and the Jihad', *OpenDemocracy*, 2011, www.opendemocracy.net/globalization/left_jihad_3886.jsp (accessed 6 May 2014).
25. Chris Harman, 'The Prophet and the Proletariat', *International Socialism Journal*, vol. 2, no. 64 (1994), www.marxists.org/archive/harman/1994/xx/islam.htm (accessed 12 November 2012).
26. Bernard Lewis, *What Went Wrong? Western Impact and Middle Eastern Response*, Oxford: Oxford University Press, 2002.
27. Achcar, *The People Want*, p. 151.
28. Ibid., pp. 251–2.
29. Ibid., p. 276.
30. Hanieh, *Lineages of Revolt*, p. 171.
31. Ibid., pp. 168, 171.
32. Philip Marfleet, 'Egypt: The Workers Advance', *International Socialism Journal*, vol. 2, no. 139 (2013), www.isj.org.uk/?id=904 (accessed 13 October 2013); Philip Marfleet, '"Never Going Back": Egypt's Continuing Revolution', *International Socialism Journal*, vol. 2, no. 137 (2013) www.isj.org.uk/?id=866 (accessed 6 May 2014).
33. Michael R. Gordon, 'Egyptians Following Right Path, Kerry Says', *New*

York Times, 3 November 2013, World/Middle East section, www.nytimes. com/2013/11/04/world/middleeast/kerry-egypt-visit.html (accessed 28 April 2014).

34. Nicholas Watt, 'David Cameron Orders Inquiry into Activities of Muslim Brotherhood', *Guardian*, 1 April 2014, World News section, www. theguardian.com/world/2014/apr/01/cameron-muslim-brotherhood-orders-inquiry-extremism (accessed 28 April 2014).

35. Harman, 'The Prophet and the Proletariat'.

36. Sameh Naguib, *Al-Ikhwan Al-Muslimun: Ru'iya Ishtarakiyya*, Cairo: Markaz Al-Dirasat Al-Ishtarakiyya, 2006.

37. Ibid., pp. 40–43.

38. Ibid.

39. Harman, 'The Prophet and the Proletariat'.

40. Marsha Pripstein Posusney, *Labor and the State in Egypt: Workers, Unions, and Economic Restructuring*, New York: Columbia University Press, 1997, p. 16.

41. Richard Hyman, *Industrial Relations: A Marxist Introduction*, London: Macmillan, 1975; Tony Cliff and Donny Gluckstein, *Marxism and Trade Union Struggle: The General Strike of 1926*, London: Bookmarks, 1986; Ralph Darlington and Martin Upchurch, 'A Reappraisal of the Rank-and-File versus Bureaucracy Debate', *Capital & Class* 36 (2012), pp. 77–95, http://dx.doi.org/10.1177/0309816811430369.

42. Cliff and Gluckstein, *Marxism and Trade Union Struggle*.

43. Darlington and Upchurch, 'A Reappraisal of the Rank-and-File versus Bureaucracy Debate', p. 91.

44. Ibid., p. 80.

45. Jeffrey R Webber, *Rebellion and Reform in Bolivia: Class Struggle, Indigenous Liberation, and the Politics of Evo Morales*, Chicago: Haymarket, 2011.

46. Davidson, *How Revolutionary Were the Bourgeois Revolutions?*, p. 147.

47. Choonara, 'The Relevance of Permanent Revolution'; Davidson, *How Revolutionary Were the Bourgeois Revolutions?*

48. Lenin, *The State and Revolution*, ch. 3.

49. Choonara, 'The Relevance of Permanent Revolution'.

CHAPTER 1

1. Gamal Essam El-Din, 'A New Boost for Privatisation', *Al-Ahram Weekly*, 7 December 2000, http://weekly.ahram.org.eg/2000/511/ec5.htm.

2. Kathryn C. Lavelle, *The Politics of Equity Finance in Emerging Markets*, Oxford: Oxford University Press, 2004, p. 176.

3. Ayman Ibrahim, 'Ummal Al-Tirsana Bayna Ta'suf Al-Idara Wa Tawata Al-Niqaba', *www.e-Socialists.net*, 23 May 2007, http://revsoc.me/workers-farmers/ml-ltrsn-byn-tsf-ldr-wtwtw-lnqb.

4. *Sabah Dream: Dina Abd-Al-Rahman Taqrir an Tirsana Al-Iskandaria Libinaa Al-Sufun*, 2011, www.youtube.com/watch?v=wYNwKarDftw&feature=youtube_gdata_player.

5. Lavelle, *The Politics of Equity Finance in Emerging Markets*.

6. Paul Mason, *Why It's Kicking off Everywhere: The New Global Revolutions*,

London; New York: Verso, 2012, p. 18.

7. *Sabah Dream.*

8. Citadel Capital, 'NRTC to Receive 10 River Barges Assembled by Alexandria Shipyard', 17 July 2012, http://citadelcapital.com/in-the-news/nrtc-to-receive-10-river-barges-assembled-by-alexandria-shipyard.

9. Adam Hanieh, *Lineages of Revolt: Issues of Contemporary Capitalism in the Middle East*, Chicago: Haymarket Books, 2013, p. 141.

10. Wahdat al-Dirasat, 'Tahawwulat Al-Iqtisad Al-Misri (Muladhat Awliyya)', *Al-Tariq Al-Ishtaraki* 1 (1999), pp. 5–51.

11. Anne Alexander, *Leadership in the National Movements of Egypt and Iraq 1945–63*, Ph.D. thesis, University of Exeter, 2007.

12. Joel Beinin and Zachary Lockman, *Workers on the Nile: Nationalism, Communism, Islam, and the Egyptian Working Class, 1882–1954*, London: I.B. Tauris, 1988.

13. Michael Kidron, *A Permanent Arms Economy*, London: Socialist Workers Party, 1989; Chris Harman, *Zombie Capitalism: Global Crisis and the Relevance of Marx*, Chicago: Haymarket Books, 2010.

14. Beinin and Lockman, *Workers on the Nile.*

15. Ibid., p. 139.

16. Ibid., p. 146.

17. Alexander, 'Leadership in the National Movements of Egypt and Iraq 1945–63'.

18. Ibid.

19. Ibid.; Beinin and Lockman, *Workers on the Nile.*

20. Alexander, 'Leadership in the National Movements of Egypt and Iraq 1945–63'.

21. Singapore Free Press, 'Egyptians Boycott Dutch Ship', *Singapore Free Press*, 4 August 1947.

22. Alexander, 'Leadership in the National Movements of Egypt and Iraq 1945–63'.

23. Tariq al- Bishri, *Al-haraka al-siyasiya fi Misr, 1945–1952*, al-Qahira: Dar as-Shuruq, 2002.

24. Beinin and Lockman, *Workers on the Nile*, p. 427; Alexander, 'Leadership in the National Movements of Egypt and Iraq 1945–63'.

25. Marsha Pripstein Posusney, *Labor and the State in Egypt: Workers, Unions, and Economic Restructuring*, New York: Columbia University Press, 1997, p. 44.

26. Ibid.; Alexander, 'Leadership in the National Movements of Egypt and Iraq 1945–63'.

27. Posusney, *Labor and the State in Egypt*, pp. 62–3.

28. Ibid., pp. 73–9; Joel Beinin, 'Labor, Capital, and the State in Nasserist Egypt, 1952–1961', *International Journal of Middle East Studies*, vol. 21, no. 1 (February 1989), pp. 71–90.

29. John Waterbury, 'The "Soft State" and the Open Door: Egypt's Experience with Economic Liberalization, 1974–1984', *Comparative Politics*, vol. 18, no. 1 (October 1985), p. 65.

30. Robert Mabro and Samir Muhammad Radwan, *The Industrialization of*

Egypt, 1939–1973: Policy and Performance, Oxford: Clarendon Press, 1976, p. 144.

31. Beinin, 'Labor, Capital, and the State in Nasserist Egypt, 1952–1961', p. 86.

32. Joel Beinin, *The Struggle for Worker Rights in Egypt*, Washington DC: Solidarity Center, 2010, p. 12.

33. Alan Richards and John Waterbury, *A Political Economy of the Middle East*, Boulder CO: Westview Press, 2008, p. 189; Wahdat al-Dirasat, 'Tahawwulat Al-Iqtisad Al-Misri (Muladhat Awliyya)'.

34. Waterbury, 'The "Soft State" and the Open Door', p. 70.

35. Anne Alexander, 'Mubarak in the International Arena', in Philip Marfleet and Rabab El-Mahdi, eds, *Egypt: The Moment of Change*, London: Zed Books, 2009, pp. 136–50.

36. Omar El Shafei, *Workers, Trade Unions and the State in Egypt, 1984–1989*, Cairo: American University in Cairo Press, 1995.

37. Posusney, *Labor and the State in Egypt*, p. 223.

38. Klaus Enders, 'IMF Survey: Egypt: Reforms Trigger Economic Growth', 13 February 2008, www.imf.org/external/pubs/ft/survey/so/2008/car021308a.htm.

39. Reda Eissa, *Al-'Adala al-Daribiyya, Al-Markaz al-Masry lil-Huquq al-Iqtisadiyya wal-Igtima'iyya*, Cairo, 2010, p. 34.

40. See Timothy Mitchell, 'Dreamland: The Neoliberalism of Your Desires', *Middle East Report* 210 (April 1999), pp. 28–33, for an exploration of the relationship between state and private capital in this process during the 1990s.

41. World Bank, Operations Evaluation Department, 'Egypt Country Assistance Evaluation', Washington DC: World Bank, 26 June 2000, pp. 1–2.

42. OECD, 'Business Climate Development Strategy: Phase 1 Policy Assessment – Privatisation Policy and Public Private Partnerships', July 2010, p. 4, www.oecd.org/dataoecd/49/55/46340470.pdf.

43. Ibid.

44. Ibid.

45. M. Hassan and C. Sassanpour, 'Labor Market Pressures in Egypt: Why Is the Unemployment Rate Stubbornly High?', *Journal of Development and Economic Policies*, vol. 10, no. 2 (2008), p. 13.

46. Mona Said, 'Compensating Differentials and Queue For Public Sector Jobs: Evidence from Egyptian Household Survey Data', Department of Economics Working Papers, SOAS, 2004, www.soas.ac.uk/economics/research/workingpapers/file28843.pdf.

47. Mostafa Bassiouny, 'Dirasat Al-Niqabat', unpublished paper, 2009, p. 11.

48. Mariz Tadros, 'State Welfare in Egypt since Adjustment: Hegemonic Control with a Minimalist Role', *Review of African Political Economy*, vol. 33, no. 108 (June 2006), p. 237.

49. Ibid., p. 240.

50. Ibid., p. 241.

51. Jeremy M. Sharp, *Egypt–United States Relations*, Washington DC: Congressional Research Service, 2005, p. 11.

52. Ray Bush, *Counter-Revolution in Egypt's Countryside: Land and Farm-*

ers in the Era of Economic Reform, London and New York: Zed Books, 2002; US Embassy in Cairo, 'Reform Fatigue at the Housing Ministry', WikiLeaks', 10 July 2008, www.telegraph.co.uk/news/wikileaks-files/egypt-wikileaks-cables/8327026/Reform-Fatigue-At-The-Housing-Ministry.html.

53. Bush, *Counter-Revolution in Egypt's Countryside*.
54. Robert Springborg, *Mubarak's Egypt : Fragmentation of the Political Order*, Boulder CO: Westview Press, 1989, p. 107.
55. Ibid., p. 113.
56. Ibid., p. 110.
57. Shana Marshall and Joshua Stacher, 'Egypt's Generals and Transnational Capital', *Middle East Report* 262 (Spring 2012), www.merip.org/mer/mer262/egypts-generals-transnational-capital.
58. Zeinab Abul-Magd, 'The Egyptian Republic of Retired Generals', *Foreign Policy*, 12 May 2012, http://mideast.foreignpolicy.com/posts/2012/05/08/the_egyptian_republic_of_retired_generals.

CHAPTER 2

1. Alex Callinicos and Chris Harman, *The Changing Working Class: Essays on Class Structure Today*, London and Chicago: Bookmarks, 1987, p. 6.
2. Chris Harman, 'The Workers of the World', *International Socialism Journal* 96, vol. 2, no. 96 (2002), http://pubs.socialistreviewindex.org.uk/isj96/harman.htm.
3. S. Sabry, *Poverty Lines in Cairo*, Poverty Reduction in Urban Areas Series, Working Paper 21, International Institute for Environment and Development, London, May 2009.
4. Using data from household surveys, Armanious and El-Hossiny argue that there is a significant correlation between increased household size and increased incidence of poverty, with households defined as chronically poor counting an average of 8 members, compared to an average of 4.6 members for those defined as 'never poor'. Taking into account a national average of 2.85 births per woman, a female workforce participation rate of 23 per cent, and a rate of youth unemployment of around 29 per cent on average for 2004–08, estimating an average of 4 dependants per wage worker seems a relatively conservative assumption. Dina Armanious and Yasmine El-Hossiney, 'Main Determinants of the Dynamics of Poverty (Chronically and Transient Poverty) in Egypt between 1998–2006', conference paper presented at the Population Association of America 2012 Annual Meeting Program, http://paa2012.princeton.edu/papers/121119 (accessed 8 August 2014); World Bank database, data.worldbank.org, http://data.worldbank.org/indicator/SL.UEM.1524.ZS.
5. Callinicos and Harman, *The Changing Working Class*, p. 64.
6. Ibid.
7. This is of course an understanding of combined development that differs from Trotsky's original formulation, which saw combination taking place across capitalist and pre-capitalist forms of production. See Chapter 1 of Trotsky, *History of the Russian Revolution* (New York: Pathfinder, 1992) for more detail.

8. F. Tregenna, 'Characterising Deindustrialisation: An Analysis of Changes in Manufacturing Employment and Output Internationally', *Cambridge Journal of Economics*, vol. 33, no. 3 (November 2008), pp. 433–66.

9. Ibid.

10. Gilbert Achcar, *The People Want: A Radical Exploration of the Arab Uprising*, London: Verso, 2013.

11. Ahmed Ghoneim, 'Promoting Competitive Markets in Developing Economies (The Case of Egypt)', 2005, International Development Research Center, Ottawa, p. 8, http://idl-bnc.idrc.ca/dspace/bitstream/10625/35100/1/127158.pdf.

12. Ibid.

13. UNCTAD, *Commodities at a Glance – Special Issue on Energy*, February 2012, p. 41, http://unctad.org/en/PublicationsLibrary/suc2011d6_en.pdf; World Bank, 'Natural Gas Rents (% of GDP)', 2011, http://data.worldbank.org/indicator/NY.GDP.NGAS.RT.ZS?page=6.

14. Ray Bush, 'Politics, Power and Poverty: Twenty Years of Agricultural Reform and Market Liberalisation in Egypt', *Third World Quarterly*, vol. 28, no. 8 (January 2007), p. 1600.

15. Ibid., p. 1609.

16. Women's wages for public administration were not provided in this dataset. Establishments over ten persons only.

17. Ayman Riad, 'The Cement Industry in Egypt: Between Monopoly and the Need for Development Construction', 25 October 2011, www.zawya.com/story/Egypts_cement_industry-zawya20111025054229.

18. Ibid.

19. Ministry of Finance, *Profile of M/SMEs in Egypt – Update Report*, October 2005, www.mof.gov.eg/MOFGallerySource/English/SME/Research_studies/24.pdf.

20. A. El-Haddad, *Effects of the Global Crisis on the Egyptian Textiles and Clothing Sector: A Blessing in Disguise?*, working paper, International Labour Organization, Geneva, 2010, p. 2, http://natlex.ilo.ch/public/english/region/afpro/cairo/downloads/textileenglish.pdf.

21. Ibid.; Sameh Naguib, *Labour, Markets and Industrial Development: Garment Production in the City of Shubra El-Kheima*, Ph.D. thesis, University of London, 2006.

22. El-Haddad, *Effects of the Global Crisis on the Egyptian Textiles and Clothing Sector*, p. 5.

23. Ibid.

24. Naguib, *Labour, Markets and Industrial Development*, p. 125.

25. Gherzi, *Strategy and Action Plan Project for the Egyptian Textile and Clothing Industry – Inception Report*, Industrial Modernisation Centre, July 2006, www.cabdirect.org/abstracts/19541603857.html.

26. Faiza Rady, 'Esco Ordeal Ends', *Al-Ahram Weekly*, 2 June 2005, p. 7, http://weekly.ahram.org.eg/2005/745/eg9.htm.

27. El-Haddad, *Effects of the Global Crisis on the Egyptian Textiles and Clothing Sector*, p. 13.

28. Markaz al-dirasat al-ishtarakiyya, *Tabaqa Amila Misriyya Gadida*, Awraq

Ummaliyya, March 2005, www.e-socialists.net; Jochen Möller, 'Working and Living in 10th of Ramadan City: The Perspective of Workers in Small Industries', *Égypte/Monde Arabe*, vol. 1, no. 33 (1998), http://ema.revues.org/index1575.html.

29. Markaz al-dirasat al-ishtarakiyya, *Tabaqa Amila Misriyya Gadida*.

30. Data on the location of firms in 10th of Ramadan City was compiled from the crowd-sourced mapping platform Wikimapia, which represents an exceptionally rich source of information about the industrial landscape of Egypt. The information was cross-referenced with searches in online trade directories and company websites, and with a research visit to 10th of Ramadan City on 1 June 2013. The data for plot A2 can be found at http://wikimapia.org/#lat=30.2794436&lon=31.794605&z=15&l=0&m=b, while the data for plot A3 can be found at http://wikimapia.org/#lat=30.296453&lon=31.8062887&z=17&l=0&m=b.

31. General Motors, 'Egypt', 2013, http://careers.gm.com/worldwide-locations/africa/egypt.html; Robert Springborg, *Mubarak's Egypt : Fragmentation of the Political Order*, Boulder CO: Westview Press, 1989, p. 109.

32. Seoudi Group, 'Founder', 2013, www.seoudi.com/founder.php.

33. 'Aboul Fotouh, 'Speranza Egypt – Aboul Fotouh', 2013, www.speranza-egypt.com.

34. Naguib, 'Labour, Markets and Industrial Development'.

35. KPMG, *Strategic Study to Upgrade Egypt's Automotive Sector: Executive Summary and Overview*, Cairo: Industrial Modernisation Centre, January 2005, www.imc-egypt.org/studies/ExecutiveSummaries/Automotive%20Sector%20Development%20Strategy_EN.pdf; Akhbar el Yom, 'Automech Akhbar El Yom – Market Background', 2011, www.automech-online.com/MarketBackground.aspx.

36. Tom Gara, 'Egypt: Chinese Cars Coming', *Financial Times*, 21 February 2012, http://blogs.ft.com/beyond-brics/2012/02/21/egypt-chinese-cars-coming.

37. Anne Alexander, *Leadership in the National Movements of Egypt and Iraq 1945–63*, Ph.D. thesis, University of Exeter, 2007; Joel Beinin and Zachary Lockman, *Workers on the Nile: Nationalism, Communism, Islam, and the Egyptian Working Class, 1882–1954*, London: I.B. Tauris, 1988.

38. ILO, 'Concepts and Definitions of Informality', 2012, http://laborsta.ilo.org/informal_economy_E.html.

39. Privatization Coordination Support Unit, 'The Results and Impacts of Egypt's Privatization Program', Carana Corporation, August 2002, pp. 38–9.

40. Vincenzo Comito, *PPP & Concession Agreements in the Mediterranean Countries: Overview and Perspectives*, EuroMed Transport Project, 20 July 2010, p. 6, www.euromedtransport.eu/En/image.php?id=1139.

41. Ikram Al Yacoub, 'What's in a Tuk-Tuk? Happy Egyptians Paying Low Fares, of Course', 12 October 2012, http://english.alarabiya.net/articles/2011/05/16/149296.html.

42. Hadeel Al Sayegh, 'Ghabbour to Cash in on Egypt Taxi Overhaul', *The National*, 22 August 2010, www.thenational.ae/business/markets/ghabbour-to-cash-in-on-egypt-taxi-overhaul.

43. Suez Canal Authority, 'Suez Canal Traffic Statistics', 2013, www.suezcanal. gov.eg/TRstat.aspx?reportId=4.

44. Ahram Online, 'Cairo Microbus Drivers Begin Partial Strike', *Ahram Online*, 2 October 2012, http://english.ahram.org.eg/NewsContent/1/64/54525/ Egypt/Politics-/Cairo-microbus-drivers-begin-partial-strike.aspx.

45. Alison Meuse, 'Selling Protection', *Business Monthly*, July 2011, http://amcham.org.eg/resources_publications/publications/business_monthly/issue. asp?sec=4&subsec=selling%20protection&im=7&iy=2011.

46. Leila Hassanin, 'Egypt', 2007, www.giswatch.org/en/country-report/ civil-society-participation/egypt.

47. Reuters, 'Egypt to Grant Telecom Egypt a Mobile License', *Reuters*, 26 December 2012, www.reuters.com/article/2012/12/26/egypt-telecom egypt-idUSL5E8NQ3JU20121226.

48. Alin Popescu, 'Deja Vu All Over Again: Cables Cut in the Mediterranean – Renesys Blog', 19 December 2008, www.renesys.com/blog/2008/12/deja-vu-all-over-again-cables.shtml.

49. James Cowie, 'Egypt Leaves the Internet – Renesys Blog', 27 January 2011, www.renesys.com/blog/2011/01/egypt-leaves-the-internet.shtml.

50. World Bank database: primary school enrollment, http://data.worldbank. org/indicator/se.prm.enrr; adult literacy rate, http://data.worldbank.org/ indicator/se.adt.litr.zs (both accessed 8 August 2014).

51. Ministry of Education, *National Strategic Plan For Pre-University Education Reform in Egypt 2007/8–2011/12*, 2007, p. 31, http://planipolis.iiep. unesco.org/upload/Egypt/EgyptStrategicPlanPre-universityEducation.pdf; Helen Chapin Metz, 'Education', in *Egypt: A Country Study*, Washington DC: Library of Congress, 1990, http://countrystudies.us/egypt/71.htm.

52. Teacher activists, 10 September 2011.

53. Teacher activists, June 2012.

54. Hala Talaat, interview, Cairo, 5 April 2012; Mariz Tadros, 'State Welfare in Egypt since Adjustment: Hegemonic Control with a Minimalist Role', *Review of African Political Economy*, vol. 33, no. 108 (June 2006), pp. 237–54.

55. Hala Talaat, interview,.

56. Guy Standing, *The Precariat: The New Dangerous Class*, London: Bloomsbury Academic, 2011; Kevin Doogan, *New Capitalism?: The Transformation of Work*, Cambridge: Polity Press, 2009.

57. Claire Ceruti, 'One Class or Two? The Labour Reserve and "Surplus Population" in Marx and Contemporary Soweto', *South African Review of Sociology*, vol. 41, no. 2 (June 2010), pp. 77–103.

58. Jackline Wahba, 'The Impact of Labor Market Reforms on Informality in Egypt', *Gender and Work in the MENA Region Working Paper Series*, August 2009, www.populationcouncil.us/pdfs/wp/mena/03.pdf.

59. Ibid., p. 13.

60. Diego F. Angel-Urdinola and Kimie Tanabe, *Micro-Determinants of Informal Employment in the Middle East and North Africa Region*, World Bank, Washington DC, January 2012, pp. 12–13, http://siteresources.worldbank. org/socialprotection/Resources/SP-Discussion-papers/Labor-Market-DP/1201.pdf.

CHAPTER 3

1. Operations Evaluation Department World Bank, 'Egypt Country Assistance Evaluation', World Bank, Washington DC, 26 June 2000, p. 1.
2. Rosa Luxemburg, *The Mass Strike, the Political Party and the Trade Unions, 1906: Rosa Luxemburg*, trans. Patrick Lavin, London: Merlin Press, 1964.
3. Rabab El-Mahdi, 'The Democracy Movement: Cycles of Protest', in Rabab El-Mahdi and Philip Marfleet, eds, *Egypt: The Moment of Change*, London: Zed Books, 2009, pp. 87–103.
4. Luxemburg, *The Mass Strike, the Political Party and the Trade Unions, 1906*.
5. El-Mahdi, 'The Democracy Movement: Cycles of Protest'.
6. Fatemah Farag, 'Child Murder Sparks Campus Fury', *Al-Ahram Weekly*, 5 October 2000, http://weekly.ahram.org.eg/2000/502/eg5.htm.
7. Vickie Langohr, 'Cracks in Egypt's Electoral Engineering', *Middle East Research and Information Project*, 7 November 2000, www.merip.org/mero/mero110700.
8. Anti-war activist, 21 March 2003.
9. Hisham Bastawisi and Mahmoud Mekki, 'When Judges Are Beaten', *Guardian*, 10 May 2006, www.guardian.co.uk/commentisfree/2006/may/10/comment.egypt.
10. Hisham Fouad, 'Qiraa Awliyya Fi Al-Ihtigagat Al-Ummaliyya Al-Rahina', www.e-Socialists.net, 8 November 2004, www.e-socialists.net/node/1425; Joel Beinin, *The Struggle for Worker Rights in Egypt*, Washington DC: Solidarity Center, 2010, p. 16; Markaz Awlad al-Ard, 'Hasad al-harakah al-ummaliyya fi am 2010', www.ecesr.com, 2010.
11. Marsha Pripstein Posusney, *Labor and the State in Egypt: Workers, Unions, and Economic Restructuring*, New York: Columbia University Press, 1997, pp. 263–7.
12. Egyptian Trade Union and Workers Watch, 'Shahr Fibrayir Am 2007', 1 March 2007, www.e-socialists.net/taxonomy/term/150/all?page=2.
13. Joel Beinin and Hossam El-Hamalawy, 'Egyptian Textile Workers Confront the New Economic Order', Middle East Research and Information Project, 25 March 2007, www.merip.org/mero/mero032507; Egyptian Trade Union and Workers Watch, *Shahr Fibrayir Am 2007*.
14. Egyptian Workers and Trade Union Watch (EWTUW), 'Shahr Abril 2007', May 2007, http://arabist.net/arabawy/wp-content/uploads/2007/05/may-case-studymasrespain.pdf; Beinin and El-Hamalawy, 'Egyptian Textile Workers Confront the New Economic Order'.
15. Eman Morsi, 'Strikes in Egypt: Female Workers on the Frontline', www.babelmed.net, 16 April 2008, www.babelmed.net/Countries/Mediterranean/strikes_in.php?c=3143&m=9&l=en.
16. EWTUW, 'Shahr Abril 2007'.
17. EWTUW, 'Al-Usbu'a Al-Thalith Walra'ba' Min Shahr Uktubir 2007', October 2007, http://arabist.net/arabawy/wp-content/uploads/2007/11/3-4-actober.pdf.

18. International Trade Union Confederation (ITUC), *Report for the WTO General Council Review of the Trade Policies of Egypt*, Brussels, 26 July 2011.
19. Workers' placard in the September 2007 strike at Misr Spinning, Mahalla.
20. Human Rights Watch, 'Egypt: Release Dozens of Protestors Held Without Charge', 18 July 2008, www.hrw.org/news/2008/07/17/egypt-release-dozens-protestors-held-without-charge.
21. Luxemburg, *The Mass Strike, the Political Party and the Trade Unions, 1906.*
22. US Embassy in Cairo, 'Mahalla One Year after the Strike', WikiLeaks, 12 March 2009, http://wikileaks.org/cable/2009/03/09CAIRO428.html#.

CHAPTER 4

1. Joel Beinin and Zachary Lockman, *Workers on the Nile: Nationalism, Communism, Islam, and the Egyptian Working Class, 1882–1954*, London: I.B. Tauris, 1988; Joel Beinin, 'Labor, Capital, and the State in Nasserist Egypt, 1952–1961', *International Journal of Middle East Studies*, vol. 21, no. 1 (February 1989), pp. 71–90; Marsha Pripstein Posusney, *Labor and the State in Egypt: Workers, Unions, and Economic Restructuring*, New York: Columbia University Press, 1997.
2. Posusney, *Labor and the State in Egypt.*
3. Ibid., p. 28.
4. Beinin and Lockman, *Workers on the Nile*; Anne Alexander, *Leadership in the National Movements of Egypt and Iraq 1945–63*, Ph.D. thesis, University of Exeter, 2007; A. Alexander, 'Leadership and Collective Action in the Egyptian Trade Unions', *Work, Employment and Society*, vol. 24, no. 2 (June 2010), pp. 241–59; Anne Alexander, 'Analysing Activist Cultures in the Egyptian Workers' Movement', in Jude Howell, ed., *Non-Governmental Public Action and Social Justice*, Basingstoke: Palgrave Macmillan, 2013.
5. Government of Egypt, 'Qanun Al-Niqabat Al-Ummaliyya Raqm 12 Lisana 1995', Al Jazeera, 1995, www.aljazeera.net/specialfiles/pages/536961d8-8f73-4687-9c7e-3de45711cd70.
6. Al-Mahkama al-Dusturiyya al-Uliya, 'Dustur 1964', www.hccourt.gov.eg/Constitutions/Constitution64.asp.
7. Inter-Parliamentary Union, 'Egypt (Majlis Al-Chaab)', IPU Parline Database, 2010, www.ipu.org/parline-e/reports/2097_arc.htm.
8. Posusney, *Labor and the State in Egypt.*
9. Muhammad Al-Agrudi, 'Megawer: Nuqif Bil-Marsad Did Tazwir Shihadat Al-Sifa Al-Ummaliyya', Al-Ahram Digital, 10 September 2010, http://digital.ahram.org.eg/articles.aspx?Serial=249159&eid=707.
10. Inter-Parliamentary Union, 'Egypt (Majlis Al-Chaab) Elections in 2005', IPU Parline Database, 2010, www.ipu.org/parline-e/reports/arc/2097_05.htm.
11. 'Murashahu Al-Ikhwan Bil-Qahira', Ikhwanonline.net, 2005, www.ikhwanonline.net/data/baralman2005/ikhwan3.htm; 'Murashahu Al-Ikhwan Fi Al-Iskandaria', Ikhwanonline.net, 2005, www.ikhwanonline.net/data/baralman2005/ikhwan1.htm.
12. 'Murashahu Al-Ikhwan Bil-Qahira'.

13. 'Murashahu Al-Ikhwan Fi Al-Iskandaria'.
14. Posusney, *Labor and the State in Egypt*.
15. Ibid.
16. Mostafa Bassiouny, 'Dirasat Al-Niqabat', unpublished paper, 2009, p. 24.
17. Muhammad Azuz, 'Fashl Al-Idirab Al-Shara'i Al-Awwal Fi Misr Li Tanta Lil-Kitan … Wa Ittihad Al-Ummal Yuqarrir Ta'liq Al-Itisam', *Al-Masry Al-Youm*, 12 August 2008, http://today.almasryalyoum.com/article2.aspx?Art icleID=222268&IssueID=1495.
18. Bassiouny, 'Dirasat Al-Niqabat', p. 24.
19. Azuz, 'Fashl Al-Idirab Al-Shara'i Al-Awwal Fi Misr Li Tanta Lil-Kitan … Wa Ittihad Al-Ummal Yuqarrir Ta'liq Al-Itisam'; Lagna al-tadamun ma ummal tanta lil-kitan, 'Megawer Wa Al-Gawhari Yukhawnun Ummal Tanta Lil-Kitan Wa Al-Ummal Yurfudun Qarar Taliq Al-Idirab Wa Yuqataun Al-Tariq Al-Sariaa', *Markaz Al-Dirasat Al-Ishtarakiyya*, 10 August 2008, www.e-socialists.net/node/4041.
20. CTUWS, *Waqai Ma Gara Al-Intikhabat Al-Niqabiyya Dawra 2006–2011*, 2006, www.ctuws.com/uploads/Books/The-Trade-Union-Elections/Arabic/Facts-Ar.pdf.
21. Kamal Abu Aita, 29 March 2008.
22. Fatma Ramadan and Egyptian Trade Union and Workers Watch, 'Shahr Abril 2007', May 2007, www.e-socialists.net/sites/default/files/pdf/7.pdf.
23. Hisham Fouad, 'Al-Burkan Al-Ummaly Lan Yuhda', *Markaz Al-Dirasat Al-Ishtarakiyya*, 3 March 2007, http://revsoc.me/workers-farmers/lbrkn-lmly-ln-yhd.
24. Taha Sa'ad Uthman, *Min Tarikh Ummal Masr – Kifah Ummal Al-Nasig*, al-Qahira: Maktabat al-Madbuli, 1983, pp. 71–2; Fathallah Mahrus, 9 July 2009; Alexander, 'Analysing Activist Cultures in the Egyptian Workers' Movement'.
25. Eva Bellin, *Stalled Democracy: Capital, Labor, and the Paradox of State-Sponsored Development*, Ithaca NY: Cornell University Press, 2002, p. 106.
26. Mohamed Sghaeir Saihi, 12 November 2012.
27. Mostafa Bassiouny, 'Azmat Al-Tandhim Al-Niqabi Fi Masr', *Awraq Ishtarakiyya*, November 2009, www.e-socialists.net/node/5115.
28. Magdi Sharara, *Al-Haraka al-Niqabiyya al-Misriyya: Dirasa Tahliliyya li-Nata'ig Intikhabat Al-Niqabiyya: Al-Dawra Al-Thalith Ashr 2006–2011*, Cairo, Al-Ittihad Al-Am Li-Niqabat, 2007, p. 54.
29. Ibid., p. 57.
30. Bassiouny, 'Azmat Al-Tandhim Al-Niqabi Fi Masr'.
31. US Embassy in Cairo, 'Labor Strikes: GOE Approach Unsuccessful in Stemming Protests', WikiLeaks, 29 May 2007, http://wikileaks.org/cable/2007/05/07CAIRO1595.html#.
32. Erin Snider and David Faris, 'The Arab Spring: U.S. Democracy Promotion in Egypt', *Middle East Policy*, vol. XVIII, no. 3 (2011), http://mepc.org/journal/middle-east-policy-archives/arab-spring-us-democracy-promotion-egypt?print.
33. Solidarity Center, 'Programme of Assistance to the Egyptian Trade Union Federation (ETUF) – Final Report', 2003, http://pdf.usaid.gov/pdf_docs/

PDABZ006.pdf.

34. Mohammed Shafiq, "'The Union Is a Shield and Our Sword Is the Strike'", *Socialist Review*, December 2011, www.socialistreview.org.uk/article. php?articlenumber=11845.
35. Hilmi Al-Gazzar, 'Ra'is Al-Hurriya Wal-Adala', *Al-Masry Al-Youm*, 8 October 2012, www.almasryalyoum.com/node/1163016.
36. Shafiq, "'The Union Is a Shield and Our Sword Is the Strike'".
37. Ibid.

CHAPTER 5

1. US Embassy in Cairo, 'Egypt Labor Update: GOE Shuts Down Labor NGO', 2 May 2007, http://wikileaks.org/cable/2007/05/07CAIRO1283. html#.
2. Ibid.
3. Ralph Darlington and Martin Upchurch, 'A Reappraisal of the Rank-and-File versus Bureaucracy Debate', *Capital & Class*, vol. 36, no. 1 (February 2012), pp. 77–95.
4. Many of the details in this section are based on Mostafa Bassiouny's personal engagement with the strike as a journalist and an activist. We have also provided references to Gamal Uwayda's account of the property tax collectors' movement (*Malahama 'itisam muwadhafiy al-dara'ib al-aqariyya*, Cairo: Markaz al-dirasat al-Ishtarakiyya, 2008).
5. Ibid., pp. 16–19.
6. Ibid., p. 27.
7. Ibid., p. 29.
8. Ibid., p. 30.
9. Ibid., p. 39.
10. Ibid., p. 40.
11. Ibid., pp. 45–6.
12. Ibid., p. 53.
13. Ibid., pp. 53–4.
14. Ibid., p. 62.
15. Ibid., p. 63.
16. Kamal Abu Aita, 'Ma Ba'd Al-Lagna Al-Uliyya Lil Idrab?', *Nubat Sahyan*, October 2008.
17. Ibid.
18. Ibid.
19. Uwaydah, *Malahama 'itisam muwadhafiy al-dara'ib al-'aqariyya*, pp. 108–10.
20. 'Niqabat Al-Bunuk Ayala Lil Suqut Istiqala Ha'it Maktab Lagna Al-Dahaqiliyya', *Nubat Sahyan*, 4th edn, May 2009.
21. Nubat Sahyan, 'Waintisarna', *Nubat Sahyan*, 4th edn, May 2009, p. 1.
22. US Embassy in Cairo, 'Founder of Egypt's First Independent Union on Labor Activism', Telegraph, WikiLeaks, 1 October 2009, www.telegraph. co.uk/news/wikileaks-files/egypt-wikileaks-cables/8327162/Founder-Of-Egypts-First-Independent-Union-On-Labor-Activism.html.

23. Kamal Abu Aita, 'Khitab Musagil B'ilm Al-Wusul: Ism Al-Rasil Al-Dara'ib Al-Aqariyy ... Ism Al-Mursil Ilihu Ummal Al-Barid ... Al-Ainwan Bir Masr', *Al-Ishtaraki*, 1 July 2009, www.e-socialists.net/node/3700.

24. Ibid.

25. Ministry of Education, *National Strategic Plan For Pre-University Education Reform in Egypt 2007/8–2011/12*, 2007, p. 32, http://planipolis.iiep. unesco.org/upload/Egypt/EgyptStrategicPlanPre-universityEducation.pdf.

26. Hala Talaat, 5 April 2012.

27. Ibid.

28. Niqaba al-mihan al-talimiyya, 'Tarikh Niqaba Al-Mihan Al-Talimiyya', http://ets.eg/Syndicate/history.htm (accessed 1 June 2014).

29. Hala Talaat, interview.

30. Hatim Salam, 'Al-Mu'alimin Tu'alin Ta'sis Niqaba "Mustaqilla" Raghm Al-Rafd Al-Hukumi', *Youm* 7, 15 July 2010, www.youm7.com/News. asp?NewsID=254276.

31. Ahmed El-Sayyed,interview with Ahmed el-Sayyed, Health Technicians' Union, 18 March 2011.

32. Ibid.

33. Ibid.

34. Naamat Gaber, interview with Naamat Gaber, civil aviation worker, 4 April 2012.

35. Hisham Fouad, 'Al-Mahalla: Al-Fursa Al-Da'iyya', *Al-Ishtaraki*, 33rd edn, April 2009.

36. A. Alexander, 'Leadership and Collective Action in the Egyptian Trade Unions', *Work, Employment & Society*, vol. 24, no. 2 (June 2010), pp. 241–59.

37. Centre for Trade Union and Workers Services (CTUWS), 'The Visa and Immigration Section in the Canadian Embassy Refrained from According an Entry Visa to CTUWS General Coordinator. Sequenced Abstruse Demeanors Have Been an Object of Queries', 27 June 2010, www.ctuws.com/ Default.aspx?item=501.

38. AFL–CIO, 'The George Meany–Lane Kirkland 2009 Human Rights Award', 3 March 2010, http://blog.aflcio.org/About/Exec-Council/EC-Statements/ The-George-Meany-Lane-Kirkland-2009–Human-Rights-Award.

39. CTUWS, 'Ta'rif Al-Dar', 17 April 2013, www.ctuws.com/about/ story/?item=14.

40. CTUWS, 'Tasalam Al-Dar Al-Khidamat Ga'izat Al-Gumhuriyya Al-Faransiyya Lihuquq Al-Insan Li-Am 1999', 17 April 2013, www.ctuws.com/about/ story/?item=100; Unison, 'Act Now – Call on Mubarak to Revoke Closure of Unison-Supported Organisation in Egypt', 2007, www.unison.org.uk/ international/pages_view.asp?did=5186; Solidar, 'Past Winners Archive 2000–2008', 2013, www.solidar.org/Past-Winners-Archive-2000–2008. html; Catherine Essoyan, 'Centre for Trade Union and Workers Services (CTUWS) (Egypt)', Oxfam, accessed 17 April 2013, www.ctuws.com/uploads/CTUWS-back/Solidarities/International/English/Oxfam-Novib_ english.pdf.

41. Solidarity Center, 'Court Decision Restores Egyptian Worker Rights Organization', 2007, www.solidaritycenter.org/content.asp?contentid=772.

CHAPTER 6

1. V.I. Lenin, 'The Collapse of the Second International II', 1915, www.marxists.org/archive/lenin/works/1915/csi/ii.htm.
2. Sameh Naguib, *The Egyptian Revolution*, London: Bookmarks, 2011.
3. Sayed Abd-al -Rahman, 20 March 2011.
4. Ibid.
5. ANHRI, *Duwa Fi Darb Al-Hurriya: Shuhada Thawrat 25 Yanayir*, 2012, www.anhri.net/wp-content/uploads/2012/05/book-2.pdf.
6. Egyptian Journalists Union, 'Al-Qawa'im Ba'd Al-Ta'dil', edited list of injured and killed during the 18-Day uprising against Mubarak', unpublished document, 2013.
7. Abd-al -Rahman, interview.
8. Naguib, *The Egyptian Revolution*.
9. Mu'assisat Awlad al-Ard and Markaz al-masry lil huquq al-iqtisadiyya wa al-igtima'iyya, *Al-Ummal Wa Al-Thawra Al-Masriyya – Ru'iyya Huquqiyya*, Cairo: Markaz al-masry lil huquq al-iqtisadiyya wa al-igtima'iyya, 16 February 2011.
10. The details of strike action by workers during this period are based on Mostafa Bassiouny's personal experience and discussions with leading worker activists during the 18 Days.
11. Muhammad Salah and Sharif Al-Dib, 'Bil-Suwwar ... Al-Itisamat Tatawasil Bi Addad Min Qita'at Al-Dahaqiliyya', *Youm 7*, 13 February 2011, www.youm7.com/News.asp?NewsID=351252#.UnUlUFOwDts.
12. Usama Ahmad, 'Tullab Masr Yu'akidun ... Al-Thawra Mustamira', *Masr Al-Thawriyya*, 15 March 2011, www.e-socialists.net/node/6655.
13. AFP, 'Mahalla's Misr Spinning and Weaving Workers Strike', *Ahram Online*, 16 February 2011, http://english.ahram.org.eg/News/5695.aspx.
14. Mu'assisat Awlad al-Ard and Markaz al-masry lil huquq al-iqtisadiyya wa al-igtima'iyya, *Al-Ummal Wa Al-Thawra Al-Masriyya – Ru'iyya Huquqiyya*.
15. Sarah Raslan, 'Cairo Bus Drivers Partially Suspend Strike after 18 Days', *Ahram Online*, 4 October 2011, http://english.ahram.org.eg/NewsContent/1/64/23343/Egypt/Politics-/Cairo-bus-drivers-partially-suspend-strike-after--.aspx; MENAsolidarity, 'Egypt: Teachers Tell Generals "Meet Our Demands ... or No School This Year"', *MENA Solidarity Network*, 13 September 2011, http://menasolidaritynetwork.com/2011/09/13/egypt-teachers-tell-generals-meet-our-demands-or-no-school-this-year.
16. This table is derived from data compiled by Awlad al-Ard for its monthly reports on workers' collective action. Awlad al-Ard uses press reports and therefore includes estimated numbers of participants for a large proportion, but not all, of if its reports on workers' strikes and protests. In order to estimate the total number of participants per month, episodes of collective action are categorised by size (under 100, 100–499, 500–999, 1,000–4,999 and so on), and the proportion of strikes calculated, with recorded numbers of participants who fell into each category. It is assumed that strikes *without* recorded numbers of participants would fall into the same pattern, thus allowing estimation of the total number of participants per month. This method has only been applied to strikes with under 5,000 participants,

assuming that strikes with over 5,000 participants – as these remained relatively rare – were likely to have been reported on in detail by the media. See Awlad al-Ard, 'Hasad al-Haraka al-Ummaliyya', March–September 2011, for the original reports.

17. Joel Beinin, *The Struggle for Worker Rights in Egypt*, Washington DC: Solidarity Center, 2010, p. 16.

18. Egyptian independent trade unionists, 'Egypt: Demands of the Workers in the Revolution', *Socialist Worker*, 19 February 2011, http://socialistworker. co.uk/art/23553/Egypt%3A+Demands+of+the+workers+in+the+revolution.

19. MENA Solidarity, 'Egypt: Teachers Tell Generals "Meet Our Demands ... or No School This Year"', *MENA Solidarity Network*, 2011 http://menasolidaritynetwork.com/2011/09/13/egypt-teachers-tell-generals-meet-our-demands-or-no-school-this-year/ (accessed 1 December 2013).

20. 'Ummal wa Amilat ghazl al-mahalla, 'Min Ummal Wa Amilat Ghazl Al-Mahalla', 3 September 2011, www.e-socialists.net/node/7361.

21. CAPMAS, *Al-Nashra Al-Rabaa Sanawiyya Li Bahath Al-Quwa Al-Amila*, October 2011.

22. Anne Alexander, 'The Egyptian Workers' Movement and the 25 January Revolution', *International Socialism Journal* 133 (January 2012), www.isj. org.uk/index.php4?id=778&issue=133.

23. Zeinab El Gundy, 'Political Parties and Powers to Approve El-Selmi Document, on Condition It Is Amended', *Ahram Online*, 16 November 2011, http://english.ahram.org.eg/NewsContent/1/64/26754/Egypt/Politics-/Political-parties-and-powers-to-approve-ElSelmi-do.aspx; Tamir Moustafa, *Drafting Egypt's Constitution: Can A New Legal Framework Revive a Flawed Transition?*, Brookings Doha Center, Stanford Project on Arab Transitions, Brookings Institute, March 2012, www.brookings.edu/~/media/research/files/papers/2012/3/12%20egypt%20constitution%20moustafa/new1%20drafting%20egypts%20new%20constitutionenr03.pdf.

24. Ashraf Umar, 'Musharika Ummaliyya Mahduda Fi 11 Febrayir ... Limadha?', *Al-Ishtaraki*, 15 February 2012, www.e-socialists.net/node/8310.

25. Sarah Carr, 'A Firsthand Account: Marching from Shubra to Deaths at Maspero', *Egypt Independent*, 10 October 2011, www.egyptindependent. com/news/firsthand-account-marching-shubra-deaths-maspero; Ekram Ibrahim, 'Justice Denied: Egypt's Maspero Massacre One Year on', *Ahram Online*, 9 October 2012, http://english.ahram.org.eg/News/54821.aspx.

26. CAPMAS, *Al-Nashra Al-Rabaa Sanawiyya Li Bahath Al-Quwa Al-Amila*, October 2011; CAPMAS, *Al-Nashra Al-Rabaa Sanawiyya Li Bahath Al-Quwa Al-Amila*, January 2013.

27. CAPMAS, *Al-Bahith Al-Dakhl Wal-Infaq Wal-Istihilak Li-Am 2010-2011*, November 2012.

CHAPTER 7

1. Ahmad Mahmoud Ahmad, 5 April 2012.

2. Ibid.

3. Tariq Al-Beheiry, 1 November 2012.

4. Hala Talaat, 5 April 2012.

5. Ibid.

6. Al-lagna al-tansiqiyya lidrab al-arish, 'Bayan Mu'tamir Ligan Idrab Al-Mu'alimin Bil-Arish', E-Socialists.net, 22 September 2011, http://revsoc. me/workers-farmers/byn-mwtmr-ljn-drb-lmlmyn-blrysh.

7. Teacher activists, 10 September 2011.

8. Mohammed Shafiq and Doctors without Rights activists, October 2011; Mohammed Shafiq, '"The Union Is a Shield and Our Sword Is the Strike"', *Socialist Review*, December 2011, www.socialistreview.org.uk/article. php?articlenumber=11845.

9. Anne Alexander, 'The Egyptian Workers' Movement and the 25 January Revolution', *International Socialism Journal*, vol. 2, no. 133 (Winter 2012), www.isj.org.uk/index.php4?id=778&issue=133 (accessed 29 April 2012).

10. Kamal Abu Aita, 27 October 2011.

11. *Ummal Al-Sikkat Al-Hadid Awzin Niqaba Mustaqilla Li?*, 2011, www.you-tube.com/watch?v=E10IzcERSSM&feature=youtube_gdata_player.

12. Oil union activist, 27 October 2011; teacher activists, June 2012.

13. Haitham Muhammadain, 'Al-Yawm: Al-Ilan an Niqaba Mustaqilla Bi-mustashfa Al-Du'aa Wa Ukhra Fi Sikkak Haddid Al-Wasta', 4 May 2011, www.e-socialists.net/node/6848.

14. Al-Masry Al-Youm, 'Makatib Shubra Al-Kheima Wa Kafr Al-Shaykh Wa Qena Wal Gharbiyya Tandum Lidrab Al-Barid', *Al-Masry Al-Youm*, 4 September 2011, www.almasryalyoum.com/node/492345; Al-Ishtaraki, 'Al-Barid Yuwasil Idrabu an Al-Aml Lilyawm Al-Thalith Ala Al-Tawala', *Al-Ishtaraki*, 4 September 2011, www.e-socialists.net/node/7377.

15. Ahram Online, 'Egypt's Ain Sokhna Port to Reopen as 2-Week-Old Strike Ends', *Ahram Online*, 24 October 2012, http://english.ahram.org.eg/News-Content/3/12/56466/Business/Economy/Egypts-Ain-Sokhna-port-to-reo-pen-as-weekold-strike.aspx.

16. Rifaat Arafat, 19 December 2012.

17. Hind Abdel-Gawad, 2 June 2013.

18. MENAsolidarity, 'Egypt: Locked-out IFFCO Food Workers Con-tinue Strike', *MENA Solidarity Network*, 5 June 2013, http://mena solidaritynetwork.com/2013/06/05/egypt-locked-out-iffco-food-workers-continue-strike.

19. EFITU, 'Egypt: New Unions' Declaration of Independence', MENA Soli-darity Network, 28 June 2011, http://menasolidaritynetwork.com/2011/07/05/ egypt-new-unions-declaration-of-independence.

20. Kamal Abu Aita, interview; Noha Mohamed Murshid, 27 October 2011.

21. Fatma al-Zahra'a Muhammad, 'Al-Ittihad Al-Masri Lil Niqabat Al-Musta-qilla Yuaqid Mu'atamr Al-Ta'sisi Bimadinat Al-Intag Al-Ilami Ghadan', *El-Fagr*, 27 January 2012, http://new.elfagr.org/Detail.aspx?nwsId=116754 &secid=1&vid=2.

22. Islam Muhammad Ali, 'Ta'sis Awwal Ittihad Mahalli Liniqabat Al-Ummal Al-Mustaqilla Bil-Suways', *Suez Online*, 21 January 2012, http://revsoc. me/workers-farmers/tsys-wl-thd-mhl-lnqbt-lml-lmstql-blswys; Rasha Al-Naggar, '17 Niqaba Min Al-Mansura Tu'alin Ta'sis Al-Ittihad Al-Masry Lil Niqabat Al-Mustaqilla', *Al-Ahram Digital*, 9 May 2012, http://digital.ahram.

org.eg/articles.aspx?Serial=894618&eid=368.

23. CTUWS, 'Ta'sis Mu'atamr Ummal Masr Al-Dimuqrati', 14 October 2011, www.anhri.net/?p=41654.

24. CTUWS, 'Ham Wa Agil ... Al-Mu'atamr Al-Ta'sisi Limu'atamr Ummal Masr Al-Dimuqrati', 2013; Amira Wahba, 'Ummal Masr Yu'aqid Mu'tamru Al-Ta'sisi Bihudur 300 Niqaba Bilsahafiyyin Ayyam 24 wa 25 wa 26 Abril', *Al-Ahram*, 28 March 2013, http://gate.ahram.org.eg/News/326830.aspx.

25. GFETU, 'Al-Ittihad Al-Am Lilniqabat Al-Ummaliyya Al-Masriyya', 1 December 2013, www.gfetu.com.

26. Al-Beheiry, interview.

27. Muhammad Al-Anwar and Al-Biramawwi Sharif, 'Al-Ilan an Ta'sis Al-Ittihad Al-Masry Lil-Niqabat Al-Mustaqilla', *Al-Dustur Al-Asly*, 13 August 2011, www.masress.com/dostor/50955.

28. MENA, 'Tagmid Tawqiyyat Maglis Idara Ittihad Al-Ummal Al-Munhall Hata Taskhil Lagna Tudiru Maliyan', 7 August 2011, www.masrawy.com/news/egypt/politics/2011/august/7/workers_sign.aspx?ref=rss; Youm 7, 'Ta'raf Ala Wuzzara Hukumatak Al-Gadida ... Al-Sira Al-Thatiyya Al-Kamila Lil-Wuzzara Al-Guddad', *Youm* 7, 5 August 2012, www1.youm7.com/News.asp?NewsID=749060#.UpvIoiewDts.

29. Shaima'a Galal, 'Al-Lagna Al-Mu'aqita Tungah Fi Hall Azma Ummal Al-Mahalla', 8 September 2011, www.ikhwanonline.com/new/print.aspx?ArtID=90829&SecID=230.

30. Joel Beinin, *The Rise of Egypt's Workers*, Carnegie Endowment for International Peace, Washington DC, 2012, http://carnegieendowment.org/2012/06/28/rise-of-egypt-s-workers.

31. Rana Taha, 'Workers' Movements Unite to Push for Syndicates' Freedom Law', *Daily News Egypt*, 15 October 2012, www.dailynewsegypt.com/2012/10/15/workers-movements-unite-to-push-for-syndicates-freedom-law.

32. MENAsolidarity, 'Egypt: "Trade Union Rights Are Our Way to Social Justice"', MENA Solidarity Network, 14 November 2012, http://mena solidaritynetwork.com/2012/11/14/egypt-trade-union-rights-are-our-way-to-social-justice-new-leaflet.

33. Ibid.

CHAPTER 8

1. Nasma Ali, 'Ai'sha: La Nuhtag Ila Maqa'id Al-Ummal Idha Indamagu Fi Al-Ahzab', 12 October 2010, www.almasryalyoum.com/node/268280.

2. *Takhsis Nisba Min Maqa'id Maglis Al-Sha'ab Al-Masry Lil-Ummal Wal-Fallahin*, 2010, www.youtube.com/watch?v=6kn_sMyyyOA&feature=youtube_gdata_player.

3. Karl Marx, 'Marx to Dr Kugelmann Concerning the Paris Commune', 12 April 1871, www.marxists.org/archive/marx/works/1871/letters/71_04_12.htm.

4. Peyman Jafari, 'Rupture and Revolt in Iran', *International Socialism Journal* 124 (September 2009), www.isj.org.uk/?id=585.

5. IFES, *Elections in Egypt: Analysis of the 2011 Parliamentary Electoral System*, International Foundation for Electoral Systems, 1 November 2011, p.

2, www.ifes.org/~/media/Files/Publications/White%20PaperReport/2011/ Analysis_of_Egypts_2011_Parliamentary_Electoral_System.pdf.

6. Jadaliyya, 'How Are Seat Winners Determined in the Egyptian Elections?', www.jadaliyya.com/pages/index/3361/how-are-seat-winners-determined-in-the-egyptian-el (accessed 17 October 2012).

7. IFES, *Elections in Egypt*, p. 8.

8. Muhammad Al-Agrudi, 'Manah 8500 Shihada Amil Wa Istiba'd Kamal Abbas', *Al-Ahram Digital*, 15 October 2011, http://digital.ahram.org.eg/ articles.aspx?Serial=669545&eid=707.

9. Ibid.

10. Radwa Hisham, 'Ra'is Al-Niqabat Al-Mustaqilla Yu'alin Tarshihu Lil Ma-glis Al-Sha'ab ... Wa 650 Shihada Lil Raghibin Fi Al-Tarshih', 13 October 2011, www.hoqook.com/18989.

11. Mahmud Abd-al -Ghani, 'Waqfa Amam Mahkama Al-Giza Did Rafd Mu-rashahi Al-Niqabat Al-Mustaqilla', *Youm 7*, 31 October 2011, www.youm7. com/News.asp?NewsID=524202&SecID=65&IssueID=0.

12. Al-Masry Al-Youm, 'Murashah Ikhwan Shamal Al-Giza: Nahnu Aqrab Lil Nas ... Wal-Libraliyyun Tafraghu Lmuwaghatna', *Al-Masry Al-Youm*, 12 December 2011, www.almasryalyoum.com/node/545761.

13. Abd-al -Ghani, 'Waqfa Amam Mahkama Al-Giza Did Rafd Murashahi Al-Niqabat Al-Mustaqilla'.

14. Yasmin Al-Giyushi, 'Al-Karama Tataqadum Bi 15 Murashahan Lil-In-tikhabat Al-Nasiri Taqdim Bi 214 Murashahan', *Al-Tahrir*, 24 October 2011, http://tahrirnews.com; Al-Masry Al-Youm, 'Murashah Ikhwan Shamal Al-Giza: Nahnu Aqrab Lil Nas ... Wal-Libraliyyun Tafraghu Lmuwaghatna'.

15. Muhammad Faris, 'Al-Quda'a Yu'akid Ahqiyya Al-Niqabat Al-Mustaqilla Fi Manah Shihadat Al-Sifa Al-Ummaliyya Limurashahi Al-Intikhabat', *Al-Masry Al-Youm*, 16 November 2011, www.almasryalyoum.com/node/ 515204; Noha Mohamed Murshid, 4 June 2012; Tarek Mostafa, 4 June 2012.

16. Mamduh Sha'aban, Sa'ad Tantawi and Ali Muhammad, '235 Maqa'id Lil-Hurriya Wal-Adala Wa Hulafa'ahu Wa 123 Lil-Nur Wa 38 Lil Wafd Wa 34 Lil-Kutla Fi Barlaman Al-Thawra', *Al-Ahram Digital*, 22 January 2012, http://digital.ahram.org.eg/Policy.aspx?Serial=774569.

17. BBC, 'Egypt's Islamists Win Elections', BBC News online, 21 January 2012, www.bbc.co.uk/news/world-middle-east-16665748.

18. Masrawy, 'Abu Hamid: Al-Barlaman La Yuatabir An Al-Shari'a ... Wal-Kurdy: Huwa Al-Midan Al-Shari'yy', *Masrawy.com*, 31 January 2012, www. masrawy.com/news/egypt/politics/2012/january/31/4774240.aspx.

19. Muhammad Al-Tuhami, 'Abu-Al-Futuh Yungah Fi Ta'liq Itisam Um-mal', 23 February 2012, www.ikhwanonline.com/Article.aspx?ArtID= 102009&SecID=250.

20. 'Al-Hurriya Wal-Adala Biaswan Yungah Ti Fakk Idrab Ummal Kima', Ikhwanonline.com, 23 February 2012, www.ikhwanonline.com/Article. aspx?ArtID=102013&SecID=250.

21. Ahmad Sayf-al-Nasr, 'Na'ib Al-Hurriya Wal-Adala Bil-Fayyum Yunsif Ummal Al-Kima'wiyyat', Ikhwanonline.com, 24 February 2012, www. ikhwanonline.com/Article.aspx?ArtID=102068&SecID=253.

22. Hamdi Taha, 'Salah Musa Yufadd Itisam Ummal Wadi Kom Ombo Bias-
    wan', Ikhwanonline.com, 26 February 2012, www.ikhwanonline.com/new/
    print.aspx?artID=102150&SecID=0.

23. See, for example, Usama Abd-al-Salam, 'Ittihad tullab al-azhar yunfa mush-
    arikatihu fi idirab 11 fibrayir', Ikhwanonline.com, 5 February 2012, http://
    ikhwanonline.com/Article.aspx?artID=100675&SecID=304;   Ahmad
    Morsi, 'Ataba'a masr yurfidun al-idirab wa yu'awidunu ziyada liahtiqan
    al-watan', Ikhwanonline.com, 7 February 2012, http://ikhwanonline.com/
    Article.aspx?artID=100811&SecID=230; Usama Abd-al-Salam, 'Khubara':
    idirab 11 fibyarir khitta litadmir al-iqtisad', Ikhwanonline.com, 10 February
    2012, http://ikhwanonline.com/Article.aspx?ArtID=100983&SecID=230.

24. Umar, 'Musharika Ummaliyya Mahduda Fi 11 Febrayir … Limadha?'

25. 'Electoral Commission Upholds Ban on 10 Presidential Candidates',
    Ahram Online, 17 April 2012, http://english.ahram.org.eg/NewsCon-
    tent/36/122/39510/Presidential-elections-/Presidential-elections-news/
    Electoral-commission-upholds-ban-on--presidential-.aspx.

26. Roula Khalaf and Heba Saleh, 'Egypt: From Shadows to Spotlight', Finan-
    cial Times, 21 May 2012, www.ft.com/cms/s/0/2a3a0bb2-a03c-11e1-88e6-
    00144feabdc0.html#axzz2mGBRRa00.

27. Zeinab El Gundy, 'Abdel-Moneim Abul-Fotouh', Ahram Online, 2 April
    2012, http://english.ahram.org.eg/News/36854.aspx.

28. Muhammad Ahmad and Ahmad Imbabi, 'Al-Dusturiyya Al-Uliyya Bi-Masr
    Tuqda Bi-Adm Dusturiyyat Qanun Al-Azl Wa Tuhal Maglis Al-Sha'ab', Al-
    Sharq Al-Awsat, 15 June 2012, www.aawsat.com/details.asp?section=4&arti
    cle=681960&issueno=12253#.Uh8Jv3-29c4.

29. Dalia Uthman, 'Al-Shurta Al-Askariyya Tumaris Al-Dubatiyya Al-
    Quda'iyya Wa Tunshur Kama'in Bil-Mayadin Al-Kubra', Al-Masry Al-Youm,
    15 June 2012, www.almasryalyoum.com/node/920201.

30. David D. Kirkpatrick, 'Blow to Transition as Court Dissolves Egypt's
    Parliament', New York Times, 14 June 2012, www.nytimes.com/2012/06/15/
    world/middleeast/new-political-showdown-in-egypt-as-court-invalidates-
    parliament.html.

31. MENA, 'Morsi Has No Intentions to Reinstate Parliament, Spokesperson
    Says', Al-Masry Al-Youm, 13 August 2012, www.egyptindependent.com/
    news/morsy-has-no-intentions-reinstate-parliament-spokesperson-says.

32. 'English Text of President Morsi's New Egypt Constitutional Declaration',
    Ahram Online, 12 August 2012, http://english.ahram.org.eg/News/50248.
    aspx.

33. Samar Nasr, 'Intilaq Utubisat Hamdeen Sabahi Ila Sina'a Lil-Musharika
    Fi Ihtifalat Al-Tahrir', Al-Ahram, 25 April 2012, http://gate.ahram.org.eg/
    News/200640.aspx.

34. Tarek Mostafa, interview.

35. Joel Beinin, 'Workers, Trade Unions and Egypt's Political Future', Middle
    East Report Online, 18 January 2013, www.merip.org/mero/mero011813.

36. Eric Schewe, 'A First Look at First Round Egypt Presidential Election Dis-
    trict Results', 26 July 2012, http://ericschewe.wordpress.com/2012/07/26/a-
    first-look-at-first-round-egypt-presidential-district-results.

37. Ibid.
38. Quotations from Mohamed Morsi's presidential electoral programme, archived online, 'Al-Barnamag Al-Ri'aysi … Mohamed Morsi 2012', *Ikhwanwiki*, www.ikhwanwiki.com/index.php?title (accessed 1 December 2013).
39. Al-Beheiry, interview.
40. Voting data collated from documents giving district-level voting figures for the run-offs in the presidential elections, from www.elections.eg, 29 June 2012.
41. Schewe, 'A First Look at First Round Egypt Presidential Election District Results'.
42. Al-ligan al-sha'abiyya bisaft al-laban, 'Shabab Saft Al-Laban Yad Wahida', August 2012, www.facebook.com/SaftElLaban.
43. Al-Beheiry, interview.
44. 'English Text of President Morsi's New Egypt Constitutional Declaration'.
45. Ahmad Al-Naggar, 'Limadha Nurfad Mashru'a Al-Dustur Al-Mushabwa', 14 December 2012.
46. Tom Ginsburg, 'The Real Winner in the Egyptian Constitution? The Military', *Huffington Post*, 7 December 2012, www.huffingtonpost.com/ tom-ginsburg/egypt-draft-constitution-military_b_2259798.html.
47. Yasmine Saleh and Tom Perry, 'Islamists Stamp Mark on Egypt's Draft Constitution', Reuters, 30 November 2012, www.reuters.com/article/2012/11/30/ us-egypt-constitution-idUSBRE8AT08K20121130.
48. CEIP, 'Controversial Articles in the 2012 Egyptian Constitution – Egypt's Transition', 2013, http://egyptelections.carnegieendowment.org/2013/01/04/ controversial-articles-in-the-2012–egyptian-constitution.
49. Human Rights Watch, 'Egypt: New Constitution Mixed on Support of Rights', 30 November 2012, www.hrw.org/news/2012/11/29/egypt-new-constitution-mixed-support-rights; No Military Trials, 'The Presidency Lies', 23 December 2012, http://en.nomiltrials.com.
50. No Military Trials, 'The Presidency Lies'.
51. MENAsolidarity, 'Egypt', 14 November 2012.
52. 'The Full Unofficial Results of Egypt's Constitutional Referendum: A Visual Breakdown', *Ahram Online*, 23 December 2012, http://english.ahram. org.eg/NewsContent/1/64/61119/Egypt/Politics-/The-full-unofficial-results-of-Egypts-Constitution.aspx.
53. Mary Mourad, 'Truth in Numbers: How Much Legitimacy Is Legitimate?', *Ahram Online*, 7 July 2013, http://english.ahram.org.eg/News Content/1/64/75844/Egypt/Politics-/Truth-in-numbers-How-much-legitimacy-is-legitimate.aspx.
54. CEIP, 'Results of Shura Council Elections', 2012, http://egyptelections. carnegieendowment.org/2012/02/29/results-of-shura-council-elections.
55. MENA, 'Nuwab Al-Shura Yutalibun Bi Qanun Limukafahat Al-Shaghab Wa Manah Al-Dubatiyya Al-Quda'iyya Lil Gaysh', 27 January 2013, www. almasryalyoum.com/node/1423361.
56. Al-Masry Al-Youm, 'Islamists Form Community Police Militias', *Egypt Independent*, 12 March 2013, www.egyptindependent.com/news/islamists-form-community-police-militias.

CHAPTER 9

1. Hugh Roberts, 'The Revolution That Wasn't', *London Review of Books*, 12 September 2013; Stephen Cook, 'Mubarak Still Rules', *Foreign Policy*, 14 August 2013, www.foreignpolicy.com/articles/2013/08/14/why_hosni_mubarak_still_rules_egypt?page=full.

2. Yezid Sayigh, *Above the State: The Officers' Republic in Egypt*, Carnegie Endowment for International Peace, August 2012, www.carnegieendowment.org/files/officers_republic1.pdf; Zeinab Abul-Magd, 'The Egyptian Republic of Retired Generals', *Foreign Policy*, 12 May 2012, http://mideast.foreignpolicy.com/posts/2012/05/08/the_egyptian_republic_of_retired_generals.

3. Samuel P. Huntington, *The Third Wave: Democratization in the Late Twentieth Century*, Norman: University of Oklahoma Press, 1991; Thomas Carothers, 'The End of the Transition Paradigm', *Journal of Democracy*, vol. 13, no. 1 (2002), pp. 5–21.

4. Vladimir Lenin, *The State and Revolution* (1917), ch. 3, www.marxists.org/archive/lenin/works/1917/staterev/ch03.htm.

5. Charles Levinson and Matt Bradley, 'Before Morsi's Ouster, Egypt's Top Generals Met Regularly with Opposition Leaders', *Wall Street Journal*, 19 July 2013, http://online.wsj.com/news/articles/SB10001424127887324425204578601700051224658; Issandr El Amrani, 'Sightings of the Egyptian Deep State', Middle East Research and Information Project, *Middle East Report Online*, 1 January 2012, www.merip.org/mero/mero010112; Nathan J. Brown, 'Egypt's Wide State Reassembles Itself', *Foreign Policy Blogs*, 17 July 2013, http://mideast.foreignpolicy.com/posts/2013/07/17/egypt_s_wide_state_reassembles_itself?wp_login_redirect=0.

6. Yezid Sayigh, *Above the State: The Officers' Republic in Egypt*, Carnegie Endowment for International Peace, Washington DC, August 2012, www.carnegieendowment.org/files/officers_republic1.pdf (accessed 30 September 2012); Zeinab Abul-Magd, 'The Egyptian Republic of Retired Generals', *Foreign Policy*, 2012 http://mideast.foreignpolicy.com/posts/2012/05/08/the_egyptian_republic_of_retired_generals (accessed 17 May 2012).

7. 'Atif Hilmi', Wikipedia (Arabic), 5 November 2013, http://ar.wikipedia.org/w/index.php?title.

8. Hazem Kandil, *Soldiers, Spies and Statesmen: Egypt's Road to Revolt*, London: Verso, 2012, pp. 179–81.

9. Human Rights Watch, 'Egypt: Military Court Convicts Opposition Leaders', 16 April 2008, www.hrw.org/en/news/2008/04/15/egypt-military-court-convicts-opposition-leaders.

10. As Human Rights Watch noted in 2011, 'Since taking over the government, the military appears to consider the whole country "controlled by the military" and therefore everyone is potentially subject to military trials.' Human Rights Watch, 'Egypt: Retry or Free 12,000 After Unfair Military Trials', Human Rights Watch, 10 September 2011, www.hrw.org/news/2011/09/10/egypt-retry-or-free-12000-after-unfair-military-trials.

11. Ahmad Imbabi, 'Al-Qadi Faruq Sultan … Ragil Al-Aqdar', *Al Sharq Al-Awsat*, 29 June 2012.

12. Kandil, *Soldiers, Spies and Statesmen*.

13. 'Ahmed Abdeen', Wikipedia, 28 August 2013, http://en.wikipedia.org/w/ index.php?title=Ahmed_Abdeen&oldid=570462999.

14. Amir Al-Sawwaf, 'Adil Labib: Fakhur Bintima'i Lamn Al-Dawla', *Al-Wafd*, 12 August 2011.

15. Rasha Al-Gamal, 'Al-Alaf Yutadhahirun Fil Fayyum Wal-Isma'iliyya Limatlaba Birahil Al-Muhafidhin', *Al-Badil*, 4 March 2011; Sami Abd al-Radi, 'Imad Mikha'il Shahata Min Luwa'a Mahbub … Ila Muhafidh Marfud', *Al-Masry Al-Youm*, 19 April 2011; Mohamed Hamdi et al., '2000 Mutadhahir Fi Miliyniyya Al-Karama Bi Qena Wa Guma'a Al-Tathir Bi Sina'a Tutalib Bi Iqala Al-Fasidin', *Al-Masry Al-Youm*, 29 April 2011.

16. Ashraf Badr, 'Sharaa Yu'ad Bita'dil Wizari Wa Harakat Al-Muhafidhin Wa Istiba'd Al-Matuwartin Fi Gara'im Did Al-Thuwar', *Al-Ahram*, 11 July 2011.

17. Rosa Luxemburg, *The Mass Strike, the Political Party and the Trade Unions, 1906: Rosa Luxemburg*, trans. Patrick Lavin, London: Merlin Press, 1964.

18. Carter Goodrich, *The Frontier of Control: A Study in British Workshop Politics*, New York: Harcourt, Brace & Howe, 1920, http://archive.org/ details/frontierofcontro00gooduoft.

19. Peter Robinson, 'Portugal 1974–75', in Colin Barker, ed., *Revolutionary Rehearsals*, 2nd edn, Chicago: Haymarket, 2008.

20. Assef Bayat, *Workers and Revolution in Iran*, London: Zed Books, 1987.

21. Jeffrey R. Webber, *Rebellion and Reform in Bolivia: Class Struggle, Indigenous Liberation, and the Politics of Evo Morales*, Chicago: Haymarket, 2011.

22. Hisham Fouad, 'Ummal Al-Naql Al-Am Yuhasirun Maglis Al-Wuzara', May 2011, www.e-socialists.net/node/7566; Mitwalli Salim, Yusif Al-Awami and Sara Nur-al-Din, 'Idrab Al-Naql Al-Am Yushall Al-Murur Fil-Qahira Wal-Mutalib: Al-Huwafidh Wa Taghiyyar Al-Utubisat Al-Muthalika', 2 May 2011, www.almasryalyoum.com/node/421453.

23. Al-Ishtaraki, 'Ummal Al-Naql Al-Am Yutaghun Lita'liq Al-Idrab', 27 September 2011, www.e-socialists.net/node/7576.

24. *Al-Naql Al-Am 3 Sanawat Min Al-Ihtigag*, 2012, www.youtube.com/watch ?v=neefu3RoMNQ&feature=youtube_gdata_player.

25. Marwa Al-Shafa'i, 'Idrab Guzi'i Bigaraj Tayyiba Al-Taba'a Liha'it Al-Naql Al-Am Wa Idrab 9 Ummal an Al-Ta'am', *Al-Shorouq*, 29 June 2012.

26. Haitham Muhammadain, 'Yawm Ma'a Shaykh Tariq … Wa Ummal Al-Naql Al-Am', *Al-Ishtaraki*, 18 September 2012.

27. *Shahid: 'Itisam Hi'at Al-Naql Al-Am*, 2013, www.youtube.com/watch?v=2 krJBi1F5gw&feature=youtube_gdata_player.

28. *Itisam Ummal Hi'at Al-Naql Al-Am*, 2013, www.youtube.com/watch?v= WnXj9nIQ-iM&feature=youtube_gdata_player.

29. Muhammad Mugahid and Muhammad Faris, 'Muwadhfu Al-Masriyya Lil-Itisalat Yubda'un Idraban Maftuhan Wa Yuhadidun Biquta'a Al-Tilifunat Al-Ardiyya', *Al-Masry Al-Youm*, 15 October 2011, www.almasryalyoum. com/node/505385.

30. Muhammad Mahir, 'Al-Amilun Bil-Masiryya Lil-Itisalat Yutalibun Mursi Biqalat Bashir Wa Tathir Al-Hi'at', *Al-Masry Al-Youm*, 2012, www.almasry-

alyoum.com/node/1108906; Muhammad Mahir, 'Al-Mustaqilla Lil-Amilin Bil-Itisalat Turahib Bi-Istiqalat Bashir: Bidaya Litathir Al-Hi'at', *Al-Masry Al-Youm*, 25 September 2012.

31. Hala Kamal, June 2012.
32. Shaden Shehab, 'First-year German U', *Al-Ahram Weekly*, 2 October 2003, http://weekly.ahram.org.eg/2003/658/eg9.htm.
33. Usama Ahmad, 'Al-Gama'at Al-Masriyya Tastakamil Al-Thawra', *Markaz Al-Dirasat Al-Ishtarakiyya*, 7 April 2011.
34. Al-Ishtaraki, 'Waqfa Ihtigagiyya Litullab Gama'at Al-Mansura Li Mutlaba Bi-Iqalat Al-Qiyadat Al-Gama'iyya Wa Tard Al-Haras Al-Gama'ai', *Al-Ishtaraki*, 13 September 2011.
35. 'Egypt: University Workers Co-Ordinate National Strike', MENA Solidarity Network, 17 September 2012, http://menasolidaritynetwork.com/2012/09/17/egypt-university-workers-co-ordinate-national-strike.
36. Muhammad Al-Shuwadfi, 'Istiqala Ra'is Gama'at Ain Shams Wa Gami'a Umada'a Kuliyatiha', *Al-Ahram*, 4 October 2011, http://gate.ahram.org.eg/NewsContent/13/55/123066; Daha Salah, 'Istiqala Ra'is Gama'at Assiyut Min Mansibihi', *Youm* 7, 9 October 2011.
37. Mohamed Hilali, 'Al-Irada Al-Thawriyya Tuntasir Ala Al-Baltagiyya Wa Ummala Amn Al-Dawla Bi-Gama'at Ain Shams', 14 April 2013, http://revsoc.me/students/lrd-lthwry-tntsr-l-lbltjy-wml-mn-ldwl-bjm-yn-shms; *Al-Yawm Al-Thalith Min Mudhahirat Handasat Iskandariyya Abril 2013 Lil Tathir Wa Ilan Al-Mizaniyya*, 2013, www.youtube.com/watch?v=OMOvTzrSPIs&feature=youtube_gdata_player.
38. Fatma Zahra'a Abd-al-Hamid, 27 October 2011.
39. Mohamed Shafiq and Doctors Without Rights activists, interview, in Arabic and English, 30 April 2011; Mohamed Shafiq, '"The Union Is a Shield and Our Sword Is the Strike"', *Socialist Review*, December 2011, www.socialistreview.org.uk/article.php?articlenumber=11845 (accessed 14 October 2013).
40. *Idrab Masana'a Al-Sukkar Min Agl Tathir Al-Bilad*, 2011, https://ar-ar.facebook.com/Gabhetattagheer.ESIIC (accessed 15 December 2011).
41. Sugar Factories Front for Change, 'Front for Change in the Sugar Factories and Refineries: Facebook Page', 9 December 2011, file:///C:/Users/User/Documents/egyptian%20revolution%20sources/facebook%20data/sugar%20factories%20front%20for%20change/Gabhetattagheer.ESIIC.htm.
42. Bawaba al-aqsar al- akhbariyya, 'Bakri Wa Ragah Yunhagan Fi Fadd Itisam Masna'a Sukkar Armant', *Al-Aqsar Al-Yawm*, 2 January 2012, www.luxortoday.com.
43. Rafiq Nasif, 'Ummal Ghazl Al-Mahalla Wal-Ma'shat Yusharikaun Fi Guma'a Al-Tathir', *Al-Wafd*, 5 July 2011, www.alwafd.org.
44. Mustafa Al-Naggar, '"Ummal Ghazl Al-Mahalla Yuqadimun Mudhakira Li Silmi Li-Iqalat Al-Gaylani', *Youm* 7, 15 October 2011, www.youm7.com/News.asp?NewsID=513276&SecID=296#.UnUDEVOwDts.
45. Adil Durra, 'Umumiyya Ghazl Al-Mahalla Tuqarir Iqalat Al-Gibali Wa Maglis Idaratuhu ... Wa Tuhallihum Ila Niyabat Al-Amwal Al-Ama', *Al-*

Masry Al-Youm, 27 November 2007, http://today.almasryalyoum.com/article2.aspx?ArticleID=84474.

46. Muhammad Mabruk, 'Bil-Suwwar ... Ummal Al-Mahalla: Munhana Mursi Fursa Kafiyya ... Wa Nushtarat Tahqiq Mutalibina Qabl Inha'a Al-Itisam', *Al-Ahram*, 15 July 2012, http://gate.ahram.org.eg/News/231171.aspx.

47. Mustafa Al-Naggar, 'Abd-Al-Alim Ra'isan Lil-Qabida Lil-Ghazl Khalfan Lil-Gaylani', *Youm 7*, 28 May 2012, www1.youm7.com/News.asp?NewsID =690654&SecID=24&IssueID=0.

48. Subhi Abd-al -Salam, Ahmad Fathi and Rafiq Nasif, 'Ummal Ghazl Al-Mahalla Yuhaddidun Bi Shall Al-Dalta', *Al-Watan*, 12 October 2013, www.elwatannews.com/news/details/339317; Radwa Khidr, 'Idrab Ummal Ghazl Al-Mahalla Lil Matlaba Bi Rahil Ra'is Al-Sharika Al-Qabida', *Al-Wafd*, 26 August 2013, www.alwafd.org.

49. *Local Council Workers in Egypt Choose Their Own Boss*, 2011, www.youtube.com/watch?v=XOd5X7rR_X8&feature=youtube_gdata_player.

50. Muhammad Abu al -Ainayn, 'Al-Iskandariyya: Hayy Gharb Yu'alan Al-Asyan Al-Madani Al-Thalatha' Lil Matlaba Bi-Iqala Salam Wa Sharaf Wa Al-Nu'amani', *Al-Masry Al-Youm*, 11 July 2011, www.almasryalyoum.com/node/476582; Al-Nahar, 'Ta'gil Qadiyya Muwafadhin Hayy Gharb Ila 30 Abril', 1 April 2012, www.alnaharegypt.com/t~67311; Rihab Abdallah, 'Bira'a 11 Muwadhafan Wa Amilan Bihayy Gharb Al-Iskandariyya Min Tuhma Al-Tahrid Ala Al-Idrab', *Al-Watan*, 21 October 2012, www.elwatannews.com/news/details/65099.

51. Yusif Al-Awami et al., 'Istimrar Al-Ihtigagat Al-Fi'awiyya Fil-Qahira Wal-Muhafidhat ... Wa 3 Alaf Muwadhaf Fil-Tayyaran Yutadhahirun Lil-Matlaba Bistiba'ad Mana'a Wa Qiyadat Al-Wizara', *Al-Masry Al-Youm*, 6 March 2011, www.almasryalyoum.com/node/341567.

52. Mu'assisat Awlad al-Ard, 'Hasad Al-Haraka Al-Ummaliyya Fi Shahr Maris', www.e-socialists.net/node/6793 (accessed 2 August 2012).

53. DPA, 'Wazir Al-Tayyaran Al-Masry Yustalim Muham Mansibihi Wast Mudhahirat Hashida', 21 July 2011, www.masrawy.com/News/Egypt/Politics/2011/july/21/aviation.aspx.

54. DPA, 'Ta'iyin Madani Ra'isan Li Matar Al-Qahira Al-Dawly Liawwal Marra Mundhu 50 Aman', 25 July 2011, www.masrawy.com/news/egypt/politics/2011/july/25/cairo_airport.aspx?ref=rss.

55. MENA, 'Tadhahir Addad Min Muwadhafi Sharikat Mina'a Al-Qahira Al-Gawy', *Al-Wafd*, 2 February 2012, www.alwafd.org.

56. Hisham Fouad, 'Al-Amilun Bil Mattarat Yumna'un Al-Ra'is Al-Askari Al-Gadid Min Dukhul Al-Sharika', 5 January 2012, http://revsoc.me/workers-farmers/lmlwn-blmtrt-ymnwn-lryys-lskry-ljdyd-mn-dkhwl-lshrk; Yusif Al-Awami and Hisham Yasin, 'Mudhahira Al-Muwadhafin Tutih Bi-Ra'is Al-Masriyya Lil-Mattarat Wal-Irsad Tuhaddid Bil-Idrab Shamil', *Al-Masry Al-Youm*, 4 January 2012, www.almasryalyoum.com/node/585051.

57. BBC Arabic, "Irga'a 48 rihla bisabbab idrab al-mudayfin al-gawiyyin fi sharika masr lil-tayyaran.', BBC Arabic, 7 September 2012, www.bbc.co.uk/arabic/middleeast/2012/09/120907_egyptairstrike.shtml.

58. DPA, 'Tahwil Rihalat Masr Lil-Tayyaran Limabna Al-Mattar Al-Qadim

Ba'd Fashl Inha'a Idrab Ummal Al-Haqa'ib', *Al-Masry Al-Youm*, 19 May 2013, www.almasryalyoum.com/node/1759226.

59. Meeting with EFITU officials, June 2013

60. 'Egypt: Airport Workers' Battle against the Generals' Candidate', MENA Solidarity Network, 17 June 2012, http://menasolidaritynetwork. com/2012/06/17/egypt-airport-workers.

61. Hisham Fouad, 'Al-Amilun Bil-Mattar Yuhtifun: Shalu Tayyar Gabu Tayyar ... Barra Barra Ya Maglis Ar', 11 June 2012, http://revsoc.me/politics/ lmlwn-blmtr-yhtfwn-shlw-tyr-jbw-tyr-brh-brh-y-mjls-r.

62. Al-Badil, 'Wizarat Al-Tayyaran Al-Madani ... Wizara Alati Yusa'ab Ikhwanatiha', *Al-Badil*, 24 January 2013, http://elbadil.com/?p=100309.

63. 'Egypt: "We're Paid by the Penny" – Rail Strikers Tell Their Stories', MENA Solidarity Network, 12 April 2013, http://menasolidaritynetwork.com/2013/04/12/ egypt-were-paid-by-the-penny-rail-strikers-tell-their-stories.

64. 'Egypt: Independent Unions, Revolutionary Activists Slam Conscription of Rail Strikers', MENA Solidarity Network, 10 April 2013, http:// menasolidaritynetwork.com/2013/04/10/egypt-independent-union-federation-condemns-conscriptio.

65. Interview with labour lawyer Haitham Mohamedain, in Arabic, Cairo, 10 September 2011.

66. Sherif Mansour, 'On the Divide: Press Freedom at Risk in Egypt', Committee to Protect Journalists, 14 August 2013, http://cpj.org/reports/2013/08/ on-divide-egypt-press-freedom-morsi.php, (accessed 25 November 2013).

67. Legend Youth, 'Bayan Miliyuniyya Tahir Al-Ilam'.

68. MENA and Ahram Online, 'Newspaper Editor's Trial for Insulting Morsi to Begin Thursday' , *Ahram Online*, 21 August 2012, http://english.ahram. org.eg/NewsContent/1/64/50921/Egypt/Politics-/Newspaper-editors-trial-for-insulting-Morsi-to-beg.aspx (accessed 25 November 2013).

69. Ahram Online, 'Morsi Approves New Press Council Appointments, Attaches SIS to Egypt Presidency', *Ahram Online*, 6 September 2012, http:// english.ahram.org.eg/NewsContent/1/64/52180/Egypt/Politics-/Morsi-approves-new-press-council-appointments,-att.aspx (accessed 25 November 2013).

70. Mansour, 'On the Divide: Press Freedom at Risk in Egypt'; ANHRI, *Al-Muwad Al-Muqida Lihuriyya Al-Ta'bir Bil-Qawanin Al-Masriyya – Ta'dilat Maqtaraha*, Arabic Network for Human Rights Information, 14 January 2013, http://www.anhri.net/?p=67898 (accessed 25 November 2013).

71. Mohamed Gabr, 'Istimrar Itisam Al-Alaf Amam Al-Intag Al-Ilami Lil-Matlaba Bil-Tathir', 2012, www.ikhwanonline.com/Article.aspx?ArtID= 131140&SecID=230 (accessed 25 November 2013); FJP, 'Tuwas'ia Da'irat Itisam Madinat Al-Intag Al-Ilami Ila Babawa 2', 2012, www.fj-p.com/article. php?id=34520 (accessed 25 November 2013).

72. Mansour, 'On the Divide: Press Freedom at Risk in Egypt'.

73. Mahmud Mekki and Hisham Bastawisi, 'When Judges Are Beaten', *Guardian*, 10 May 2006, www.theguardian.com/commentisfree/2006/may/10/comment. egypt (accessed 25 November 2013).

74. Nathan Brown, 'The Battle over Egypt's Judiciary', *Sada*, Carnegie

Endowment for International Peace, 8 May 2013, http://carnegieendowment.org/sada/2013/05/08/battle-over-egypt-s-judiciary/g2nb (accessed 25 November 2013).

75. Ahram Online, 'Salafist Nour Party Meets with Egypt's NSF in Closed-Door Talks', *Ahram Online*, 14 February 2013, http://english.ahram.org.eg/NewsContent/1/64/64827/Egypt/Politics-/Salafist-Nour-Party-meets-with-Egypts-NSF-in-close.aspx (accessed 25 November 2013).

76. Youm 7, 'Al-Ikhwan Yughliqun Bab Dar Al-Quda'a Bil-Lafita "Al-Sha'ab Yurid Iqalat Wazir Al-Adl"', 19 April 2013, http://videoyoum7.com/?p=109523 (accessed 25 November 2013).

77. 'Justice Minister Mekki's Resignation Letter', *Ahram Online*, 21 April 2013, http://english.ahram.org.eg/NewsContent/1/64/69798/Egypt/Politics-/Justice-Minister-Mekkis-resignation-letter-Text.aspx (accessed 25 November 2013).

78. Paul Taylor, 'Update: Revolt Mounts against Egypt's Mursi over Judges', Reuters, 23 April 2013, http://en.aswatmasriya.com/news/view.aspx?id=4066fc36-cea2-40f0-a871-c0c81358d479 (accessed 25 November 2013).

79. Chris Harman, 'The Prophet and the Proletariat', *International Socialism Journal*, vol. 2, no. 64 (Autumn 1994), www.marxists.org/archive/harman/1994/xx/islam.htm (accessed 12 November 2012).

80. Hugh Roberts, 'The Revolution That Wasn't', *London Review of Books*, 12 September 2013, pp. 3–9.

81. Philip Marfleet, 'Egypt: Revolution Contained?', *Socialist Review*, September 2013, www.socialistreview.org.uk/article.php?articlenumber=12379.

82. Anne Alexander, *Leadership in the National Movements of Egypt and Iraq 1945–63*, Ph.D. thesis, University of Exeter, 2007.

83. Al-Ishtarakiyyin al-Thawriyyun, 'Yusqat Hukm Al-Askar … La Li Awdat Al-Filul … La Li Awdat Al-Ikhwan', 15 August 2013, http://revsoc.me/letters-to-comrades/ysqt-hkm-lskr-l-lwd-lflwl-l-lwd-lkhwn.

84. Al-Badil, 'Wizarat Al-Tayyaran Al-Madani … Wizara Alati Yusa'ab Ikhwanatiha'.

CONCLUSION

1. Mahmoud Badr, 'Reply to Egypt's Detractors', *Ahram Online*, 27 April 2014, http://english.ahram.org.eg/NewsContentPrint/4/0/99874/Opinion/0/Reply-to-Egypts-detractors.aspx.

2. Vladimir Lenin, *The State and Revolution* (1917), ch. 1, p. 46, www.marxists.org/archive/lenin/works/1917/staterev/ch01.htm.

3. E.P. Thompson, *The Making of the English Working Class*, London: Penguin, 1991.

4. 'Tamarod Movement to Turn into a Political Party after Presidential Elections', *Ahram Online*, 29 April 2014, http://english.ahram.org.eg/NewsContent/1/64/100104/Egypt/Politics-/Tamarod-movement-to-turn-into-a-political-party-af.aspx; 'Egypt's Tamarod Split Widens', *Ahram Online*, 11 February 2014, http://english.ahram.org.eg/NewsContent/1/0/94026/Egypt/0/Egypts-Tamarod-split-widens-.aspx; Badr, 'Reply to Egypt's Detractors'.

5. Adam Hanieh, *Capitalism and Class in the Gulf States*, Basingstoke: Palgrave Macmillan, 2011; Adam Hanieh, *Lineages of Revolt: Issues of Contemporary Capitalism in the Middle East*, Chicago: Haymarket Books, 2013.
6. Hanieh, *Lineages of Revolt*, p. 9.
7. Eberhard Kienle, *A Grand Delusion: Democracy and Economic Reform in Egypt*, London: I.B. Tauris, 2000.
8. Hal Draper, *Karl Marx's Theory of Revolution*, Volume 2: *The Politics of Social Classes*, New York: Monthly Review Press, 1978, p. 286.
9. Ibid., pp. 366, 305.
10. Ibid., p. 310.
11. Neil Davidson, *How Revolutionary Were the Bourgeois Revolutions?*, Chicago: Haymarket Books, 2012, p. 147.
12. Anne Alexander, 'The Growing Social Soul of Egypt's Democratic Revolution', *International Socialism Journal* 131 (June 2011), www.isj.org.uk/?id=741.
13. For a guide to the decision-making and assembly facilitation practices adopted by some activists in the 15 May movement, see Carolina, 'Quick Guide on Group Dynamics in People's Assemblies', 31 July 2011, Thttp://takethesquare.net/2011/07/31/quick-guide-on-group-dynamics-in-peoples-assemblies. For contrasting discussions of the Argentinian experience of organising neighbourhood assemblies, see Chris Harman, 'Spontaneity, Strategy and Politics', *International Socialism Journal*, vol. 2, no. 104 (9 October 2004); Marina Sitrin, *Everyday Revolutions: Horizontalism and Autonomy in Argentina*, London: Zed Books, 2012.
14. Hazel Haddon et al., 'Live Updates: Millions on Streets in Egypt as Defiant Morsi Addresses Nation', *Ahram Online*, 2 July 2013, http://english.ahram.org.eg/News/75511.aspx.

Bibliography

Abdallah, Rihab, 'Bira'a 11 Muwadhafan Wa Amilan Bihayy Gharb Al-Iskandari-yya Min Tuhma Al-Tahrid Ala Al-Idrab', *Al-Watan*, 21 October 2012, www.elwatannews.com/news/details/65099.

Aboul Fotouh, 'Speranza Egypt – Aboul Fotouh', 2013, www.speranzaegypt.com.

Abul-Magd, Zeinab, 'The Egyptian Republic of Retired Generals', *Foreign Policy*, 2012, http://mideast.foreignpolicy.com/posts/2012/05/08/the_egyptian_republic_of_retired_generals.

Achcar, Gilbert, *The People Want: A Radical Exploration of the Arab Uprising* (London: Saqi Books, 2013).

Adil, Du'aa, *Mu'shir Al-Dimuqratiyya: Fibrayir 2013*, International Development Center, Cairo, March 2013, http://idceg.blogspot.co.uk.

——, *Mu'shir Al-Dimuqratiyya: Maris 2013*, International Development Center, Cairo, April 2013, http://idceg.blogspot.co.uk.

——, *Mu'shir Al-Dimuqratiyya: Abril 2013*, International Development Center, Cairo, May 2013, http://idceg.blogspot.co.uk.

——, *Mu'shir Al-Dimuqratiyya: Mayu 2013*, International Development Center, Cairo, June 2013, http://idceg.blogspot.co.uk.

AFL–CIO, 'The George Meany-Lane Kirkland 2009 Human Rights Award', 2010, http://blog.aflcio.org/About/Exec-Council/EC-Statements/The-George-Meany-Lane-Kirkland-2009–Human-Rights-Award.

AFP, 'Mahalla's Misr Spinning and Weaving Workers Strike', *Ahram Online*, 16 February 2011, http://english.ahram.org.eg/News/5695.aspx.

Al-Agrudi, Muhammad, 'Manah 8500 Shihada Amil Wa Istiba'd Kamal Abbas', *Al-Ahram Digital*, 15 October 2011, http://digital.ahram.org.eg/articles.aspx?Serial=669545&eid=707.

——, 'Megawer: Nuqif Bil-Marsad Did Tazwir Shihadat Al-Sifa Al-Ummaliyya', *Al-Ahram Digital*, 10 September 2010, http://digital.ahram.org.eg/articles.aspx?Serial=249159&eid=707.

Ahmad, Muhammad, and Ahmad Imbabi, 'Al-Dusturiyya Al-Uliyya Bi-Masr Tuqda Bi-Adm Dusturiyyat Qanun Al-Azl Wa Tuhal Maglis Al-Sha'ab', *Al-Sharq al-Awsat*, 15 June 2012, www.aawsat.com/details.asp?section=4&artic le=681960&issueno=12253#.Uh8Jv3-29c4.

Ahmad, Usama, 'Al-Gama'at Al-Masriyya Tastakamil Al-Thawra', *Markaz al-dirasat al-ishtarakiyya*, 2011, http://revsoc.me/students/ljmt-lmsry-tstkml-lthwr.

———, 'Tullab Masr Yu'akidun ... Al-Thawra Mustamira', *Masr al-Thawriyya*, 15 March 2011, www.e-socialists.net/node/6655.

Ahram Online, 'Cairo Microbus Drivers Begin Partial Strike', *Ahram Online*, 2 October 2012, http://english.ahram.org.eg/NewsContent/1/64/54525/Egypt/ Politics-/Cairo-microbus-drivers-begin-partial-strike.aspx.

———, 'Egypt's Ain Sokhna Port to Reopen as 2–Week-Old Strike Ends', *Ahram Online*, 24 October 2012, http://english.ahram.org.eg/NewsContent/ 3/12/56466/Business/Economy/Egypts-Ain-Sokhna-port-to-reopen-as-week old-strike.aspx.

———, 'Egypt's Tamarod Split Widens', *Ahram Online*, 11 February 2014, http:// english.ahram.org.eg/NewsContent/1/0/94026/Egypt/0/Egypts-Tamarod split-widens-.aspx.

———, 'Electoral Commission Upholds Ban on 10 Presidential Candidates – Presidential Elections News – Presidential Elections 2012 – Ahram Online', 17 April 2012, http://english.ahram.org.eg/NewsContent/36/122/39510/Presidential elections-/Presidential-elections-news/Electoral-commission-upholds-ban on--presidential-.aspx.

———, 'English Text of President Morsi's New Egypt Constitutional Declaration – First 100 Days – Egypt – Ahram Online', *Ahram Online*, 12 August 2012, http://english.ahram.org.eg/News/50248.aspx.

———, 'Justice Minister Mekki's Resignation Letter', *Ahram Online*, 21 April 2013, http://english.ahram.org.eg/NewsContent/1/64/69798/Egypt/Politics-/ Justice-Minister-Mekkis-resignation-letter-Text.aspx.

———, 'Morsi Approves New Press Council Appointments, Attaches SIS to Egypt Presidency', *Ahram Online*, 6 September 2012, http://english.ahram.org.eg/ NewsContent/1/64/52180/Egypt/Politics-/Morsi-approves-new-press-council appointments,-att.aspx.

———, 'Salafist Nour Party Meets with Egypt's NSF in Closed-Door Talks', *Ahram Online*, 14 February 2013, http://english.ahram.org.eg/NewsContent/1/64/64827/Egypt/Politics-/Salafist-Nour-Party-meets-with-Egypts-NSF in-close.aspx.

———, 'Tamarod Movement to Turn into a Political Party after Presidential Elections', 29 April 2014, http://english.ahram.org.eg/NewsContent/1/64/100104/ Egypt/Politics-/Tamarod-movement-to-turn-into-a-political-party-af.aspx.

———, 'The Full Unofficial Results of Egypt's Constitutional Referendum: A Visual Breakdown', *Ahram Online*, 23 December 2012, http://english.ahram. org.eg/NewsContent/1/64/61119/Egypt/Politics-/The-full-unofficial-results of-Egypts-Constitution.aspx.

Abu al-Ainayn, Muhammad, 'Al-Iskandariyya: Hayy Gharb Yu'alan Al-Asyan Al-Madani Al-Thalatha' Lil Matlaba Bi-Iqala Salam Wa Sharaf Wa Al-Nu'amani', *Al-Masry Al-Youm*, 11 July 2011, www.almasryalyoum.com/node/476582.

Abu Aita, Kamal, 'Khitab Musagil B'ilm Al-Wusul: Ism Al-Rasil Al-Dara'ib Al-Aqariyy … Ism Al-Mursil Ilihu Ummal Al-Barid … Al-Ainwan Bir Masr', *Al-Ishtaraki*, 1 July 2009 edition, www.e-socialists.net/node/3700.

——, 'Ma Ba'd Al-Lagna Al-Uliyya Lil Idrab?', *Nubat Sahyan*, October 2008.

Akhbar el Yom, 'Automech Akhbar El Yom – Market Background', 2011, www.automech-online.com/MarketBackground.aspx.

Alazar, Abdelhady, 'Ashiq Sina'a: Suwwar Wa Fidiyu Guma'a Tathir Sina'a Min Al-Arish', *Abdelhadyy*, 2011, http://abdelhadyy.blogspot.co.uk/2011/04/2011429.html.

Al-Badil, 'Wizarat Al-Tayyaran Al-Madani … Wizara Alati Yusa'ab Ikhwanatiha', *Al-Badil*, 24 January 2013, http://elbadil.com/?p=100309.

Alexander, A., 'Leadership and Collective Action in the Egyptian Trade Unions', *Work, Employment & Society*, 24 (2010), 241–59, http://dx.doi.org/10.1177/0950017010362144.

Alexander, Anne, 'Analysing Activist Cultures in the Egyptian Workers' Movement', in Jude Howell, ed., *Non-Governmental Public Action and Social Justice* (Basingstoke: Palgrave Macmillan, 2013).

——, *Leadership in the National Movements of Egypt and Iraq 1945–63* (Ph.D. thesis, Exeter University, 2007.

——, 'Mubarak in the International Arena', in Philip Marfleet and Rabab El-Mahdi, eds, *Egypt: The Moment of Change* (London: Zed Books, 2009), pp. 136–50.

——, 'The Egyptian Workers' Movement and the 25 January Revolution', *International Socialism Journal*, 2012, www.isj.org.uk/index.php4?id=778&issue=133.

——, 'The Growing Social Soul of Egypt's Democratic Revolution', *International Socialism Journal*, 2011, www.isj.org.uk/?id=741.

Ali, Ahmad, 'Man Yuzara'a Al-Ta'ifiyya?', *Al-Ishtaraki*, 22 April 2011, http://revsoc.me/politics/mn-yzr-ltyfy.

Ali, Nasma, 'Ai'sha: La Nuhtag Ila Maqa'id Al-Ummal Idha Indamagu Fi Al-Ahzab', 2010, www.almasryalyoum.com/node/268280.

El Amrani, Issandr, 'Sightings of the Egyptian Deep State ', *Middle East Report Online*, 2012, www.merip.org/mero/mero010112.

Angel-Urdinola, Diego F., and Kimie Tanabe, *Micro-Determinants of Informal Employment in the Middle East and North Africa Region* (World Bank, January 2012), http://siteresources.worldbank.org/SocialProtection/Resources/SP-Discussion-papers/Labor-Market-DP/1201.pdf.

ANHRI, *Al-Muwad Al-Muqida Lihuriyya Al-Ta'bir Bil-Qawanin Al-Masriyya – Ta'dilat Maqtaraha*, 14 January 2013, www.anhri.net/?p=67898.

——, *Duwa Fi Darb Al-Hurriya: Shuhada Thawrat 25 Yanayir* (ANHRI, 2012), www.anhri.net/wp-content/uploads/2012/05/book-2.pdf.

Al-Anwar, Muhammad, and Al-Biramawwi Sharif, 'Al-Ilan an Ta'sis Al-Ittihad Al-Masry Lil-Niqabat Al-Mustaqilla', *Al-Dustur al-Asly*, 13 August 2011, www.masress.com/dostor/50955.

Al-Awami, Yusif, Huda Rashwan, Abu al-Sa'ud Muhammad, Ahmad Al-Buhairi, Muhsin Samika and Basant Zayn-al-Din, 'Istimrar Al-Ihtigagat Al-Fi'awiyya Fil-Qahira Wal-Muhafidhat … Wa 3 Alaf Muwadhaf Fil-Tayyaran Yutadhahirun Lil-Matlaba Bistiba'ad Mana'a Wa Qiyadat Al-Wizara', *Al-Masry Al-Youm*, 6 March 2011, www.almasryalyoum.com/node/341567.

Al-Awami, Yusif, and Hisham Yasin, 'Mudhahira Al-Muwadhafin Tutih Bi-Ra'is Al-Masriyya Lil-Mattarat Wal-Irsad Tuhaddid Bil-Idrab Shamil', *Al-Masry Al-Youm*, 4 January 2012, www.almasryalyoum.com/node/585051.

Ayman Riad, 'The Cement Industry in Egypt: Between Monopoly and the Need for Development Construction', 2011, www.zawya.com/story/Egypts_cement_ industry-ZAWYA20111025054229.

Azuz, Muhammad, 'Fashl Al-Idirab Al-Shara'i Al-Awwal Fi Misr Li Tanta Lil-Kitan ... Wa Ittihad Al-Ummal Yuqarrir Ta'liq Al-Itisam', *Al-Masry Al-Youm*, 12 August 2008, http://today.almasryalyoum.com/article2.aspx?ArticleID=2 22268&IssueID=1495.

Badr, Ashraf, 'Sharaa Yu'ad Bita'dil Wizari Wa Harakat Al-Muhafidhin Wa Istiba'd Al-Matuwartin Fi Gara'im Did Al-Thuwar', *Al-Ahram*, 11 July 2011, http://gate.ahram.org.eg/News/93140.aspx.

Badr, Mahmoud, 'Reply to Egypt's Detractors', *Ahram Online*, 27 April 2014, http://english.ahram.org.eg/NewsContentPrint/4/0/99874/Opinion/0/Reply-to-Egypts-detractors.aspx.

Barker, Colin, 'A Note on the Theory of Capitalist States', *Capital & Class* 2 (1978), 118–26.

——, 'The State as Capital', *International Socialism Journal*, vol. 2, no. 1 (1978), 16–42.

Bassiouny, Mostafa, 'Azmat Al-Tandhim Al-Niqabi Fi Masr', *Awraq Ishtarakiyya*, November 2009, www.e-socialists.net/node/5115.

——, 'Dirasat Al-Niqabat (unpublished Paper)' (2009).

Bastawisi, Hisham, and Mahmoud Mekki, 'When Judges Are Beaten', *Guardian*, 10 May 2006, www.guardian.co.uk/commentisfree/2006/may/10/comment. egypt.

Bawaba al-aqsar al- akhbariyya, 'Bakri Wa Ragah Yunhagan Fi Fadd Itisam Masna'a Sukkar Armant', *Al-Aqsar al-Yawm*, 2 January 2012, www.luxor-today.com.

Bayat, Assef, *Workers and Revolution in Iran* (London: Zed Books, 1987).

BBC, 'Egypt's Islamists Win Elections', *BBC*, 21 January 2012, section Middle East, www.bbc.co.uk/news/world-middle-east-16665748.

BBC Arabic, 'Irga'a 48 rihla bisabbab idrab al-mudayfin al-gawiyyin fi sharika masr lil-tayyaran.', *BBC Arabic*, 7 September 2012, www.bbc.co.uk/arabic/ middleeast/2012/09/120907_egyptairstrike.shtml.

Beblawi, Hazem, and Giacomo Luciani, *The Rentier State* (London: Croom Helm, 1987).

Beinin, Joel, 'Labor, Capital, and the State in Nasserist Egypt, 1952–1961', *International Journal of Middle East Studies* 21 (1989), 71–90.

——, *The Rise of Egypt's Workers* (Carnegie Endowment for International Peace, 2012), www.carnegieendowment.org/files/chandler_clean_energy_final.pdf.

——, 'The Struggle for Worker Rights in Egypt', Solidarity Center, 2010.

——, 'Workers, Trade Unions and Egypt's Political Future', *Middle East Report Online*, 2013, www.merip.org/mero/mero011813.

Beinin, Joel, and Zachary Lockman, *Workers on the Nile: Nationalism,*

Communism, Islam, and the Egyptian Working Class, 1882–1954 (London: I.B.Tauris, 1988).

Beinin, Joel, and El-Hamalawy, Hossam, 'Egyptian Textile Workers Confront the New Economic Order', Middle East Research and Information Project, 2007, www.merip.org/mero/mero032507.

Bellin, Eva, *Stalled Democracy: Capital, Labor, and the Paradox of State-Sponsored Development* (Ithaca NY: Cornell University Press, 2002).

Bishri, Tariq al-, *Al-haraka al-siyasiya fi Misr, 1945–1952* (al-Qahira: Dar as-Shuruq, 2002).

Brown, Nathan, 'The Battle over Egypt's Judiciary', *Carnegie Endowment for International Peace*, 2013, http://carnegieendowment.org/sada/2013/05/08/battle-over-egypt-s-judiciary/g2nb.

———, 'Egypt's Wide State Reassembles Itself', *Foreign Policy Blogs*, 2013, http://mideast.foreignpolicy.com/posts/2013/07/17/egypt_s_wide_state_reassembles_itself?wp_login_redirect=0.

Bukharin, Nikolai, *Imperialism and World Economy* (New York: H. Fertig, 1967).

Bush, Ray, *Counter-Revolution in Egypt's Countryside: Land and Farmers in the Era of Economic Reform* (London: Zed Books, 2002).

———, 'Politics, Power and Poverty: Twenty Years of Agricultural Reform and Market Liberalisation in Egypt', *Third World Quarterly* 28 (2007), 1599–1615.

Callinicos, Alex, *Imperialism and Global Political Economy* (Cambridge: Polity Press, 2009).

———, *Marxism and the New Imperialism* (London: Bookmarks, 1994).

Callinicos, Alex, and Chris Harman, *The Changing Working Class: Essays on Class Structure Today* (London: Bookmarks, 1987).

CAPMAS, *Al-Nashra Al-Rabaa Sanawiyya Li Bahath Al-Quwa Al-Amila*, October 2011.

———, *Al-Nashra Al-Rabaa Sanawiyya Li Bahath Al-Quwa Al-Amila*, January 2013.

Carothers, Thomas, 'The End of the Transition Paradigm', *Journal of Democracy* 13 (2002), 5–21, http://dx.doi.org/10.1353/jod.2002.0003.

Carr, Sarah, 'A Firsthand Account: Marching from Shubra to Deaths at Maspero', *Egypt Independent*, 10 October 2011, www.egyptindependent.com/news/firsthand-account-marching-shubra-deaths-maspero.

CEIP, 'Controversial Articles in the 2012 Egyptian Constitution – Egypt's Transition', 2013, http://egyptelections.carnegieendowment.org/2013/01/04/controversial-articles-in-the-2012-egyptian-constitution.

———, 'Results of Shura Council Elections – Egypt's Transition', 2012, http://egyptelections.carnegieendowment.org/2012/02/29/results-of-shura-council-elections.

Ceruti, Claire, 'One Class Or Two? The Labour Reserve and "Surplus Population" in Marx and Contemporary Soweto', *South African Review of Sociology* 41 (2010), 77–103, http://dx.doi.org/10.1080/21528586.2010.490386.

Chapin Metz, Helen, 'Education', in *Egypt: A Country Study* (Washington DC: Library of Congress, 1990), http://countrystudies.us/egypt/71.htm.

Choonara, Joseph, 'The Relevance of Permanent Revolution: A Reply to Neil Davidson', *International Socialism Journal*, 2011, www.isj.org.uk/?id=745.

Citadel Capital, 'NRTC to Receive 10 River Barges Assembled by Alexandria Shipyard Citadel Capital', 2012, http://citadelcapital.com/in-the-news/nrtc-to-receive-10-river-barges-assembled-by-alexandria-shipyard.

Cliff, Tony, and Donny Gluckstein, *Marxism and Trade Union Struggle: The General Strike of 1926* (London: Bookmarks, 1986).

Comito, Vincenzo, *PPP & Concession Agreements in the Mediterranean Countries: Overview and Perspectives*, EuroMed Transport Project, 20 July 2010, www.euromedtransport.eu/En/image.php?id=1139.

Cook, Steven A., 'Mubarak Still Rules', *Foreign Policy*, 14 August 2013, www.foreignpolicy.com/articles/2013/08/14/why_hosni_mubarak_still_rules_egypt?page=full.

Cowie, James, 'Egypt Leaves the Internet – Renesys Blog', 2011, www.renesys.com/blog/2011/01/egypt-leaves-the-internet.shtml.

CTUWS, 'Ham Wa Agil … Al-Mu'atamr Al-Ta'sisi Limu'tamr Ummal Masr Al-Dimuqrati', 2013, www.ctuws.com/?item=1286.

——, 'Ta'rif Al-Dar', 2013, www.ctuws.com/about/story/?item=14.

——, 'Ta'sis Mu'atamr Ummal Masr Al-Dimuqrati', *ANHRI.net*, 2011, www.anhri.net/?p=41654.

——, 'Tasalam Al-Dar Al-Khidamat Ga'izat Al-Gumhuriyya Al-Faransiyya Lihuquq Al-Insan Li-Am 1999', 2013, www.ctuws.com/about/story/?item=100.

——, 'The Visa and Immigration Section in the Canadian Embassy Refrained from According an Entry Visa to CTUWS General Coordinator… Sequenced Abstruse Demeanors Have Been an Object of Queries – CTUWS', 2010, www.ctuws.com/Default.aspx?item=501.

——, *Waqai Ma Gara Al-Intikhabat Al-Niqabiyya Dawra 2006–2011* (CTUWS, 2006), www.ctuws.com/uploads/Books/The-Trade-Union-Elections/Arabic/Facts-Ar.pdf.

Daragahi, Borzou, 'Human Rights: Egypt's Black Holes', *Financial Times*, 22 April 2014, www.ft.com/cms/s/0/b0ac6ccc-c97e-11e3-99cc-00144feabdc0.html?siteedition=uk#axzz2zhAMLzqE.

Darlington, Ralph, and Martin Upchurch, 'A Reappraisal of the Rank-and-File versus Bureaucracy Debate', *Capital & Class* 36 (2012), 77–95, http://dx.doi.org/10.1177/0309816811430369.

Davidson, Neil, *How Revolutionary Were the Bourgeois Revolutions?* (Chicago: Haymarket Books, 2012).

Doogan, Kevin, *New Capitalism?: The Transformation of Work* (Cambridge: Polity Press, 2009).

DPA, 'Ta'iyin Madani Ra'isan Li Matar Al-Qahira Al-Dawly Liawwal Marra Mundhu 50 Aman', 25 July 2011, www.masrawy.com/news/egypt/politics/2011/july/25/cairo_airport.aspx?ref=rss.

——, 'Tahwil Rihalat Masr Lil-Tayyaran Limabna Al-Mattar Al-Qadim Ba'd Fashl Inha'a Idrab Ummal Al-Haqa'ib', *Al-Masry Al-Youm*, 19 May 2013, www.almasryalyoum.com/node/1759226.

——, 'Wazir Al-Tayyaran Al-Masry Yustalim Muham Mansibihi Wast Mudhahirat Hashida', 21 July 2011, www.masrawy.com/News/Egypt/Politics/2011/july/21/aviation.aspx.

Draper, Hal, *Karl Marx's Theory of Revolution II, The Politics of Social Classes*

(New York: Monthly Review Press, 1978).

Durra, Adil, 'Umumiyya Ghazl Al-Mahalla Tuqarir Iqalat Al-Gibali Wa Maglis Idaratuhu ... Wa Tuhallihum Ila Niyabat Al-Amwal Al-Ama', *Al-Masry Al-Youm*, 27 November 2007, http://today.almasryalyoum.com/article2.aspx?ArticleID=84474.

EFITU, 'Egypt: New Unions' Declaration of Independence', *MENA Solidarity Network*, 2011, http://menasolidaritynetwork.com/2011/07/05/egypt-new-unions-declaration-of-independence.

Egyptian independent trade unionists, 'Egypt: Demands of the Workers in the Revolution', *Socialist Worker*, 19 February 2011, http://socialistworker.co.uk/art/23553/Egypt%3A+Demands+of+the+workers+in+the+revolution.

Egyptian Journalists Union, 'Al-Qawa'im Ba'd Al-Ta'dil' (Edited List of Injured and Killed during the 18-Day Uprising against Mubarak), unpublished document, 2013.

Egyptian Trade Union and Workers Watch, *Shahr Fibrayir Am 2007*, Egyptian Trade Union and Workers Watch, 1 March 2007, www.e-socialists.net/taxonomy/term/150/all?page=2.

Eissa, Reda, *Tax Justice in Egypt: A Tax-Payer's Perspective*, 2010, www.almaglesalwatany.org.

Al-Eissawi, Ibrahim, Al-*Iqtisad Al-Masry Fi 30 Aman* (Cairo: Al-Maktaba Al-Akadimiyya, 2007).

Enders, Klaus, 'IMF Survey: Egypt: Reforms Trigger Economic Growth', 2008, www.imf.org/external/pubs/ft/survey/so/2008/car021308a.htm.

Essam El-Din, Gamal, 'A New Boost for Privatisation', *Al-Ahram Weekly*, 7 December 2000, 511 edn, http://weekly.ahram.org.eg/2000/511/ec5.htm.

Essoyan, Catherine, 'Centre for Trade Union and Workers Services (CTUWS) (Egypt)' (Oxfam), www.ctuws.com/uploads/CTUWS-back/Solidarities/International/English/Oxfam-Novib_English.pdf.

EWTUW, 'Al-Usbu'a Al-Thalith Walra'ba' Min Shahr Uktubir 2007' (Egyptian Workers and Trade Union Watch, 2007), http://arabist.net/arabawy/wp-content/uploads/2007/11/3-4-actober.pdf.

——, 'Shahr Abril 2007' (Egyptian Workers and Trade Union Watch, 2007), http://arabist.net/arabawy/wp-content/uploads/2007/05/may-case-studymasrespain.pdf.

Ezz Steel, 'Ezz Steel At a Glance', www.ezzsteel.com/main.asp?pageID=17.

Farag, Fatemah, 'Child Murder Sparks Campus Fury', *Al-Ahram Weekly*, 5–11 October 2000, http://weekly.ahram.org.eg/2000/502/eg5.htm.

Faris, Muhammad, 'Al-Quda'a Yu'akid Ahqiyya Al-Niqabat Al-Mustaqilla Fi Manah Shihadat Al-Sifa Al-Ummaliyya Limurashahi Al-Intikhabat', *Al-Masry Al-Youm*, 16 November 2011, www.almasryalyoum.com/node/515204.

Fatma al-Zahra'a Muhammad, 'Al-Ittihad Al-Masri Lil Niqabat Al-Mustaqilla Yuaqid Mu'atamr Al-Ta'sisi Bimadinat Al-Intag Al-Ilami Ghadan', *El-Fagr*, 27 January 2012, http://new.elfagr.org/Detail.aspx?nwsId=116754&secid=1&vid=2.

FJP, 'Tuwas'ia Da'irat Itisam Madinat Al-Intag Al-Ilami Ila Babawa 2', 2012, www.fj-p.com/article.php?id=34520.

Fouad, Hisham, 'Al-Amilun Bil Mattarat Yumna'un Al-Ra'is Al-Askari Al-Gadid

Min Dukhul Al-Sharika', *revsoc.me*, 2012, http://revsoc.me/workers-farmers/
lmlwn-blmtrt-ymnwn-lryys-lskry-ljdyd-mn-dkhwl-lshrk.

———, 'Al-Amilun Bil-Mattar Yuhtifun: Shalu Tayyar Gabu Tayyar … Barra
Barra Ya Maglis Ar', 2012, http://revsoc.me/politics/lmlwn-blmtr-yhtfwn-shlw-
tyr-jbw-tyr-brh-brh-y-mjls-r.

———, 'Al-Burkan Al-Ummaly Lan Yuhda', *Markaz al-dirasat al-ishtarakiyya*,
2007, http://revsoc.me/workers-farmers/lbrkn-lmly-ln-yhd.

———, 'Al-Mahalla: Al-Fursa Al-Da'iyya', *Al-Ishtaraki*, April 2009, 33 edn, 6.

———, 'Qiraa Awliyya Fi Al-Ihtigagat Al-Ummaliyya Al-Rahina', 2004, www.e-
socialists.net/node/1425.

———, 'Ummal Al-Naql Al-Am Yuhasirun Maglis Al-Wuzara'a', 2011, www.e-
socialists.net/node/7566.

Gaber, Naamat, interview with Naamat Gaber, Civil Aviation worker, 2012.

Gabr, Muhammad, 'Istimrar Itisam Al-Alaf Amam Al-Intag Al-Ilami Lil-
Matlaba Bil-Tathir', 2012, www.ikhwanonline.com/Article.aspx?ArtID=1
31140&SecID=230.

Galal, Shaima'a, 'Al-Lagna Al-Mu'aqita Tungah Fi Hall Azma Ummal Al-Mahalla', 2011, www.ikhwanonline.com/new/print.aspx?ArtID=90829&SecID=230.

Al-Gamal, Rasha, 'Al-Alaf Yutadhahirun Fil Fayyum Wal-Isma'iliyya Limatlaba Birahil Al-Muhafidhin', *Al-Badil*, 4 March 2011, www.masress.com/
elbadil/23024.

Gara, Tom, 'Egypt: Chinese Cars Coming', *Financial Times*, 2012, http://blogs.
ft.com/beyond-brics/2012/02/21/egypt-chinese-cars-coming.

Al-Gawhari, Muhammad, 'Mudhahirat Fi Beni Soueif Tunadid Bi Ta'iyin Al-
Dumyati Muhafidhan Watuhadid Bmana'ahu Min Dukhul Al-Diwan', *Al-
Ahram*, 15 April 2011, http://gate.ahram.org.eg.

Al-Gazzar, Hilmi, 'Ra'is Al-Hurriya Wal-Adala: "3-1"', *Al-Masry Al-Youm*, 8
October 2012, www.almasryalyoum.com/node/1163016.

General Motors, 'Egypt', 2013, http://careers.gm.com/worldwide-locations/africa/
egypt.html.

GFETU, 'Al-Ittihad Al-Am Lilniqabat Al-Ummaliyya Al-Masriyya', 2013, www.
gfetu.com.

Abd-al-Ghani, Mahmud, 'Waqfa Amam Mahkama Al-Giza Did Rafd Murashahi
Al-Niqabat Al-Mustaqilla', *Youm 7*, 31 October 2011, www.youm7.com/News.
asp?NewsID=524202&SecID=65&IssueID=0.

Gherzi, *Strategy and Action Plan Project for the Egyptian Textile and Clothing
Industry – Inception Report* (Industrial Modernisation Centre, July 2006),
www.cabdirect.org/abstracts/19541603857.html.

Ghoneim, Ahmed, *Promoting Competitive Markets in Developing Economies: The
Case of Egypt*, 2005, http://idl-bnc.idrc.ca/dspace/bitstream/10625/35100/1/
127158.pdf.

Gigi Ibrahim, *Idrab Masnaa Al-Sukkar Bi-Armant*, 2011, www.youtube.com/wa
tch?v=FJNe5Wu3oaQ&feature=youtube_gdata_player.

Ginsburg, Tom, 'The Real Winner in the Egyptian Constitution? The Military',
Huffington Post, 2012, www.huffingtonpost.com/tom-ginsburg/egypt-draft-
constitution-military_b_2259798.html.

Al-Giyushi, Yasmin, 'Al-Karama Tataqadum Bi 15 Murashahan Lil-Intikhabat

Al-Nasiri Taqdim Bi 214 Murashahan', *Al-Tahrir*, 24 October 2011, http://tahrirnews.com.

Goodrich, Carter, *The Frontier of Control: A Study in British Workshop Politics* (New York: Harcourt, Brace & Howe, 1920), http://archive.org/details/frontierofcontro00gooduoft.

Gordon, Michael R., 'Egyptians Following Right Path, Kerry Says', *New York Times*, 3 November 2013, www.nytimes.com/2013/11/04/world/middleeast/kerry-egypt-visit.html.

Government of Egypt, 'Qanun Al-Niqabat Al-Ummaliyya Raqm 12 Lisana 1995', Al Jazeera, 1995, www.aljazeera.net/specialfiles/pages/536961d8-8f73-4687-9c7e-3de45711cd70.

El Gundy, Zeinab, 'Abdel-Moneim Abul-Fotouh – Meet the Candidates – Presidential Elections 2012', *Ahram Online*, 2 April 2012, http://english.ahram.org.eg/News/36854.aspx.

——, 'Political Parties and Powers to Approve El-Selmi Document, on Condition It Is Amended', *Ahram Online*, 16 November 2011, http://english.ahram.org.eg/NewsContent/1/64/26754/Egypt/Politics-/Political-parties-and-powers-to-approve-ElSelmi-do.aspx.

El-Haddad, A., *Effects of the Global Crisis on the Egyptian Textiles and Clothing Sector: A Blessing in Disguise?*, Working Paper, 2010, http://natlex.ilo.ch/public/english/region/afpro/cairo/downloads/textileenglish.pdf.

Haddon, Hazel, Salma Shukrallah, Osman El-Sharnoubi, Nada Radwan and Tarek Sherif, 'Live Updates: Millions on Streets in Egypt as Defiant Morsi Addresses Nation', *Ahram Online*, 2 July 2013, http://english.ahram.org.eg/News/75511.aspx.

Halliday, Fred, *Islam and the Myth of Confrontation: Religion and Politics in the Middle East* (London and New York: I.B. Tauris, 1996).

——, 'The Left and the Jihad', OpenDemocracy, 2011, www.opendemocracy.net/globalization/left_jihad_3886.jsp.

Hamdi, Muhammad, Sa'id Nafi', Salah Al-Balak, Ahmad Abu Dara'a, Mamduh Arafa, and Amal Abbas, '2000 Mutadhahir Fi Miliyniyya Al-Karama Bi Qena Wa Guma'a Al-Tathir Bi Sina'a Tutalib Bi Iqala Al-Fasidin', *Al-Masry Al-Youm*, 29 April 2011, www.almasryalyoum.com/node/417587.

Hanieh, Adam, *Capitalism and Class in the Gulf States* (Basingstoke: Palgrave Macmillan, 2011).

——, *Lineages of Revolt: Issues of Contemporary Capitalism in the Middle East* (Chicago: Haymarket Books, 2013).

Harman, Chris, 'The Prophet and the Proletariat', *International Socialism Journal*, 1994, www.marxists.org/archive/harman/1994/xx/islam.htm.

——, 'The State and Capitalism Today', *International Socialism Journal*, vol. 2, no. 51 (1991), 3–54.

——, 'The Workers of the World', *International Socialism Journal*, 2002, http://pubs.socialistreviewindex.org.uk/isj96/harman.htm.

——, *Zombie Capitalism: Global Crisis and the Relevance of Marx* (Chicago: Haymarket Books, 2010).

Hashmat, Dina, 'Ahlan Bikum Fi Midan Al-Tahrir … Gumhuriyya Al-Ahlam Al-Mumkina', *Al-Akhbar*, 8 February 2011, www.al-akhbar.com/node/3842.

Hassan, M., and C. Sassanpour, 'Labor Market Pressures in Egypt: Why Is the Unemployment Rate Stubbornly High?', *Journal of Development and Economic Policies* 10 (2008).

Hassanin, Leila, 'Egypt | GISWatch', 2007, www.giswatch.org/en/country-report/civil-society-participation/egypt.

Hilali, Muhammad, 'Al-Irada Al-Thariyya Tuntasir Ala Al-Baltagiyya Wa Ummala' Amn Al-Dawla Bi-Gama'at Ain Shams', 2013, http://revsoc.me/students/lrd-lthwry-tntsr-l-lbltjy-wml-mn-ldwl-bjm-yn-shms.

Hisham, Radwa, 'Ra'is Al-Niqabat Al-Mustaqilla Yu'alin Tarshihu Lil Maglis Al-Sha'ab ... Wa 650 Shihada Lil Raghibin Fi Al-Tarshih', 2011, www.hoqook.com.

Human Rights Watch, 'Egypt: Military Court Convicts Opposition Leaders ', 2008, www.hrw.org/en/news/2008/04/15/egypt-military-court-convicts-opposition-leaders.

———, 'Egypt: New Constitution Mixed on Support of Rights', 2012, www.hrw.org/news/2012/11/29/egypt-new-constitution-mixed-support-rights.

———, 'Egypt: Release Dozens of Protestors Held Without Charge', 2008, www.hrw.org/news/2008/07/17/egypt-release-dozens-protestors-held-without-charge.

———, 'Egypt: Retry or Free 12,000 After Unfair Military Trials, 2011, www.hrw.org/news/2011/09/10/egypt-retry-or-free-12000-after-unfair-military-trials.

Huntington, Samuel P., *The Third Wave: Democratization in the Late Twentieth Century* (Norman: University of Oklahoma Press, 1991).

Hyman, Richard, *Industrial Relations: A Marxist Introduction* (London: Macmillan, 1975).

Ibrahim, Ayman, 'Ummal Al-Tirsana Bayna Ta'suf Al-Idara Wa Tawata' Al-Niqaba', 2007, http://revsoc.me/workers-farmers/ml-ltrsn-byn-tsf-ldr-wtwtw-lnqb.

Ibrahim, Ekram, 'Justice Denied: Egypt's Maspero Massacre One Year on', *Ahram Online*, 9 October 2012, http://english.ahram.org.eg/News/54821.aspx.

Idrab Masana'a Al-Sukkar Min Agl Tathir Al-Bilad, 2011, www.youtube.com/watch?v=Wqf-2I-wU-w&feature=youtube_gdata_player.

IFES, *Elections in Egypt: Analysis of the 2011 Parliamentary Electoral System*, International Foundation for Electoral Systems, 1 November 2011, www.ifes.org/~/media/Files/Publications/White%20PaperReport/2011/Analysis_of_Egypts_2011_Parliamentary_Electoral_System.pdf.

Ikhwanonline.com, 'Al-Hurriya Wal-Adala Biaswan Yungah Ti Fakk Idrab Ummal Kima', 23 February 2012, www.ikhwanonline.com/Article.aspx?ArtID=102013&SecID=250.

Ikhwanonline.net, 'Murashahu Al-Ikhwan Bil-Qahira', 2005, www.ikhwanonline.net/data/baralman2005/ikhwan3.htm.

———, 'Murashahu Al-Ikhwan Fi Al-Iskandaria', 2005, www.ikhwanonline.net/data/baralman2005/ikhwan1.htm.

Ikhwanwiki, 'Al-Barnamag Al-Ri'aysi ... Mohamed Morsi 2012', www.ikhwanwiki.com.

ILO, 'Concepts and Definitions of Informality', 2012, http://laborsta.ilo.org/informal_economy_E.html.

Imbabi, Ahmad, 'Al-Qadi Faruq Sultan ... Ragil Al-Aqdar', *Al Sharq al-Awsat*, 29 June 2012, www.aawsat.com/details.asp?section=45&article=683991&iss

ueno=12267#.UoahLCewDtt.

Inter-Parliamentary Union, 'IPU Parline Database: EGYPT (Majlis Al-Chaab) Elections in 2005', 2010, www.ipu.org/parline-e/reports/arc/2097_05.htm.

——, 'IPU Parline Database: Egypt (Majlis Al-Chaab)', Historical Election Archives', 2010, www.ipu.org/parline-e/reports/2097_arc.htm.

Al-Ishtaraki, 'Al-Barid Yuwasil Idrabu an Al-Aml Lilyawm Al-Thalith Ala Al-Tawala', *Al-Ishtaraki*, 4 September 2011, www.e-socialists.net/node/7377.

——, 'Ummal Al-Naql Al-Am Yutaghun Lita'liq Al-Idrab', 2011, www.e-socialists.net/node/7576.

——, 'Waqfa Ihtigagiyya Litullab Gama'at Al-Mansura Li Mutlaba Bi-Iqalat Al-Qiyadat Al-Gama'iyya Wa Tard Al-Haras Al-Gama'ai', *Al-Ishtaraki*, 13 September 2011, http://revsoc.me/students/wqf-htjjy-ltlb-jm-lmnswr-llmtlb-bql-lqydt-ljmy-wtrd-lhrs-ljm.

Al-Ishtarakiyyin al-Thawriyyun, 'Yusqat Hukm Al-Askar ... La Li Awdat Al-Filul ... La Li Awdat Al-Ikhwan', 2013, http://revsoc.me/letters-to-comrades/ysqt-hkm-lskr-l-lwd-lflwl-l-lwd-lkhwn.

Itisam Shabab Al-Thawra Bi-Sina'a Amam Diwan Al-Muhafidh Fil-Arish, 2011, www.youtube.com/watch?v=cIo39p29pqw&feature=youtube_gdata_player.

Itisam Ummal Hi'at Al-Naql Al-Am, 2013, www.youtube.com/watch?v=WnXj9nIQ-iM&feature=youtube_gdata_player.

ITUC, 'Report for the WTO General Council Review of the Trade Policies of Egypt', International Trade Union Conferederation, 2011.

Jadaliyya, 'How Are Seat Winners Determined in the Egyptian Elections?', www.jadaliyya.com/pages/index/3361/how-are-seat-winners-determined-in-the-egyptian-el.

Jafari, Peyman, 'Rupture and Revolt in Iran', *International Socialism Journal*, 2009, www.isj.org.uk/?id=585.

Kandil, Hazem, *Soldiers, Spies and Statesmen: Egypt's Road to Revolt* (London: Verso, 2012).

Khalaf, Roula, and Heba Saleh, 'Egypt: From Shadows to Spotlight', *Financial Times*, 21 May 2012, www.ft.com/cms/s/0/2a3a0bb2-a03c-11e1-88e6-00144fe-abdco.html#axzz2mGBRRa00.

Khidr, Radwa, 'Idrab Ummal Ghazl Al-Mahalla Lil Matlaba Bi Rahil Ra'is Al-Sharika Al-Qabida', *Al-Wafd*, 26 August 2013, www.alwafd.org.

Kidron, Michael, *A Permanent Arms Economy* (London: Socialist Workers Party, 1989).

Kienle, Eberhard, *A Grand Delusion: Democracy and Economic Reform in Egypt* (London: I.B. Tauris, 2000).

Kirkpatrick, David D., 'Blow to Transition as Court Dissolves Egypt's Parliament', *New York Times*, 14 June 2012, www.nytimes.com/2012/06/15/world/middle east/new-political-showdown-in-egypt-as-court-invalidates-parliament.html.

Kishk, Hassanein, 'Al-Buniya Al-Mutaghayrira Lil Tabaqa Al-Amila Al-Misiryya: Mulahazhat Awliyya', 2009.

KPMG, *Strategic Study to Upgrade Egypt's Automotive Sector: Executive Summary and Overview*, Industrial Modernisation Centre, January 2005, www.imc-egypt.org/studies/ExecutiveSummaries/Automotive%20Sector%20Development%20Strategy_EN.pdf.

Lagna al-tadamun ma ummal tanta lil-kitan, 'Megawer Wa Al-Gawhari Yukhaw-nun Ummal Tanta Lil-Kitan Wa Al-Ummal Yurfudun Qarar Taliq Al-Idirab Wa Yuqataun Al-Tariq Al-Sariaa', *Markaz al-dirasat al-ishtarakiyya*, 2008, www.e-socialists.net/node/4041.

Langohr, Vickie, 'Cracks in Egypt's Electoral Engineering', *Middle East Research and Information Project*, 2000, www.merip.org/mero/mero110700.

Lavelle, Kathryn C., *The Politics of Equity Finance in Emerging Markets* (Oxford: Oxford University Press, 2004).

Legend Youth, 'Bayan Miliyuniyya Tathir Al-Ilam', Facebook, 2012.

Lenin, V. I., 'The Collapse of the Second International II', 1915, www.marxists.org/archive/lenin/works/1915/csi/ii.htm.

Lenin, Vladimir, *The State and Revolution* . ch. 1, in *The State and Revolution*, www.marxists.org/archive/lenin/works/1917/staterev/ch01.htm.

Levinson, Charles, and Matt Bradley, 'Before Morsi's Ouster, Egypt's Top Generals Met Regularly with Opposition Leaders', *Wall Street Journal*, 19 July 2013, http://online.wsj.com/news/articles/SB10001424127887324425204578601700051224658.

Lewis, Bernard, *What Went Wrong?: Western Impact and Middle Eastern Response* (Oxford: Oxford University Press, 2002).

Local Council Workers in Egypt Choose Their Own Boss, 2011, www.youtube.com/watch?v=XOd5X7rR_X8&feature=youtube_gdata_player.

Luxemburg, Rosa, *The Mass Strike, the Political Party and the Trade Unions, 1906: Rosa Luxemburg* (London: Merlin Press, 1964).

Mabro, Robert, and Samir Muhammad Radwan, *The Industrialization of Egypt, 1939–1973: Policy and Performance* (Oxford: Clarendon Press, 1976).

Mabruk, Muhammad, 'Bil-Suwwar ... Ummal Al-Mahalla: Munhana Mursi Fursa Kafiyya ... Wa Nushtarat Tahqiq Mutalibina Qabl Inha'a Al-Itisam', *Al-Ahram*, 15 July 2012, http://gate.ahram.org.eg/News/231171.aspx.

Magdi, Walid, 'Sharaf Yugmid Nashat Muhafidh Qena Al-Gadid Wa Yukalaf Al-Sikratir Al-Am Bimuhamahu', *Al-Masry Al-Youm*, 25 April 2011, www.almasryalyoum.com/node/412721.

El-Mahdi, Rabab, 'The Democracy Movement: Cycles of Protest', in Rabab El-Mahdi and Philip Marfleet, eds, *Egypt: the Moment of Change* (London: Zed Books, 2009), 87–103.

Mahir, Muhammad, 'Al-Amilun Bil-Masiryya Lil-Itisalat Yutalibun Mursi Biqalat Bashir Wa Tathir Al-Hi'at', *Al-Masry Al-Youm*, 2012, www.almasryalyoum.com/node/1108906.

——, 'Al-Mustaqilla Lil-Amilin Bil-Itisalat Turahib Bi-Istiqalat Bashir: Bidaya Litathir Al-Hi'at', *Al-Masry Al-Youm*, 25 September 2012, www.almasryalyoum.com/node/1135776.

Al-Mahkama al-Dusturiyya al-Uliya, 'Dustur 1964', 2012, www.hccourt.gov.eg/Constitutions/Constitution64.asp.

Mansour, Sherif, *On the Divide: Press Freedom at Risk in Egypt*, Committee to Protect Journalists, 14 August 2013, http://cpj.org/reports/2013/08/on-divide-egypt-press-freedom-morsi.php.

Mansouracity, 'Muhafidh Al-Daqahiliyya Al-Gadid: Al-Liwa'a Muhammad Muhsin Hafdhi', www.mansouracity.com/pge-50.html.

Marfleet, Philip, 'Egypt: Revolution Contained?', *Socialist Review*, September 2013, www.socialistreview.org.uk/article.php?articlenumber=12379.

——, 'Egypt: The Workers Advance', *International Socialism Journal*, 2013, www.isj.org.uk/?id=904.

——, '"Never Going Back": Egypt's Continuing Revolution', *International Socialism Journal*, vol. 2, no. 137 (2013), www.isj.org.uk/?id=866.

Markaz al-dirasat al-ishtarakiyya, *Tabaqa Amila Misriyya Gadida*, Awraq Ummaliyya, March 2005, www.e-socialists.net.

Markaz Awlad al-Ard, 'Hasad al-harakah al-ummaliyya fi am 2010', www.ecesr. com, 2010.

Marshall, Shana, and Joshua Stacher, 'Egypt's Generals and Transnational Capital', *Middle East Report*, 2012, www.merip.org/mer/mer262/egypts-generals-transnational-capital.

Marx, Karl, 'Marx to Dr Kugelmann Concerning the Paris Commune', 1871, www.marxists.org/archive/marx/works/1871/letters/71_04_12.htm.

Marx, Karl, and Frederick Engels, *The Manifesto of the Communist Party*, 1848, https://www.marxists.org/archive/marx/works/1848/communist-manifesto/ch01.htm.

Al-Masry Al-Youm, 'Islamists Form Community Police Militias', *Egypt Independent*, 12 March 2013, www.egyptindependent.com/news/islamists-form-community-police-militias.

——, 'Makatib Shubra Al-Kheima Wa Kafr Al-Shaykh Wa Qena Wal Gharbiyya Tandum Lidrab Al-Barid', *Al-Masry Al-Youm*, 4 September 2011, www. almasryalyoum.com/node/492345.

——, 'Murashah Ikhwan Shamal Al-Giza: Nahnu Aqrab Lil Nas ... Wal-Libraliyyun Tafraghu Lmuwaghatna', *Al-Masry Al-Youm*, 12 December 2011, www.almasryalyoum.com/node/545761.

Mason, Paul, *Why It's Kicking off Everywhere: The New Global Revolutions* (London: Verso, 2012).

Masrawy, 'Abu Hamid: Al-Barlaman La Yuatabir an Al-Shari'a ... Wal-Kurdy: Huwa Al-Midan Al-Shari'yy', 31 January 2012, www.masrawy.com/news/ egypt/politics/2012/january/31/4774240.aspx.

Massey, Doreen, 'Industrial Restructuring as Class Restructuring: Production Decentralization and Local Uniqueness', *Regional Studies* 17 (1983), 73–89, http://dx.doi.org/10.1080/09595238300185081.

Mekki, Mahmud, and Hisham Bastawisi, 'When Judges Are Beaten', *Guardian*, 10 May 2006, www.theguardian.com/commentisfree/2006/may/10/comment. egypt.

MENA, 'Morsy Has No Intentions to Reinstate Parliament, Spokesperson Says', *Al-Masry Al-Youm*, 13 August 2012, www.egyptindependent.com/news/ morsy-has-no-intentions-reinstate-parliament-spokesperson-says.

——, 'Nuwab Al-Shura Yutalibun Bi Qanun Limukafahat Al-Shaghab Wa Manah Al-Dubatiyya Al-Quda'iyya Lil Gaysh', 2013, www.almasryalyoum. com/node/1423361.

——, 'Tadhahir "Addad Min Muwadhafi Sharikat Mina'a Al-Qahira Al-Gawy', *Al-Wafd*, 2 February 2012, www.alwafd.org/%D8%A7%D9%82%D8%AA%D8% B5%D8%A7%D8%AF/157144.

———, 'Tagmid Tawqiyyat Maglis Idara Ittihad Al-Ummal Al-Munhall Hata Taskhil Lagna Tudiru Maliyan', 7 August 2011, www.masrawy.com/news/egypt/politics/2011/august/7/workers_sign.aspx?ref=rss.

MENA and Ahram Online, 'Newspaper Editor's Trial for Insulting Morsi to Begin Thursday', *Ahram Online*, 21 August 2012, http://english.ahram.org.eg/NewsContent/1/64/50921/Egypt/Politics-/Newspaper-editors-trial-for-insulting-Morsi-to-beg.aspx.

MENA Solidarity Network, 'Egypt: Airport Workers' Battle against the Generals' Candidate', 2012, http://menasolidaritynetwork.com/2012/06/17/egypt-airport-workers.

———, 'Egypt: University Workers Co-ordinate National Strike', 2012, http://menasolidaritynetwork.com/2012/09/17/egypt-university-workers-co-ordinate-national-strike.

MENA Solidarity Network, 'Egypt: Independent Unions, Revolutionary Activists Slam Conscription of Rail Strikers', 2013, http://menasolidaritynetwork.com/2013/04/10/egypt-independent-union-federation-condemns-conscriptio.

———, 'Egypt: Locked-out IFFCO Food Workers Continue Strike', 2013, http://menasolidaritynetwork.com/2013/06/05/egypt-locked-out-iffco-food-workers-continue-strike.

———, 'Egypt: Teachers Tell Generals "Meet Our Demands ... or No School This Year"', 2011, http://menasolidaritynetwork.com/2011/09/13/egypt-teachers-tell-generals-meet-our-demands-or-no-school-this-year.

———, 'Egypt: "Trade Union Rights Are Our Way to Social Justice" – New Leaflet', 2012, http://menasolidaritynetwork.com/2012/11/14/egypt-trade-union-rights-are-our-way-to-social-justice-new-leaflet.

———, 'Egypt: "We're Paid by the Penny" – Rail Strikers Tell Their Stories', 2013, http://menasolidaritynetwork.com/2013/04/12/egypt-were-paid-by-the-penny-rail-strikers-tell-their-stories.

Meuse, Alison, 'Selling Protection', *Business Monthly*, July 2011, http://amcham.org.eg/resources_publications/publications/business_monthly/issue.asp?sec=4&subsec=selling%20protection&im=7&iy=2011.

Ministry of Education, *National Strategic Plan For Pre-University Education Reform in Egypt 2007/8–2011/12*, 2007, http://planipolis.iiep.unesco.org/upload/Egypt/EgyptStrategicPlanPre-universityEducation.pdf.

Ministry of Finance, *Profile of M/SMEs in Egypt – Update Report*, October 2005, www.mof.gov.eg/MOFGallerySource/English/SME/Research_studies/24.pdf.

Mitchell, Timothy, 'Dreamland: The Neoliberalism of Your Desires', *Middle East Report*, 1999, 28–33, http://dx.doi.org/10.2307/3012500.

Möller, Jochen, 'Working and Living in 10th of Ramadan City: The Perspective of Workers in Small Industries', *Égypte/Monde Arabe*, vol. 1, no. 33 (1998), http://ema.revues.org/index1575.html.

Morsi, Eman, 'Strikes in Egypt: Female Workers on the Frontline', 2008, www.babelmed.net/Countries/Mediterranean/strikes_in.php?c=3143&m=9&l=en.

Mourad, Mary, 'Truth in Numbers: How Much Legitimacy Is Legitimate?', *Ahram Online*, 7 July 2013, http://english.ahram.org.eg/NewsContent/1/64/75844/Egypt/Politics-/Truth-in-numbers-How-much-legitimacy-is-legitimate.aspx.

Moustafa, Tamir, *Drafting Egypt's Constitution: Can A New Legal Framework Revive a Flawed Transition?*, Brookings Doha Center – Stanford Project on Arab Transitions, Brookings Institution, March 2012, www.brookings.edu/~/media/research/files/papers/2012/3/12%20egypt%20constitution%20moustafa/new1%20drafting%20egypts%20new%20constitutionenr03.pdf.

Mu'assisat Awlad al-Ard, *48 Itisaman Wa 17 Idrab Wa 32 Tadhahira Wa 23 Waqfa Ihtigagiyya Wa Tagumhurin Ithnain Wa Wafa Amil Wahid Wa Isaba 9 Ummal Wa Fasl Wa Tarshid 12 Amil Hasad Al-Haraka Al-Ummaliyya Fi Shahr Maris*, April 2011, www.e-socialists.net/node/6793.

Mu'assisat Awlad al-Ard, and Markaz al-masry lil huquq al-iqtisadiyya wa al-igtima'iyya, *Al-Ummal Wa Al-Thawra Al-Masriyya – Ru'iyya Huquqiyya* Markaz al-masry lil huquq al-iqtisadiyya wa al-igtima'iyya, 16 February 2011.

Mugahid, Muhammad, and Muhammad Faris, 'Muwadhfu Al-Masriyya Lil-Itisalat Yubda'un Idraban Maftuhan Wa Yuhadidun Biquta'a Al-Tilifunat Al-Ardiyya', *Al-Masry Al-Youm*, 15 October 2011, www.almasryalyoum.com/node/505385.

Muhammad Ali, Islam, 'Ta'sis Awwal Ittihad Mahalli Liniqabat Al-Ummal Al-Mustaqilla Bil-Suways', *Suez Online*, 21 January 2012, http://revsoc.me/workers-farmers/tsys-wl-thd-mhl-lnqbt-lml-lmstql-blswys.

Muhammadain, Haitham, 'Al-Yawm: Al-Ilan an Niqaba Mustaqilla Bimustashfa Al-Du'aa Wa Ukhra Fi Sikkak Haddid Al-Wasta', 2011, www.e-socialists.net/node/6848.

——, 'Yawm Ma'a Shaykh Tariq … Wa Ummal Al-Naql Al-Am', *Al-Ishtaraki*, 18 September 2012, http://revsoc.me/workers-farmers/ywm-m-lshykh-trq-wml-lnql-lm-0.

Al-Naggar, Ahmad, 'Limadha Nurfad Mashru'a Al-Dustur Al-Mushabwa', 2012.

Al-Naggar, Mustafa, ' Ummal Ghazal Al-Mahalla Yuqadimun Mudhakira Li Silmi Li-Iqalat Al-Gaylani', *Youm 7*, 15 October 2011, www.youm7.com/News.asp?NewsID=513276&SecID=296#.UnUDEVOwDts.

——, 'Abd-Al-Alim Ra'isan Lil-Qabida Lil-Ghazl Khalfan Lil-Gaylani', *Youm 7*, 28 May 2012, www1.youm7.com/News.asp?NewsID=690654&SecID=24&IssueID=0.

Al-Naggar, Rasha, '17 Niqaba Min Al-Mansura Tu'alin Ta'sis Al-Ittihad Al-Masry Lil Niqabat Al-Mustaqilla', *Al-Ahram Digital*, 9 May 2012, http://digital.ahram.org.eg/articles.aspx?Serial=894618&eid=368.

Naguib, Sameh, *Al-Ikhwan Al-Muslimun: Ru'iya Ishtarakiyya* (Markaz al-dirasat al-ishtarakiyya, 2006).

——, *The Egyptian Revolution* (London: Bookmarks, 2011).

Al-Nahar, 'Ta'gil Qadiyya Muwafadhin Hayy Gharb Ila 30 Abril', 1 April 2012, www.alnaharegypt.com/t~67311.

Al-Naql Al-Am 3 Sanawat Min Al-Ihtigag, 2012, www.youtube.com/watch?v=ne efu3RoMNQ&feature=youtube_gdata_player.

Nasif, Rafiq, 'Ummal Ghazl Al-Mahalla Wal-Ma'shat Yusharikaun Fi Guma'a Al-Tathir', *Al-Wafd*, 5 July 2011, www.alwafd.org.

Nasr, Samar, 'Intilaq Utubisat Hamdeen Sabahi Ila Sina'a Lil-Musharika Fi Ihtifalat Al-Tahrir', *Al-Ahram*, 25 April 2012, http://gate.ahram.org.eg/News/200640.aspx.

Niqaba al-mihan al-talimiyya, 'Tarikh Niqaba Al-Mihan Al-Talimiyya', http://ets.eg/Syndicate/history.htm.

No Military Trials, 'The Presidency Lies', 2012, http://en.nomiltrials.com.

Nubat Sahyan, 'Niqabat Al-Bunuk "Ayala Lil Suqut" Istiqala Ha'it Maktab Lagna Al-Dahaqiliyya', *Nubat Sahyan*, May 2009, 4, p. 2.

——, 'Waintisarna', *Nubat Sahyan*, May 2009, 4, p. 1.

OECD, 'Business Climate Development Strategy: Phase 1 Policy Assessment – Privatisation Policy and Public Private Partnerships', OECD, 2010, www.oecd.org/dataoecd/49/55/46340470.pdf.

Popescu, Alin, 'Deja Vu All Over Again: Cables Cut in the Mediterranean – Renesys Blog', 2008, www.renesys.com/blog/2008/12/deja-vu-all-over-again-cables.shtml.

Posusney, Marsha Pripstein, *Labor and the State in Egypt: Workers, Unions, and Economic Restructuring* (New York: Columbia University Press, 1997).

Privatization Coordination Support Unit, 'The Results and Impacts of Egypt's Privatization Program', Carana Corporation, 2002.

Abd-al -Radi, Sami, 'Imad Mikha'il Shahata Min Luwa'a Mahbub … Ila Muhafidh Marfud', *Al-Masry Al-Youm*, 19 April 2011, www.almasryalyoum.com/node/406495.

Rady, Faiza, 'Esco Ordeal Ends', *Al-Ahram Weekly*, 2 June 2005, 745, http://weekly.ahram.org.eg/2005/745/eg9.htm.

Ramadan, Fatma, and Egyptian Trade Union and Workers Watch, *Shahr Abril 2007*, May 2007, www.e-socialists.net/sites/default/files/pdf/7.pdf.

Raslan, Sarah, 'Cairo Bus Drivers Partially Suspend Strike after 18 Days', *Ahram Online*, 4 October 2011, http://english.ahram.org.eg/NewsContent/1/64/23343/Egypt/Politics-/Cairo-bus-drivers-partially-suspend-strike-after--.aspx.

Rassd Network, 'Abu-Al-Fotouh: Adly Mansour Wa Awanuhu Hawwalu Masr Li Gumhuriyat Al-Khawf', *Rassd*, 2014, http://rassd.com.

Reuters, 'Egypt to Grant Telecom Egypt a Mobile License', *Reuters*, 26 December 2012, www.reuters.com/article/2012/12/26/egypt-telecomegypt-idUSL5E8NQ3JU20121226.

Richards, Alan, and John Waterbury, *A Political Economy of the Middle East* (Boulder CO: Westview Press, 2008).

Roberts, Hugh, 'The Revolution That Wasn't', *London Review of Books*, 12 September 2013, 3–9.

Robinson, Peter, 'Portugal 1974–75', in Colin Barker, ed., *Revolutionary Rehearsals*, 2nd edn (Chicago: Haymarket Books, 2008).

Sabah Dream: Dina Abd-Al-Rahman Taqrir an Tirsana Al-Iskandaria Libinaa Al-Sufun, 2011, www.youtube.com/watch?v=wYNwKarDftw&feature=youtube_gdata_player.

Said, Mona, 'Compensating Differentials and Queue For Public Sector Jobs: Evidence from Egyptian Household Survey Data', Department of Economics Working Papers, SOAS, 2004, www.soas.ac.uk/economics/research/workingpapers/file28843.pdf.

Salah, Daha, 'Istiqala Ra'is Gama'at Assiyut Min Mansibihi', *Youm 7*, 9 October 2011, www.youm7.com/News.asp?NewsID=508776&SecID=296#.UpsmZiewDts.

Salah, Muhammad, and Sharif Al-Dib, 'Bil-Suwwar ... Al-Itisamat Tatawasil Bi Addad Min Qita'at Al-Dahaqiliyya', *Youm 7*, 13 February 2011, www.youm7. com/News.asp?NewsID=351252#.UnUlUFOwDts.

Salam, Hatim, '"Al-Mu'alimin" Tu'alin Ta'sis Niqaba "Mustaqilla' Raghm Al-Rafd Al-Hukumi', *Youm 7*, 15 July 2010, www.youm7.com/News.asp?NewsID =254276.

Abd-al -Salam, Subhi, Ahmad Fathi, and Rafiq Nasif, 'Ummal Ghazl Al-Mahalla Yuhaddidun Bi Shall Al-Dalta', *Al-Watan*, 12 October 2013, www.elwatan-news.com/news/details/339317.

Saleh, Yasmine, and Tom Perry, 'Islamists Stamp Mark on Egypt's Draft Constitu- tion', *Reuters*, Cairo, 30 November 2012, www.reuters.com/article/2012/11/30/ us-egypt-constitution-idusbre8ato8k20121130.

Salim, Mitwalli, Yusif Al-Awami, and Sara Nur-al-Din, 'Idrab Al-Naql Al-Am Yushall Al-Murur Fil-Qahira Wal-Mutalib: Al-Huwafidh Wa Taghiyyar Al-Utubisat Al-Muthalika', 2011, www.almasryalyoum.com/node/421453.

Sameh Naguib, 'Labour, Markets and Industrial Development – Garment Produc- tion in the City of Shubra El-Kheima', University of London, 2006.

Al-Sawwaf, Amir, 'Adil Labib: Fakhur Bintima'i Lamn Al-Dawla', *Al-Wafd*, 12 August 2011, www.alwafd.org.

Al Sayegh, Hadeel, 'Ghabbour to Cash in on Egypt Taxi Overhaul', *The National* (UAE), 22 August 2010, www.thenational.ae/business/markets/ ghabbour-to-cash-in-on-egypt-taxi-overhaul.

Sayf-al-Nasr, Ahmad, 'Na'ib Al-Hurriya Wal-Adala Bil-Fayyum Yunsif Ummal Al-Kima'wiyyat', *Ikhwanonline.com*, 24 February 2012, www.ikhwanonline. com/Article.aspx?ArtID=102068&SecID=253.

Sayigh, Yezid, *Above the State: The Officers' Republic in Egypt*, Carnegie Endow- ment for International Peace, August 2012, www.carnegieendowment.org/ files/officers_republic1.pdf.

El-Sayyed, Ahmed, Health Technicians Union, interview, 2011.

Schewe, Eric, 'A First Look at First Round Egypt Presidential Election Dis- trict Results', *Eric Schewe*, 2012, http://ericschewe.wordpress.com/2012/07/26/ a-first-look-at-first-round-egypt-presidential-district-results.

Seoudi Group, 'Founder', 2013, www.seoudi.com/founder.php.

Sha'aban, Mamduh, Sa'ad Tantawi and Ali Muhammad, '235 Maqa'id Lil-Hurriya Wal-Adala Wa Hulafa'ahu Wa 123 Lil-Nur Wa 38 Lil Wafd Wa 34 Lil-Kutla Fi Barlaman Al-Thawra', *Al-Ahram Digital*, 22 January 2012, http://digital. ahram.org.eg/Policy.aspx?Serial=774569.

Al-Shafa'i, Marwa, 'Idrab Guzi'i Bigaraj Tayyiba Al-Ta'ba'a Liha'it Al-Naql Al-Am Wa Idrab 9 Ummal an Al-Ta'am', *Al-Shorouq*, 29 June 2012, http://shorouk-news.com/news/view.aspx?cdate=29062012&id=eea0893a-d17b-45e4-bf29- dd5cd9f61e3d.

Shafei, Omar El, *Workers, Trade Unions and the State in Egypt, 1984-1989* (Cairo: American University in Cairo Press, 1995).

Shafiq, Mohammed, '"The Union Is a Shield and Our Sword Is the Strike"', *So- cialist Review*, December 2011, www.socialistreview.org.uk/article.php?article number=11845.

Shahid: 'Itisam Hi'at Al-Naql Al-Am, 2013, www.youtube.com/watch?v=2krJBi1

F5gw&feature=youtube_gdata_player.

Sharp, Jeremy M., *Egypt-United States Relations* (Washington DC: Congressional Research Service, 2005).

Shehab, Shaden, 'First-Year German U', *Al-Ahram Weekly*, 2 October 2003, http://weekly.ahram.org.eg/2003/658/eg9.htm.

Al-Shuwadfi, Muhammad, 'Istiqala Ra'is Gama'at Ain Shams Wa Gami'a Umada'a Kuliyatiha', *Al-Ahram*, 4 October 2011, http://gate.ahram.org.

Singapore Free Press, 'Egyptians Boycott Dutch Ship', *Singapore Free Press*, 4 August 1947, p. 1.

Snider, Erin, and David Faris, 'The Arab Spring: U.S. Democracy Promotion in Egypt', *Middle East Policy* 18 (2011), http://mepc.org/journal/middle-east-policy-archives/arab-spring-us-democracy-promotion-egypt?print.

SOLIDAR, 'Past Winners Archive 2000–2008 – SOLIDAR', 2013, www.solidar.org/Past-Winners-Archive-2000–2008.html.

Solidarity Center, 'Court Decision Restores Egyptian Worker Rights Organization', 2007, www.solidaritycenter.org/content.asp?contentid=772.

——, 'Programme of Assistance to the Egyptian Trade Union Federation (ETUF) – Final Report', 2003, http://pdf.usaid.gov/pdf_docs/PDABZ006.pdf.

Springborg, Robert, *Mubarak's Egypt: Fragmentation of the Political Order* (Boulder CO: Westview Press, 1989).

Standing, Guy, *The Precariat: The New Dangerous Class* (London: Bloomsbury Academic, 2011).

Suez Canal Authority, 'Suez Canal Traffic Statistics', 2013, www.suezcanal.gov.eg/TRstat.aspx?reportId=4.

Sugar Factories Front for Change, 'Front for Change in the Sugar Factories and Refineries: Facebook Page', 2011.

Tadros, Mariz, 'State Welfare in Egypt since Adjustment: Hegemonic Control with a Minimalist Role', *Review of African Political Economy* 33 (2006), 237–54, http://dx.doi.org/10.1080/03056240600842701.

Taha, Hamdi, 'Salah Musa Yufadd Itisam Ummal Wadi Kom Ombo Biaswan', 26 February 2012, www.ikhwanonline.com/new/print.aspx?ArtID=102150&SecID=0.

Taha, Rana, 'Workers' Movements Unite to Push for Syndicates' Freedom Law', *Daily News Egypt*, 15 October 2012, www.dailynewsegypt.com/2012/10/15/workers-movements-unite-to-push-for-syndicates-freedom-law.

Takhsis Nisba Min Maqa'id Maglis Al-Sha'ab Al-Masry Lil-Ummal Wal-Fallahin, 2010, www.youtube.com/watch?v=6kn_sMyyyOA&feature=youtube_gdata_player.

Taylor, Paul, 'Update: Revolt Mounts against Egypt's Mursi over Judges – News – Aswat Masriya', *Reuters*, 23 April 2013, http://en.aswatmasriya.com/news/view.aspx?id=4066fc36–cea2–40f0–a871–c0c81358d479.

Thompson, E.P, *The Making of the English Working Class* (Harmondsworth: Penguin, 1991).

Tregenna, F., 'Characterising Deindustrialisation: An Analysis of Changes in Manufacturing Employment and Output Internationally', *Cambridge Journal of Economics* 33 (2008), 433–66, http://dx.doi.org/10.1093/cje/ben032.

Trotsky, Leon, *The History of the Russian Revolution* (New York: Pathfinder Press, 1992).

Al-Tuhami, Muhammad, 'Abu-Al-Futuh Yungah Fi Ta'liq Itisam Ummal', 23 February 2012, www.ikhwanonline.com/Article.aspx?ArtID=102009&SecID =250.

Umar, Ashraf, 'Musharika Ummaliyya Mahduda Fi 11 Febrayir ... Limadha?', *Al-Ishtaraki*, 15 February 2012, www.e-socialists.net/node/8310.

Ummal Al-Sikkat Al-Hadid Awzin Niqaba Mustaqilla Li?, 2011, www.youtube. com/watch?v=E10IzcERSSM&feature=youtube_gdata_player.

Ummal wa Amilat ghazl al-mahalla, 'Min Ummal Wa Amilat Ghazl Al-Mahalla', *www.e-socialists.net*, 2011, www.e-socialists.net/node/7361.

UNCTAD, *Commodities at a Glance – Special Issue on Energy*, February 2012, http://unctad.org/en/PublicationsLibrary/suc2011d6_en.pdf.

UNISON, 'Act Now – Call on Mubarak to Revoke Closure of UNISON-Supported Organisation in Egypt', 2007, www.unison.org.uk/international/ pages_view.asp?did=5186.

US Embassy in Cairo, 'Egypt Labor Update: GOE Shuts Down Labor NGO', 2007, http://wikileaks.org/cable/2007/05/07CAIRO1283.html#.

——, 'Founder Of Egypt's First Independent Union on Labor Activism', 2009, www.telegraph.co.uk/news/wikileaks-files/egypt-wikileaks-cables/8327162/ Founder-Of-Egypts-First-Independent-Union-On-Labor-Activism.html.

——, 'Labor Strikes: GOE Approach Unsuccessful In Stemming Protests', WikiLeaks, 2007, http://wikileaks.org/cable/2007/05/07CAIRO1595.html# .

——, 'Mahalla One Year after the Strike', 2009, http://wikileaks.org/ Cable/2009/03/09Cairo428.Html.

——, 'Reform Fatigue at the Housing Ministry – Wikileaks', 2008, www.telegraph.co.uk/news/wikileaks-files/egypt-wikileaks-cables/8327026/Reform-Fatigue-At-The-Housing-Ministry.html.

——, 'Supporting Egypt's Democratic Transition', 2012, http://egypt.usembassy.gov/democracy.html.

Uthman, Dalia, 'Al-Shurta Al-Askariyya Tumaris Al-Dubatiyya Al-Quda'iyya Wa Tunshur Kama'in Bil-Mayadin Al-Kubra', *Al-Masry Al-Youm*, 15 June 2012, www.almasryalyoum.com/node/920201.

Uthman, Taha Sa'ad, *Min Tarikh Ummal Masr – Kifah Ummal Al-Nasig* (al-Qahira: Maktabat al-Madbuli, 1983).

Uwaydah, Gamal, *Mulahma 'Itisam Muwadhfi Al-Dara'ib Al-Aqariyya* (Markaz al-dirasat al-ishtarakiyya, 2008).

Wahba, Amira, 'Ummal Masr Yu'aqid Mu'atamru Al-Ta'sisi Bhudur 300 Niqaba Bil Sahariyyin Ayyam 24 Wa 25 Wa 26 Abril', *Al-Ahram*, 28 March 2013, http://gate.ahram.org.eg/News/326830.aspx.

Wahba, Jackline, 'The Impact of Labor Market Reforms on Informality in Egypt', *Gender and Work in the MENA Region Working Paper Series*, 2009, www. populationcouncil.us/pdfs/wp/mena/03.pdf.

Wahdat al-Dirasat, 'Tahawwulat Al-Iqtisad Al-Misri (Muladhat Awliyya)', *Al-Tariq al-Ishtaraki*, 1999, 5–51.

Waterbury, John, 'The "Soft State" and the Open Door: Egypt's Experience with Economic Liberalization, 1974–1984', *Comparative Politics* 18 (1985), 65–83, http://dx.doi.org/10.2307/421658.

Watt, Nicholas, 'David Cameron Orders Inquiry into Activities of Muslim Brotherhood', *Guardian*, 1 April 2014, section World News, www.theguardian.com/world/2014/apr/01/cameron-muslim-brotherhood-orders-inquiry-extremism.

Webber, Jeffrey R., *Rebellion and Reform in Bolivia: Class Struggle, Indigenous Liberation, and the Politics of Evo Morales* (Chicago: Haymarket Books, 2011).

World Bank, Operations Evaluation Department, 'Egypt Country Assistance Evaluation' (New York: World Bank, 2000).

Al Yacoub, Ikram, 'What's in a Tuk-Tuk? Happy Egyptians Paying Low Fares, of Course', 2012, http://english.alarabiya.net/articles/2011/05/16/149296.html.

Al-Yawm Al-Thalith Min Mudhahirat Handasat Iskandariyya Abril 2013 Lil Tathir Wa Ilan Al-Mizaniyya, 2013, www.youtube.com/watch?v=OMOvTz rSPIs&feature=youtube_gdata_player.

Youm 7, 'Al-Ikhwan Yughliqun Bab Dar Al-Quda'a Bil-Lafita "Al-Sha'ab Yurid Iqalat Wazir Al-Adl"', *Video7*, 19 April 2013, http://videoyoum7. com/?p=109523

———, 'Ta'raf "Ala Wuzzara' Hukumatak Al-Gadida ... Al-Sira Al-Thatiyya Al-Kamila Lil-Wuzzara' Al-Guddad', *Youm 7*, 5 August 2012, www1.youm7.com/News.asp?NewsID=749060#.UpvIoiewDts.

Index

www.ingramcontent.com/pod-product-compliance
Ingram Content Group UK Ltd.
Pitfield, Milton Keynes, MK11 3LW, UK
UKHW031249020325
455689UK00008B/143

9 781780 324302